SPOILS OF WAR IN THE ARAB EAST

SPOILS OF WAR IN THE ARAB EAST

Reconditioning Society and Polity in Conflict

Edited by
Aziz al-Azmeh, Harout Akdedian and Haian Dukhan

I.B. TAURIS
LONDON • NEW YORK • OXFORD • NEW DELHI • SYDNEY

I.B. TAURIS
Bloomsbury Publishing Plc, 50 Bedford Square, London, WC1B 3DP, UK
Bloomsbury Publishing Inc, 1385 Broadway, New York, NY 10018, USA
Bloomsbury Publishing Ireland, 29 Earlsfort Terrace, Dublin 2, D02 AY28, Ireland

BLOOMSBURY, I.B. TAURIS and the I.B. Tauris logo are
trademarks of Bloomsbury Publishing Plc

First published in Great Britain 2024
This paperback edition published 2025

Copyright © Aziz al-Azmeh, Harout Akdedian and Haian Dukhan 2024

Aziz al-Azmeh, Harout Akdedian and Haian Dukhan and Contributors have asserted their rights under the Copyright, Designs and Patents Act, 1988, to be identified as Editors of this work.

For legal purposes the Acknowledgements on p. x constitute
an extension of this copyright page.

Cover design by www.paulsmithdesign.com

All rights reserved. No part of this publication may be: i) reproduced or transmitted in any form, electronic or mechanical, including photocopying, recording or by means of any information storage or retrieval system without prior permission in writing from the publishers; or ii) used or reproduced in any way for the training, development or operation of artificial intelligence (AI) technologies, including generative AI technologies. The rights holders expressly reserve this publication from the text and data mining exception as per Article 4(3) of the Digital Single Market Directive (EU) 2019/790.

Bloomsbury Publishing Inc does not have any control over, or responsibility for, any third-party websites referred to or in this book. All internet addresses given in this book were correct at the time of going to press. The author and publisher regret any inconvenience caused if addresses have changed or sites have ceased to exist, but can accept no responsibility for any such changes.

A catalogue record for this book is available from the British Library.

Library of Congress Cataloging-in-Publication Data
Names: ʻAzmah, ʻAziz | Akdedian, Harout, editor. | Dukhan, Haian, editor.
Title: Spoils of war in the Arab East : reconditioning society and polity in conflict / edited by Aziz al-Azmeh, Harout Akdedian and Haian Dukhan.
Description: London ; New York : I.B. Tauris, 2024. |
Includes bibliographical references and index.
Identifiers: LCCN 2023024361 (print) | LCCN 2023024362 (ebook) |
ISBN 9780755649082 (hardback) | ISBN 9780755649129 (paperback) |
ISBN 9780755649099 (ebook) | ISBN 9780755649105 (epub) | ISBN 9780755649112
Subjects: LCSH: Peace-building–Iraq. | Peace-building–Syria. | Iraq–Politics and government–2003– | Syria–Politics and government–2000–
Classification: LCC JZ5584.172 S66 2024 (print) |
LCC JZ5584.172 (ebook) | DDC 327.1/7209567–dc23/eng/20230729
LC record available at https://lccn.loc.gov/2023024361
LC ebook record available at https://lccn.loc.gov/2023024362

ISBN: HB: 978-0-7556-4908-2
PB: 978-0-7556-4912-9
ePDF: 978-0-7556-4909-9
eBook: 978-0-7556-4910-5

Typeset by Newgen KnowledgeWorks Pvt. Ltd., Chennai, India

For product safety related questions contact productsafety@bloomsbury.com.

To find out more about our authors and books visit www.bloomsbury.com
and sign up for our newsletters.

CONTENTS

List of contributors	viii
Acknowledgements	x

Chapter 1
INTRODUCTION: RECONSTITUTING THE POST-CONFLICT REGISTER   1
   Aziz Al-Azmeh and Harout Akdedian

Part I
CONCEPTUAL AND GLOBAL EXPLORATION OF THE 'POST-CONFLICT' REGISTER

Chapter 2
PEACE-BUILDING: FROM LIBERAL STATE BUILDING IMPERATIVE TO
THE POST-CONFLICT REGISTER? PERSPECTIVES FROM COMPARISON   19
   Balazs Aron Kovacs

Chapter 3
CEASEFIRES IN SYRIA: RECONCILIATION, PEACE BY SUBMISSION AND
LATENT CONFLICT   45
   Marika Sosnowski

Chapter 4
PARAMILITARISM IN SYRIA AND IRAQ: THE INTERPENETRATION OF
MILITIAS AND THE STATE   59
   Uğur Ümit Üngör

Part II
RECONSTITUTION OF POWER IN SYRIA AND IRAQ: MILITARY STANDOFFS AND CONFLICT FRAGILITY

Chapter 5
FRAGMENTATION AND DEVOLUTION OF STATE FUNCTIONS IN
POST-WAR SOUTHERN SYRIA   75
   Abdullah Al-Jabassini

Chapter 6
DEVOLUTION OF STATE POWER IN SYRIA AND IRAQ: TRIBAL
AUXILIARIES FROM THE MARGINS TO THE CENTRES 91
   Haian Dukhan

Chapter 7
CONFLICTED COUNTERINSURGENCY: DAESH VERSUS IRAQ'S
SECURITY ARENA 117
   Jessica Watkins

Part III
THE POLITICAL ECONOMY AND GEOPOLITICS OF EMERGENT
ORDERS IN SYRIA AND IRAQ

Chapter 8
THE WAR ECONOMY IN SYRIA: CONSOLIDATING THE PRE-2011
DYNAMICS OF SYRIA'S POLITICAL ECONOMY 139
   Joseph Daher

Chapter 9
THE SHADOW ECONOMY OF THE SHABBIHA NETWORKS IN SYRIA 157
   Ali Aljasem

Chapter 10
THE STATE FROM TAHRIR SQUARE: UNDERSTANDING PROTESTORS'
CONCEPTIONS OF THE IRAQI STATE 171
   Irene Costantini and Yasmin Chilmeran

Part IV
THE BODY POLITIC RECONFIGURED: BETWEEN SOCIAL
ENGINEERING AND COMMUNITY RESISTANCE

Chapter 11
'AL-'ISLĀM KAMĀ 'UNZIL' – ASSAD'S ISLAM: RELIGION, THE STATE
AND REFITTING SYRIAN ISLAM 191
   Hammoud Hammoud

Chapter 12
DILEMMAS OF INTERVENTIONS IN NORTHERN SYRIA: REFUGEE
RETURN, RECONSTRUCTION AND DISPLACEMENTS 213
   Zeynep Sahin-Mencütek and Osman Bahadir Dinçer

Chapter 13
CIVILIAN RESISTANCE AND ITS LIMITS: THE CASE OF DEIR HAFER   237
  Harout Akdedian and Ali Aljasem

Index   267

CONTRIBUTORS

Harout Akdedian
Program Analyst in the Civil Rights Unit at the Oregon Department of Justice and Visiting scholar at Portland State University, Portland.

Aziz Al-Azmeh
University professor emeritus, Central European University, Vienna.

Abdullah Al-Jabassini
Max Weber Postdoctoral Fellow at the Robert Schuman Centre for Advanced Studies, European University Institute, Florence, Italy.

Ali Aljasem
PhD Candidate at the Centre for Conflict Studies, Utrecht University, Utrecht.

Yasmin Chilmeran
Research fellow at the Swedish Institute of International Affairs' Middle East and North Africa Programme, Stockholm.

Irene Costantini
Research fellow at the Department of Human and Social Science, University of Naples, Naples.

Joseph Daher
Visiting professor at University of Lausanne and part-time professor at the European University Institute, Florence.

Osman Bahadir Dinçer
Senior researcher at the Bonn International Centre for Conflict Studies, Bonn.

Haian Dukhan
Lecturer at the Department of Humanities and Social Sciences, Teeside University, Middlesbrough.

Hammoud Hammoud
Doctoral candidate, Free University of Berlin, Berlin.

Balazs Aron Kovacs
Visiting professor, United Nations-mandated University for Peace, San Jose.

Zeynep Sahin-Mencütek
Senior researcher at the Bonn International Centre for Conflict Studies, Bonn.

Marika Sosnowski
Research fellow at Melbourne Law School, Research associate at the German Institute for Global and Area Studies, Hamburg.

Uğur Ümit Üngör
Professor of Holocaust and Genocide Studies at the University of Amsterdam, Amsterdam.

Jessica Watkins
Research Associate at the German Institute for Global and Area Studies, Hamburg.

ACKNOWLEDGEMENTS

The editors are most grateful to all those involved in the Striking from the Margins (SFM) research programme, who participated in conceiving this book and in work leading eventually to its realization. This had been a protracted process, which accompanied and parried the vagaries of Covid. We worked principally at a distance, in discrete spurts across continents, rather than with the warmer continuity one likes to associate with research projects. All involved are to be congratulated on their resilience and engagement, and above all, persistent focus. This book is deeply indebted to the engagement of the SFM Co-Director Nadia Al-Bagdadi, and to research fellows and associates Bahadir Dinçer and Abdullah Al-Jabassini.

We are most appreciative of Jaafar Bambouk, the SFM coordinator, without whose keen eye, steady hand and dedication the programme – and the book – might have had rough passage. Our grateful thanks to him, and to the Center for Religious Studies at the Central European University, Vienna (previously in Budapest). This was SFM's institutional home from the beginning, and we are most grateful for the support and institutional sustenance, and especially for the engagement of Esther Holbrook.

The Carnegie Corporation of New York supported SFM most generously over a number of years. The project, with its special focus, would have been inconceivable without the Corporation's institutional backing and the personal engagement, encouragement and confidence of Hillary Wiesner and Nehal Amer.

We are pleased gratefully to acknowledge the support of the editorial team at Bloomsbury/I. B. Tauris. They have been briskly professional, and a pleasure to work with. Anonymous readers of the manuscript made some helpful suggestions.

Chapter 1

INTRODUCTION: RECONSTITUTING THE POST-CONFLICT REGISTER

Aziz Al-Azmeh and Harout Akdedian

The major outcome of this book and of the thinking that came into framing its themes is a conception of the post-war condition as one in which wartime conditions are churned into a dynamic of conflict in suspended animation. Conflict abatement may not realistically be parsed as conflict resolution. Civil war of the kind discussed in this book is more likely to produce an outwardly trucial condition sitting upon conditions of relapse, an interregnum, an interlude between a condition of war and a pending condition whose possible contours are obscured by complexity and by the imponderability of intense foreign action, both military and geopolitical. In the meantime, the spoils of war are sought, shared, extracted and fought over, with impressive endurance and determination. The example of Lebanon is instructive. Warlords apportioned the spoils of war in 1989 and have since been despoiling the country, all the while sitting on a condition which is structurally unsustainable. A condition that might be described as permanent condition of so far negotiated civil conflict, overwritten and sustained in suspended animation by the military dominance of one party continuously partitioning the spoils of war and maintaining a cold civil peace. Such conditions are discernible in Syria and Iraq as well, where political dynamics under conditions of conflict abatement are informed by processes of marginalization, including the marginalization of state authority.

Much of the discussion of the civil wars and other disturbances that have bedevilled the Arab East in past decades, and more particularly discussions of possible solutions, have tended to pay implicit homage to notions of transition to democracy that emerged during the terminal phases of the Cold War, premised on the expectation that the decay of authoritarian orders will inevitably lead to the rise of democratic systems (Bishara 2020). Readers of this book, however, will be hard-pressed to find occurrences of the word 'transition'. Although this book is motivated at least in part by an interest in a prognostic look at the outcomes of these wars as they appear at the present conjuncture, there is no question of presuming to sense what outcomes will eventually settle in durable fashion, or to prescribe sets of outcomes that are routinely enfolded into the transition paradigm. Rather, this book reveals that the nature of military standoffs in Syria and Iraq maintain conditions of potential relapse to violence but limit their manifestation to low-intensity modalities of violence. The interlocking of regional geopolitics with local political economies creates geographic protectorates with vested interests in the conditions that led to their emergence. This contributes to conflict abatement by simultaneously limiting incentives for a return to open war as well as preventing a final settlement or resolution to the conflict in its national or international formulations, due to both the ambitions of the interests vested in these protectorates, and the complex interplay and manoeuvring between external patrons active on the Syrian check-board. The book uncovers permutations of these realities through three primary questions: (1) What forms of violence and potential relapse persist despite military abatement in Syria and Iraq? (2) What conditions yield or maintain circumstances of military abatement? (3) What are the non-military forms of conflict perpetuation?

The argument

This book is situated at the junction of different disciplines, geographies and communities of knowledge. Both English and Arabic have been important mediums for knowledge production and policy discussions regarding political dynamics in the Arab Mashriq and their implications beyond. As a result, the published knowledge available about Syria and Iraq in both languages is at an unprecedented all-time high.[1] Academic databases indicate that between 2011 and 2021, scholarly publications about Syria in English from all fields of knowledge grew exponentially. For example, in those ten years, 2,372 publications featuring on JSTOR in the form of books, book chapters, journal articles and research reports focused on Syria.[2] During the prior ten years, the number of equivalent publications featured was a miserly 382.[3] Google Scholar aggregates a total of 10,200 published titles dedicated to Syria since 2011, including book reviews and other web-based scholarly publications that do not feature in academic databases such as JSTOR. This compares to a total of 2,810 in the previous ten years combined.[4] Knowledge production on Iraq follows a similar pattern when comparing periods before and after the US invasion in 2003 as well as before and after the expansion of Daesh in 2014.[5] Similarly, an unprecedented increase took place in Arabic, and in parallel. The Arab Council for the Social Sciences reveals that scholarly publications about the Middle East in Arabic, specifically from research centres and universities in the Middle East, witnessed a significant increase in volume since the 2011 uprisings in what some international institutions call the MENA region (Bamyeh 2015).[6]

One could derive a strong correlation between periods of armed conflict and patterns of knowledge production on the Middle East. Scholars such as Issam Eido (2014) and Seteney Shami and Cynthia Idris-Miller (2017: 1) point out how circumstances of armed conflict in what is often designated as the MENA region over the past twenty years, and the consequent transitions away from dearth of social scientific attention to the Middle East, introduced a new set of drawbacks in the scholarship. Amongst these are impasses of perception, description and analysis, characterized by what Eido describes as the mushrooming of attempts to plot monocausal narrative interpretations in terms of sectarianism, geopolitics, Salafi Jihadism, social mosaic models, authoritarianism, amongst others (Eido 2014). Integral to the 'explosion of explanatory narratives' are chronological periodizations of armed conflicts as attempts to capture the overall arc of their history.[7] This volume is a counterpoint to such apporaches, with its emphasis on complexity of processes, events and explanations.

Carefully considered, the chronological modelling of armed conflicts, whether as an explicit conceptual framework or an implicit method for organizing information related to the history of war and political violence, rests on conventional wisdom that situates instances, modalities and patterns of organized violence within temporal arcs broadly defined by a beginning, a middle phase and an endgame. This framework is therefore not only a method for organizing complex information but also an analytical lens that predetermines conflict dynamics to a path dependency characterized by a starting point, followed by conflict escalation climaxing either towards a debilitating stalemate for all involved, or decisive victory for some, and ultimately reaching an end. There is a measure of approximate historical truth in such depictions. No armed conflict has ever continued escalating without an eventual subduction of military engagement.

This eventual subduction in scales of violence seems to provide prospects of predictability and a deceptive comfort with linear depictions of what is in fact a constellation of multidirectional trajectories of rapid and radical transformations of polity and society during armed conflict and beyond.

Linear narratives owe their public appeal to the ease with which they provide common-sense grids with which to perceive and to come to terms with outcomes of war, while also lending prospects of hope, legibility and accessibility to that which in fact requires continually explicit caution, methodological sophistication and cognitive rigour.

In the cases of Syria and Iraq, despite the breadth of research questions or policy approaches that define the growing body of knowledge about the 'endgame' of conflict, it is evident that the impetus of the post-conflict lens is either a search for means intended to bring about an end to violence (Goldenberg and Heras 2017), or else an inquiry into how conflict termination is likely to materialize, and what forms it is likely to take (Heydemann 2022). Either way, the emphasis on distinction between periods of active armed conflict and the post-conflict is premised on a presumed point of rupture or transition in patterns of conflict and violence. This edited volume advocates to shift this emphasis towards zooming instead into moments and locations in Syria and Iraq where patterns of violence have in fact changed in scale. Through this emphasis in the collection of chapters, this volume shows that what is commonly considered to be an imminent post-conflict phase in Syria and Iraq is in fact characterized by simultaneous patterns of continuity and change in relation to dynamics of war prior to military abatement. In other words, the decline in the incidence of violence in Syria and Iraq, quite commonly taken to suggest the onset of peace or of transition to a post-conflict phase, needs to be seen as a continuation of war conditions, albeit by other means, but still internal to and constitutive of the territories controlled by various parties to the conflict.

The empirical impulse that informs the premise and motivates the questions adopted in this volume emerges from the setting of a research project titled Striking from the Margins (SFM).[8] This project has gone through two cycles, the second of which comes to an end with this book. The primary motives of the project were a setting in which it was felt that there was a need to understand the calamities that have befallen the Arab Mashreq, and other parts of the Arab World as well, and to take stock of dynamics that led very quickly for the once unthinkable to become actual – reference is made here specifically to the destruction of Iraq and the violent disarticulation of Syria. 'Disarticulation' is a key word indicating the atrophy, or the destruction, of the structural connections and vertical hinges that link regions with economies, social collectivities, cultures, administrative structures, politics and much in a way constitutive of a nation-state. It was clear that any understanding of these major historical events needed a considerable degree of reflection and self-reflection.

This book and its precedent publications continue to analytically understand improbabilities in ways that transcend common-sense reference to sectarianism, tribalism, ethnic stresses, the mosaic model and associated instruments of interpretation. We consider such explanations too simplistic, heavily laden with ideological baggage, and, together with the common refrain of a 'return' to this and that, tend to distort our empirical and documented observations of reality on the ground. In addition, 'return' is a rhetorical trope applied heedlessly and succeeds only in obscuring complex recent dynamics by reduction to various registers of ancestralism – in other words, ancestralism, a feature arising from the conditions of war, is often used paradoxically to explain itself. Further, this ancestralist mode of interpretation is itself premised on an unreflected ethnological assumption made about the region, assumption of cyclical recidivism to registers of sect and tribe and their analogues. Put more generally, such common modes of interpretation adopt unreflected culturalist explanations, often called 'essentialist'.

In this perspective, the Arab Mashreq appears beset by congenital proclivities which disallow the proper functioning of state and the failure of modernization; it is beset by congenital incapacities. It is often claimed, as reiterated by the Bush and Obama administrations, that the state itself in the Arab World is artificial, and thereby doomed – little attention is paid to this sociological absurdity, or to the fact that states belong to culture, not to nature, and are by their nature artificial. We do not find this convincing, and think not so much of congenital sectarianism, but instead of sectarianization, for instance, as a constellation of specific dynamics arising from specific conjunctures. The same could be said of religion: not so much revival, for religion was never moribund, but as reconditioning and expanding the religious sphere. There is much output on this ((https://religion.ceu.edu/striking-margins-project-i); (http://religion.ceu.edu/striking-margins-project-phase-ii)), including studies published in *Striking from the Margins: State, Religion and Devolution of Authority in the Middle East*.[9] The stresses upon state structures and other articulating instances in the body-nationals of Syria and of Iraq were likewise seen in this perspective, with a considerable distance taken from the common clichés about the failure of the Arab state, of nationalism or of secularization. Much of these claims for failure and incapacity was congruent with neoliberal reforms and the international regime of identity politics.[10]

During the first stage of SFM, we sought to contribute to a paradigm shift based on empirical research, some of it very granular indeed. The application of the normal conceptual, analytical and perspectival resources of the social sciences and the humanities to these empirical findings was at variance with exceptionalist perspectives on the region, for all their currency in both academic work and policy perspectives. Based upon the empirical work produced, exceptionalist narratives seem to be at best far-fetched and often entirely unnecessary. The same vantage point also indicates that narrative exposés in the form of glorified journalism is rarely adequate to achieving a meaningful understanding of events narrated.

This book, building on the knowledge from preceding publications, seeks to make a transition from diagnostic to a more prognostic reading of armed conflicts in the Arab World in recent years with emphasis on outcomes and consequences rather than causality. But similar to the precedent work, this book comes to offer along with the companion volume, *Spoils of War: Gendering the Body Politic*,[11] an interconnected constellation of integrated studies of conditions that have come to interject themselves, unstably yet seemingly immovably, between wars which, according to the common perception, are now more or less over, bar the shouting, and more stable and durable conditions that might eventually emerge. These conditions of interregnum are neither chaotic nor haphazard, but have internal dynamics of their own in a variety of domains explored in this and the companion volume, a process of contradictory and incompatible restructuration in different regions and social and political domains, to the extent that their durability is difficult to judge. In fact, one of the major findings of both volumes suggests the implausibility of speaking of 'post-conflict' situations as linear sets of events that might be described in terms of progression, solution, overcoming and, ultimately, transition to a salutary condition.

Clearly enough, some readers might venture to infer possible policy directions from the results of these books. Policy directions have not been part of this research project's brief, although clearly the results of empirical research no less than those of analysis might and should lend themselves to conceptions of policy.

Conceptual framework

Empirical studies in this book focus on conditions where the abeyance of war-making is hedged by proneness to relapse, conditions which nonetheless manifest emergent factors sustaining military abatement potentially, accompanied with and strategies of reconfiguring culture, society and polity and stabilizing vested interests emerging from war. Iraq and Syria make for useful comparisons. Both witnessed large-scale destruction and disarticulation. The political modus operandi devised by the United States for Iraq, inspired by Lebanese consociationalism, has become part of an international nation-building doxa adopted by many international organizations working with notions of ancestralism and identity – these figure centrally in discussions on the future of Syria. And Syria seems to lag behind Iraq in this specific respect, where such arrangements seem to have been welded into the body politic, or what is, rather, presented as a national body politic.

Post-conflict frameworks, such as the Liberal Peace Paradigm and its critical counterpoints, represent an ensemble of distinct yet interconnected interventions, measures, policies, structures and conceptual frameworks that are typically deployed either as a package or selectively at later stages or aftermath of intra-state armed conflict under the premise of conflict termination. As highlighted by Balazs Kovacs in Chapter 2, some of the most recognizable components of this register are 'post-conflict reconstruction, transitional justice and reconciliation, economic reintegration, disarmament, demobilisation, and reintegration (DDR) schemes, democratisation including most especially elections, constitutional- and security sector reform (SSR), and various transformatory approaches to help deal with the past (DWP), re-establish social cohesion, and promote cultural change'.[12] Much of this discussion around peace-building takes place within the parameters of what came to be known since the early 1990s as the 'Liberal Peace Paradigm' and its critical counterpoints known as 'post-liberal peace' (Paffenholz 2021, Richmond 2010, Mac Ginty and Richmond 2013). The fundamental criticism levelled against the Liberal Peace Paradigm, which came to prominence in the post-Soviet historical context, was that post-conflict frameworks were too often embedded in or reliant on the very same political actors that contributed to social strife in the first place, and that institutional arrangements proposed as antidotes to open conflict were counterproductive as they were superimposed in a top-down format without consideration for local specificities or needs (Kovacs and Tobias 2016: 1).

The critical counterpoint to the Liberal Peace Paradigm that came to dominate the post-conflict register in the global humanitarian field, United Nations agencies and peace-building literature centred around the importance of local peace-building rather than national state-building as a more effective operational mechanism of conflict transformation (Mac Ginty and Richmond 2013), where it came to be framed as 'a critical agenda of peace' (Mac Ginty and Richmond 2013) in peace and conflict studies. As a result, the scholarship witnessed growing and well-merited emphasis on psycho-social needs, victim-centred approaches and trauma-informed programs of social and economic rehabilitation of localities impacted by political violence. This local turn, however, did not eliminate pre-existing pitfalls (specifically in its neoliberal tendencies) and continued to be the subject of much scholarly debate within the field of Peace and Conflict Studies, itself raising questions about the role of localizing the post-conflict register in processes of power consolidation of wartime vested interests under conditions of conflict abatement.[13] One might wish to remember that the dire condition in which Lebanon finds itself today resulted from years of consociation amongst erstwhile warlords, which emptied the state of all functional and regulatory content, and made it as a resource for private interests, as is the case in Syria and Iraq as well.

Amongst the key features of post-liberal peace is its continuous reliance on para-state systems of government which reinforce state-like structures, intentionally or otherwise. In other words, the alleged post-liberal peace paradigm of analytical and policy frameworks, as applied to Syria and Iraq, further reinforce the consolidation of territorial protectorates and concurrent projects of para-state building, alongside the central state and bypassing it. Therefore one could entertain analytical frames that posit the post-conflict register, with its vocabularies, programmatic aspects and debates, as complicit with dynamics of power consolidation as armed conflicts transition towards lower-intensity cycles of violence.

Despite the semantic flexibility of peace-building frameworks, parties to armed conflict continue to rush not only to endorse but also to appropriate peace-building frameworks, to serve agendas which are only superficially compatible with stated aspirations of state-rebuilding on the part of peace-builders. Of specific mention of such frameworks that are also intimately familiar to Syria and Iraq already are post-conflict reconstruction, transitional justice, economic reintegration, democratization schemes primarily based on devising electoral laws that satisfy belligerent groups, constitutional reforms, and various transformative approaches to re-establish a veneer of social cohesion. For instance, post-invasion peace-building schemes applied in Iraq under the banner of consociationalism as a conflict resolution strategy not only led to the further destabilization of Iraq, but also reinforced processes of sectarianization in the country, with a complex social and regional geography (Dodge 2021: 459–60). The outcome was the direct empowerment of factional and sectarian contenders for political power who captured key state institutions at the expense of 'the coherence of the state' as well as its autonomy (Dodge 2021: 459). Consequently, predatory dynamics against public interest, as in a general population as well as public institutions, remained uninterrupted (Akdedian 2023).

The increased bureaucratization and professionalization of the international aid industry has been a contributing factor in this instrumentalization of peace-building for purposes of power consolidation regardless of the ideological or semantic acrobatics of the humanitarian field. Peace-building frameworks have been ritualized and canonized such that they conceal, at face value, their innate political tendencies. It is this context of bureaucracy that power groups aiming to consolidate control are able to appropriate tools and resources of peace-building. Aspirations of actual peace-building may still be partially fulfilled through those endeavors. The political ambitions and idealistic aspirations of local actors enacting peace-building frameworks are not mutually exclusive. Utopian endeavors or achievements do not negate their political functions. Rather, the multiplicity of functions offered by peace-building toolkits reveals the legitimizing potential of such frameworks for political powers in place. The legitimizing functions of the peace-building framework will suit and serve the dominant political classes of Syria and Iraq that will continue to partition the spoils of war going forward.

Conflict transformation in Syria and Iraq: A background

The transition from open conflict in Syria and Iraq towards episodes of low-intensity violence does not represent a post-conflict phase. Instead, military contests can be seen as mutating and expanding into non-military fields. Despite the substantial reduction in scales of violence, conflict-transformation under conditions of military abatement represent a crucial transformational state of affairs where military exploits translate into action in non-military institutional domains – bearing in mind that "transformation" is here used in the sense of an interregnum, without clear indications of what the transformation is likely to lead to. These include the appropriation of state institutions, state functions and state resources by new intermediaries and warlords, which in turn shape the future of state-society relations.

Since 2011, the multiple atrophies of the fields in which state power had been exercised, and the deregulation and outsourcing of state prerogatives – military, legal, social, cultural – engendered a disarticulated multitude of centres of power, constituted alongside emergent or pre-existing subaltern pockets of organized social, religious, military or political activism, both in Iraq and Syria. The process of disarticulating the constituent structural elements of the nation state is in a further stage of decay in Syria than it is in Iraq. The most visible actors in this process of disarticulation are Salafi and Salafi-Jihadi currents among Sunnis, and analogous movements among Shiites, often ignored in studies of the region and assumed implicitly to be generically distinct. These forces gained capacity to reconfigure religious norms and political practices by means of decisionist action in areas where they achieved uncontested or stable military control. These are paralleled by the expansion of the religious sphere by deliberate state and para-state action in both Syria and Iraq.

The vertical hinge of these developments are processes of atrophy and disarticulation of state functions which devolved to a multitude of contested territories, agencies and institutional domains vying for supremacy. The outcome is manifest in the reconfiguration of polities: legal orders; economic transactions and infrastructures (including significant predatory and tributary exactions); ideologies, systems of education and norms of sociality that shape individual conduct; the re-socialization of communities into religious practices that had long been in abeyance or that had been invented in the heat of battle; and the institutionalization of emergent hierarchies of power, with an associated social and religious habitus. Syria and Iraq diverge in their experiences with regard to the outcomes of reconfigurations of polities. Both, however, are reconfigured in ways that rendered pre-conflict polities hardly recognizable.

With the devolution of the monopoly of violence throughout the armed conflicts in Syria and Iraq, security functions and military activities were outsourced in ways that attributed economic and sociocultural functions to security actors. This process of fragmentation that is still proceeding in Syria and Iraq, is noticeable in both government-held areas as well as in other areas, carved out by various formations, sometimes with tacit agreements with the formal government of the country (Akdedian and Hasan 2020). Either way, geographies of territorial control witnessed a thrust towards establishing para-state structures aiming to achieve a regulatory supremacy over institutional domains through the military field, and specifically on the part of those commanding available coercive capacities and economic resources based on networks of patronage, translocal support and local extraction of rent and tribute. Processes of power consolidation and reconstitution of authority also implicated areas beyond those that were contested militarily, as the devolution of centralized modes of social organization and government is intimately connected to peripheries as much as to centres of power. For example, as the coercive capacities of Assad's rule shrank due to sustained losses as well as geographic expansion on various fronts, areas that had not been contested militarily still witnessed transformations and new bargaining processes within local hierarchies, both institutional (such as the growing role of the religious domain) as well as clientelist (in local patronage and privileges).[14].

If we were to identify the moment when para-state building projects came to define the Syrian and Iraqi conflicts, it would be in the very moment that peaceful protests in Syria were forced and encouraged to transition towards military activism aimed at territorial control rather than the ouster of the Assad government, and the moment that private militias in Iraq were deemed legitimate partners in the military struggle against Daesh as it attempted to establish its own state structures. It is in this period, throughout the years 2012 and 2014 in Syria, and 2014 onwards in Iraq, that parallel statelets proliferated. Territorial divisions in Iraq are more complex, and less visible to outsiders, than those in Syria. In both cases, however, military groups scrambled for territorial control by either establishing state-like regulatory structures or capturing existing state institutions and functions with varying degrees of success and durability, depending upon coercive capacity, resources and support. Integral to such efforts were programs and efforts of reconfiguring society and culture by emergent groups within contested territories, such as Hay'at Tahrir al-Sham (HTS), Kurdish militants, Shi'ite militias in Iraq and in parts of Syria, and the Syrian state's outsourced military formations in areas subject to a variable geometry of central and devolved privateering control. Attempts at re-socializing entire areas and populations came about through the introduction of educational, societal, legal and cultural systems which are likely further to solidify under conditions of conflict abatement.[15]

Of specific relevance for illustrative purposes here is the role of Turkey as guarantor of stability in the Syrian Northwest in HTS-controlled (the rebranded Al-Nusra Front) Idlib while being the main protagonist in continuous military incursions and demographic engineering in Northeast Syria.[16] Similarly, the Russian role as guarantor of stability in the Syrian South (Dar'a) is in sharp contrast to its leading role in military intervention on the frontlines between HTS-controlled Idlib and territories controlled by the Syrian state and its allies.[17] Proxies of the Islamic Republic of Iran, such as the Hashd, had a leading role in defeating Daesh in Iraq but their personnel in the east and north-east, and in western and southern Syria, are also on the frontlines of conflict escalation, including the violent suppression of peaceful anti-sectarian demonstrations.[18] Lebanese Hezbollah forces too, while no longer leading military excursions on frontlines inside Syria, continue to bolster their presence in geo-strategically significant areas that can facilitate future military mobilization, internally or externally. Geographically contained and periodic military operations of low intensity continue to be manifest as part of the bargaining process over spoils of war partitioned according to the asymmetries of military powers at play.[19] Meanwhile, emergent political economies associated with those territorial protectorates along with internal sociocultural and demographic engineering efforts within each emergent territorial protectorate at the subnational level create the circumstances for sustained territorial segmentation, sustaining political, social, economic, legal and cultural segmentation within the national territory of Syria.

The acquisition and accumulation of spoils of war, as economic, political, ideological and societal rewards coveted by the surviving participants in armed conflict are in this perspective largely independent of an eventual final settlement of armed contestation. Rather, as the economic activities and predatory practices of paramilitary groups in Syria and Iraq show,[20] the contest over spoils of war have been integral to the history of the conflict. But it is the soldering into place consolidating the sway of vested interests enjoying the spoils of war that continuously escalates, as the intensity of organized violence subsides.

The concept of the state as an institutional domain, deployed here and through the flow of this volume, is defined as a field of power that consists of the authority and relative capacity to regulate other domains primarily through unmatched access to administrative and coercive force (al-Azmeh et. al. 2021, Abdelrahim 2006, Weber 1978: 236–7). It is through its regulatory coercive capacity that it gains further presence beyond the military field as 'political and administrative instances of command, coercion, coordination, regulation and, occasionally, of mediation' (al-Azmeh and al-Bagdadi 2021: 7–8). The authority of para-state territories in Syria and Iraq also stems from military capacities in place (al-Azmeh et. al. 2021). In this sense, as armed conflicts in Syria and Iraq transition towards low-intensity cycles of violence, the state, despite the institutional atrophy and reconfiguration of pre-conflict state structures, once again emerges as the major horizon and reward. In other words, the state emerges as a reward in and of itself due to its capacity to institutionalize the extraction of wealth and power by a set of 'private interests, or … concordant or discordant oligarchies" comprised of warlords and hoarders of capital during armed conflict (Magyar 2018: 139–40). In this sense, activities that are generally described as corrupt in common parlance emerge in Syria and Iraq, similar to other war-impacted contexts, to constitute a structuring element in the very system of appropriation of state structures and state functions, rather than an institutional derangement or alleged cultural attribute.[21] The post-conflict register in its peace-building endeavors is at times complicit with the entrenchment of this system of private appropriation of public functions and decision-making processes as a mechanism of conflict resolution.

Structure of the book

This volume is organized around four dimensions of conflict transformation pertaining to Syria and Iraq. Part I of the book highlights analytical and policy frameworks of conflict termination. Its purpose is to aggregate vocabularies of conflict transformation through a juxtaposition of post-conflict paradigms of knowledge against the emergent realities of military abatement in Syria and Iraq. Part II addresses the issue of perpetuating forms of violence and potential relapse by looking at circumstances of military standoffs. Part III of this volume looks into political economies and geopolitics of conflict transformation, with the reinforcement of territorial protectorates under conditions of military stalemate in view. This section indicates conditions that sustain the transition of conflicts in Syria and Iraq to low-intensity events of violence. Finally, Part IV focuses on efforts of sociocultural and political engineering that reconfigure the body politic under circumstances of military stalemate. These actions represent non-military forms of conflict perpetuation.

In Part I , entitled 'Conceptual and Global Exploration of the "Post-conflict Register", the focus is placed on empirical and analytical inconsistencies of post-conflict frameworks through a focus on the fundamental pillars of the framework: (1) peace-building (Balazs Aron Kovacs), (2) ceasefires (Marika Sosnowski) and (3) (de)militarization (Uğur Ümit Üngör). Balazs Aron Kovacs looks into the peace-builiding paradigm, in theory and practice, from a comparative perspective with instances from the Philippines, Nepal, Sri Lanka and Timor-Leste as case studies where variations of the liberal peace paradigm and its derivatives (including critical perspectives) have been attempted. This chapter introduces vocabularies of post-conflict frameworks and provides an empirical investigation that highlights *their* functional implications. The second chapter, by Marika Sosnowski, focuses on ceasefires and their function in processes of conflict transformation in Syria. The third chapter of this section by Uğur Ümit Üngör looks into the role of paramilitarism in contexts of war and peace and dynamics of conflict perpetuation in Syria and Iraq.

Part II, 'Reconstitution of Power in Syria and Iraq: Military Standoffs and Conflict Fragility', focuses on military conditions of relapse to military conflict in Iraq and Syria under circumstances of conflict abatement. Abdullah Al-Jabassini analyses conditions of security fragmentation and the frailty of reconciliation settlements in Syria, highlighting challenges to service-provision as well as overall processes of reconstitution of state authority in the Syrian south. Haian Dukhan concentrates on the rise of tribal military groups and the consolidation of their military capacities in areas beyond urban centres in Iraq and Syria. The chapter highlights the predatory implications of this rise for civilians through patterns of sequestration of properties during conditions of military stalemate. Jessica Watkins's chapter discusses the contexts and implications of counterinsurgency dynamics in Iraq where Daesh had a stronghold.

Part III of the book, 'The political Economy and Geopolitics of emergent Orders in Syria and Iraq', turns to war economies and current proxy dynamics of power through economic means and economic protectorates in Syria and Iraq.

Joseph Daher highlights the war and post-war economic contexts that continue to reinforce economic disparities and strengthen social inequities, regional disparities and generalized corruption which led to the protest movements in Syria in the first place but at the same time created opportunities for Assad's power consolidation, relative to specific geographies and milieux, during crisis. The chapter also highlights how post-conflict reconstruction efforts are a continuation of war by other means. Ali Aljasem's chapter provides documentation of the shadow economy of paramilitary networks and groups, and shows how these reinforce war economies, local systems of patronage, war-lordism and foreign sponsorship under conditions of conflict abatement. The final chapter in this section, by Irene Costantini and Yasmin Chilmeran, offer perspectives for understanding Iraqi protestors' conceptions of the Iraqi state and its socio-economic roles. The chapter argues that reading the Iraqi protests through the multi-layered socio-economic and socio-political failures of the post-conflict state building model of Iraq (post-US invasion), provides insight into the persistence of this model of state, as well as of the state-society issues that gave rise to Daesh in the first place.

The last three chapters of Part IV, entitled 'The Body Politic Reconfigured: Between Social Engineering and Community Resistance', look at the dynamics of social engineering, and at contestations over the reconfiguration of the body politic in Syria and Iraq during and in the aftermath of violent conflict. Hammoud Hammoud presents the strategies of power consolidation over the religious field by the Assad state. Zeynep Sahin-Mencütek and Osman Bahadir Dinçer focus on Interventions and efforts of social engineering targeting the Syrian north and displaced Syrians. Harout Akdedian and Ali Aljasem look at civilian initiatives to resist conditions of war through a case study that highlights the limits to civilian agency and collective transformative capacity during conditions of military stalemate.

Notes

1 Rates of knowledge production in the English language are suggestive due to the language's position as a global language of consumption of social-scientific material, thus indicating trends beyond areas speaking English as a native or primary academic language. See Hanafi and Arvanatis (2016).
2 Search results from JSTOR on publications dedicated to Syria in part or in total, accessed 22 December 2021: https://www.jstor.org/action/doAdvancedSearch? group=none&q0=Syria&q1=&q2=&q3=&q4=&q5=&q6=&sd=2011&ed=2021&pt=&isbn=&f0=ti&c1= AND&f1=all&c2=AND&f2=all&c3=AND&f3= all&c4=AND&f4=all&c5=AND&f5=all&c6=AND&f6=all&acc=off&la=eng+OR+en&ar=on&bk= on&rr=on&so=rel.
3 Search results from google scholar for publications dedicated to Syria in part or in total, accessed 22 December 2021: https://www.jstor.org/action/doAdvancedSearch? group=none&q0=Syria&q1=&q2=&q3= &q4=&q5=&q6=&sd=2000&ed=2010&pt= &isbn=&f0=ti&c1=AND&f1=all&c2=AND&f2=all&c3= AND &f3=all&c4=AND&f4=all&c5=AND&f5=all&c6=AND&f6= all&acc=off&la=eng+OR+en&ar=on&bk=on&rr=on&so=rel.

4 https://scholar.google.com/scholar?start=60&q=allintitle:+syria&hl=en&as_sdt=0,38&as_ylo=2000&as_yhi=2010&as_vis=1.
5 Between 1992 and 2002, 30,061 publications featuring on JSTOR in the form of books, book chapters, journal articles and research reports were dedicated to Iraq. https://www.jstor.org/action/doAdvancedSearch? group=none&q0=Iraq &q1=&q2=&q3=&q4= &q5=&q6=&sd=1992&ed=2002&pt=&isbn= &f0=all& c1=AND&f1=all&c2=AND&f2=all&c3=AND&f3= all&c4=AND&f4=all&c5= AND&f5=all&c6= AND&f6=all&acc=off&la=&so=rel; during the subsequent ten years, the number of equivalent publications featured was 114,551; see https://www.jstor.org/action/doAdvancedSearch? group=none&q0=Iraq&q1 =&q2=&q3=&q4= &q5=&q6=&sd=2003&ed=2013&pt=&isbn= &f0=all&c1 =AND&f1=all&c2=AND&f2=all&c3= AND&f3=all&c4=AND&f4=all&c5= AND&f5=all&c6=AND&f6=all&acc=off&la= &so=rel.
6 This rise is not only in the number of publications but also in the number of research centres and professional societies. See Bamyeh (2015).
7 For a sample of explicit linear narratives described above, see Allard and Fazal (2019), Kahl, Goldenberg and Heras (2017) and Bull and Ollivant (2022). For narratives of implied linear trajectories or projections, see also Sharif (2019), Gani and Hinnebusch (2022) and Watkins and Hasan (2021). For a sample of similar projections in the humanitarian field, see United Nations (2021) and International Crisis Group (2019).
8 This project was supported generously by the Carnegie Corporation of New York, and based at the Central European University.
9 Edited by Aziz Al-Azmeh, Nadia Al-Bagdadi, Harout Akdedian and Harith Hasan (2021). The Introduction sketches the conceptual framework of the whole project (https://saqibooks.com/books/saqi/striking-from-the-margins/).
10 See, for instance, the critical comments of Gilbert Achcar, 'Hegemony, Domination, Corruption and Fraud in the Arab Region', *Middle East Critique*, 2021 (https://doi.org/10.1080/19436149.2021.1875173).
11 Edited by Nadia Al-Bagdadi and Valentina Zagaria.
12 Balazs Kovacs, Chapter 1
13 For specific explorations on Syria and Iraq in relation to the Liberal Peace Paradigm and its counterpoints, see Paffenholz (2021) and Dodge (2021), respectively. For a broader overview, see special issue (Kovacs and Tobias 2016: 1–105).
14 Akdedian (2021).
15 See Chapter 12 by Hammoud Hammoud.
16 See Chapter 13 by Zeynep Sahin and Bahadir Dincer
17 See Chapters 5 and 6 by Abdullah Al-Jabassini and Haian Dukhan, respectively.
18 See Chapter 10 by Costantini and Chilmeran.
19 The latest episodes of such confrontations were amongst factions within Turkish backed forces in the Syrian North (Oweis 2022).
20 See Chapter 9, by Ali Aljasem.
21 See Chapter 2 by Balazs Kovacs.

Bibliography

Abdelrahim, H. (2006). *Al-Zubuniyya al-siyasiyya fi al-mujtama' al-'arabi: Qira'a ijtima'iyya siyasiyya fi tajribat al-bina' al-watani bi-Tunis* [Political clientelism in the

Arab society: a socio-political reading of the national building experience in Tunisia]. Beirut: Riyad al-Rayyis.

Achcar, Gilbert, R. (2021). 'Hegemony, Domination, Corruption and Fraud in the Arab Region, *Middle East Critique.* https://doi.org/10.1080/19436149.2021.1875173 (accessed 9 June 2023).

Akdedian, H. (2021). 'Stifling the Public Domain in Syria: Religion and State from Neoliberalism to State Atrophy'. In A. al-Azmeh, N. al-Bagadadi, H. Akdedian and H. Hasan (eds), *Striking from the Margins: State, Religion and Devolution of Authority in the Middle East* (91–118). London: Saqi Books.

Akdedian, H. (2023). *State Atrophy in Syria: War, Society and Institutional Changes.* Edinburgh: Edinburgh University Press.

Akdedian, H., and Hasan, H. (2020). 'State Atrophy and the Reconfiguration of Borderlands in Syria and Iraq: Post-2011 Dynamics'. *Political Geography*, 80: 1–10.

al-Azmeh, A., and al-Bagdadi, N. (2021). 'Introduction'. In A. al-Azmeh, N. al-Bagdadi, H. Akdedian and H. Hasan (eds), *Striking from the Margins: State, Religion and Devolution of Authority in the Middle East* (1–24). London: Saqi Books.

al-Azmeh, A., Al-Bagdadi, N., Akdedian, H., and Hasan, H. (2021). *Striking from The Margins: State, Religion and Devolution of Authority in the Middle East.* London: Saqi Books.

Allard, B., Fazal, T. M. (2019). 'How Syria's Civil War May End'. *Washington Post.* 28 August.https://www.washingtonpost.com/politics/2019/08/28/how-syr ias-civil-war-may-end/ (accessed 24 April 2022).

Bamyeh, M. (2015). *Social Sciences in the Arab World: Forms of Presence.* Beirut: Arab Social Science Monitor.

Bishara, Azmi (2020). *al-Intiqal al-dimuqrati wa-ishkaliyatuh dirasah nazariyah wa-tatbiqiyah muqaranah* [Problems of democratization: A comparative theoretical and applied study]. Beirut: al-Markaz al-Arabi lil-Abhath wa-Dirasat al-Siyasat.

Bull, B., and Ollivant, D. (2022). 'Iraq After ISIS: What to Do Now'. *New America.* 12 April. newamerica.org/international-security/reports/iraq-after-isis-what-do-now/ (accessed April 2018).

Dodge, T. (2021). 'The Failure of Peacebuilding in Iraq: The Role of Consociationalism and Political Settlements'. *Journal of Intervention and Statebuilding* 15(4): 459–75.

Eido, I. (2014). 'ISIS: The Explosion of Narratives – the Land of the Revolution between Political and Metaphysical Eternities'. *Jadaliyya.* 3 October. https://www.jadaliyya.com/Details/31290 (accessed 15 February 2022).

Gani, J. K., and Hinnebusch, R. (2022). *Actors and Dynamics in the Syrian Conflict's Middle Phase: Between Contentious Politics, Militarization and Regime Resilience.* London: Routledge.

Hanafi, S., and Arvanatis, R. (2016). *Knowledge Production in the Arab World: The Impossible Promise.* London: Routledge.

Heydemann, S. (2022). 'Assad's normalization and the politics of erasure in Syria'. *Brookings Institute.* 13 January. https://www.brookings.edu/blog/order-from-chaos/2022/01/13/assads-normalization-and-the-politics-of-erasure-in-syria/ (accessed April 2022).

International Crisis Group. (2019). 'Exiles in Their Own Country: Dealing with Displacement in Post-ISIS Iraq'. *Middle East Briefing.* 19 October. https://www.crisisgroup.org/middle-east-north-africa/gulf-and-arabian-peninsula/iraq/b79-exiles-their-own-country-dealing-displacement-post-isis-iraq (accessed April 2022).

Kahl, C. H., Goldenberg, I., and Heras, N. A. (2017). 'A Strategy of Ending the Syrian Civil War'. *Center for a New American* Security. 1 June. https://www.jstor.org/stable/resrep06 269?seq=3 (accessed April 2022).

Kovacs, B., and Tobias, P. (2016). 'Questioning Peace Infrastructure and Peace Formation'. *Peace and Conflict Review* 9(1): 1–11.

Mac Ginty, R., and Richmond, O. (2013). 'The Local Turn in Peace Building: A Critical Agenda for Peace'. *Third World Quarterly* 34(5): 763–83.

Magyar, B. (2018). 'Towards a Terminology for Post-Communist Regimes'. In B. Magyar (ed.), *Stubborn Structures: Reconceptualizing post-Communist Regimes* (139–40). Budapest: Central European University.

Oweis, K. Y. (2022). 'Militant Group Aligned with Turkey Flexes Muscles after Fighting in Northern Syria'. *The National*. 19 June. https://www.thenationalnews.com/mena/syria/2022/06/19/militant-group-aligned-with-turkey-flexes-muscles-after-fighting-in-northern-syria/ (accessed une 2022).

Paffenholz, T. (2021). 'Perpetual Peacebuilding: A New Paradigm to Move Beyond the Linearity of Liberal Peacebuilding'. *Journal of Intervention and peacebuilding* 15(3): 367–85.

Richmond, O. (2010). 'Resistance and the Post-liberal Peace'. *Journal of International Studies* 38(3): 665–92.

Shami, S., and Miller-Idriss, C. (2017). *Middle East Studies for the New Millennium: Infrastructures of Knowledge*. New York: New York University Press.

Sharif, S. (2019). 'Predicting the End of the Syrian Conflict: From Theory to the Reality of a Civil War'. *Studies in Conflict & Terrorism* 44(4): 326–45.

United Nations. (2021). 'Ending Syria's War Is Our Collective Responsibility, UN Chief Tells Donor Conference'. *UN News*. 30 March. https://news.un.org/en/story/2021/03/1088672 (accessed 8 April 2022).

Watkins, J., and Hasan, M. (2021). 'Post-ISIL Reconciliation in Iraq and the Local Anatomy of National Grievances: The Case of Yathrib. *peacebuilding*. 1 July. https://www.tandfonline.com/doi/full/10.1080/21647259.2021.1940434 (accessed April 2022).

Weber, M. (1978). *Economy and Society*. Los Angeles: University of California Press.

Part I

CONCEPTUAL AND GLOBAL EXPLORATION OF THE 'POST-CONFLICT' REGISTER

Chapter 2

PEACE-BUILDING: FROM LIBERAL STATE BUILDING IMPERATIVE TO THE POST-CONFLICT REGISTER? PERSPECTIVES FROM COMPARISON

Balazs Aron Kovacs

Introduction

This chapter investigates how the broad field of peace-building, ostensibly seeking to create conditions in conflict-affected societies that would reduce the likelihood of relapse to violent conflict through addressing its root causes, transforming the structures that generate and drive it, came to be so easily overtaken by pervasive conflict actors – including the state. In particular, how certain of its approaches are appropriated by the state – or, to be more precise, governments in charge of the state apparatus and local power brokers mediating it – in conflict-affected countries to serve agendas superficially compatible with peace-building's stated aspirations while sometimes even undermining them.

What this volume refers to as 'the post-conflict register' is this ensemble of distinct yet interconnected interventions, measures, policies, structures and processes – sometimes even referred to as 'tools' – typically deployed as a package at the later stages or aftermath of internal – that is, waged within the internationally-recognized boundaries of formally sovereign states – armed conflict. Some of its most recognizable components are post-conflict reconstruction; transitional justice and reconciliation; economic reintegration; disarmament, demobilisztion and reintegration (DDR) schemes; democratization including most especially elections; constitutional- and security sector reform (SSR); and various transformatory approaches to help dealing with the past (DWP), re-establish social cohesion and promote cultural change.

It began taking shape at the winding down of the Cold War through an evolutionary process in an ecosystem of UN agencies, inter-governmental organizations, international and domestic NGOs, academic research institutions, think tanks, social movements and – at least formally – sovereign states of widely divergent levels of power and capacity. It is an idiosyncrasy that, due to its origins in the post-Cold War moment, much of the ideological content of these interventions is pervasively liberal in nature – in the political-constitutional and economic senses of the term – to the point that the literature and practice refer to it as the liberal peace-building paradigm.

Much critical attention has been paid to this feature of the project, taking particular aim at its blueprint-based social engineering; its lack of cultural, social and political awareness and sensitivity, and even its supposed imperialism (e.g. Chandler 2006; Schellhaas and Seegers 2009). Such criticism, indeed, prompted theoretical and institutional responses seeking to reform peace-building. These include the emergence of 'the local turn' (Leonardsson and Rudd 2015; Roger Mac Ginty and Richmond 2013) in critical peace and conflict studies, initiatives like 'localization' (e.g. Barakat and Milton 2020; International Alert 2020) seeking to channel a greater proportion of international donor funding to local responders to crises, the 'sustaining peace' agenda and the humanitarian-development-peace nexus, both originating in the UN, to expand the scope of peace-building and mainstreaming it in all areas of the organization's work, and most recently a growing bottom-up demand to decolonize aid and peace-building. Yet, the depth and significance of this liberalism should not be overstated, as it is only part of peace-building's ideological baggage, and arguably an eroding one.

From the outset, institutional peace-building has sought to (re)constitute the state, seen as the default organizer of society and guarantor of international stability. Even though this was explicitly stated in an Agenda for Peace (UNSG 1992), the defining document of the entire project, the statism inherent in it went unquestioned for considerably longer than liberalism, and allowed for a near-complete identification of peace-building with state-building (Cubitt 2013). In this chapter I trace how the state-building imperative came to dominate peace-building, how it eventually allowed for a (re-)definition of peace as having state authority in place – liberal or not – and, finally, how the tools of the post-conflict register have in some cases been usurped by governments and local leaders mediating the state to pursue their agenda while securing a veneer of respectability and legitimacy through the use of the language and forms of international peace-building.

Two developments are of particular concern here. The first is institutional peace-builders' increasing alignment with, and in some cases subordination to, the narrowly defined interests of governments seeking to dominate societies, including the UN whose legitimacy at least partially stems from being a champion of universal norms, many of which seek to limit states' capacity to do that (Warnecke 2020). This tension is particularly visible in the case of the UN, which simultaneously seeks to uphold these universal norms and the primacy of the state as the organizer of societies. It has, on numerous occasions, proffered ideas and approaches which sought to de-centre the state and focus on human flourishing, such as human development instead of economic development as the measure of progress, or human security instead of state security. At the same time, it reaffirms the centrality of the state, and (also) measures its success by the extent it is able to support states in carrying out their policies. To a lesser extent, and in somewhat different ways, civil society peace-building also faces similar dilemmas, having to make compromises with states and at times non-state actors to be able to operate in a given country or area within a country (Hayes et al. 2017).

The second is the way conflict-affected states themselves adopt the rhetoric of liberal peace-building and its forms – the post-conflict register – and deploy these as tools of domination. A prominent example of this is the Philippines where a negotiated agreement between the government and the major secessionist armed group is in place with a light international footprint. This peace process coexists with a separate, long-running ideological insurgency (Angstrom 2001), which the current government is attempting to handle through an aggressive counterinsurgency campaign, lending it for fruitful comparative analysis. It can be observed in other diverse settings too. For instance, in Nepal, where a negotiated peace agreement resulted in significant international involvement (Robins 2012), so much so that it was effectively turned into a laboratory of international organizations to test their latest ideas. In Sri Lanka, where war was terminated through military victory, the involvement of international peace-building has been limited (Höglund and Orjuela 2012). Or in Timor-Leste, where the UN established a protectorate to bring an end to armed conflict, sparking intense protest among the locals, and which eventually became, according to Freedom House, the most democratic country in the region (Arthur 2020). The key element of the appropriation of the post-conflict register by governments and strongmen is a cycle of de- and re-politicization. It is a process in which specific forms of intervention become canonized and formalized, losing their inherently political character. This is then followed by a re-politicization by the state and powerful political leaders who use what are now neutral tools for their own ends.

The landscape we see emerging here is one increasingly dominated by states or their local surrogates that speak the language of peace-building and use its tools to consolidate their power. The peace that they build is often a bleak, negative peace, which may be preferable to war, but still a far cry from the emancipatory aspirations of the pioneers of peace-building, the UN and other peace-building interveners, to achieve 'positive peace'.

The post-conflict register

One does not need to be a specialist in peace and conflict studies, peace-building, or any adjacent area of scholarship to recognize the individual features of this landscape. They are familiar to anyone who follows the politics of any number of countries embroiled in internal armed conflict or recovering from one. They populate the reports of the UN, aid agencies, local and international non-governmental organizations (INGOs), sometimes the governments of the countries in question. Some even make it to the news, like the various transitional justice mechanisms ranging from the likes of the Extraordinary Chambers in the Court of Cambodia and the Truth and Reconciliation Commission of South Africa to high-profile post-conflict elections to the highly controversial Provincial Reconstruction Teams in Afghanistan. These are some of the major, macro-level components of the post-conflict register. In their practical application they are broken down to hundreds of discrete and categorized activities, canonized through a constantly evolving repository of 'best-practices', passed down through specialized university programmes, workshops and training, and consolidated by the donors and major peace-building actors. Below, three very different components are discussed briefly, including how they are conceived and taken over by governments and local elites to pursue their power interests.

The monopoly of violence: Disarmament, demobilization and reintegration

Disarmament, Demobilization and Reintegration (DDR) programmes seek to address the problems that arise in the aftermath of a peace agreement in relation to the fighters – typically rank-and-file and lower ranks – whose organizations are dismantled, downsized or integrated into the security services of the state (Kilroy 2021; Muggah 2009). It is related to other peace-building interventions, such as SSR (Brzoska 2005), stabilization and economic development, and itself contains many more specific activities or tools (livelihood projects, trauma healing, community dialogues, etc.). Disarmament means the collection and disposal of arms and ammunition and similar materials from combatants, and often from the civilian population as well. Demobilization is the formal and controlled discharge of active (and in some cases former or retired) combatants from non-state armed groups, sometimes including some form of 'reinsertion' assistance, with the aim of effectively dismantling the military structure of these groups. Reintegration is a process by which ex-combatants are led back to civilian life, with support to obtaining sustainable employment or other legal source of income (e.g. self-employment or entrepreneurship), the victims of the conflict, the dependents and families of these, so-called civilian returnees and the communities where the reintegration takes place. It is a political, social and economic process with an open time frame, primarily taking place in communities at the local level (United Nations, n.d.).

DDR directly serves the restoration of statehood and the securing of the monopoly of the state over violence. It began in the 1970s and became a mainstay of UN peace operations by the 1990s. Over the decades, operations have increased in scope, reach, complexity and methods. At a minimum, it is concerned with security, the removal of arms, the people who wield them and the structures which enable them to challenge the state in an organized and violent manner. At a maximum it seeks to create opportunities for (economic) development and conflict transformation. There is variation in how and by whom the collection and disposal of weapons is taken care of; the specific arrangements to reduce the overall number of armed personnel and transform or disband non-state armed forces; how the reintegration or reinsertion of former combatants is carried out, what package the DDR implementers offer them and so on.

By reducing the available weapons and dismantling structures capable of sustained armed combat, DDR serves the prevention focus of peace-building. Its more recent focus on community violence reduction is a particular case in point as it is conducted even before a formal DDR process, and as such can contribute to conflict transformation. Yet, in a broader perspective, the removal of arms from non-state actors – individuals and groups – and the elimination of organized groups specialized in violence independent of the state has been an integral part of the modern state-building project (Tilly 1985), as it is essential to establishing the state's monopoly of force. As such, while it is not always framed thus, DDR is inseparable from the state-building agenda of contemporary peace-building. This is not to argue against DDR per se. But in the absence of a state which respects human rights, which does not provide genuine avenues for the peaceful contestation for power, or where the armed forces and other components of the state's violence apparatus are not entirely under civilian control, a well-implemented DDR programme may reduce the capacity to rebel while conserving the root causes of conflict. Vice versa, since this prospect is not lost on non-state armed groups, they may decide to create hidden arms caches as an insurance against oppression or reprisals. This, in turn, means that instability is conserved.

DDR is at one level an evolving, complex approach to deal with a specific challenge of post-conflict peace-building – itself is part of the post-conflict register. At another, it is broken down to discrete tasks – tools – which are sometimes less than optimally coordinated or at cross-purposes with each other. These tasks often overlap with other areas, particularly in development. Accordingly, states and other local actors with the ability to do so sometimes cherry-pick from these and use them for purposes beyond peace-building.

For instance, the Philippine government runs several distinct DDR programmes targeting various non-state armed groups. Two of the major processes have targeted the major Muslim insurgencies, the Moro National Liberation Front (MNLF) and its splinter group, the Moro Islamic Liberation Front (MILF), neither of which was explicitly called as such, for reasons of political sensitivity – nevertheless, they have this function. While the earlier one with the MNLF only included the reintegration component accompanied by a voluntary weapon buy-back scheme (Makinano and Lubang 2001), the more recent, currently ongoing process with the MILF (called 'Normalization') does include 'decommissioning' – the removal of combatants from the military structure and the surrender of weapons – along with reintegration (Crisis Group 2021). One of the strains on the broader peace process is exactly the fact that the government is pushing for disarmament while lagging on other key components of importance to the MILF, most crucially the dismantling of private armies of local strongmen (Engelbrecht 2021), a direct threat to their political survival once their arms are surrendered.

Another one of these, the Enhanced Comprehensive Local Integration Program (E-CLIP), targets the communist New People's Army with which the government is in open war. In other words, the Philippine government took the key components of DDR – a reintegration package, a gun buy-back scheme, a broad range of livelihoods assistance including skills training and loan schemes, assistance to receiving communities, and others – and turned them into counterinsurgency measures. Arguably, by the standards of the UN it would not qualify as a DDR programme, but the point is exactly this: a government appropriates the tools along with the rhetoric of peace-building (the E-CLIP programme is run by the Office of the Presidential Adviser on the Peace Process, the Philippines's 'peace ministry', discussed in more detail later), and more recently that of the war on terror, too, and uses them for counterinsurgency.

In all cases there has been an apparent, but selective, concern with securing the state's monopoly of violence. In fact, the E-CLIP programme is arguably a more comprehensive DDR programme than the Normalization. Inasmuch as it concerns potential politico-military challenges against the regime, state-run DDR programmes pursue disarmament with increasing élan. Not so much when non-state armed groups are aligned with the regime. For instance, in the Mindanao peace process the private armies of local political clans, which have long-standing accommodations with Manila (and present a direct existential threat to an unarmed MILF), the state is not exerting much effort to implement the DDR. Similarly, while the E-CLIP programme actively seeks to entice communist insurgents to disarm and demobilize, it also tolerates private armies, meanwhile the Armed Forces of the Philippines actively trains the private militias of business corporations in areas of active insurgency.

At the same time, the Normalization process stipulates the transformation of six MILF camps to civilian-economic functions, as part of generating 'peace dividends' for ex-combatants and the broader conflict-affected population through economic development projects in these areas. Apart from it progressing slower than expected and generating new conflicts with local indigenous communities, in some of these camps local commanders of the MILF appear to be using this opportunity to transform themselves, along with their camps, into major landlords, an example of how a DDR process can be used to accumulate capital and establish economic-political power in a post-conflict context by the elite members of a non-state armed group.

East Timor and Sri Lanka present two other examples where DDR has been closely interlinked with state-building agendas. In the former, independent statehood was created through direct tutelage by the UN. This included an SSR programme, which absorbed some of the former combatants, while the others went through a series of initiatives, led by INGOs, some UN agencies and eventually the new independent government (De Almeida 2017). In this sense, the DDR (and SSR) processes were not usurped by any particular actor as much as they were key constituting elements of the state-building effort. In Sri Lanka, where war termination was achieved through military victory, DDR has been a tool to re-impose state rule over the vanquished population, albeit with some – tokenistic – consultation with UN agencies and international donors to learn the know-how of DDR from them, and to legitimize the process (Molloy 2011: 120).

In contrast, SSR by definition targets the state's broadly understood violence apparatus with the dual aim of improving its capacity to provide physical protection to the state and its citizens, and to do it in a way that is coherent with the norms of democratic states such as civilian control and respect for human rights. In theory, DDR and SSR should form a continuum, whereby the removal of violent challengers from the state would segue into the transformation of the state's use of its violence apparatus. The successful integration of DDR and SSR processes could, in theory, help address the kind of security dilemma of non-state armed groups described earlier, and compel them to genuinely disarm and dismantle its military structure. From the outset a consistent criticism of SSR has been its very close connection with an externally driven state-building agenda and a technocratic approach that disregarded local context and actors outside the state (e.g. Jackson 2011, 2018; Kurtenbach and Ansorg 2020). Stojanović Gajić and Pavlović (2021) identify the security sector as a distinct target for state capture, in particular by political actors to secure impunity, securitization and the selective use of the justice system and security provision with the aim of exerting social and political control. Beyond the theoretical criticism, SSR's track record has been considered poor as well, which in turn led to thinking about ways to reconceptualize (Sedra 2018). Similarly to other areas of peace-building, SSR, in theory albeit less in practice, is moving towards increased contextualization, localization and integration of relevant societal actors within the state and without (Donais 2018).

Civil society

A very different, and even more burgeoning area of peace-building is civil society support and civil society-led interventions. The fact is that arguably by far the greatest number and most innovative of peace-building activities originate from genuine local civil society organizations, which seek to address the pressing concerns of their constituencies. Many of these do not ever get in contact with international or state-led institutional peace-building. These are not the focus of the following paragraphs, although they sometimes are the origin of new approaches in peace-building.

The support for and development of civil society has been an integral, often discussed and conceptually contested component of peace-building. Civil society in the context of international peace-building is usually understood in one of three ways. First, and in its broadest sense, as a social space of discourse where ideas emerge, are debated, where ideologies are compared and where, eventually, a social contract is composed (Kaldor 2003). Second, as the 'arena of voluntary – uncoerced – collective action around shared interests, purposes and values' (Pouligny 2005: 497). Third and most narrowly, as particular kinds of organizations, which are, at least legally, independent from the state, from for-profit organizations (businesses, 'the market'), and from those institutions of society, which are considered to comprise the 'private' sphere (the family).

Paffenholz (2009: 60) points out that 'historically the concept of "civil society" has been an almost purely Western concept, tied to the political emancipation of European citizens from former "feudalistic" ties, monarchy, and the state during the 18th and 19th centuries'. While civil society in its broadest sense is found in any society of sufficient organizational complexity, peace-builders do not necessarily find it (Pouligny 2005: 498–9). It is either because they are not prepared to find it due to their insufficient local knowledge; they are professionalized to the point that they would not recognize anything lacking expected level of formality, even if they saw it, or would dismiss it as unacceptable and lacking credibility; or they face such pressures – time, resources, expected performance – which preclude lengthy and energy-consuming engagement with such indigenous civil society (see Ballesteros 2020).

The substantial reasons for emphasizing the creation and strengthening of civil society are varied. Some see civil society organizations as the space to regenerate social capital (Putnam 2000), or a Tocquevillian 'school of democracy' (Putnam, Leonardi and Nanetti 1993). A similar expected function is bridging groups in divided societies, such as formerly hostile communities. Others see civil society as a counterbalance against the state – which is one of its supposed roles in established democratic states. Civil society organizations are expected to hold the state accountable to internationally accepted norms of democracy, to ensure transparency, or to advocate causes of public interest. For Lederach (1997), civil society is where many of those mid-level leaders are found who can bridge the gap between elites and grassroots and thus serve as tier two in a peace process, including post-conflict peace-building. The diverse expectations of civil society at times lead to internal contradictions in peace-building missions between civil society strengthening and state-building.

The historical and philosophical origins of civil society in Europe as understood by peace-builders matter. First, the earlier mentioned inability or unwillingness of peace-builders to recognize (in both senses of the word) locally existing forms of civil society is because they seek what is familiar to them and if they do not find it, they go on and create it. This is as true of the substance of civil society (its goals, values, culture) as of its form (trade unions, NGOs, etc.).

Second, the internal contradictions between civil society and state-building are not incidental. They are not the products of faulty sequencing or inefficient coordination. Rather, they stem from the very logic of this European history, where indeed, the organizations today recognized as civil society emerged out of resistance to the state and state-building, or at least to influence the state to serve certain desirable ends. In this sense, working towards a well-functioning civil society can be an empowering or a disempowering thing. It could help develop the spaces and avenues for people to discuss their common affairs and pursue their interests in the public sphere peacefully and constructively, or it could be a mechanical creation of 501(c) – clones that meet the formal requirements of international donors and call that civil society. It follows that activities under this heading may be part of a state-building project or not, depending on the approach one takes.

Having said all this, 'civil society' became both an end in itself of, and an entry point for, peace-building. Through local NGOs, which are (assumed to be) legitimate to both the originators and the recipients of interventions, conflict-affected communities can be reached. This makes them the implementers of many other 'tools' of peace-building from organizing dialogue and reconciliation workshops to livelihood projects to delivering basic social (and even supposedly state) services.

Civil society organizations thus play a particular role in the economy and politics of peace-building. Especially in international peace-building, resources are channelled through a limited set of institutions. Prominent among these is the UN and regional intergovernmental organizations, embassies of donor countries, a select group INGOs and finally the governments of the states in question. The ultimate recipient of most of these resources is also the state in some form, either as direct beneficiary or as distributor to target communities. A still significant portion of funding and other resources, however, go to local civil society organizations, in part for the ideological/political reasons discussed above, and in part because they are the actual implementers of the programmes and projects of the INGOs, the UN and other primary conduits of donor funding. In order to boost their legitimacy, capture more resources, promote their political agenda with a degree of deniability and to crowd out critical organizations, states and local strongmen make use of pseudo-civil society organizations (for uncivil civil society, see Glasius (2010); for the limiting of genuine civil society space, see Hayes et al. (2017)), and so does virtually every insurgent group for the same reasons. For example, in the Philippines mayors are known to create such local organizations in order to ensure that the civil society representation required by law in decision-making and oversight processes is amenable to them, and to channel public funds to their families and clients.

Institutionalizing peace-building: Infrastructures for peace

The concept and practice of infrastructures for peace is illustrative of the entire cycle of the emergence of an approach to address conflict, its 'discovery' by scholarship, intentional replication leading to it becoming a tool, which is then appropriated by states and local elite actors to proffer their own agenda.

In the 1980s, in disparate parts of the world, people caught up in the violent conflicts of the era – often embedded in the Cold War, subject to forces way beyond anything they could hope to control – experimented with ground-up, local initiatives not to end the conflict as a whole but to ensure that violence ceases visiting their communities. These local peace committees were invented and designed by people in those contexts, who intimately knew their social, political and geographical environment, as well as the conflict actors physically present in their area.

Based on his direct observations of these local initiatives, particularly in Nicaragua and Somalia, John Paul Lederach coined the term 'infrastructures for peace' and proposed to make it the basis of his conflict transformation framework (Lederach 1997). Lederach, thus, took these highly contextually determined examples and distilled an abstract model from them, which could be used in other – potentially any – conflict context. At this point infrastructures for peace was not a template, much less a blueprint, not the least because Lederach's elicitive approach to conflict transformation is highly context-sensitive. It was, at this stage, an idea that would help peace advocates better organize their work towards reconciliation by enabling them to resolve conflicts locally, network with each other for mutual support and help transform communal relationships and cultures of violence. It was not explicitly mentioned as such, it rather provided, as Lederach intended, a framework, a form of scaffolding, which helped doing the actual work of reconciliation in divided societies.

Around 2010 this changed, when the concept was 'discovered' by the Intergovernmental Authority on Development (IGAD) and UNDP, following reports of the success of a local initiative in Northern Kenya, the Wajir Peace and Development Committee (Berkley Center for Religion 2010; Ibrahim Abdi 2001). International workshops, conferences and a flurry of publications ensued (e.g. Kumar and De la Haye 2012; Paladini Adell 2013; Unger, Lundström, Planta and Austin 2013; van Tongeren 2011), including a special issue of the *Journal of Peacebuilding and Development* and a Berghof Foundation Dialogue Series (both important platforms for developing and assessing concepts in peace-building). With few exceptions, these promoted a very different idea of infrastructures for peace, one which serves the building up and consolidation of state capacity to surveil, control and order society, and to penetrate its hitherto unreached segments. As the focus shifted from reconciliation to state-building, infrastructures for peace (by this time it was conveniently acronymized as I4P) was transformed from a general framework in the background of conflict transformation to a specific tool, more often than not used for state-building rather than reconciliation as originally intended (for a more detailed account of the transformation of the concept, see: Kovács 2019), promoted in more than three dozen countries by UNDP (Giessmann 2016).

One of the first examples of this process was the case of Kenya itself. Shortly after the success of the Wajir Peace and Development Committee came to prominence, the various actors, including the Kenyan government, began a process of replicating it in other districts, in the case of the government in a top-down manner (Odendaal 2010). Unlike in the Wajir District, however, these artificially created simulacra failed to reproduce the success of the original, not the least because of the lack of rootedness in the context, and at times ended in elite take-over.

Infrastructures for peace have since been created by a wide array of actors in conflict and post-conflict situations, in diverse, though recognizable forms – for example, government institutions and programmes, peace committees at various levels and sites of memorialization. These include grassroots and epistemic communities, and civil society in very much the same vein as they did in the 1980s. International organizations are active in the creation and/or support of infrastructures for peace. Sometimes they work directly with local initiatives or with governments to set up their own, and in some cases they promote or create new ones. Finally, many are either created by the states themselves or as part of international peace-building interventions upon the recommendation of international actors such as INGOs or the UN, especially UNDP.

Other examples of state-centred, top-down infrastructures for peace include the creation of 'peace ministries' (Hopp-Nishanka 2012), government units to handle some – or most – aspects of the negotiations with insurgent groups, and connected measures by the government, like the Secretariat for Coordinating the Peace Process (SCOPP) functioning between 2002 and 2009 in Sri Lanka, the Office of the Presidential Adviser on the Peace Process in the Philippines (OPAPP) or in Kenya the early warning system Uwiano Platform to prevent election-related violence (Chuma and Ojielo 2012). In Nepal the creation of a national peace infrastructure was part of the internationally led peace-building process and it was a – theoretically at least – fully vertically integrated one, reaching from the central government's Ministry of Peace and Reconstruction to the level of villages with a great variety of local-level components (Suurmond and Sharma 2013). Some of these local-level components were newly created, other already existing ones integrated into the new structure, and according to research they were subject to elite domination by political parties and local elites (Coyle and Dalrymple 2011). In the Philippines, genuinely local peace infrastructures such as zones of peace (Avruch and Jose 2007; Garcia 1997; Hancock 2021; Macaspac 2018) coexist with state-organized forms like the ones created through the government's PAMANA programme, which seek to address armed conflicts ranged along various stages of conflict resolution from ones where so-called completion agreements are in place to others where counterinsurgency is ongoing (Haim, Fernandez and Cruz 2019). The PAMANA programme, particularly in the areas of the New People's Army, is used by the government to penetrate hitherto unreached segments of society, break up insurgent areas and provide entry points for the agents of the state to establish themselves in the communities. Similarly to the aforementioned E-CLIP programme, PAMANA is coordinated by OPAPP, the individual programmes and projects are carried out by various line agencies of the government fitting a whole-of-government approach, and the projects themselves are targeted by the Philippine military (Kovács 2019).

In what follows, I trace the process of how the post-conflict register emerged, often from organic, context-driven attempts to address the root causes of conflict and foster sustainable positive peace, and its appropriation.

The emergence of the post-conflict register

While the absence of war ('negative peace') is fairly easy to define, 'peace' (or 'positive peace') is, arguably, an essentially contested concept (Gallie 1956), but one that is simultaneously profoundly political and of overwhelming practical import. Its presence and quality in a particular context such as a polity is literally a question of life or death for individuals, their communities, political regimes and, in extreme cases, the state itself. This significance gives the question of peace, and of its bringing about, an urgency and practicality that make its deliberate pursuit necessary. The combination of the impossibility of definitively settling on an agreed notion of peace and the need to create it generates a tension, which can only be managed, not conclusively resolved. This tension makes peace-building a contested space. The contestation, within the field and over the meaning of peace-building, is ideological, theoretical, organizational and political. It takes place in an ecosystem of diverse entities – states, intergovernmental- and non-governmental organizations, research institutions, grassroots groups and political movements – within which ideas emerge, compete, are manifested in physical and institutional forms, get appropriated and reinterpreted.

Nothing is new about any of this. As far as we can look back into the past, people have always sought peace through managing and resolving their conflicts, creating and transforming social, economic and political structures. The activity we call peace-building, however, is much more recent. It is traceable directly to the pioneering work of Johan Galtung (1976) who originally coined the term and, crucially, readjusted its focus from inter-state to intra-state conflict, at once consolidating scholarly enquiry on this topic outside international relations and opening the way to practically engaging with conflicts on various levels using similar approaches adjustable to the locus of intervention. It is to be noted that Johan Galtung did not 'invent' peace and conflict studies, it emerged from the experiences of the two world wars of the twentieth century. Galtung built on earlier scholarship where the shift of attention from international to domestic conflict was already well underway (for a concise summary of this, see Ramsbotham, Woodhouse and Miall (2016: ch. II)). The importance of the 'invention' of peace-building is thus found in the way it allowed for connecting levels of analysis and intervention (from global to local), the transferability of the understanding of conflict (itself, arguably, an essentially contested concept) as a universally applicable concept on these levels using the same terminology and conceptual set, and the same approaches to address it. It made the emergence of a post-conflict register conceptually possible. Other factors, to which I turn briefly later are the 'deductive approach' (Cousens 2001) of organizations to how they define the actual content of peace-building, and its evolution within the ecosystem of these organizations.

With the intellectual foundations and some practical experience from initiatives in the many intra-state conflicts of the 1970s and 1980s (e.g. Lederach 1997; Mouly 2013) already in place, institutional peace-building emerged as a distinct type of peace operation at the turn of the 1980s and 1990s. For this to happen, the winding down and eventual end of the Cold War was necessary, for the kind of deep intervention in the domestic affairs of states was hardly possible under its circumstances. It did not take a long time for it to turn around completely, the question whether to intervene or not giving way to how to intervene (Woodward 2007: 145).

In turn, the historical moment, the end-of-history triumphalism of Western liberal democracy and Reaganite neoliberalism (Fukuyama 1989) significantly influenced the ideological, political and economic content of what is now called liberal peace-building. It helped that this new, interventionist peace project meshed well with the existing modernization-focused international development agenda (Schellhaas and Seegers 2009). Major institutional structures have been built, and vested interests formed around it since.

These structures grew from four main roots, creating the peace-building ecosystem. First, the agencies of the broad United Nations system, including the World Bank, began adapting to the new needs and opportunities in the immediate aftermath of the Cold War. This process is far from concluded. Its most recent development is the creation of the UN Peacebuilding Architecture (PBA), comprising the Peacebuilding Commission, The Peacebuilding Fund, and the Peacebuilding Support Office, which seeks to bolster the UN's capacity and coordinate some of the work in this area. The existence of the PBA does not mean some kind of centralization of functions and work – the individual UN agencies continue to pursue their related programming. Due to its size, prestige, resources, global reach and role as a donor to many other organizations, the UN continues to play an outsized role in developing the theory and practice of peace-building. This happens through two principal mechanisms. In some cases the UN develops and champions a concept, idea or approach. This was the case with the concept of human security (UNDP 1994), which remains a core concept. The other mechanism is when a concept developed in another domain – such as academia or civil society – is taken on board by the UN and promoted. Examples of this include peace-building itself, originally proposed by Galtung, or peace infrastructures (Kovács 2020), which emerged from local peace initiatives in a variety conflict contexts to be later proposed as a distinct approach to peace-building by John Paul Lederach (1997). Over time, some intergovernmental organizations joined the ranks of the UN agencies, principally the African Union and the OSCE.

Second, a wide range of civil society organizations – from INGOs employing hundreds of staff members and working in dozens of countries to grassroots community-based organizations (CBOs) in remote locations – have been active in peace-building work even during the Cold War and since (Fischer 2011). Due to this diversity, civil society actors cannot be treated as a homogenous group. Their concerns can be drastically different, so is their embeddedness in the international system and their place in the peace-building ecosystem; their criteria of recruitment and pool of recruits and therefore their epistemologies can differ greatly; and more often than not, their relationships are fraught (See e.g.: Pouligny 2005; Verkoren and van Leeuwen 2013). What connects actors which approximate this ideal type is, first, their general view of peace-building as a bottom-up approach rooted in a tradition of social justice, and, second, the fact that many innovations in peace-building originate from them. The latter is a function of these organizations being on the 'frontlines' of peace-building – they work directly with conflict-affected populations and confront their needs, understand their capacities and dilemmas – and thanks to this they are the ones experimenting with new approaches. Some of these become part of the post-conflict register, such as using arts and sports for peace-building, other community-level interventions including consultations, dialogues and Track 2 and Track 3 peace processes.

Third, research institutions – universities, think tanks and research-oriented NGOs like ACCORD in South Africa, the Berghof Foundation in Germany or Saferworld in the UK – have been key in generating new concepts and approaches, synthesizing and critiquing praxis, and therefore contribute to the emergence, spread or abandonment of these, and by extension to the consolidation of the post-conflict register and its evolution over time.

Fourth, states have always been part of the peace-building ecosystem, but their involvement cannot be so easily categorized as the others. This is due, in part, to the great power differential of the states involved. Powerful core states clearly play a different role, one of agenda setting, even pursuing imperial ambitions (Kfir 2012; Monshipouri 2003, 2005; Spears 2012) according to some critics (Chandler 2006; Schellhaas and Seegers 2009), or at least to protect their interest in the status quo of the international system (Hameiri 2014). On the other end of this spectrum, conflict-affected states, typically developing and on the periphery of the international system – notable exceptions include Northern Ireland and the Basque Country – are often the sites of external intervention and social engineering of varying intrusiveness. What is important to keep in mind here is that contrary to the apparent asymmetry of power between a poor, conflict-affected state and intervening international peace-building actors, ultimately it is the former that has greater influence over shaping the peace being built due to their better familiarity with the context, stronger commitment and for the simple fact of being around indefinitely as opposed to the transience of external interveners. Part of this process of adaptation was the adoption of the language and tools of peace-building for different purposes.

Parallel with the growth in the number of actors involved in peace-building, its thematic scope grew as well. This was the result of the progressive recognition of the inherent complexity of the task, the reflection on and co-optation of much of the critique peace-building received, and the increasing diversity of the actors themselves. Already An Agenda for Peace set out to address programmatically a considerably broader set of issues than the UN and others had previously done, including arms proliferation, primordialism, environmental degradation and related concerns such as the thinning of the ozone layer, the disintegration of traditional social structures, population growth, burgeoning debt burdens, trade barriers, migration, drug use and trade, poverty and inequality, diseases, political oppression and despair as well as the causes of these identified as a lack of respect for human rights, sustainable economic and social development, the existence of weapons of mass destruction–and more (UNSG 1992 paras 5 and 11–13). Over the nigh thirty years since, the list has expanded further as, for example, climate change gathered pace and attention, the role of the violence apparatus of the state in peace transitions got better understood and articulated, and as broader conflict dynamics including local-level ones came into focus.

Arguably, this is simply the reflection of the complexity of change in conflict-affected societies. For example, one of the most overused terms by peace-building practitioners, especially those of a spiritual bent, is 'holism' – the idea that conflict, rooted in multiple causes, can only be truly addressed if intervention takes into account all of societies' sub-systems from the political to the economic to the ideological to the cultural to the religio-spiritual, and so on. Less expansive but similar approaches seek to integrate various types of interventions. For instance, human rights, development, and peace were brought together under concepts such as human development and human security. A more recent proposal is the humanitarian-development-peace nexus (itself preceded by other 'nexuses' such as the humanitarian-development and the development-peace). The evolution of the relatively straightforward peacekeeping mission of the Cold War into the contemporary multidimensional peacekeeping operation, which incorporates a wide range of interventions beyond force separation, is another example.

The recognition of the interconnectedness of arenas of social, economic, cultural and political life, all relevant to the reconstitution of peaceful society, is in sharp contrast with the way the whole enterprise is organized. The actual reality is one of fragmented actors and epistemologies, siloing, and competition for scarce resources including, among other things, financing and attention. Here emerge the discrete, well-delineated and self-contained activities that coalesced into the post-conflict register. This 'emergence' and subsequent consolidation happens through two primary mechanisms. One is a deductive approach (Cousens 2001) in which organizations designate or 'tweak' whatever they do to be at best adapted, at worst labelled as peace-building. In practice this is often the result of a combination of donor pressure to work on peace or at least include it in programming which can be relatively easily achieved through this kind of 'rebranding' and institutional inertia.

Cousens (2001) contrasts this with an inductive approach, which is based on the identification of 'root causes of conflict' and 'peace-building needs' and designing interventions that address these. This is the basis of the other mechanism, wherein innovations by peace-building actors, typically the ones directly working in conflict-affected areas, are co-opted by more powerful institutional actors at higher levels, including the UN, major INGOs and most importantly donor agencies, which then impose them henceforth. This process of co-optation is often mediated by academia and research conducted by think tanks and NGOs.

What happens here is that successful initiatives are noticed, studied, 'harvested' as 'best practices' (or as its recent, more modest iteration goes, 'good practices') and canonized by said institutions through their policy papers, calls for funding proposals, and so on. Once this happens, organic responses – that is, responses to conflict formulated by those directly involved in and affected by it – are formalized and turned into 'tools'. They are now imported and 'contextualized', in some cases they may even be re-imported in slightly different forms. One consequence of this is that peace-builders in conflict-affected contexts now have to adapt to these expectations, the irony of which is that new approaches are typically adopted in response to the criticism of blueprint-based top-down peace-building. Another is that, once decontextualized and 'tool-ified', they can be adopted and appropriated by nearly any political actor.

With the growth in complexity of peace-building operations, a correspondingly diverse set of approaches emerged. These cover virtually every aspect of political, social, economic, cultural and community life (Barnett, Kim, O'Donnell and Sitea 2007; Call and Cousens 2008; Chetail 2009b). Not only are they expansive, though, they are also broken down to hundreds of very small components – activities, activity lines – which are eventually implemented in practice (Woodward 2007: 163). This ensemble of discrete components, recognizable, transmissible, cut to a manageable size to be administered within project time-frames, is the post-conflict register.

Key components of the process in which specific approaches and activities became tools have been the increasing bureaucratization and professionalization of the international aid sector as a whole, including peace-building, a perhaps inevitable consequence of the central role of major institutions in it. Bureaucratization implies a need for quantifiability and categorizability. And, in turn, bureaucracies need professional staff trained to purpose. Thus, increasingly, the people who carry out peace-building work in this institutional framework prepare for a career in the field through formalized training – in innumerable master's programmes around the world – further entrenching the approaches and tools canonized by major bureaucracies. The effects of this radiate beyond these institutions and the international NGOs, which follow the same modus operandi, through a combination of norm-setting and generating models on the one hand, and the control of the flow of resources as the conduits between institutional donors and local civil society, on the other.

This is, then, what peace-builders do, and therein lies a paradox between peace-building's high – at times bordering hubristic – ambitions of social transformation, and its mundane reality of constructing 'LogFrames' and 'Theories of Change', applying for short-horizon donor funding with these, and then implementing hundreds of projects which end up mostly disconnected from each other, not to mention their transformatory aspirations. It is this space of technocracy, mundanity and routine where state-building and power-consolidating actors appropriate the tools of peace-building.

The appropriation of the post-conflict register

From almost the very beginning, thus, a strain of peace-building developed with the – explicit or implicit – aim of building the state in war-torn countries, and within it many standard activities emerged. These are now found in nearly every context where peace-building is undertaken, informed by the statist idea that, at the end of day, things like shared narratives, a culture of peace, reconciliation and so on notwithstanding, the most reliable way to secure peace is to have a modern state in place (Call and Cousens 2008; Call and Wyeth 2008; Chetail 2009a: 9; Fukuyama 2005; G7+ 2011; Ghani and Lockhart 2008; OECD 2011; Paris 2004; UNSG 2001: paras 10–11, 2005: para 19, 2014: para 6; World Bank 2011).

The initial element, therefore, of the process of appropriation by the government and the local surrogates of the state is that peace-building is very much biased in their favour – it does not take much effort to adapt these tools as long as they are used for state-building or what at least appears to be that, and make it look legitimate internationally as well as in the eyes of large swathes of domestic public opinion.

The second, key, element is the cycle of politicization-depoliticization-repoliticization, which resulted from the interplay of a series of factors. It is useful to begin with the experience of the first two decades of contemporary peace-building, and especially the criticism levelled against it.

Peace-building is not a monolithic, unified enterprise. It is true that the UN in particular has an outsized influence on the development of theory and practice, but by no means is peace-building equivalent to what the UN does – nor is the UN's way of building peace monolithic or even coherent. Various 'peace-buildings' coexist in tension, sometimes in direct conflict with each other. For example, Edward Newman (2009: 46–51) distinguishes three trends within contemporary peace-building. Realist peace-building is mainly concerned with systemic stability; transformatory peace-building is concerned with changing the relationships of actors, institutions and constituencies, from conflictual to peaceful; and liberal peace-building, which has two sub-types, the Wilsonian, which seeks to create liberal democratic states seen as the guarantor of peace and stability, and hegemonic neoliberal peace-building interested in integrating 'dysfunctional' states into the global capitalist economy. John Heathershaw (2008), in turn, talks about liberal peace as 'a tripartite international discursive environment' (597). Heathershaw distinguishes between what he calls peace-building via democratic reform or 'democratic peacebuilding', peacebuilding via civil society or 'civil society', and peacebuilding-via-statebuilding or 'statebuilding', which correspond to different conceptions of peace and graduations of the liberal peace (603–4).

All this diversity notwithstanding, for the reasons mentioned earlier, the liberal was the dominant form of peace-building, in both practice and scholarly attention. Liberal peace-building is ideological – openly about its liberalism, implicitly about its statism. Its ideology, as well as much of its funding, and the individuals filling the ranks of its core institutions, originated overwhelmingly from the developed core countries of the North Atlantic. As a result of this, it tends to come with blueprint solutions prescribing the creation of a modern liberal state enmeshed in global capitalism, with biases in favour of maintaining a particular world order, and the blind spots that accompany these. In other words, it was a highly politicized project (Heathershaw 2008: 602). And it came under thorough criticism for all this. For its suspected imperialism (Chandler 2006; Schellhaas and Seegers 2009), its lack of understanding of local realities (Boege, Brown, Clements and Nolan 2008; Clements, Boege, Brown, Foley and Nolan 2007; Mac Ginty 2010), its disempowering of the common people (Jabri 2013;. Mac Ginty and Firchow 2016; Richmond 2010) and for its entrenchment of reactionary politics (Pogodda 2020).

This criticism did not go unheeded, especially in light of the mixed track record of peace-building that nearly two decades of evidence indicated (Mason 2007). The system did shift to become more inclusive and participatory, allowing for greater input from the so-called beneficiaries of peace-building interventions, and trying to contextualize interventions better, even if some of this new openness was more instrumentalist than emancipatory (Leonardsson and Rudd 2015). The kind of incremental change seen here is indicative of the system's capacity to adjust. At the same time, the empirical evidence of the success rate of peace-building interventions and the criticism – coming from scholarship and from civil society – weakened the ideological certitude undergirding liberal peace-building. This, I argue, is the first component of the depoliticization of peace-building as a project.

A number of other circumstances have played into the process, which deepened the depoliticization of peace-building, and fostered its subsequent repoliticization of which two stand out as of particular consequence, the global war on terror and the recent revival of sovereignism in both core and conflict-affected states. The global war on terror, from the early 2000s, profoundly reframed international intervention into conflict-affected states. More than any other factor, it contributed to the securitization of peace, which reinforced peace-building's inherent statist tendencies vis-à-vis its liberalism, prioritizing the reinforcing states' capacity to provide hard security and stability, and to suppress populations perceived to pose a risk to the international order and the security of states in the global core. The two most significant consequences of this reframing are the way claiming to fight terrorism gives a leeway to states cracking down on a wide range of opposition, justifying often egregious human rights violations, and the way counter-terrorism has permeated and corrupted the UN (Altiok and Street 2020), particularly but not solely its response to conflict (15–17). Another impact of the war on terror has been the overall weakening of multilateralism as an approach of addressing conflict and international crises, and by extension the UN. Beyond the corrosive effect of the permeation of the UN by counter-terrorism, the general decline of multilateralism, the UN's capacity to serve as an effective peace-builder is further curtailed by the periodically occurring cuts or threats to cut, withholding, and earmarking of funding by states (Baumann and Weinlich 2020; Bond 2003). This erodes the organization's relevance, which it seeks to maintain – paradoxically – by becoming increasingly subservient to states' interests. This is reflected in, among things, how resident coordinators and heads of agencies are incentivized to cater to host governments' needs. In more disparate and less visible ways, INGOs are struggling with the same challenges.

The above situation is exacerbated by the recently resurgent sovereignism (arguably partially engendered by the decline of multilateralism) by which I mean the resurgent demand for the protection and reassertion of state sovereignty – and often national identity – in the face of (economic) globalization and intervention in states' internal affairs by powerful actors and inter- or supranational organizations. This phenomenon is not limited to weak, post-colonial or conflict-affected states; it is evinced in highly developed, powerful countries as well, including the United Kingdom, China, Germany, the United States and many others. But crucially, it is present in many conflict-affected countries from the Philippines, Thailand and Sri Lanka to Venezuela and Nicaragua to name a few. Albeit in different forms, this challenge comes from both the political Right and Left. Its right-wing variety tends to be nationalistic, sometimes espousing ethnic nationalism, and seeks to strengthen borders and the control of the government over how external actors engage with their citizens, political and civil society actors. Left-wing sovereignism, especially outside Western Europe and North America, reaches back to the anti-colonialist and anti-imperialist traditions of the Left, and is characterized by economic nationalism and ideas of genuine popular sovereignty and democracy. A tangible manifestation of this in the aid sector has been an increasingly visible movement to decolonize peace-building (Paige 2021; Sabaratnam 2017), which seeks to change the relations of power between institutions of the Global North and South. Considering that in the absence of a chapter VII peace operation, peace-building actors, be they UN agencies or INGOs, can only operate in conflict-affected countries with the approval of the state, their position as neutral and impartial brokers is increasingly more untenable (Warnecke 2020).

The combination of the post-conflict register with its already apolitical yet geared for state-building tools at anyone's disposal, the mixed track record, the sustained intellectual and political criticism, the erosion of the independence of its central actors along with their capacity to resist pressure, and states' reassertion of their authority has led to a significant depoliticization of international peace-building. As a result, some peace-building interventions lack in the way of discernible impact and function more as ritual than effective instruments of change. At the same time, this state of affairs opens a broader space for enterprising actors to fill peace-building with new political content, to repoliticize peace-building.

At one level, creative new initiatives are emerging from conflict contexts. There is increasing horizontal communication and exchange across countries between peace-builders working outside the remit of institutional peace-building. This can make peace-building less centralized, more robust, and increase its emancipatory potential. Inversely, the UN itself is working towards addressing some of the problems discussed here, by launching initiatives such as the 'sustaining peace' agenda, localization, the creation of the position of peace and development advisers, and the triple nexus approach, which seek to break down artificial siloes and make conflict interventions more sensitive to context, including the attempts to repurpose peace-building.

At another level, however, governments and local strongmen use this constellation to repoliticize peace-building in a different way, to deploy its language and forms to achieve their own political objectives. On the face of it, these actors are engaged in state-building exercises, which they wrap in the rhetoric of peace-building and partially pursue using its tools as well. The rhetoric and familiar tools provide a veneer of respectability and legitimacy to these exercises both internationally and domestically. This is made easier because it meshes well with the discourse and practices of defensive peace-building (Hameiri 2013), the primary concern of which is systemic stability and the management of the (perceived) risk posed by weak states, and the kind of sovereign pluralism, which has characterized frontier governance since the mid-late nineteenth century (Hopkins 2020). It allows for the emergence – or continuation – of diverse forms of rule and politics internally while still maintaining a seeming uniformity and standardization internationally. More often than not, however, a mediated state (Waldner 1999) reasserts itself since the central government lacks the capacity to penetrate society. Thus, attempts at state-building in the context of peace-building interventions end up reinforcing it further (Barnett and Zürcher 2009).

What happens under the surface is often better described as regime consolidation rather than state-building in the sense it has been theorized in the context of post-conflict peace-building (Fukuyama 2005; Ghani and Lockhart 2008; Paris 2004; Paris and Sisk 2009). Inasmuch as it is state-building, it is building the kind of state

Weber (1948) defined as organized domination, 'a relation of men dominating men, a relation supported by means of legitimate (i.e. considered to be legitimate) violence' (78). This domination is often divided between a central government and local strongmen, but that may be enough to create sufficient stability for the international community to approve and the citizenry to accept it.

As Tobias Denskus (2009) pointed out, 'peacebuilding is a reduction of political conflicts to technical processes in line with international discourses' (57). This alignment became increasingly symbolic, it has lost its political content. And therein lies the problem. Because the peace-building tools of the post-conflict register are, at one level, indeed, just that. They have been designed to facilitate accessing communities, spread ideas, generate consensus and to create, transform and strengthen institutions. In this sense, they are apolitical and can just as well be used to penetrate, not simply access communities, to gather intelligence on groups and individuals and profile them, to order and structure society, to spread government propaganda instead of the values of a culture of peace, to cleverly swap peace education for educating to pacify and so on. They can be, and sometimes are, repurposed to establish and consolidate domination exactly because of the field's depoliticization. Peace-building has been rightly criticized for being political, because its politics was a top-down, contextually blind, hegemonic politics. It is to the credit of peace-builders – from the UN to CBOs – that they, as much as they were able, listened to the criticism. As a response, they largely gave up on politics. But it did not make peace-building itself apolitical – it just allowed others to determine its political content. Peace, however, is a political good, and if peace-builders are to salvage the project, they may need to repoliticize themselves. It should not be a return to the kind of politics that characterized the field in the 1990s and 2000s. It should be more respectful and humble, more reflective and culturally sensitive, decolonial even, but it should be politics.

Bibliography

Altiok, A., and Street, J. (2020). 'A Fourth Pillar for the United Nations?: The Rise of Counter-terrorism'. *Saferworld*. https://www.saferworld.org.uk/resources/publicati ons/1256-a-fourth-pillar-for-the-united-nations-the-rise-of-counter-terrorism (accessed 06 September 2023).

Angstrom, J. (2001). 'Towards a Typology of Internal Armed Conflict: Synthesising a Decade of Conceptual Turmoil'. *Civil Wars* 4(3): 93–116. doi:10.1080/13698240108402480.

Arthur, C. (2020). 'Post-conflict Timor-Leste'. In Oliver Richmond and Gëzim Visoka (eds), *The Palgrave Encyclopedia of Peace and Conflict Studies* (1–15). London: Palgrave Macmillan.

Avruch, K., and Jose, R. S. (2007). 'Peace Zones in the Philippines'. In L. E. Hancock and C. R. Mitchell (eds), *Zones of Peace* (51–69). Bloomfield, NJ: Kumarian Press.

Ballesteros, M. D. M. (2020). 'Funding Eligibility Requirements: Inclusion, Exclusion, and Mediation in Peace Interventions'. *Development in Practice* 31(1): 1–10. doi:10.1080/09 614524.2020.1770700.

Barakat, S., and Milton, S. (2020). 'Localisation Across the Humanitarian-Development-Peace Nexus'. *Journal of Peacebuilding & Development* 15(2): 147–63. doi:10.1177/1542316620922805.

Barnett, M., Kim, H., O'Donnell, M., and Sitea, L. (2007). 'Peacebuilding: What Is in a Name?'. *Global Governance* 13: 35–58.

Barnett, M., and Zürcher, C. (2009). 'The Peacebuilder's Contract: How External Statebuilding Reinforces Weak Statehood'. In R. Paris and T. D. Sisk (eds), *The Dilemmas of Statebuilding: Confronting the Contradictions of Postwar Peace Operations* (23–52). London: Routledge.

Baumann, M.-O., and Weinlich, S. (2020). 'Funding the UN: Support or Constraint?'. In S. Browne and T. G. Weiss (eds), *Routledge Handbook on the UN and Development* (151–64). London: Taylor & Francis.

Berkley Center for Religion, P. W. A. (2010). A Discussion with Dekha Ibrahim, Founder, Wajir Peace and Development Committee, Kenya. Berkley Center for Religion, Peace & World Affairs. http://berkleycenter.georgetown.edu/interviews/a-discussion-with-dekha-ibrahim-founder-wajir-peace-and-development-committee-kenya.

Boege, V., Brown, A., Clements, K. P., and Nolan, A. (2008). *On Hybrid Political Orders and Emerging States: State Formation in the Context of 'Fragility'* (1–21). Berlin: Berghof Research Centre for Constructive Conflict Management.

Bond, A. (2003). 'U.S. Funding of the United Nations: Arrears Payments as an Indicator of Multilateralism'. *Berkeley Journal of International Law* 21: 703–14.

Brzoska, M. (2005). 'Embedding DDR Programmes in Security Sector Reconstruction'. In A. Bryden and H. Hänggi (eds), *Security Governance in Post-Conflict Peacebuilding* (95–113). Münster: LIT.

Call, C. T., and Cousens, E. M. (2008). 'Ending Wars and Building Peace: International Responses to War-Torn Societies'. *International Studies Perspectives* 9(1): 1–21. doi:10.1111/j.1528-3585.2007.00313.x.

Call, C. T., and Wyeth, V. (eds) (2008). *Building States to Build Peace*. Boulder: Lynne Rienner Publishers.

Chandler, D. (2006). *Empire in Denial: The Politics of State-building*. London: Pluto Press.

Chetail, V. (2009a). 'Introduction: Post-conflict Peacebuilding – Ambiguity and Identity'. In V. Chetail (ed.), *Post-Conflict Peacebuilding: A Lexicon* (1–33). Oxford: Oxford University Press.

Chetail, V. (ed.) (2009b). *Post-conflict Peacebuilding: A Lexicon*. Oxford: Oxford University Press.

Chuma, A., and Ojielo, O. (2012). 'Building a Standing National Capacity for Conflict Prevention and Resolution in Kenya'. *Journal of Peacebuilding & Development* 7(3): 25–39. doi:10.1080/15423166.2013.774790.

Clements, K. P., Boege, V., Brown, A., Foley, W., and Nolan, A. (2007). 'State Building Reconsidered: The Role of Hybridity in the Formation of Political Order'. *Political Science* 59(1): 45–56. doi:10.1177/003231870705900106.

Cousens, E. M. (2001). 'Introduction'. In E. M. Cousens and C. Kumar (eds), *Peacebuilding as Politics: Cultivating Peace in Fragile Societies*. Boulder, CO: Lynne Rienner Publishers.

Coyle, D., and Dalrymple, S. (2011). 'Snapshots of Informal Justice Provision in Kaski, Panchthar and Dhanusha Districts, Nepal'. www.saferworld.org.uk/downloads/Saferworld%20-%20Snapshots%20of%20Informal%20Justice%20Report.pdf.

Crisis Group. (2021). 'Southern Philippines: Keeping Normalisation on Track in the Bangsamoro'. https://www.crisisgroup.org/asia/south-east-asia/philippi

nes/313-southern-philippines-keeping-normalisation-track-bangsamoro (accessed 06 September 2023).

Cubitt, C. (2013). 'Constructing Civil Society: An Intervention for Building Peace?'. *Peacebuilding* 1(1): 91–108. doi:10.1080/21647259.2013.756274.

De Almeida, U. (2017). 'Reintegration of FALINTIL, Timor-Leste's Ex-Combatants, Then and Now'. *Journal of Peacebuilding & Development* 12(1): 91–6. doi:10.1080/15423166.2017.1286251.

de Waal, A. (2019). 'Africa's "Civil Wars" Are Regional Nightmares'. *Foreign Policy*. 22 October. https://foreignpolicy.com/2019/10/22/africas-civil-wars-are-regional-nightmares/

Denskus, T. (2009). 'The Fragility of Peacebuilding in Nepal'. *Peace Review* 21(1): 54–60. doi:10.1080/10402650802690078.

Donais, T. (2018). 'Security Sector Reform and the Challenge of Vertical Integration'. *Journal of Intervention and Statebuilding* 12(1): 31–47. doi:10.1080/17502977.2018.1426681.

Engelbrecht, G. (2021). 'The Normalization Process in the Bangsamoro Faces Rising Uncertainty'. *The Diplomat*. https://thediplomat.com/2021/04/the-normalization-process-in-the-bangsamoro-faces-rising-uncertainty/

Fischer, M. (2011). 'Civil Society in Conflict Transformation: Strengths and Limitations'. In H. J. Giessmann, M. Fischer and B. Austin (eds), *Advancing Conflict Transformation. The Berghof Handbook II* (287–313). Opladen/Framington Hills: Barbara Budrich.

Fukuyama, F. (1989). 'The End of History?' *National Interest*, Summer. http://www.wesjones.com/eoh.htm.

Fukuyama, F. (2005). *State-Building: Governance and World Order in the Twenty-First Century*. Croydon: Profile Books.

G7+. (2011). 'A New Deal for Engagement in Fragile States'. In *International Dialogue on Peacebuilding and Statebuilding*. file:///D:/Downloads/the_new_deal.pdf. (accessed 06 September 2023).

Gallie, W. B. (1956). 'Essentially Contested Concepts'. *Proceedings of the Aristotelian Society* 56 (1955–6): 167–98. doi:10.2307/4544562.

Galtung, J. (1976). 'Three Approaches to Peace: Peacekeeping, Peacemaking, and Peacebuilding'. In J. Galtung (ed.), *Peace, War and Defence: Essays in Peace Research* (Vol. II, 282–304). Copenhagen: Christian Ejlers.

Garcia, E. (1997). 'Filipino Zones of Peace'. *Peace Review* 9(2): 221–4. doi:10.1080/10402659708426054.

Ghani, A., and Lockhart, C. (2008). *Fixing Failed States: A Framework for Rebuilding a Fractured World*. Oxford: Oxford University Press.

Giessmann, H. J. (2016). 'Embedded Peace – Infrastructures for Peace: Approaches and Lessons Learned'. https://www.undp.org/publications/infrastructures-peace-approaches-and-lessons-learned (accessed 06 September 2023).

Glasius, M. (2010). 'Uncivil Society'. In H. K. Anheier and S. Toepler (eds), *International Encyclopedia of Civil Society* (1583–8). New York: Springer.

Haim, D., Fernandez, M. C., and Cruz, M. (2019). *Evaluation of the Payapa at Masaganang Pamayanan (PAMANA) Program*. Manila: UNDP Philippines.

Hameiri, S. (2013). 'Regulatory Statebuilding and the Transformation of the State'. In D. Chandler and T. D. Sisk (eds), *The Routledge Handbook of International Statebuilding* (52–63). London: Routledge.

Hameiri, S. (2014). 'The Crisis Of Liberal Peacebuilding and the Future of Statebuilding'. *International Politics* 51(3): 316–33. doi:10.1057/ip.2014.15.

Hancock, L. E. (2021). 'Zones of Peace'. In Oliver Richmond and Gëzim Visoka (eds), *The Palgrave Encyclopedia of Peace and Conflict Studies* (1-10). Cham: Palgrave Macmillan.

Hayes, B., Barat, F., Geuskens, I., Buxton, N., Dove, F., Martone, F., Twomey, H. and Karaman, S. (2017). *On 'Shrinking Space': A Framing Paper.*. Amsterdam, Transnational Institute.

Heathershaw, J. (2008). 'Unpacking the Liberal Peace: The Dividing and Merging of Peacebuilding Discourses'. *Millennium - Journal of International Studies* 36(3): 597-621. doi:10.1177/03058298080360031101.

Höglund, K., and Orjuela, C. (2012). 'Hybrid Peace Governance and Illiberal Peacebuilding in Sri Lanka'. *Global Governance* 18: 89-104.

Hopkins, B. D. (2020). *Ruling the Savage Periphery: Frontier Governance and the Making of the Modern State*. Cambridge, MA: Harvard University Press.

Hopp-Nishanka, U. (2012). 'Infrastructures for Peace at the Height of Violent Conflict: Lessons from Establishing Peace Secretariats for Track 1 Negotiations'. *Journal of Peacebuilding & Development* 7(3): 70-4. doi:10.1080/15423166.2013.767625.

Ibrahim Abdi, D. I. (2001). 'Mainstreaming Gender in IGAD Peace Building and Conflict Resolution Programmes: A Case Study of Community Peace Building, Wajir, Kenya'. . Paper presented at the Seminar on Women Participation in Peace Building and Mediation Processes, Khartoum, Sudan.

International Alert. (2020). 'Can We Build Peace from a Distance?: The Impact of COVID-19 on the Peacebuilding Sector'.https://www.international-alert.org/publicati ons/can-we-build-peace-from-a-distance-impact-covid-19-peacebuilding/ (accessed 06 September 2023).

Jabri, V. (2013). 'Peacebuilding, the Local and the International: A Colonial or a Postcolonial Rationality?'. *Peacebuilding* 1(1): 3-16. doi:10.1080/21647259.2013.756253.

Jackson, P. (2011). 'Security Sector Reform and State Building'. *Third World Quarterly* 32(10): 1803-22. doi:10.1080/01436597.2011.610577.

Jackson, P. (2018). 'Introduction: Second-Generation Security Sector Reform'. *Journal of Intervention and Statebuilding* 12(1): 1-10. doi:10.1080/17502977.2018.1426384.

Kaldor, M. (2003). 'The Idea of Global Civil Society'. *International Affairs (Royal Institute of International Affairs* 79(3): 583-93. doi:10.2307/3569364.

Kfir, I. (2012). ' "Peacebuilding" in Afghanistan: A Bridge Too Far?'. *Defence Studies* 12(2): 149-78. doi:10.1080/14702436.2012.699721.

Kilroy, W. (2021). 'Disarmament, Demobilization, and Reintegration (DDR)'. In Oliver Richmond and Gëzim Visoka (eds), *The Palgrave Encyclopedia of Peace and Conflict Studies* (1-5). Cham: Palgrave Macmillan.

Kovács, B. Á. (2019). *Peace Infrastructures and State-Building at the Margins*. Cham: Palgrave Macmillan.

Kovács, B. Á. (2020). 'Peace Infrastructures'. In Oliver Richmond and Gëzim Visoka (eds), *The Palgrave Encyclopedia of Peace and Conflict Studies* (1-13). Cham: Palgrave Macmillan.

Kumar, C., and De la Haye, J. (2012). 'Hybrid Peacemaking: Building National "Infrastructures for Peace" '. *Global Governance* 18(1): 13-20.

Kurtenbach, S., and Ansorg, N. (2020). 'Security Sector Reform after Armed Conflict'. In Oliver Richmond and Gëzim Visoka (eds), *The Palgrave Encyclopedia of Peace and Conflict Studies* (1-9). Cham: Palgrave Macmillan

Lederach, J. P. (1997). *Building Peace: Sustainable Reconciliation in Divided Societies*. Washington, DC: United States Institute of Peace Press.

Leonardsson, H., and Rudd, G. (2015). 'The "Local Turn" in Peacebuilding: A Literature Review of Effective and Emancipatory Local Peacebuilding'. *Third World Quarterly* 36(5): 825–39. doi:10.1080/01436597.2015.1029905.

Mac Ginty, R. (2010). 'Hybrid Peace: The Interaction between Top-Down and Bottom-Up Peace'. *Security Dialogue* 41(4): 391–412. doi:10.1177/0967010610374312.

Mac Ginty, R., and Firchow, P. (2016). 'Top-Down and Bottom-Up Narratives of Peace and Conflict'. *Politics*. doi:10.1177/0263395715622967.

Mac Ginty, R., and Richmond, O. P. (2013). 'The Local Turn in Peace Building: A Critical Agenda for Peace'. *Third World Quarterly* 34(5): 763–83. doi:10.1080/01436597.2013.800750.

Macaspac, N. V. (2018). 'Insurgent Peace: Community-Led Peacebuilding of Indigenous Peoples in Sagada, Philippines'. *Geopolitics* 24(4): 839–77. doi:10.1080/14650045.2018.1521803.

Makinano, M. M., and Lubang, A. (2001). *Disarmament, Demobilization and Reintegration: The Mindanao Experience*. Department of Foreign Affairs and International Trade of Canada.

Mason, T. D. (2007). *Sustaining the Peace after Civil War*. Carlisle: Strategic Studies Institute.

Molloy, D. (2011). 'DDR: Niger Delta and Sri Lanka: Smoke and Mirrors?'. *Journal of Conflict Transformation & Security* 1(1): 110–32.

Monshipouri, M. (2003). 'NGOs and Peacebuilding in Afghanistan'. *International Peacekeeping* 10(1): 138–55. doi:10.1080/714002393.

Monshipouri, M. (2005). 'The NGOs' Dilemmas in Post-War Iraq: From Stabilisation to Nation-Building'. In O. P. Richmond and H. F. Carey (eds), *Subcontracting Peace: The Challenges of NGO Peacebuilding*. London: Ashgate.

Mouly, C. (2013). 'The Nicaraguan Peace Commissions: A Sustainable Bottom-Up Peace Infrastructure'. *International Peacekeeping* 20(1): 48–66. doi:10.1080/13533312.2012.761833.

Muggah, R. (2009). 'Disarmament, Demobilization, and Reintegration'. In V. Chetail (ed.), *Post-Conflict Peacebuilding: A Lexicon* (123–37). Oxford: Oxford University Press.

Newman, E. (2009). '"Liberal" Peacebuilding Debates. *New Perspectives on Liberal Peacebuilding*, ed. E. Newman, R. Paris and O. P. Richmond (26–53). Tokyo: United Nations University Press.

Odendaal, A. (2010). *An Architecture for Building Peace at the Local Level: A Comparative Study of Local Peace Committees*. New York: UNDP.

OECD (2011). *Supporting Statebuilding in Situations of Conflict and Fragility: Policy Guidance*, DAC. Guidelines and Reference Series, OECD Publishing. http://dx.doi.org/10.1787/9789264074989-en (accessed 06 September 2023).

Paffenholz, T. (2009). 'Civil Society'. In V. Chetail (ed.), *Post-conflict Peacebuilding: A Lexicon* (60–73). Oxford: Oxford University Press.

Paige, S. (2021). 'Time to Decolonise Aid: Insights and Lessons from a Global Consultation'. https://www.peacedirect.org/wp-content/uploads/2021/05/PD-Decolonising-Aid_Second-Edition.pdf (accessed 06 September 2023).

Paladini Adell, B. (2013). 'From Peacebuilding and Human Development Coalitions to Peace Infrastructure in Colombia'. In B. Unger, S. Lundström, K. Planta and B. Austin (eds), *Peace Infrastructures: Assessing Concept and Practice* (44–52). Berlin: Berghof Foundation.

Paris, R. (2004). *At War's End: Building Peace after Civil Conflict*. Cambridge: Cambridge University Press.

Paris, R., and Sisk, T. D. (eds). (2009). *The Dilemmas of Statebuilding: Confronting the Contradictions of Postwar Peace Operations*. London: Routledge.

Pogodda, S. (2020). 'Revolutions and the Liberal Peace: Peacebuilding as Counterrevolutionary Practice?'. *Cooperation and Conflict* 55(3): 347–64. doi:10.1177/0010836720921881.

Pouligny, B. (2005). 'Civil Society and Post-Conflict Peacebuilding: Ambiguities of International Programmes Aimed at Building "New" Societies'. *Security Dialogue* 36(4): 495–510. doi:10.1177/0967010605060448.

Putnam, R. D. (2000). *Bowling Alone: The Collapse and Revival of American Community*. New York: Simon and Schuster.

Putnam, R. D., Leonardi, R., and Nanetti, R. Y. (1993). *Making Democracy Work: Civic Traditions in Modern Italy*. Princeton, NJ: Princeton University Press.

Ramsbotham, O., Woodhouse, T., and Miall, H. (2016). *Contemporary Conflict Resolution* (Fourth edn). Cambridge: Polity Press.

Richmond, O. P. (2010). 'Resistance and the Post-liberal Peace'. *Millennium – Journal of International Studies* 38(3): 665–92. doi:10.1177/0305829810365017.

Robins, S. (2012). 'Transitional Justice as an Elite Discourse'. *Critical Asian Studies* 44(1): 3–30. doi:10.1080/14672715.2012.644885.

Sabaratnam, M. (2017). *Decolonising Intervention: International Statebuilding in Mozambique*. London: Rowman & Littlefield International.

Schellhaas, C., and Seegers, A. (2009). 'Peacebuilding: Imperialism's New Disguise?'. *African Security Review* 18(2): 1–15. doi:10.1080/10246029.2009.9627524.

Sedra, M. (2018). 'Adapting Security Sector Reform to Ground-Level Realities: The Transition to a Second-Generation Model'. *Journal of Intervention and Statebuilding* 12(1): 48–63. doi:10.1080/17502977.2018.1426383.

Spears, I. S. (2012). 'The False Promise of Peacebuilding'. *International Journal* 67(2): 295–311. http://go.galegroup.com/ps/i.do?id=GALE%7CA299760279&v=2.1&u=dixson&it=r&p=AONE&sw=w&asid=fd0e7688683c87d3e30acc1c6ac77679.

Stojanović-Gajić, S., and Pavlović, D. (2021). 'State Capture, Hybrid Regimes, and Security Sector Reform'. *Journal of Regional Security* 16(2): 89–126. doi:10.5937/jrs0-34622.

Suurmond, J., and Sharma, P. M. (2013). 'Serving People's Need for Peace: Infrastructures for Peace, the Peace Sector, and the Case of Nepal'. In B. Unger, S. Lundström, K. Planta and B. Austin (eds), *Peace Infrastructures: Assessing Concept and Practice* (1–11). Berlin: Berghof Foundation.

Tilly, C. (1985). 'War Making and State Making as Organized Crime'. In P. Evans, D. Rueschemeyer and T. Skocpol (eds), *Bringing the State Back In* (169–91). Cambridge: Cambridge University Press.

UN Peacebuilding Support Office. (2010). UN Peacebuilding: An Orientation. New York, United Nations.

UNDP (1994). *Human Development Report 1994*.New York: United Nations Development Programme.

Unger, B., Lundström, S., Planta, K., and Austin, B. (Eds). (2013). Peace Infrastructures: Assessing Concept and Practice. Berlin: Berghof Foundation.

United Nations. (n.d.). 'Integrated Disarmament, Demobilization and Reintegration Standards'. https://www.unddr.org/the-iddrs/ (accessed 06 September 2023).

UNSG. (1992). *An Agenda for Peace: Preventive Diplomacy, Peacemaking and Peace-Keeping*. (A/47/277 – S/24111). New York: United Nations

UNSG. (1995). *Supplement to an Agenda for Peace: Position Paper of the Secretary-General on the Occasion of the United Nations*. (A/50/60-S/1995/1, 3 January 1995). New York: United Nations.
UNSG. (2001). 'No Exit without Strategy: Security Council Decision-Making and the Closure or Transition of United Nations Peacekeeping Operations'. https://digitallibrary.un.org/record/438855 (accessed 06 September 2023).
UNSG. (2005). 'In Larger Freedom: Towards Development, Security And Human Rights for All'. https://digitallibrary.un.org/record/603385?ln=en (accessed 06 September 2023).
UNSG. (2014). 'Peacebuilding in the Aftermath of Conflict'.
van Tongeren, P. (2011). 'Infrastructures for Peace'. In S. A. Nan, Z. C. Mampilly and A. Bartoli (eds), *Peacemaking: From Practice to Theory* (400–19). Oxford: Praeger.
Verkoren, W., and van Leeuwen, M. (2013). Civil Society in Peacebuilding: Global Discourse, Local Reality. *International Peacekeeping* 20(2): 159–172. doi:10.1080/13533312.2013.791560.
Waldner, D. (1999). *State Building and Late Development*. Ithaca, NY: Cornell University Press.
Warnecke, A. (2020). 'Can Intergovernmental Organizations Be Peacebuilders in Intra-State War?' *Journal of Intervention and Statebuilding* 14(5): 634–53. doi:10.1080/17502977.2020.1794132.
Weber, M. (1948). 'Politics as a Vocation'. In H. H. Gerth and C. W. Mills (eds), *From Max Weber: Essays in Sociology* (77–128). London: Routledge.
Woodward, S. L. (2007). 'Do the Root Causes of Civil War Matter? On Using Knowledge to Improve Peacebuilding Interventions'. *Journal of Intervention and Statebuilding* 1(2): 143–70. doi:10.1080/17502970701302789.
World Bank. (2011). *World Development Report 2011: Conflict, Security, and Development*. Washington, DC, The World Bank.

Chapter 3

CEASEFIRES IN SYRIA: RECONCILIATION, PEACE BY
SUBMISSION AND LATENT CONFLICT

Marika Sosnowski

Time, and the labelling of it, is a critical framing device in virtually every aspect of human endeavour. While different time periods have certain distinct characteristics, and we can adjust ourselves to distinct orderings of time, the human tendency towards the classification of time into discrete episodes – work as opposed to free time, day or night-time and, of relevance to this chapter, war versus peacetime – works to obscure important continuities between chronological periods that are labelled in the collective consciousness as being different, even opposites. In particular, this chapter invites readers to interrogate the lexicon and concepts we use to narrativize situations and events, that in thought processes hides (or at best simplifies) the way we internally and externally organize the world. My hope is that it will bring above the line of consciousness some of the 'known unknowns', or even perhaps the 'unknown unknowns', we carry.

To do this, the chapter adds to the important work already begun by Balazs Kovacs in Chapter 2 to more deeply interrogate the assumptions implicit in categorizations of war and what comes after it – often what we label as peace or post-conflict – that many of us, scholars and practitioners, have internalized and operationalized in our work. This is relevant because, as Elaine Scarry suggests, 'The relative ease or difficulty with which any given phenomenon can be *verbally represented* also influences the ease or difficulty with which that phenomenon comes to be *politically represented*' and, more importantly, interpreted (Scarry 1987: 12, emphasis added). To help unpack our understandings of war and peace, this chapter engages broadly with the literature on war-to-peace transitions, in particular critical approaches to war and conflict studies. Over the past few decades, the scholarship has evolved towards exploring the linkages between what are often classified as temporally distinct time periods, that is war and peace. Questioning the specific dynamics of conflict transformation in the Arab Mashriq, as the contributions to this book do, is a part of this important enquiry. The problem therefore is not that wars and what happens in their aftermath in the Mashriq are overlooked or absent from existing scholarship – far from it. Rather, before we continue with these important enquiries and examinations, we need to take one step back to question the vocabularies and frameworks we use to conceptualize the larger picture of how the dynamics of wartime resonate and ripple through what is often labelled as peace or described as post-conflict.

Through recourse to two examples from the Syrian civil war – legalized processes of displacement and the mandating of decentralized security – I want to show how the text of agreements that have been variously labelled truce, local ceasefire and reconciliation agreements aimed at stopping 'war' can have major ramifications for the dynamics of the subsequent 'peace' or 'post-war' environment. The examples from Syria show how the specific terms of these agreements baked in many of the inequities that led to large-scale violence in Syria in the first place particularly around sectarian identity, economic disparity and security. Practically this means that although these conflict drivers have shifted and changed in fundamental ways both during the course of the war and after government takeover, the legacies of these particular social and political dynamics continue to manifest after the abatement of military contests.[1]

The past and the post of the 'post-conflict'

Much scholarly and practical work has been done over the preceding decades on peace-building – 'as an institutionalised practice through which war-torn societies are helped by UN missions and other multi-and bilateral actors to stop armed conflicts' (Öjendal et al. 2021: 269). This includes an analysis of the personality traits of mediators, the timing of agreements, the conditions that precede a negotiated deal and the inclusion of particular terms within the agreements themselves (Martin 2006, Zartman 1995, Fortna 2004, Haysom and Hottinger 2010). All this is done with the primary aim of discovering what these agreements need to do in order to successfully stop or reduce levels of physical violence and ideally put in place the embryonic trappings of a functioning state (Galtung 1969, Milliken and Krause 2002, John 2008). Most of the scholarship on peace-building therefore tended to focus on how to stop violence and ipso facto bring about what Johan Galtung called a negative peace.

More recent literature that specifically deals with transitions between war and peace in various contexts and from various perspectives questions the underpinnings of much of this previous peace-building literature by asking the fundamental question: what is war and what is peace (Steenkamp 2011, Meagher 2012). For example, Tarak Barkawi argues from a post-colonial perspective that, in Eurocentric thought and inquiry, war and peace are sharply distinguished and that this bifurcation works as a basic organizing principle for much scholarship, policy discussions, humanitarian and development programming (Barkawi 2016: 201). This periodization of time into periods of war and peace is perhaps most obvious in the framing of the First (1914–18) and Second World Wars (1939–45) as starting and ending in specific years without consideration for the many violent dynamics that pre and post ceded these date ranges. Codifying these specific years as wartime, relies on the implicit image of war as large-scale, organized, and reciprocal violence. At a minimum, peace is the absence of such violence as Galtung has suggested. A multifaceted knowledge infrastructure that manifests in public education campaigns, memorialization and even international law reinforces this image of war and, consequently, makes the war/peace binary seem self-evident. Conventional scholarship that bifurcates scholars of war and conflict, with scholars of peace and peace-building, tends to reflect the assumption that these time periods are largely distinct from one another and therefore require their own disciplinary fields.

But, in many environments (and this is particularly relevant to countries in the Mashriq), 'the ambit is not necessarily between war and a beatific state of peace, but between armed resistance and the reign of punitive expeditions, police, spies, and death squads' (Barkawi 2016: 205). Between what outsiders may classify as war or peacetime, for those experiencing it, the violence of civil war can morph from overt warfare to repression through a process where an opponent may be defeated militarily but becomes the coercive threat behind lawful governance. This means that in many cases, whether it is war or peacetime is not necessarily easy to differentiate or delineate into particular years. What may be called peacetime by some is inevitably infused with relations of force, violence and oppression. Likewise, wartime does not only consist of direct violence, but can also be structurally, institutionally, symbolically, culturally and ideological violent (Bourgois 2004: 428). In line with this, Mary Dudziak has argued that 'built into the concept of wartime is the assumption of an inevitable endpoint' (Dudziak 2012: 12). This means that there can be a societal tendency to believe that history will move seamlessly from one kind of time period to another. However, for critical conflict scholars this sequential chapterization can be problematic not least because it is unclear what peace actually means to certain people and at certain times – is it some kind of utopian goal or simply the cessation of armed hostilities,[2] the lack of overt physical violence, something based on more holistic notions of human security or the ability by one or more parties to consolidate policies and practices that discriminate and disenfranchise others (Klem 2018, Kurtenbach 2019)? In many environments, the contradistinction between wartime and peacetime, conflict and post-conflict is not necessarily a good yardstick by which to judge violence or how secure people are from it.

Over the past few decades, various scholars have highlighted, and attempted to remedy, the numerous ways the peace and conflict lexicon (and the industry it supports) do not adequately capture the complex social, political and cultural situations that follow the end of mass, organized violence (Srinivasan 2021, Kurtenbach 2019, Steenkamp 2011, Keen 2000). A major commonality of these arguments seems to lie in the paradox and ambiguity of the immediate peace/post-war register that is not really peace, but is also not necessarily a continuation of war. This means that 'the end of war is at once a key turning point and a time of continuity' and that supposed peacetimes are often infused with very high levels of violence (Klem 2018: 234, Kurtenbach 2019: 284). Much scholarship already implicitly understands this dilemma and tends to refer to peace-with-prefixes (e.g. liberal, negative, every day, legitimate, victor's, authoritarian) or put 'peace' or 'post-war' in inverted commas signalling to readers that this time period is neither simple nor straightforward.

This problematization of the concept of the post-conflict register is relevant to the current situation in Syria because in conventional thinking about war already prevalent in diplomatic, humanitarian and policy circles, the government of Bashar al-Assad is thought to have won the Syrian civil war (O'Connor 2021, Hamidi 2021, Hall, Shaar and Othman Agha 2021, Hubbard 2021). In violently retaking control over the vast majority of the country through agreements that have been variously called truces, local ceasefires and reconciliation agreements, the state has been triumphant in reimposing its rule on the populations and territory of the vast majority of what were once rebel-held areas (Sosnowski 2020, Berti and Sosnowski 2022, Lewis, Heathershaw and Megoran 2018). Thinking about the war as being over has major ramifications for not only how academics conceptualize war and peace in Syria, but also how this impacts on the scale and type of diplomatic engagement; who is able to provide humanitarian relief, where these supplies come from and to whom they ultimately go. My point is that while the war may arguably have legally and politically ended, it would be erroneous to label the current situation in Syria as fundamentally different from what came before (Arimatsu and Choudhury 2014).[3] A major reason for this is that the original grievances that spurred the 2011 uprising did not vanish into the past but changed and morphed particularly in ongoing issues around sectarian identity, economic disparity and security. This happened due to the dynamics of the war but also due to the particular elements of the peace – namely the terms of various local agreements.

Bart Klem has argued that the end of mass violence should be understood as a *post-war transition*. This conceptualization is useful for our understanding of contemporary Syria because it emphasizes that the end of large-scale violence simultaneously denotes a break with the past while acknowledging elements of continuity that do not necessarily bring us any closer to peace. Klem argues that in the environment proceeding mass violence, the term 'post' is best understood in the same sense as the 'post' in 'post-colonial' – as an active, ongoing state rather than as something fixed to a particular static point in time (Klem 2018: 238). This type of conceptualization seems a better fit when describing contemporary Syria because it places current dynamics, changes and events in a continuum paying due attention to what influenced and precipitated them. At the same time, the idea of a post-war transition does not assume a peaceful end-state where all roads inevitably lead. Understanding the post-conflict in Syria means taking stock of dynamics of continuity, dynamism and transformation in order to recognize that elements of path dependency manifest simultaneously with the rupturing of relationships, networks and lives (Clapham 1994: 439). Accurate depictions of continuities at play therefore require uncovering path dependencies in conflict dynamics as well as the ruptures resulting from mass violence.

In the Syrian context, while there has been a meaningful break from the past due to the Assad regime's takeover of much of the country and the end of large-scale violence, describing this situation as a post-war transition implies that academics, policymakers, humanitarians and journalists pay attention to both pre-war and wartime dynamics that continue to manifest, albeit in different ways. Implicit in the idea of post conflict is that this situation is the inevitable outcome or best that can be hoped for. Instead, pursuing the logic of the post-war transition means that it is not only the violence of the pre-war and wartime that lives on in the current transitional period, but also the lessons about strategies and sources of power that will inevitably influence future events. As Yassin al-Haj Saleh suggests, 'The regime may be able to overcome the intifada by force, but such a victory will only mark the first round in a longer struggle, one in which Syrians will already have recourse to a sophisticated memory of exceptional experiences, a source of support for them in any future rounds of their liberation struggle' (Saleh 2017: 32).

Legalizing processes of displacement

Even before the founding of the modern state of Syria, who owned what land and how that land was regulated, was at the forefront of economic and political struggles. Officially, land and property in Syria falls under two categories, private land or state land. However, in reality, the tenure system over much of the land of Syria is transacted using hybrid and customary arrangements. Customary and other unofficial forms of land tenure are most common in rural and informal peri-urban settlement areas, often regarded as slums. For example, prior to 2011, approximately 40 per cent of the population of Damascus lived in informal settlements meaning they had no state-backed legal recourse to property rights (UN Habitat 2013). The drought that immediately preceded the Syrian war necessitated that many people who lived in rural areas and made their living from agriculture relocate to these peri-urban centres. Because of the political economy of the Assad rule, particularly after Bashar al-Assad became president in 2000, the human geography of the country became fundamentally linked simultaneously to sect-based social formations as well as uneven economic development (Abdel Kouddous 2011, Hanano 2011). This meant that many of the communities that opposed the regime were located in rural areas or in the peri-urban fringe of Syria's larger cities and were also Sunni Muslim. The anthropogeography of the country would have major implications for the Assad regime's strategy of using agreements – variously called truces, local ceasefires and most recently reconciliation agreements – to manage opposition populations both during the war and into the current post-war transition.

Three years after the war began, in 2014, policymakers and practitioners, including UN Special Envoy for Syria Staffan de Mistura, began to advocate for the use of local ceasefires as a conflict resolution measure aimed at alleviating violence in certain communities with a view to these agreements eventually tying into a broader national peace process (Hassan 2014).[4] The promotion of localized agreements, that were envisaged to be temporal and limited in effect, quickly became mired in controversy. This was due to the Syrian regime's strategy of establishing a siege environment around communities it wanted to subdue by starving its population and increasing military bombardment in order to impose the terms of the truce being offered on rebel-held communities (Araabi and Hilal 2016).

Agreements between opposition groups on the one side and the Syrian regime and/or Russia on the other, were reached in light of these coercive practices. Few communities could withstand these inhumane and criminal conditions for long periods. In Daraya on the outskirts of Damascus, one of the town's negotiators told Amnesty International: 'The regime would offer a truce or settlement and continue to place military pressure to force us to acquiesce. This was the concept. After we received an offer from these intermediaries, the following day there would be a military escalation to strike fear in people's hearts and make them plead for a solution' (Amnesty International 2017). Hundreds of these types of agreements have been made with different communities in Syria. Few have elements of negotiation or compromise, as the terms truce, ceasefire or reconciliation agreement suggest (Chounet-Cambas 2016, Syria Institute 2014). As Dr Nizar, a surgeon from one of the peri-urban areas of Damascus, put it, 'This [local truces] is not negotiations, this is implementing a pre-planned process of displacement' (Dlewati 2017, Sosnowski 2020).

The civil war, and the use of localized agreements, enabled the Syrian regime to effectively kill two birds with one stone. As the conflict grew and large-scale physical destruction of neighbourhoods that opposed Assad's rule (most often in those peri-urban, slum areas inhabited predominantly by Sunni Muslims) became more widespread, an 'urban renewal' option (i.e. demolition and redevelopment) was favoured over a 'contain and hold' strategy because the redevelopment option overlapped significantly with the Syrian regime's strategy to contain the civil war through demographic engineering (Clerc 2014). The local ceasefire agreements effectively gave legal cover to a highly political project the Assad regime was undertaking in order to relocate those that opposed it as a way to protect and secure itself. In 2014, the Syrian State Minister for National Reconciliation Affairs said that the idea behind local agreements 'is to restore the state of security in Syria' (Bartlett 2014).

Once populations in rebellious areas like the Old City of Homs and the outer suburbs of Damascus (such as Eastern Ghouta or the south-west like Daraya and Moadamiya) were displaced under the terms of these local ceasefire agreements, the Syrian regime resorted to both existing and new property laws to seize land on a mass scale. These include most infamously Law No. 10 that enables local authorities to designate areas for redevelopment, take control over property within these marked zones and oversee reconstruction; Decree 66 which established the initial foundations for the Assad regime's wholesale seizure of land and property; Law No. 5 of 2016, which empowers local officials to enter 'public-private partnerships'; and Decree 19 of 2015 which authorizes private holding companies to 'take over the management of assets and properties owned by cities and towns across the country'. These legal and regulatory frameworks not only provide legal cover for illegal displacement but also enable the Assad regime to reward supporters and punish opponents. Opponents are broadly understood by the

Assad regime to include not just those who were active in the opposition but large segments of Syria's pre-2011 population that happened to reside in areas that fell under opposition control. Contracts for redevelopment are offered to economic elites that support and bolster the Assad regime, and properties seized are given to government allies (e.g. Iranian citizens, Defense Force militia members) (Chulov 2017, Syria Institute 2014). In the Old City of Homs, for example, properties owned by the people expelled (Sunnis) have gone to Alawi affiliates of the Assad regime (Wimmen 2016).

Local agreements act as a keystone for strategies of legalized displacement that reward cronies, advance demographic change and consolidate the Assad regime's centres of power, particularly the capital and other major cities (Heydemann 2018: 11–12). Planned processes of displacement, undergirded by the terms of local agreements, operationalize sectarian strategies of power consolidation in the post-conflict era. This emphasizes how the current phase is more akin to a post-war transition – simultaneously linked to dynamics of identitarian mobilization during armed conflict while at the same time different because of the Assad regime's new constituent networks.

Mandating decentralized security

The Assad regime has a long history of working with various non-state actors. Hafez al-Assad adopted a pragmatic rather than an ideological strategy that saw him build relationships with an unlikely array of allies, proxies and clients. This 'long-breath' strategy was helpful in keeping relations with everyone open, even if those relations were in many cases precarious (Samaha 2017). Bashar al-Assad continued his father's tradition. However, the liberalization policies he initiated in the early years of his rule emboldened a new genre of loyalist paramilitary forces during the armed conflict. These were often headed by many of Syria's newly minted business elite who, in large part, created armed groups to protect their economic fiefdoms. For example, until they were disbanded in 2017, the Desert Hawks were led by eminent businessman Mohammad Jaber, purportedly the 'Rockefeller of Syrian businessmen' (Aboufadel 2016). These various pro-government militia groups tend to be less disciplined than the national army, and in many ways more corrupt. It has been debated by varying scholars and policymakers how much risk these groups pose to the power of the Assad regime (Grinstead 2017, Leenders and Giustozzi 2019, Samaha 2017, Schnieder 2016). Regardless of the deemed threat, the long-term strategy of the regime seems to be aimed at reconsolidating its own control over the security arena by either shutting these groups down or absorbing their members into the national army.

Russia seemingly facilitated the latter when it joined the Syrian conflict in mid-2015. A condition of Russian entry into Syria was that there be one, more traditionally structured, military command it could deal with. This necessitated various local militia groups, such as the National Defense Force and the Kataeb al-Baath, be absorbed into the Syrian army initially through the establishment of the Fourth Corps. Members were paid monthly salaries but retained the right to return to their civil jobs. Over time, Russia's relationship with the Fourth Corps became strained by the unruly behaviour of many of these militias. For example, Kataeb al-Baath refused to abide by international agreements Russia had made to allow humanitarian aid to enter the then-besieged city of Daraya (Khatib and Sinjab 2018: 22). Likewise, National Defence Force militia members linked to businessmen Sami Aubrey and the Berri clan were accused of committing a variety of abuses against civilians in Aleppo (Zambelis 2017: 7–11, Ali 2013). With the behaviour of the Fourth Corps proving erratic, Russia set up the Fifth Corps in an attempt to restructure the Syrian army around personnel who were both reliable and loyal to Russia – and also to roll back some of the influence of other militias and a new Fourth Division set up by Iran.

The terms of truce, local ceasefire and what are now ubiquitously called reconciliation agreements facilitated the integration of armed rebel groups into the Russian-led Fourth and Fifth Corps, as well as Iran's Fourth Division (Khatib and Sinjab 2018: 13). In Syrian state-run media, the idea of 'reconciliation' has become commonplace. Rebel leaders who make these deals are lauded and promoted. Once a reconciliation agreement is made, the integration process is operationalized through two specific terms. The first relates to the 'settlement of status' process whereby individuals, including civilians and military defectors, deserters and draft dodgers, are required to undergo a government-run security procedure in order to guarantee their future safety and security. The second, which was used overwhelmingly in agreements in the south of the country, explicitly relates to the incorporation of ex-rebel fighters into the Russian-led Fifth Corps or the Iranian backed Fourth Division (Al-Jabassini 2019: 12, Enab Baladi 2017).

After an agreement was reached, men in rebel-held communities who had deserted or dodged their mandatory Syrian army conscription were expected to join the Syrian army within six months or else provide a valid justification to either postpone or be exempted from military service. Because many could provide no legal justification and enrolling in the army meant leaving their families and communities, many ex-rebel fighters and other male civilians of military-age chose instead to join the Fifth Corps or the Fourth Division under the terms of reconciliation agreements. This meant not only that they would not be arrested for army desertion, they would also be paid a monthly salary of between USD 150 and USD 300 (Al-Jabassini 2019: 10, Adleh and Favier 2017: 12). As Abdullah al-Jabassini explains in more detail in Chapter 6, security provision, particularly in the south of the country, fluctuates dramatically. This hinges primarily upon the terms of the agreements made between local rebel factions and Russia, Iran and the Syrian government at what has roundly been considered the end of active hostilities in mid-2018 (International Crisis Group 2019, 3).

While these agreements aimed to end fighting and restore state control over rebel-held areas, many of the rebel factions active during the civil war but now notionally linked to Russia or Iran under the terms of local agreements continue to operate with relative freedom and impunity. This runs counterproductive to the Assad regime's presumed strategy of reconsolidating its control over the security arena. Many of these local armed groups continue to provide security to their communities, even erecting barriers at the entrances and exits of each city to prevent the entry of the Syrian Army.[5] Occasionally, armed confrontations have occurred between pro-government forces and previous opposition factions against the background of arrests or assassinations, control over resources and access to illicit economies, refusal to hand in criminals and political competition between various leaders (Tokmajyan 2021).[6] A former Syrian governor said, 'In Houran generally, there is no regime-control. It remains impossible for the regime to enter Busra al-Sham, Daraa City, Tafas and their surroundings, due to certain considerations or guaranties; but of course, there are no guarantees but their arms.'[7]

The Assad regime, Russia and Iran potentially have the ability to reign in ex-rebel groups that supposedly now operate under their control. However, there seems to be a lack of resources and will because 'imposing security in Daraa is very difficult because of the large number of actors on the ground.'[8] Despite occasional threats and in some cases action leading to the regime retaking military control, the fact that violence by a range of actors continues to escalate, service provision is minimal and the economic situation in Syria more broadly is grim makes it increasingly difficult for the Syrian government, Russia or Iran to maintain their supremacy in terms of controlling security (al-Khateb 2021, COAR 2021, Tsurkov 2020, Hubbard and Saad 2021).[9] The situation creates a paradox, particularly for the Assad regime: It needs these local security actors to provide a level of security so that citizens don't rise up against it (as they did in 2011) but it is simultaneously suspicious of them because it views any form of alternative power as an existential threat or a push for separatism (Salahi 2020).

The dispersion of power across different non-state armed actors in Syria that have been facilitated by the terms of local agreements illustrates how the current situation, even in areas considered to be post-war because of the signing of agreements, is not necessarily a case of substantive victory or effective security control on the part of any one actor. According to Noor Samaha, many senior Syrian government officials admit there is no return to the type of control over security the Assad regime exercised prior to 2011 (Samaha 2017). While the government may have a long history of navigating precarious paths with various allies, clients and proxies, the agreements that it has used to 'win' the war, in fact only mandate decentralized security.

Conclusion

Few Syrians describe the current situation in the country as being particularly stable, secure or peaceful. On the contrary, while large-scale physical violence has mostly subsided, what has emerged is, 'the dense texture of war and society relations, and the long reach of the shadows of war' (Barkawi 2016: 204). It is an environment of interlocking structures, processes and relationships composed of pre-existing actors, discourses and cultures, only some of which have been revised and reoriented by new pressures and contexts (Hills 2008: 29). Focusing too heavily on the 'post' of the post-war period, we often fail to recognize continuities of violence and other conflict dynamics. Likewise, putting the transitional and contingent nature of the current period in Syria front and centre of any analysis necessitates that we not see this period as an end point.

Now that the war is growingly branded as over by Damascus, the Assad regime has begun discussions with other governments regarding the resumption of intelligence and counterterrorism cooperation together with the reopening of embassies (Samaha 2017: 6). Likewise, the United States has proposed supplying natural gas to Lebanon through Syria with little acknowledgement regarding Assad's role in bringing about the current crisis. Jordan's King Abdullah has also been pushing Washington to re-engage with Assad (Chulov 2017). Academics, solely focusing on levels of violence, have labelled local agreements as being 'successful' without delving into the broader (violent) dynamics of these agreements (Karakus and Svensson 2020). Focusing largely on the war being over without considering the continuities and contingencies of the post-war register has meant that, for example, international attention on, and humanitarian and development programming for, the needs of the people displaced from 'reconciled' communities has been lacking. Because it is virtually impossible for humanitarian support in government-controlled areas of Syria not to be funnelled through the state, the Assad regime is able to control where and to who aid is provided (Sosnowski and Hastings 2019). By operating under the pretence that the armed conflict ended through the signing of reconciliation agreements, the Assad regime is able to mask ongoing conflict dynamics while continuing to harness a new arsenal of strategies and resources to reward its networks, consolidate power and exclude opponents – actual and presumed.

Notes

1. For a similar analysis with regard to Sri Lanka, see Thiranagama (2013: 111).
2. See, e.g. Kurtenbach (2019), where she discusses how despite most countries in Latin America being formally 'at peace' it is the most violent region in the world.
3. *Prosecutor v. Tadić*, Decision on the Defence Motion for Interlocutory Appeal, 2 October 1995, IT-94-1, para. 70, applies the two legal criteria for a non-international armed conflict (intensity of the hostilities; involvement of an organized armed group) to the onset of the civil war in Syria in 2011/2012.
4. This was a strategy promoted by prominent conflict resolution scholar and practitioner Nir Rosen and White House National Security Council member Robert Malley known as localized ceasefires or 'incremental freeze zones'. Full text of their policy recommendations can be found here: https://www.scribd.com/document/385329881/Nir-Rosen-s-influential-2014-paper-on-Syrian-conflict-de-escalation.
5. Interview with governor (AH3), January 2021; interview with local council member (NH1), December 2020.
6. Interview with local council member (NH1), December 2020.
7. Interview with governor (AH3), January 2021.
8. Interview with media activist (NH3), January 2021.

9 See also Hunadah (@Hunada5) https://twitter.com/hunada5/status/1411951976116596 738?s=24.

Bibliography

Abdel Kouddous, Sharif (2011). 'A Lifetime of Resistance in Syria.' . *The Nation*. 1 September. https://www.thenation.com/article/archive/lifetime-resistance-syria/ (accessed 24 May 2022).

Aboufadel, Leith (2016). 'Who Are the Desert Hawks?' . *AMN News*. 4 June. https://www.almasdarnews.com/article/syrian-desert-hawks/ (accessed 25 May 2022).

Adleh, Fadi, and Agnes Favier (2017) '"Local Reconciliation Agreements" in Syria: A Non-Starter for Peacebuilding'. *Middle East Directions: Research Project Report*, 1–17 June.

Ali, Muhammad Sheikh (2013). 'The Berri's: The History of the "Shabiha" Did Not Protect Them from Assad's Missiles [آل بري: تاريخ "تشبيحي" لم يحمهم من صواريخ آل الأسد]'. *Orient News*. 27 July. https://orient-news.net/ar/news_show/4601 (accessed 25 May 2022).

Al-Jabassini, Abdullah (2019). 'From Rebel Rule to a Post-Capitulation Era in Daraa Southern Syria: The Impacts and Outcomes of Rebel Behaviour during Negotiations 12'. *Middle East Directions: Working Papers*: 1–27.

Al-Khateb, Khaled (2021). 'Damascus Scrambles for More Control in Southern Syria'. . *al-Monitor*. 15 February. https://www.al-monitor.com/originals/2021/02/syria-south-tafas-regime-iran-russia-influence-tension.html (accessed 25 May 2022).

Amnesty International (2017). '"We Leave or We Die" Forced Displacement under Syria's "Reconciliation" Agreements'. *Amensty International*. 12 December. https://www.amnestyusa.org/reports/we-leave-or-we-die-forced-displacement-under-syrias-reconciliation-agreements/ (accessed 24 May 2022).

Araabi, Samer, and Leila Hilal (2016). 'Reconciliation, Reward and Revenge: Analyzing Syrian De-Escalation Dynamics through Local Ceasefire Negotiations'. *Berghof Foundation*. 10 August. https://berghof-foundation.org/library/reconciliation-reward-and-revenge-analyzing-syrian-de-escalation-dynamics-through-local-ceasefire-negotiations (accessed 25 May 2022).

Arimatsu, Louise, and Mohbuba Choudhury (2014). 'The Legal Classification of the Armed Conflicts in Syria, Yemen and Libya'. *Chatham House*. January. https://www.chathamhouse.org/sites/default/files/home/chatham/public_html/sites/default/files/20140300ClassificationConflictsArimatsuChoudhury1.pdf (accessed 24 May 2022).

Barkawi, Tarak (2016). 'Decolonising War'. *European Journal of International Security* 1(2): 199–214.

Bartlett, Eva (2014). 'As Foreign Insurgents Continue to Terrorize Syria, the Reconciliation Trend Grows'. *Dissident Voice*. 22 August. https://dissidentvoice.org/2014/08/as-foreign-insurgents-continue-to-terrorize-syria-the-reconciliation-trend-grows/ (accessed 24 May 2022).

Berti, Benedetta, and Marika Sosnowski (2022). 'Neither peace nor democracy: the role of siege and population control in the Syrian regime's coercive counterinsurgency campaign'. *Small Wars & Insurgencies* Published Online. https://doi.org/10.1080/09592318.2022.2056392.

Bourgois, Phillipe (2004). 'The Continuum of Violence in War and Peace: Post-Cold War Lessons from El Salvador'. In Nancy Scheper-Hughes and Philippe Bourgois (eds), *In Violence in War and Peace: An Anthology* (425–34). Malden: Blackwell.

Chounet-Cambas, Luc (2016). 'Ceasefires'. *GSDRC: Applied Knowledge Services*. June. http://www.gsdrc.org/wp-content/uploads/2016/06/Ceasefires_RP.pdf (accessed 24 May 2022).

Chulov, Martin (2017). 'Iran Repopulates Syria with Shia Muslims to Help Tighten Regime's Control'. *The Guardian*. 13 January. https://www.theguardian.com/world/2017/jan/13/irans-syria-project-pushing-population-shifts-to-increase-influence. (accessed 24 May 2022).

Clapham, Christopher (1994). 'Review Article: The Longue Durée of the African State'. *African Affairs* 93(372): 433–9.

Clerc, Valérie (2014). 'Informal Settlements in the Syrian Conflict: Urban Planning as a Weapon'. *Built Environment* 40(1): 34–51.

COAR (2021). 'Dar'a Siege: Russia Abouts Face, Amps Up Pressure.' *Centre For Operational Analysis and Research* . 5 July. https://coar-global.org/2021/07/05/dara-siege-russia-abouts-face-amps-up-pressure/ (accessed 25 May 2022).

Dlewati, Hiba (2017). 'Years-Long Truces End as Government Tightens Control on Damascus'. *Syria Deeply*. 18 May. https://www.newsdeeply.com/syria/articles/2017/05/18/syria-its-not-a-truce-until-government-tanks-are-in-the-square (accessed 24 May 2022).

Dudziak, Mary L (2012). *War Time: An Idea, Its History, Its Consequences*. Oxford: Oxford University Press.

Enab Baladi (2017). 'Jordanian Seal on Reconciliation Documents for Daraa Countryside ['نسر الأردن" على وثائق المصالحات في ريف درعا للمزيد']'. *Enab Baladi*. 4 March. https://www.enabbaladi.net/archives/134935 (accessed 25 May 2022).

Fortna, Virginia Page (2004). *Peace Time: Cease-Fire Agreements and the Durability of Peace*. Princeton, NJ: Princeton University Press.

Galtung, John (1969). 'Violence, Peace, and Peace Research'. *Journal of Peace Research* 6(3): 167–91.

Grinstead, Nick (2017). 'The [Last] King of Syria: The Feudalization of Assad's Rule'. . *War on the Rocks*. 22 November. https://warontherocks.com/2017/11/the-last-king-of-syria-the-feudalization-of-assads-rule/ (accessed 25 May 2022).

Hall, Natasha, Shaar, Karam, and Othman Agha, Munqith (2021). 'How the Assad Regime Systematically Diverts Tens of Millions in Aid'. . *Center for Strategic and International Studies*. 20 October. https://www.csis.org/analysis/how-assad-regime-systematically-diverts-tens-millions-aid (accessed 24 May 2022).

Hamidi, Ibrahim (2021). 'Syria's Return… "Step after Step"?'. . *Asharq Al-Awsat*. 27 November. https://english.aawsat.com/home/article/3327416/syrias-return-step-after-step (accessed 24 May 2022).

Hanano, Amal (2011). 'Portraits of a People'. . *Jadaliyya*. 31 October. https://www.jadaliyya.com/Details/24567/Portraits-of-a-People.

Hassan, Hassan (2014). 'Hope Springs in Syria? How Local Cease-fires Have Brought Some Respite to Damascus'. . *Foreign Affairs*. 22 January. https://www.foreignaffairs.com/articles/syria/2014-01-22/hope-springs-syria (accessed 24 May 2022).

Haysom, Nicholas and Hottinger, Julian (2010). ' Do's and Don'ts of Sustainable Ceasefire Agreements'.*United Nations Peacemaker*. https://peacemaker.un.org/sites/peacemaker.un.org/files/DosAndDontofCeasefireAgreements_HaysomHottinger2010.pdf (accessed 23 May 2022).

Heydemann, Steven (2018). 'Beyond Fragility: Syria and the Challenges of Reconstruction in Fierce States'. *Brookings Institute*. 6 June. https://www.brookings.edu/wp-content/uploads/2018/06/FP_20180626_beyond_fragility.pdf (accessed 4 May 2022).
Hills, Alice (2008). *Policing Post-Conflict Cities*. London: Zed Books.
Hubbard, Ben and Saad, Hwaida (2021). 'Having Won Syria's War, al-Assad Is Mired in Economic Woes'. *New York Times*. 23 February. https://www.nytimes.com/2021/02/23/world/middleeast/syria-assad-economy-food.html (accessed 25 May 2022).
Hubbard, Ben (2021). 'Bashar al-Assad Steps in from the Cold, but Syria Is Still Shattered'. *New York Times*. 11 October. https://www.nytimes.com/2021/10/11/world/middleeast/al-assad-syria.html (accessed 24 May 2022).
International Crisis Group (2019). 'Lessons from the Syrian State's Return to the South'. *Middle East and North Africa Report*. 25 February: 1–27.
John, Jonathan Di (2008). 'Conceptualising the Causes and Consequences of Failed States: A Critical Review of the Literature, No. 25.' *Working Paper*. January: 1–51.
Karakus, Dogukan Cansin, and Svensson, Isak (2020). 'Between the Bombs: Exploring Partial Ceasefires in the Syrian Civil War, 2011–2017'. *Terrorism and Political Violence* 32(4): 681–700.
Keen, David (2000). 'War and Peace: What's the Difference?'. *International Peacekeeping* 7(4): 1–22.
Khatib, Lina, and Sinjab, Lina (2018). 'Syria's Transactional State: How the Conflict Changed the Syrian State's Exercise of Power'. *Chatham House*. October. https://www.chathamhouse.org/sites/default/files/publications/research/2018-10-10-syrias-transactional-state-khatib-sinjab.pdf.
Klem, Bart (2018). 'The Problem of Peace and the Meaning of "Post-War"'. *Conflict, Security & Development* 18(3): 233–55.
Kurtenbach, Sabine (2019). 'The Limits of Peace in Latin America'. *Peacebuilding* 7(3): 283–96.
Leenders, Reinoud, and Giustozzi, Antonio (2019). 'Outsourcing State Violence: The National Defence Force, "Stateness" and Regime Resilience in the Syrian War.' *Mediterranean Politics* 24(2): 157–80.
Lewis, David, Heathershae, John, and Megoran Nick (2018). 'Illiberal Peace? Authoritarian Modes of Conflict Management'. *Cooperation and Conflict* 53(4): 486–506.
Martin, Harriet (2006). *Kings of Peace, Pawns of War: The Untold Story of Peace-Making*. London: Continuum.
Meagher, Kate (2012). 'The Strength of Weak States? Non-State Security Forces and Hybrid Governance in Africa'. *Development and Change* 43(5): 1073–101.
Milliken, Jennifer, and Krause, Keith (2002). 'State Failure, State Collapse, and State Reconstruction: Concepts, Lessons and Strategies'. *Development and Change* 33(5): 753–74.
Öjendal, Joakim, Jan Backmann, Maria Stern and Hanna Leonardsson. (2021). 'Introduction–Peacebuilding Amidst Violence'. *Journal of Intervention and Statebuilding* 15(3): 269–88.
O'Connor, Tom (2021). 'Syria's Bashar al-Assad Returns to World Stage in Defeat for US, Win for its Foes'. *NewsWeek*. 13 October. https://www.newsweek.com/2021/10/22/syrias-bashar-al-assad-returns-world-stage-defeat-us-win-its-foes-1637831.html (accessed 24 May 2022).
Salahi, Reem (2020). 'Bridging the Gap: Local Governance Committees in "Reconciled" Areas of Syria'. *Chatham House Analysis*. April. https://syria.chathamhouse.org/research/bridging-the-gap-in-reconciled-areas-of-syria (accessed 25 May 2022).

Saleh, Yassin al-Haj (2017). *The Impossible Revolution: Making Sense of the Syrian Tragedy.* London: Hurst.
Samaha, Nour (2017). 'Survival Is Syria's Strategy'. *The Century Foundation.* 8 February. https://tcf.org/content/report/survival-syrias-strategy/?agreed=1 (accessed 25 May 2022).
Scarry, Elaine (1987). *The Body in Pain: The Making and Unmaking of the World.* Oxford: Oxford University Press.
Schnieder, Tobias (2016). 'The Decay of the Syrian Regime is Much Worse Than You Think'. *War on the Rocks.* 31 August. https://warontherocks.com/2016/08/the-decay-of-the-syrian-regime-is-much-worse-than-you-think/ (accessed 25 May 2022).
Sosnowski, Marika, and Hastings, Paul (2019). 'Exploring Russia's Humanitarian Intervention in Syria'. *Washington Institute.* 25 June. https://www.washingtoninstitute.org/policy-analysis/exploring-russias-humanitarian-intervention-syria (accessed 25 May 2022).
Sosnowski, Marika (2020). 'Reconciliation Agreements as Strangle Contracts: Ramifications for Property and Citizenship Rights in the Syrian Civil War'. *Peacebuilding* 8(4): 460–75.
Srinivasan, Sharath (2021). *When Peace Kills Politics: International Intervention and Unending Wars in the Sudans.* London: Hurst.
Steenkamp, Christina (2011). 'In the Shadows of War and Peace: Making Sense of Violence after Peace Accords'. *Conflict, Security & Development* 11(3): 357–83.
The Syria Institute (2014). 'No Return to Homs – A Case Study on Demographic Engineering in Syria'. *Pax for Peace.* 5 March. https://paxforpeace.nl/media/download/pax-tsi-no-return-to-homs.pdf (accessed 24 May 2022).
Thiranagama, Sharika (2013). 'Claiming the State: Postwar Reconciliation in Sri Lanka'. *Humanity: An International Journal of Human Rights, Humanitarianism, and Development* 4(1): 93–116.
Tokmajyan, Armenak (2021). 'Pawnography in Southern Syria'. *Diwan: Carnegie Middle East Centre.* 15 February. https://carnegie-mec.org/diwan/83873 (accessed 25 May 2022).
Tsurkov, Elizabeth (2020). 'Syria's Economic Meltdown'. *New Lines Institute.* 15 June. https://newlinesinstitute.org/syria/syrias-economic-meltdown/ (accessed 25 May 2022).
UN Habitat (2013). 'Emergency Response to Housing Land and Property Issues in Syria'. *Housing, Land and Property (HLP).* January: 1–4.
Wimmen, Heiko (2016). 'Syria's Path from Civic Uprising to Civil War'. *Carnegie Endowment for International Peace.* 22 November. https://carnegieendowment.org/2016/11/22/syria-s-path-from-civic-uprising-to-civil-war-pub-66171 (accessed 24 May 2022).
Zambelis, Chris (2017). 'Institutionalized "Warlordism": Syria's National Defense Force'. *Terrorism Monitor* 15(6): 7–11.
Zartman, William (1995). *Elusive Peace: Negotiating an End to Civil War.* Washington, DC: Brookings Institution.

Chapter 4

PARAMILITARISM IN SYRIA AND IRAQ: THE INTERPENETRATION OF MILITIAS AND THE STATE

Uğur Ümit Üngör

Introduction: Paramilitarism and the State

Paramilitarism is a system in which a state has relationships with irregular armed organizations that carry out violence. These armed groups have different forms and types of relationships with the state, but nevertheless are linked to it. Paramilitarism affects the state in many ways: it hinders the institution-building process and de-institutionalizes the state in at least three ways. First, liability for paramilitary violence is not traceable up the formal chain of command. It affects the formal hierarchies of the state and sows confusion and conflict among government officials. Second, the victims of paramilitary violence are unable to claim their rights through the courts fearing the wrath of the paramilitaries, which weakens the judiciary. Finally, political parties that oppose paramilitarism often run into trouble, as many paramilitary groups have political constituencies, which do not generate them votes. The net result is that the extent and depth of a state's symbiotic ties to the paramilitaries are becoming more entrenched. Paramilitarism is a global phenomenon and not limited to the classical examples of Colombia, Indonesia or Northern Ireland. Although these countries are of course politically and culturally very different, their paramilitary systems have a lot in common. In the triangular relationship between government agencies, political parties and intelligence services, patronage networks often arise, which can form militias outside the regular government agencies. This type of networking is often cultivated through informal interpersonal trust common in politics, organized crime or tribal ties. These types of relationships can explain the ability of political actors to maintain paramilitary networks. In both Iraq and Syria, these conditions have been created by war, exploited by politicians *and* deliberately fuelled.

The major distinction between paramilitarism and militias is that the former contains the prefix 'para', which means 'beside' as well as 'on behalf of' or 'beyond', and suggests its dynamic and relational proximity to the state. The suffix -ism denotes wider societal and political implications, but not an ideology. The insular term 'militias' focuses myopically on the armed group of men in relative isolation, and it includes not only those armed groups that fight for decidedly non-state groups, such as rebel groups in general, but also political parties or unions in democracies, neighbourhood vigilantes in societies with the right to bear arms and others, without the ties to the state. This definition focus on different elements of paramilitarism, including their military and political functions, aims and objectives, and especially the nature of their relationships with the state. This chapter focuses on the state, because paramilitaries' arrangements with the state is not necessarily placed front and centre in the wider literature on paramilitarism. Some have even argued that pro-government militias in fact have a lot in common with anti-government rebels, as they defect back and forth.

However, the centrality of the state has been recognized by many experts on paramilitarism. Hristov offers a typology of different paramilitary actors (death squads, vigilantes, warlords) and argues that 'the steady features across the different cases is the paramilitary groups' pro-state stance – in other words their favourable attitude towards the state or the political party in power – as well as the state's tolerance, support or promotion of these groups' (2016: 38). Kalyvas and Arjona treat paramilitarism as a complex and multifaceted phenomenon and define them as follows: 'Paramilitaries are armed groups that are directly or indirectly with the state and its local agents, formed by the State or tolerated by it, but that are outside its formal structure' (Kalyvas and Arjona 2005: 25). They identify four types of paramilitarism (vigilantes, death squads, home guards, and militias, and paramilitary armies) and conceptualize two dimensions as crucial: the resources of the state and the height of the threat. Their principal argument is that paramilitarism is related to state-building, in that the emergence of paramilitaries depends on the complex interplay between state resources and threat levels (Kalyvas and Arjona 2005: 25–45).

Like many other studies, this chapter too departs from still widespread, common understandings of the state as a static and uniform Weberian construct. In that traditional interpretation, these types of armed groups are seen as the discordant 'lumps in the dough' of the state's otherwise ostensibly smooth and homogenous monopoly of violence. The state's perceived monopoly on violence is temporary and reversible, and 'oligopoly' of violence has often been used as a better alternative to 'monopoly'. Indeed, even the state/non-state dichotomy has limited use: state formation ('statification' and 'de-statification') is a process, and state sovereignty is always a patchwork of interlocking, overlapping and competing agencies and apparatuses of coercion. Only a focus on these intra-state dynamics can elucidate paramilitarism. Therefore, a more promising line of research not only looks at the militias themselves but takes a broader view and examines their institutional environment and embeddedness in the state. Many scholars have recognized that the institutional environment and political interests is vital to identifying and understanding militias (Engels 2010: 69–87). Staniland has taken the argument even farther, arguing that instead of approaching militias as a discrete, apolitical phenomenon isolated from their institutional environment, a better understanding can only be pursued by integrating research on a host of interconnected themes such as insurgencies, electoral violence, state-building and examining 'armed politics' (2015: 694–705). This chapter follows this strategy, because ultimately paramilitarism is about politics: the distribution of intrasocietal power.

When following this road map, two important pitfalls need to be avoided: approaching the state as a monolith and seeing paramilitaries as a static phenomenon. For example, Aliyev's distinction between 'state-parallel' and 'state-manipulated' paramilitaries offers a snapshot of two types of militias that simply have differing political and institutional distance to the state at a certain moment of time, but paramilitaries can shift in their relative position to the state (Aliyev 2016: 498–516). Therefore, these static distinctions disappear if one takes a processual, continuous approach. Arnaut rightly claims that militias benefit from 'proximity to the regular defence and security forces', by which he indicates 'physical co-presence during training, on the front lines, and aspirations of the youngsters – as holders of secure employment and as icons of social success' (Arnaut 2012: 81). But 'proximity' cannot be a static given, as violent conflict continuously restructures the constellation of the militias and the state. Second, the undifferentiated use of the terms 'state', 'regime' and 'government' postulate the state as a monolith, instead of a processual, fluctuating set of networks in which particular agencies, institutions or informal alliances are involved in organizing paramilitaries.

Another example is Staniland's useful distinction of four strategies that states can deploy relating to militias: suppression, containment, collusion, incorporation (2015: 770–93). However, 'the state' is no monolith: whereas one arm of the government can suppress certain militias, another can expend resources to support militias covertly or overtly. Tactical operations are often run by different agencies, institutions and levels of the state, which should not be homogenized but aggregated and problematized. The resultant is a state which can be at war with itself, or successive governments can deal differently with the (nominally same) paramilitary group. The underlying problem with some of these conceptualizations is that the nature of paramilitary-state relationships is highly dynamic, even volatile, and snapshot distinctions between 'informal' or 'semi-official' ties disregard their historical and changeable nature. Paramilitaries and militias are social groups with 'biographies' that can extend decades. What can begin as a rebel group can transform into an informal militia, and become regimented and formalized within a state's security sector.

Syria: 'We are the state'

In 2011, paramilitarism became a prominent feature of the Syrian conflict. From the outbreak of the uprising in March 2011, the Syrian government's violent response to the mass protests became more extensive and intensive. Within a decade, a civil war had devastated economic and civic life, killed over 500,000 people, reached military and political stalemate and fragmented Syrian territory. A key aspect of the Assad rule's repression against the population was its use of paramilitary forces, in popular parlance generically called Shabbiha, a catch-all category for irregular militias dressed in civilian gear and linked organically to the Syrian government. From March 2011 onwards, their acts were well-documented in video clips, leaks, confessions, defections and victim testimonies. The Shabbiha carried out storming of neighbourhoods, dispersion of demonstrations, as well as property crimes, torture, kidnapping, assassination and massacre (Starr 2012: 12–13). The Assad's rule condoned, absorbed, incited, steered and gradually organized and reorganized the Shabbiha, first in 2011 into the 'Popular Committees' (لجان شعبيه), then in 2012 into the 'National Defense Forces' (قوات الدفاع الوطني). This transformation of paramilitary forces introduced a formalization of their structures, a devolution of state power and a further criminalization of the conflict. Whereas the Shabbiha seem to have appeared out of the blue, they had a clear prehistory: these networks had been engaging in illegal activities (protection rackets, smuggling, gambling) before 2011, including during the Lebanese civil war. The Syrian government connived with them and maintained them 'on retainer' through its elaborate patronage system (Saleh 2017: 45–64). The rank-and-file of the militias is largely drawn from young unemployed men from particular sections of Syrian society, in many cities especially from the predominantly Alawite neighbourhoods. Its victims are a broad range of individuals and groups that are targeted for a variety of reasons.[1]

The city of Homs is a key example of Shabbiha activity, and for a snapshot of Shabbiha thinking it is instructive to look at an example of an interaction with a Shabbih from before the Syrian uprising. During the revolution in Tunisia, a female student in the Syrian city of Homs was having a coffee at a café in the overall pro-government neighbourhood of Zahra. The café was owned by a man whose cousin was an officer in one of the Assad rule's intelligence agencies, collectively known by their Arabic vernacular term as 'Mukhabarat'. As the discussions in the café revolved around the demonstrations in Tunisia, the student asked the café owner whether he was not concerned that such demonstrations would also occur in Syria. "No," the man lashed out, 'Bashar is great, and he would kill all the demonstrators. If he won't kill them, we will kill them, and Bashar too.'[2] This answer, in a nutshell, captures a range of issues relevant in Shabbiha thinking and activity in 2011. A few months after that interaction, Homs was buzzing with unrest weekly. On Friday 18 March 2011, after online calls for a "Friday of Dignity" (جمعة الكرامة), thousands of Homsis demonstrated in the streets of the city. In the Khaled ibn al-Walid mosque in the largely working-class Sunni neighbourhood of Khalidiyya, 2,000 people gathered and demonstrated, but the security forces and Shabbiha militias assaulted and arrested a number of them. A Friday later, on 25 March, crowds gathered on the central and symbolic Clock Tower Square (ساحة الساعة), where it must have been clear to everyone this was going to become a demonstration or a sit-in. It became both, and more: the security forces and militias again arrested and beat hundreds of demonstrators. From then on, Homsis demonstrated regularly on Fridays, which turned deadlier and deadlier, and by early April, every week dozens of demonstrators were killed or arrested. By the end of 2011, the Shabbiha had committed countless massacres against civilians in the city and countryside of Homs, thereby contributing to a rapid escalation of the conflict into a civil war.

In the first two years of the conflict, the Assad rule's official narrative went from denial of the existence of the Shabbiha, to a denial of their violence, to a denial of their relationship with the state. The relationship with the state began to stand central in public discussions and in the scholarship theorizing the Shabbiha. A comprehensive Carter Center report on pro-government paramilitarism concluded that the National Defense Forces (NDF) met a number of the state's needs: low defection rates, manpower boost and asymmetrical counterinsurgency skills (Carter Center 2013: 8). Chabkoun argued they fulfil four functions: 'armed support for regime offensives in strategic areas, local implementation of the regime's scorched earth policy, creating a general environment of suppression and terror among civilians, particularly secondary and university students, and finally, a way to divert blame for massacres and other violence away from the regime' (2014). Giustozzi and Leenders's cogent study of the paramilitarization in Syria and the impact it had on the functioning of the state traces the prehistory of the NDF to the state's adaptability in its authoritarian governance. The Syrian government's paramilitary formations then were borne out of its ingenious ability to respond to the uprising by outsourcing the repression; this did not damage the government's 'stateness' but did lead to a heterarchical security order (Leenders and Giustozzi 2019: 157–80). The issue of the involvement and debilitation of the state due to the militias' expanding power and subversive activities remained a bone of contention. Landis for example, argued that 'the regime is increasingly being taken over by the shabiha', whereas Ziadeh disagreed and posited that 'they are under the full control and coordination with the security and the army' (Abouzeid 2012). Finally, as the prominent paramilitary commanders formerly known as Shabbiha entrenched themselves in the Syrian economy, arguments emerged of their 'warlordism'. Zambelis examined their localized and personalized character and concluded that 'NDF commanders have carved out lucrative fiefdoms' (2017: 11). Nick Grinstead scoped out NDF fighters' motives ranging from the ideological to the pragmatic, and also looked at the two main implications following from their increased autonomy: committing unauthorized violence within the state, and engaging in extractive rent-seeking (Grinstead 2017).

Most studies of the Shabbiha employ explicit or implicit explanatory models of their emergence and functioning. These approaches include instrumentalism (the state *needed* them), sectarianism (Alawites mobilized primordially), materialism (mercenaries motivated by short-term gains), warlordism (local strongmen staking out fiefdoms), sexism (hypermasculinity and libidinal energy unleashed), criminality (organized crime gangs seizing opportunities) and upgraded authoritarianism (institutional duplication as coup-proofing). All of these analytical frameworks are valid in themselves, but they also missed several crucial opportunities and details and only partly addressed the many paradoxes that underlie the Shabbiha phenomenon. For example, these groups are quite secretive and covert organizations, but nevertheless carry out very visible violence: they torture, maim and kill their victims in public, and often publicize their activities. Also, their visual self-representations in terms of menacing posture, militaristic dress, steroid-fuelled muscles and general scene-setting is meant to send a threatening message to potential dissenters and demonstrators. Second, the Shabbiha offer a paradox of discipline versus unruliness: national security should be based on reliability of personnel and predictability of outcome, whereas the Shabbiha are neither and are known for being capricious and volatile (Wedeen 2018: 49). A third paradox is how a poor and disadvantaged class of low-status workers turned into fanatical protectors of the interests and privileges of a wealthy political elite (Saleh 2014: 3). Fourth: in full acknowledgement that the Assad's rule is a personalistic set of networks, many think-tank reports, long-form articles and NGO reports use charts, graphs and data to reflect formal structures and schematic representations of entirely informal and elusive networks. Finally, the central and most pressing paradox of the Shabbiha has still not been resolved: if the Assad's rule has such an expansive security apparatus at its disposal, including several seemingly omnipotent intelligence agencies, why did it mobilize and militarize civilians in Shabbiha militias?

Finally, one crucial distinction that needs to be made is networks of command: different Shabbiha groups were recruited, formed and deployed by different sponsors. Some were a profoundly local phenomenon, and then in 2017 literally morphed into the 'Local defence Forces' (قوات الدفاع المحلي). Others were a more national formation and enjoyed stature and authority to move across Syria and had direct access to Assad's (para)military elite, such as Bassam al-Hassan or Fadi Saqqar. Furthermore, the differing (indeed competing) factions within the Syrian state led to factionalism among Shabbiha groups, for example private groups funded by Christian businessmen in the Wadi Nasara ran their own militia, and external sponsorship led to dependence on foreign actors, especially from Iranian paramilitary bosses. Under the ostensibly uniform appearance of a united armed force in military fatigues, this led to a proliferation of aspirations and motives, as well as forms of violence. Whereas some Shabbiha were uniformed NDF members who fought on the fronts, others were unabashed in exhibiting their gangsterism in the streets of Syria.

Iraq: 'We are all Hashd'

The US invasion of Iraq in 2003 is often marked as the 'starting point' of Iraqi state erosion and the rise of paramilitaries. Paramilitaries have almost become a stereotypical depiction of the Iraqi insurgency or of Iraqi politics, as if there was something inevitable or essentialist about them. This picture needs to be nuanced and critiqued. The Iraqi Ba'ath party was a vanguard party based on secular nationalism with millenarian undertones, a movement that believed in a coming fundamental transformation of society through forceful action. This already gave it a fairly violent nature, but when it came under the influence of Saddam Hussein, from the 1970s on, its paramilitary wings multiplied and became more influential. Its 'Popular Army' (al-*Jaysh al-Shaabi*) party militia terrorized the streets of Iraqi cities, and two other paramilitary wings, the 'National Guard (*Haras al-Qawmi*) and 'Saddam's Men of Sacrifice' (*Fedayeen Saddam*) carried out assassinations and rioted against other political parties, especially the Iraqi Communist Party, and was backed by the CIA (*Coughlin*, 2005: 62–3, 197).[3]

Once the Ba'ath Party came into power through a *coup d'état* on 17 July 1968, these militias went from a street-fighting gang to a militia set to protect the state, both against internal opposition and against any coup attempt by the regular Iraqi army. Having seized the Iraqi state institutions, the Popular Army grew from a few thousand members in 1970 to an estimated 650,000 in 1987 (Al-Marashi and Salama 2008: 124–6). The fact that Jaysh al-Shaabi was subordinated to the party, meant that it functioned not only as a reserve, but as an anti-army to offset the power of the Ministry of Defense and offer the state control of the civilian population in the interior rather than the fronts. In other words, the militia was a coup-proofing device, as was the case for many paramilitary groups (Ash 2016: 703–28). As a post-colonial modern republic, Baathist Iraq also relied on tribal paramilitaries, for example Saddam Hussein enlisted Arab tribes in the 'Tribal Army' (*Jaish al-Asha'ir*), an auxiliary force. These groups started as counterinsurgency forces due to their mobilizational capacity, since there are many very large Iraqi tribes that could be enticed to remake themselves into tribal militias. To be sure, it would be wrong to assume there was a pre-existing infrastructure of a well-organized tribal hierarchy ready to take up arms. Rather, Saddam's call for a tribal militia produced a mobilization along ostensibly tribal lines on a local level. The men who self-represented and self-fashioned as 'tribal leaders' were made into tribal leaders by virtue of the state's approval. In other words, tribal militias weren't born – they were spawned, and gradually became the tribal 'interface' of the Iraqi state, functioning as the main interlocutors between local communities and the state (Blaydes 2018: 287).

The invasion and breakdown of the Iraqi military, police and intelligence services only accelerated this process. After 2003, armed conflicts arose in which paramilitary groups were created as armed wings of political movements. Large Shia militias emerged, such as the Mahdi army of Muqtada al-Sadr or the Badr Organization of Hadi al-Amiri, which kept politics in a stranglehold and often clashed with each other. The formation of this type of party militias was officially a flagrant violation of the Iraqi constitution of 2005 (Article 9(B)), which prohibited 'the formation of paramilitary militias outside the framework of the armed forces'. When Iraqis began demonstrating massively in February 2011, on the eve of the Syrian crisis and rise of Daesh, this paramilitary system was already deeply entrenched in national politics.

The rise of ISIS bolstered Iraqi paramilitarism well beyond the point of no return. On 13 June 2014, Grand Ayatollah Ali al-Sistani issued a rare fatwa for the mass mobilization of Iraqi men against ISIS. Sistani, a major authority in the Shia world, proclaimed the 'collective obligation' of Iraqi men to defend the nation from the threat of ISIS. Sistani's fatwa followed the Iraqi government's push for paramilitary mobilization. Initially, the ruling Dawa party opposed the proliferation of paramilitaries, but the rise of ISIS changed its attitude. When the Iraqi military collapsed in June 2014, Prime Minister Nouri al-Maliki signed a decree to create the Popular Mobilization Forces (*al-Hashd al-Sha'abi*). While Sistani's fatwa was intended to motivate men to join mainstream security forces and not as a fiat for blanket paramilitarization, the two decrees legitimized seven pre-existing paramilitary units and ratified several new ones. Now, long-standing Shia paramilitary groups could operate in total freedom, and about 100,000 men gathered under the new banner of the *Hashd*.

The faces of this new Iraqi paramilitarism were not Saddam's many intelligence bosses who had characterized and terrorized his state, but Shia paramilitary leaders with enormous power. Qais al-Khazali, the head of the Asa'ib Ahl al-Haq group, even suggested that they branch outside the security sector and take over other state functions. 'We are all Hashd', he concluded in a blatant expression of para-state aspirations. Another example was Abu Mahdi al-Muhandis (1954–2020), who had long-standing ties to the Iranian Revolutionary Guard in the 1980s and became a member of parliament for the Dawa party after 2003 and deputy chairman of the Hashd Commission. Abu Mahdi started the Kata'ib Hezbollah, the Iraqi counterpart of the Lebanese Hezbollah, and was killed by a US attack on 3 January 2020. These old and new paramilitary groups fought against the US military, ISIS and Syrian rebel groups; but they also arrested and killed civilians in residential areas in Syria and Iraq, and are therefore widely feared by Sunni communities across both countries. After militarily defeating ISIS, most of the Hashd fighters returned to their hometowns in the south and began operating as a parallel state. The circle of paramilitarism was now complete.

Much of Iraqi paramilitarism bears the imprint of Iranian paramilitarism and transnational influence, embodied by Major General Qasem Suleimani (1957–2020), Major General in the Revolutionary Guards and commander of the Iranian Quds Force, Suleimani's aims were a complex mix between Iranian nationalism, anti-Israeli and anti-American geopolitical considerations, revanchism for the Iran–Iraq war, and unmistakably sectarian appropriations, or put simply, Shia nationalism (Filkins 2013). The consequences for Syria and Iraq are serious, and his deep influence and powerful imperative continue to be felt in the vast lands between Beirut and Tehran.[4] In the twenty-first century, both Syria and Iraq, countries with fairly parallel histories and dynamics of state and society, collapsed into violent conflicts that differed significantly.[5] Iraq was occupied from abroad; Syria experienced a grassroots uprising. One central factor became and remained prominent in both countries as they imploded in civil war: paramilitarism. There are clear differences between the cases: Syria is still the security state, where the various intelligence agencies reign supreme and Russia supports the Syrian army as a powerful foreign backer. But there are similarities as well: strong Iranian influence, empowerment of paramilitaries due to the persistent conflicts and sectarianization due to the conduct of pro-government militias. The recent pasts of both countries attests to the durability of paramilitarism: once it nestles into the political system, it is notoriously difficult to exorcise.

Discussion: In the shadow of the state

Paramilitarism is fundamentally a matter of the state, and the starting point in any examination of their relationships must be the assumption that the state is neither a monolithic nor an organic entity. It is reductive to think of the state as a Moloch, for it is a hodgepodge of bureaucracies and actors with competing and often contradictory goals, interests and beliefs. States consists of a complex set of institutions that operate alongside, above, under and beyond each other, and therefore must be disaggregated so their influence and dynamics can be properly examined. These institutions are both formally existing physical agencies, encapsulated in buildings and ministries, but also intangible social institutions that comprise networks, cells, cultures and norms that differ substantially in scope, purpose and resources (Migdal 1994: 7–34). Considering the complexity of modern and contemporary states, how can we theorize the state's relationships to paramilitarism? In various national and historical settings, paramilitaries have been seen as self-sustaining *non-state* armed groups that operate on their own behalves and motives, *pro-state* actors that are fully accountable under the state's official structures, agents of the *dual state* as formulated by Ernst Fraenkel (Fraenkel, 1941: XIII)[6] shadowy figures and groups who operated on behalf of an autonomous *deep state*, or *para-state* characters that were formed beyond regular state institutions. Although these characterizations all bear a modicum of truth, they are also incomplete and do not sufficiently cover the variation within global paramilitarism.

These notions of vague power centres and disfigurations of the state loom large in the popular imagination. In American political jargon, a 'smoke-filled room' is used to describe secret political gatherings of an inner circle of powerful, well-connected, cigar-smoking regents that make the 'real' decisions against the democratic will of the population. The similar notion of 'shadow government' or 'cryptocracy' veers towards conspiracy theories that base themselves on the idea that actual political power resides not with publicly elected representatives but with shadowy power brokers who operate behind the scenes. These (often paranoid) theories do attempt to explain the phenomena of paramilitarism and paramilitary violence, but blame it on the Freemasons, 'international Jewry', ostensibly omnipotent intelligence agencies, or other secret societies. Ostensibly, these omniscient and omnipotent groups manipulate state policy in their own interests, and therefore paramilitary violence cannot be attributed to the state. The problem with all these interpretations, both the serious and absurd ones, is that they are too monolithic and static. The relationships between the state and paramilitarism must be seen as a dynamic process. The deep state in Turkey, para-institutional state-building in Mexico, the dual state dynamic in Myanmar or the weak state accusations of Central African Republic all forego the conclusion that these are fundamentally processes, not snapshots, and that the secretive nature of paramilitary networks does not automatically mean that the separate actors and groups involved are secret.

Furthermore, the fact that paramilitarism can be deeply rooted and paramilitary violence spectacular and influential should not lead us to the facile conclusion that the state therefore must be weak. Indeed, discussions of paramilitarism have often departed from weak state theory or variations thereof, and whereas weak state theory is helpful in understanding (aspects of) the dynamics of the onset of civil war, it sets limits to our knowledge (Fearon and Laitin 2003: 75–90). Even paramilitary leaders themselves often mention state weakness and foreground their roles as strongmen. Aldo Civico's ethnographic fieldwork on Colombian paramilitaries painted a piercing portrait of murderous AUC commander Fabio Acevedo, who legitimized the existence of strongmen by admitting: 'We were illegal, but honestly, it was because of the inefficiency of the state, its inability to protect the maximum well-being of every citizen and its lack of presence in these communes' (2016: 168). Acevedo's comments are telling, because he alleges state weakness and acknowledges the illegality of paramilitaries, but at the same time recognizes the legitimacy of the state. Jenny Pearce wrote that across Latin America, the state's lack of monopoly over the means of violence is not a case of state weakness, but of legitimacy, as criminal disorder or civil unrest provide the justification for the state to violently impose order (2010: 286–306).

Indeed, the term 'weak' itself must be criticized, for what is state 'weakness'? Charles Tilly defined strength and weakness of states as government capacity, 'the extent to which governmental agents control resources, activities, and populations within the government's territory' (2003: 41). Michael Mann famously distinguished government strength as divided between infrastructural power and despotic power, in which weakness in either would constitute weakness in general (1986: 170). Neither can weakness be conceptualized only from the state's own weakness. Resistance from societal actors, such as NGOs, tribes, unions or notables affects state capacity just as much. Joel Migdal theorized that states' capacities to mobilize the public and implement social policies depends on and relates to the structure of society. According to him, state ineffectiveness 'has stemmed from the nature of the societies they have confronted – from the resistance posed by chiefs, landlords, bosses, rich peasants, clan leaders, *za'im*, *effendi*s, *agha*s, *cacique*s, *kulaks*' (Migdal 1988: 33). The state has to contend with these 'strongmen', some of whom are social bandits or mob bosses who command fully illegal structures, others are chieftains of tribes in informal power hierarchies, and again others are heads of the state's own agencies, who oppose certain policies. The strongman is a holder of local authority in the framework of a traditional social organization, attempts to survive against the grain of state power and is in control of a clientelist patronage network. Indeed, some scholars have argued that secret patron-client relations are the main instrument to engender the plausibly deniability that paramilitarism requires (Manwaring 2012: 41). Of course, the state itself actively allows or produces strongmen, and it is in the perverse state formation of these social figurations where paramilitarism thrives. Hence it makes sense to look closely into the coercive capacities of states in which paramilitarism was prevalent.

So too, in the twin cases of paramilitary violence in Syria and Iraq, in which the entire region has been very critically affected by the destruction wrought by paramilitarism, we can hardly call these states 'weak'. A 'weak paramilitary state' sounds much like the often-used term 'weak dictator'. However, clearly a state can be weak in some areas, but strong in others, not just territorially and temporally, but institutionally. A state like Syria might perhaps appear weak in some areas, for example in its capacity to insure state employees or manage higher education, but it is astoundingly strong in other areas; for example, it commands over a dozen intelligence agencies and prisons, not to mention a host of paramilitary organizations. A state like Iraq may seem weak in its inability to provide basic services like electricity, public transportation or legal accountability, but through its security forces it can penetrate particular constituencies and easily draw considerable paramilitary manpower from them. Paramilitarism became embedded in these two societies in different ways. In Iraq, the 2003 invasion and concomitant de-institutionalization of the state was a caesura following the Baathist tradition of militia mobilization, and prompted paramilitary activity across the country. In Syria, the 2011 Assad's rule response to the mass demonstrations was a sufficient catalyst for paramilitary activity, which then in and of itself engendered processes of violent mobilization and counter-violence.

Notes

1 In a forthcoming book I will offer an elaborate examination of the Shabbiha phenomenon: *Assad's Militias and Mass Violence in Syria* (Cambridge: Cambridge University Press, 2024).
2 Interview with Noura al-Ameer Jizawi, 9 January 2016, Istanbul.
3 A similar process occurred to the 'Special Apparatus' (*Jihaz al-Khaas*), the Ba'ath party's intelligence organization. Saddam was in charge of it in the 1960s, and after the 1968 coup, he expanded it and integrated it with the existing Intelligence (*Mukhabarat*) system in Iraq. Ibid., 85–9.
4 For a comprehensive overview of Shi'ite militias in Lebanon, Syria and Iraq, see Phillip Smyth, 'The Shia Militia Mapping Project' *Washington Institute*, May 2019, https://www.washingtoninstitute.org/policy-analysis/view/the-shia-militia-mapping-project (accessed 10 September 2019).
5 For a concise but deft analysis of both countries' descent into violence, see William Harris, *Quicksilver War: Syria, Iraq and the Spiral of Conflict* (Oxford: Oxford University Press, 2018).
6 Fraenkel defined Nazi Germany as a dual state, in which a *normative* state was the closest to a rule-of-law state (a *Rechtsstaat*), and a *prerogative* state, a 'governmental system which exercises unlimited arbitrariness and violence unchecked by any legal guarantees'. The Nazis' paramilitary and secret service structures then were part and parcel of the prerogative state.

Bibliography

Abouzeid, Rania (2012). 'The Wrath of the Shabiha: The Assad Regime's Brutal Enforcers'. *Time*. 11 June. https://world.time.com/2012/06/11/the-wrath-of-the-shabiha-the-assad-regimes-brutal-enforcers/ (accessed 28 May 2022).

Aliyev, Huseyn (2016). 'Strong Militias, Weak States and Armed Violence: Towards a Theory of 'State-Parallel' Paramilitaries'. *Security Dialogue* 47(6): 498–516.

Arnaut, Karel (2012). 'Corps habillés, Nouchis and subaltern Bigmanity in Côte d'Ivoire'. In Mats Utas (ed.), *African Conflicts and Informal Power: Big Men and Networks* (81). London: Zed.

Ash, Konstantin (2016). 'Threats to Leaders' Political Survival and Pro-Government Militia Formation'. *International Interactions* 42(5): 703–28.

Blaydes, Lisa (2018). *State of Repression: Iraq under Saddam Hussein*. Princeton, NJ: Princeton University Press.

Carter Center (2013). *Pro-Government Paramilitary Forces* (8). Atlanta, GA: Carter Center.

Chabkoun, Malak (2014). 'Pro-Regime Militias in Syria: SAA Unit or Ad-Hoc Apparatus?'. *Al Jazeera Center for Studies*. 24 July. http://studies.aljazeera.net/en/reports/2014/07/201472494759578879.html (accessed 28 May 2022).

Civico, Aldo (2016). *The Para-state: An Ethnography of Colombia's Death Squads*. Berkeley: University of California Press.

Coughlin, Con (2005). *Saddam: His Rise and Fall*. New York: HarperCollins.

Engels, Bettina (2010). 'Mapping the Phenomenon of Militias and Rebels in Africa'. In Wafula Okumu and Augustine Ikelegbe (eds.), *Militia, Rebels and Islamist Militants: Human Insecurity and State Crisis in Africa* (69–87). Pretoria: Institute for Security Studies.

Fearon, James, and David Laitin (2003). 'Ethnicity, Insurgency, and Civil War'. *American Political Science Review* 97(1): 75–90.

Filkins, Dexter (2013). 'The Shadow Commander'. *New Yorker*. 23 September. https://www.newyorker.com/magazine/2013/09/30/the-shadow-commander (accessed 28 May 2022).

Fraenkel, Ernst (1941). *The Dual State: A Contribution to the Theory of Dictatorship*. New York: Oxford University Press.

Grinstead, Nick (2017). *Assad Rex?: Assessing the Autonomy of Syrian Armed Groups Fighting for the Regime*. The Hague: Clingendael Institute.

Harris, William (2018). *Quicksilver War: Syria, Iraq and the Spiral of Conflict*. Oxford: Oxford University Press.

Hristov, Jasmine (2016). *Paramilitarism and Neoliberalism*, 38. Pluto Press.

Kalyvas, Stathis, and Ana Arjona (2005). 'Paramilitarismo: Una Perspectiva Teórica'. In Alfredo Rangel (ed.), *El Poder Paramilitar* (25–45). Bogotá: Planeta.

Leenders, Reinoud, and Antonio Giustozzi (2019). 'Outsourcing State Violence: The National Defence Force, "Stateness" and Regime Resilience in the Syrian War'. *Mediterranean Politics* 24(2): 157–80.

Mann, Michael (1986). *The Sources of Social Power: Volume 1, A History of Power from the Beginning to AD 1760*. Cambridge: Cambridge University Press.

Manwaring, Max G. (2012). *Gangs, Pseudo-Militaries, and Other Modern Mercenaries: New Dynamics in Uncomfortable Wars*. Oklahoma, OK: University of Oklahoma Press.

Al-Marashi, Ibrahim, and Sammy Salama (2008). *Iraq's Armed Forces: An Analytical History*. London: Routledge.

Migdal, Joel S. (1988). *Strong Societies and Weak States: State-Society Relations and State Capabilities in the Third World*. Princeton, NJ: Princeton University Press.

Migdal, Joel S. (1994). 'The State in Society: An Approach to Struggles for Domination'. In Joel S. Migdal, Atul Kohli and Vivienne Shue (eds), *State Power and Social Forces: Domination and Transformation in the Third World* (7–34). Cambridge: Cambridge University Press.

Pearce, Jenny (2010). 'Perverse State Formation and Securitized Democracy in Latin America'. *Democratization* 17(2): 286–306.

Saleh, Yassin al-Haj (2014). 'The Syrian Shabiha and Their State'. *Heinrich Böle Stiftung*. 3 March. https://lb.boell.org/en/2014/03/03/syrian-shabiha-and-their-state-statehood-participation (accessed 28 May 2022), 3.

Saleh, Yassin al-Haj (2017). *The Impossible Revolution: Making Sense of the Syrian Tragedy*. London: Haymarket.

Smyth, Phillip (2019). 'The Shia Militia Mapping Project'. *Washington Institute*. May https://www.washingtoninstitute.org/policy-analysis/view/the-shia-militia-mapping-project (accessed 28 May 2022).

Staniland, Paul (2015). 'Armed Groups and Militarized Elections'. *International Studies Quarterly* 59(4): 694–705.

Staniland, Paul (2015). 'Militias, Ideology, and the State'. *Journal of Conflict Resolution* 59(5): 770–93.

Starr, Stephen (2012). 'Shabiha Militias and the Destruction of Syria'. *CTC Sentinel* 5: 12–13.

Tilly, Charles (2003). *The Politics of Collective Violence*. Cambridge: Cambridge University Press.

Ungor, Ugur (2024). *Assad's Militias and Mass Violence in Syria*. Cambridge: Cambridge University Press.

Wedeen, Lisa (2018). *Authoritarian Apprehensions*. Chicago, IL: University of Chicago Press.

Zambelis, Chris (2017). 'Institutionalized "Warlordism": Syria's National Defense Force'. *Jamestown Foundation Terrorism Monitor*, 7–11.

Part II

RECONSTITUTION OF POWER IN SYRIA AND IRAQ: MILITARY STANDOFFS AND CONFLICT FRAGILITY

Chapter 5

FRAGMENTATION AND DEVOLUTION OF STATE FUNCTIONS IN POST-WAR SOUTHERN SYRIA

Abdullah Al-Jabassini

Introduction

In June 2018, the Syrian state backed by Russia launched a military operation in order to recapture the rebel-held areas of southern Syria.[1] To mitigate the danger of regional escalation in an area that sits at the intersection of the Israeli-occupied Golan Heights and Jordan, and is consequently subject to intense geopolitical turbulence, Russia forged a relatively lenient approach to counterinsurgency. As the state was encroaching on rebel turf and recapturing territory by military means, Russian interlocutor offered rebels the opportunity to engage in negotiations the outcome of which facilitated the return of the state institutions, but not of the military and security services.

The immediate consequence of this necessarily disjointed implementation of two fundamentally divergent approaches was the emergence of an archipelago of micro-territorial political orders, across which the state's authority ranged from strong to weak. While the state's use of armed force coerced rebels into surrender and allowed for a reassertion and reproduction in many hamlets of the exercise of authoritarian power by the state and its agencies or extensions, the Russian-led negotiations demarcated areas of limited statehood and granted former rebels a margin of manoeuvre to continue the exercise, under surveillance, of limited violence, restricting the states authority. For Russia, the main objective of orchestrating and safeguarding a fragmented landscape was to fulfil regional understandings to prevent an influx of Iranian-backed forces to this border region.

Drawing on the notion that conflicts are generally not solved and that contemporary asymmetric, protracted and complex violent conflicts require more than the reframing of positions and the identification of win-win outcomes (Galtung 1995: 53; Miall 2004: 70), the conceptual backbone of this chapter rests on the assumption that the defeat of a rebellion does not necessarily allow the state to reconstitute its full political authority. Instead, this study operates in the analytical terms of evolution and transformation of internal armed conflict. More precisely, it looks into the causes and effects of the transition from an open 'insurgency', defined as 'asymmetric warfare' (Kalyvas and Balcells 2010: 415–29) and 'a process of competitive state building', (Kalyvas 2006: 218) to a 'low-intensity conflict',[2] an euphemism for irregular, guerrilla warfare in which combatants affiliated to various actors, including the state and non-state armed organisms, continue to exhibit brief, limited and small-scale episodes of violence in a battle for influence and control (Al-Jabassini 2021).

While under the earlier phase of the present condition the state has managed to reconstitute and reassert its authoritarian power in parts of the region, I argue that the process of conflict transformation orchestrated by Russia has generated areas of limited statehood. These are zones in which the central authorities 'lack the ability to implement and enforce rules and decisions and/or in which they do not command a legitimate monopoly over the means of violence' (Börzel et al. 2018: 7). In spite of conditions of constrained domestic sovereignty, areas of limited statehood are not ungoverned spaces and public goods, such as security and justice, are provided by a constellation of actors (Risse 2015: 152–68). Building on what has been stated, this chapter explores patterns of devolution of state functions to a variety of non-state local actors. This includes ordinary civilians, clan sheikhs and former rebels operating in the realms of security, justice and the healthcare economics.

Empirically, this chapter employs a sub-national research design focusing on the Daraa governorate in southern Syria. Drawing on original qualitative and quantitative data collected through rare access to private archives of classified and unpublished documents, in addition to eighty semi-structured interviews conducted between June 2018 and October 2021 with ordinary civilians, clan sheikhs, military officers, senior former rebel commanders, (un)reconciled former rebels and civilian opposition figures, this chapter sets itself two tasks. First, it describes in great depth how regional politics persuaded Russia to forge an approach by which it allowed a restricted state return, engendered territorial Daraa fragmentation, and fuelled small-scale violence. Second, by focusing on eastern, this study explores the ways in which a process of conflict transformation has demarcated areas of limited statehood, devolution of security functions to former rebels and creation of an autonomous sphere for locals to contribute to managing their own affairs.

The time span of the empirical analysis covers the period between June 2018, when the state launched its military offensive against the region under consideration, and September 2021, when changes in regional politics led to a renewed series of agreements that recast order in southern Syria (Al-Jabassini 2021). Given the volatile situation in southern Syria at the time of writing, and to ensure the safety of the interviewees, names and personal identifying information is omitted. Finally, I refrain from divulging sensitive and confidential evidence that could trigger or exacerbate dormant or continuing local conflicts and heighten vulnerability of populations caught up in the precarious security climate of southern Syria.

The anomalous mode of state return to Daraa governorate

Daraa is a governorate named after its principal town and is located in Syria's south-west, and figures as the so-called cradle of the revolution that broke out in the city of Daraa in 2011. The governorate is part of the Hauran Plain that, prior to the Sykes-Picot agreement which divided the Ottoman legacy in 1916, extended from southern Damascus to Ajlon in northern Jordan (Fandi 2005: 10). Daraa is a predominantly clan-based governorate, in which the clan provides a major source of social cohesion and identity and is composed of organizationally disconnected clans or 'houses' (*bayt*) (Leenders and Heydemann 2012: 139–59). Al-Zu'bi, Al-Hariri, Al-Masalmeh, Abu Zeid, Al-Mahamid and Al-Miqdad, and their associated families, collectively represent the vast majority of the population residing in the governorate.[3] While the phenomenon of the 'paramount chief' seems to have vanished by the early 1970s (Batatu 1999: 26), the leading members of the clans and the families in Daraa governorate are referred to as 'sheikh.' The sheikhs are renowned for their knowledge of broadly accepted social customs and norms to serve a multitude of functions; they regulate interactions, resolve conflicts and maintain a degree of local order and social cohesion.[4]

When war erupted in 2011, concepts such as collective responsibility, revenge and honour ignited the willingness of many locals to pick up arms and defend their hometowns against potential threats. Because state institutions have vanished in many localities, many civilians rushed to established local councils and to help in the provision and delivery of services in their communities in order to help fulfil the needs of its members. Clan sheikhs advised and offered suggestions on rebel military activities and supervised the civilian administration to ensure effective service provision. More often than not, they competed with other civilian and armed actors and took the upper hand over existing or emerging judicial institutions in many localities in Daraa governorate. Clan sheikhs broadly intervened in the judicial realm and adjudicated disputes, be it between ordinary civilians, between rebels or rebel leaders or between civilians and rebels. On balance, the roles clan sheikhs have played under rebel rule in Daraa governorate between 2011 and 2018 are well documented (Al-Jabassini 2020).

During the civil war, the state and insurgent groups each controlled distinct territories and fought back and forth along variable frontlines in Daraa governorate. In 2017, however, the landscape began to change along more durable lines of division. In May 2017, the rebel-held parts of Daraa governorate were designated by Russia, Turkey and Iran as a 'de-escalation zone', one of four such areas, within which there would be a halt of hostilities between rebel groups and the Syrian military forces.[5] The fear of an influx of Iranian-backed proxies to an area wedged between Jordan and the Israeli-occupied Golan Heights necessitated separate and additional agreements for southern Syria. In July and November 2017, the United States, Russia and Jordan covered Syria's southwest with supplementary agreements. The consecutive deals affirmed that no foreign forces shall be allowed to establish a foothold in the neighbouring governorates of Daraa and Quneitra governorates. At their core, and by excluding Iran's participation, these tripartite agreements were meant to appease growing concerns of Jordan and Israel about Iranian military ambitions to establish a foothold in the border area, by keeping all forces pinned to their current positions (Tokmajyan 2020; *Times of Israel* 2017).

In 2018, the Syrian state, backed by its Russian and Iranian allies, began to turn the tide in the civil war. By combining negotiations with civilian opposition figures and rebel leaders with unrestrained and indiscriminate use of violence, Russia has been able to enforce what the Syrian state official termed, 'reconciliation agreements'. Defined by their major outcomes – disarmament of rebel groups, displacement of local population, removal of opposition local governance structures – (Adleh and Favier 2017) such as 'carrot-and-stick' approach had succeeded in compelling the rebels to surrender in Eastern Ghouta (March–April 2018) and in Northern Homs (May 2018), and allowed the state to restore full authority and enforce absolute control over recovered territory and over the remaining population still residing in it (Ezzi 2020; Al-Rai 2019; Reuters 2018). While the state, on many occasions, adopted a heightened bellicose rhetoric and asserted its intent to recapture all areas outside of its control, the durability of the agreements and the future of the southwest remained in question. Having pushed rebels to capitulate, and upon recapturing areas in Syria's western interior, on 13 June 2018, President Bashar Al-Assad stated that 'what was proposed after the liberation of [Eastern] Ghouta was to head to the south' (Syrian Ministry of Foreign Affairs and Expatriates 2018). Together with deployment of forces to southern fronts, Al-Assad's statement clearly indicated that the Daraa governorate would be the next area of operation.

Indeed, in June 2018, fighting escalated in the northeast corner of Daraa governorate between the state's armed forces and rebel groups. While Russian war jets began bombing rebel positions in support of state forces, the fear of regional escalation and increasing concerns of Israel and Jordan about the flow of Iranian and pro-Iranian forces into a border region pushed Russia to forge a milder and more plastic approach to state return (Tokmajyan 2021). As the state was advancing and recapturing territory using the force of arms, Russia brokered negotiations between, on the one side, state representatives, and, on the other, rebel leaders and civilian opposition figures. Convened in the city of Busra al-Sham, 37 km to the east of Daraa, Russian-brokered negotiations between state representatives and opposition delegation headed by Ahmad al-Oda, a former rebel leader of the *Quwwat Shabab al-Sunna* (QSS) (or Shabab al-Sunna Forces), led the rebels to declare their surrender on 7 July. Following the example of al-Oda, rebel leaders in Tafas city, 12 km to the west of Daraa, accepted a Russian-negotiated surrender one 8 July.[6]

In return for a comprehensive and immediate ceasefire and a handover to the state of heavy and medium weapons, the agreement stipulated (1) the return of people displaced by the recent military operations to their localities, (2) restoring the official state Syrian flag simultaneously with the reopening of civilian state institutions and the resumption of service provision, (3) the release of detainees who had been captured up to three months prior to the start of the military campaign, that is, March 2018, (4) resolving the status of wanted individuals, including military defectors and draft dodgers, (5) integrating of former rebels in the Russian-backed Fifth Corps of the Syrian army and a commitment to fight the Daesh (the Islamic State),[7] (6) the return of dismissed employees to their government posts and (7) the displacement of rejectionists to Syria's north-west rebel stronghold, the Idlib governorate.[8]

In the eyes of Russia, however, the core of the agreement was to prevent the access of the state's military and security forces, or their presence, in areas covered by these agreements, and specifically the Daraa al-Balad districts of Daraa city, and the towns of Busra al-Sham, Tafas, and their surrounding localities.[9] By 1 August, the state announced bringing the region under its control following the recapture of the last locality held by *Jayish Khalid bin al-Walid* (or Khalid bin al-Walid Army), the Daesh affiliate that operated in the Basin of al-Yarmouk river, in Daraa governorate's far south-western corner (Syrian Arab News Agency 2018). By the end of the campaign, the state exhibited varying degrees of control across Daraa governorate. While the use of armed force has allowed the state to reproduce its authoritarian power, the Russian-led negotiations demarcated areas of limited statehood and has allowed former rebels to assume important roles in Daraa governorate's post-war local politics.

An archipelago of political orders

Although the complex and multifaceted insurgency was defeated, the conflict in southern Syria was far from over. The parallel yet disjointed processes of state return have transformed Daraa's map into an archipelago of distinct and contested micro-political orders determining which actors are present and which territories they control. Based on the strategy of state return, Daraa governorate can be divided into three main areas of control. First, localities recaptured by the state using the force of arms. The strategy allowed the state to reconstitute its authority and paved the way for the return of its military and security forces with no limitations of restrictions imposed on their presence or activities. The landscape of such territories was further complicated by the expansion of Iranian-backed armed groups, including the Lebanese Hezbollah. The multiplication of actors, their lack of coordination and the competition for local influence and access to former rebel recruitment pools have created lawlessness and made a clear pattern of control difficult to define.

The second type of areas includes localities covered in the Russian-led negotiations and was characterized by a return of civilian state institutions, but not of the Syrian military and security forces. Localities in this category fell into two further sub-categories: those with 'limited Russian protection', and those in the more precarious situation of 'full Russian protection'. Areas of limited Russian protection are those covered by the 2018 negotiations and represented by the so-called Central Negotiations Committee (CNC). In Tafas city and Daraa al-Balad district of Daraa city, an aggregation of civilian opposition figures and ex-rebel leaders have come together to form two distinct CNCs which, since July 2018, have acted as the main interlocutors of Russia and the Syrian state to ensure implementation of the 2018 agreement terms. The defiant or indecisive, vacillating behaviour of former rebel leaders vis-à-vis their Russian interlocutors during the 2018 negotiations (for instance, Adham al-Akrad and Murshid al-Baradan) resulted in their localities being deprived of full protection (Al-Jabassini 2019). While the CNC has gradually become a trusted broker called upon by the local population to voice their concerns to the government, yet without genuine Russian patronage to exercise pressure on the state to meet its demands, it has remained decidedly ineffective, and its meetings with state officials or state security officers were rarely fruitful. Inside these localities, many ex-rebels remained clustered and rejected the reconciliation of their status with the state. Others have accommodated themselves and reset their status and joined the state's military and security services to avoid state reprisals in the aftermath of the insurgency.

Finally, areas of full Russian protection include localities in eastern Daraa governorate that were collectively represented by al-Oda during the Russian-brokered negotiations with the Syrian state. As with the previous category, the state's military and security forces are prohibited from having access to these localities and their presence remains limited to agreed checkpoints stationed at their outskirts, at junctions that connect them to national highways. Unlike former rebel leaders elsewhere in Daraa governorate, al-Oda's demonstrable interest in the 2018 negotiations, coupled with his high mobilization capacities, have earned him genuine Russian patronage that maximized the privilege that he, civilians and former rebels obtained in the post-insurgency epoch – as the next section will detail.

Compounded with such a fragmented politico-territorial landscape, post-war Daraa governorate witnessed a resurgence of violence. This included intermittent state-led military escalations against localities in which networks of resistance remained operational. Moreover, private conflicts, personal gain, vendettas and the settling of old scores continued to trigger cycles of violence –a situation that the state did not witness in any other area in Syria it had recovered. Several factors created a fertile ground and fuelled localized, small-scale episodes of violence. First, one must mention the concepts and principles which are embedded in the governorate's strong clan-based social structure: honour, solidarity, collective responsibility and revenge. Second, the abundance of weapons and the right of former individual rebels to keep their light firearms. Third, the high number of former rebels who remained in Daraa governorate were a significant pool of latent manpower.[10]

Often perpetrated by unidentified actors, cyclical patterns of assassinations, kidnappings and drive-by shootings have prevailed and targeted ordinary civilians, government employees, reconciled rebels, unreconciled rebels, former opposition figures, Baath Party officials, state security members, soldiers and officers, and Iranian-backed militants and collaborators (Figure 5.1). Noteworthy was an apparent spatial variation in the level and intensity of violence across the Daraa governorate, with fewer cases recorded in the eastern region where the state

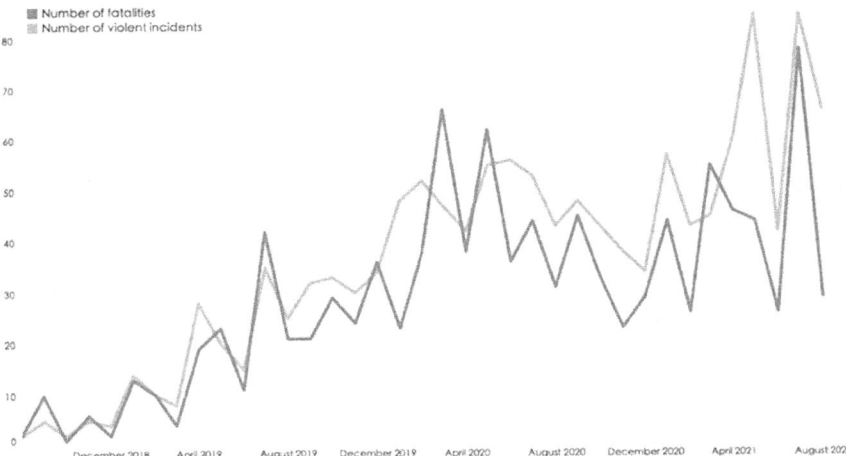

Figure 5.1 Violent incidents and fatalities in post-war Daraa (1 August 2018–1 September 2021). Note: Data collected, verified, and coded by the author. Violent incidents include, but not limited to, armed clashes, kidnappings, assassinations, and Improvised Explosive Device (IED) attacks. Fatalities are civilian and military actors on all sides.

had only a shallow presence and tenuous security grip. The next section shifts focus to the empirical case of eastern Daraa. It moves the locus of analysis to the micro-level and investigates how conflict transformation has created areas of limited statehood and opened avenues for devolution of functions to local and transnational actors.

Eastern Daraa: The stronghold of the Eighth Brigade

Eastern Daraa covers swathes of territory adjacent to the predominantly Druze governorate of Sweida and the Jordanian border, including the city of Busra al-Sham and its surrounding localities. While they had previously fallen to the QSS rebel organization, the localities of Daraa's far south-eastern corner were covered by the 2018 Russian-led negotiations that prevented a full reconstitution of state authority. Ever since the conclusion of the surrender deal, the state was able to achieve only a low degree penetration into the local communities of eastern Daraa, where it exhibited an inability fully to reinstate complete control over resources, territory and resident population.[11] Owing to a full Russian protection against state violations and a new role granted to former rebels at odds with the state, the immediate consequences were (1) devolution of security affairs to former rebels, (2) an effective intermediary role played by former rebels between the local population and state institutions with regard to improving service delivery and (3) the creation of an autonomous sphere for locals to contribute to managing their local affairs in parallel with activities carried out by local state institutions.

Devolution of security functions

Following the conclusion of the 2018 deal, Russia sought to create a local armed actor whose backbone is made up of former local rebels at odds with the state, endowed with the military capacity to use or threaten to use violence. While rebel integration into the Russian-backed Fifth Corps of the Syrian army was one of the main promises made during the 2018 negotiations, for Russia, the underlying objective was to limit state authority and prevent an influx of Iranian-backed forces to Daraa governorate. In October 2018, Russia established the Eighth Brigade, a subdivision of the Fifth Corps of the Syrian army,[12] and entrusted al-Oda, the former leader of the dissolved QSS, with its command. The commitment exhibited by al-Oda to Russia's mediation overtures, his early surrender, and the high mobilization capacities he maintained, earned him genuine Russian patronage that portrayed him as a reliable figure.[13] 'Al-Oda is pragmatic, rational and intelligent. He was the only [rebel] leader who understood the long-term rewards of the negotiations', according to a former rebel leader whose group was – along the QSS – a component of the disbanded 'Southern Front' rebel coalition.[14]

Since its formation, and under Russia's direct supervision, the Eighth Brigade selectively integrated ex-rebels who were largely descendants from Busra al-Sham and its surrounding localities into its sub-units. As of October 2021, nearly 1,600 fighters, about 900 of whom are former rebels of QSS from Busra al-Sham and its surrounding localities, were incorporated in the ranks of the Eighth Brigade.[15] From Russia's point of view, the main focus of rebel integration in eastern Daraa governorate had a logic with roots in wartime. The intervention made by the Lebanese Hezbollah in Busra al-Sham in 2012 to suppress the protests, the recruitment of the city's Shi'a youth into its ranks, and the support it later provided to the state in its military operations against rebel-held areas, together created deeply rooted hostilities against Iran and its proxies.[16] By granting local former rebels a margin of manoeuvre to inflict controllable small-scale violence, Russia sought to alter the agenda of formal rebels to impede the expansionist endeavours of the Iran-backed forces in parts of the south. For the Iran-backed forces in the south, weakening the Eighth Brigade has emerged as a priority in the post-war period. This is mainly to expand the presence of its forces and penetrate the city of Busra al-Sham, the main Shi'a population hub in southern Syria.[17] As a consequence, the Eighth Brigade participated in a reciprocal, cyclical pattern of mutual kidnappings, assassinations and drive-by shootings against militants and collaborators with the Iran-backed Hezbollah. 'The state is back and we have to deal with it in one way or another. Today, our battle is with Iran, its militias, and local collaborators', as put by a senior commander in the Eighth Brigade.[18]

The relationship between the Eighth Brigade and the state remained erratic and opaque. The Brigade recognized the return of the state and, covertly, the legitimacy of the Syrian president, Bashar al-Assad, behind closed doors.[19] It deployed forces to defend the state in armed confrontation with armed contenders in several locations in northern Latakia, Deir ez-Zor and Sweida governorates.[20] Yet Eighth Brigade emerged as a bulwark against an expanding of the state authority in areas that fell under its control in eastern Daraa. 'We accepted the return of the state and the reopening of its institutions. We are no longer interested in defeating the state. However, our duty is now to contain its expansionist ambitions in parts of the south,' explained a senior commander in the Eighth Brigade.[21] The absence of the state's military and security forces allowed the Eighth Brigade to fill the vacuum and assume security functions in localities that fell under its direct control. The Eighth Brigade maintained order by running regular patrols on main roads and highways, managing checkpoints, countering illicit drug trafficking and enforcing a degree of weapon control. 'Despite the presence of the state institutions, the Eighth Brigade is the one that protects the people and their properties from gangs and criminal groups.' as explained by a local from Busra al-Sham.[22]

Simultaneously, the Eighth Brigade did not hesitate to turn against and confront the state's military and security forces, for example for mistreating or detaining civilians or former rebels. On many occasions, the Eighth Brigade deployed contingents of its fighters to free civilians and its rebels-turned-soldiers from military and security checkpoints where they were arbitrarily detained. While many of these interventions have resulted in the nonviolent and immediate release of captured individuals, in several instances the situation had quickly escalated and broken out into armed confrontations against state forces, leading to deaths and injuries.[23] 'I was detained at a checkpoint staffed by the Air Force Intelligence. They informed me that my name was on a list of wanted persons and asked me to surrender my weapon. Rapidly, the headquarters sent an armed convoy and was able to free me,' related by an Eighth Brigade fighter.[24] As a consequence, and despite available economic incentives, security guarantees has enticed more former rebels to join the ranks of the Eighth Brigade. In the words of a former rebel: 'I receive a monthly salary of $200, however, I registered to join the Brigade mainly to protect myself against arrest by the state.'[25]

Participation in local government

Enabling state institutions to resume effective service provision was one core promise that Russia had promised to fulfil. However, a dramatic macroeconomic deterioration, a sharp decline in the availability of labour due to civilian flight, death and injury, and the state institutions struggle to recover have posed a daunting challenge to the fulfilment of this task. Despite restrictions imposed on its presence, the state aimed to enhance service provision in a variety of ways. First, while it abolished structures of control and service provision that existed under rebel control, the state co-opted projects installed by the opposition local councils and NGOs. For example, the state's water establishment co-opted the water plan previously implemented by the Busra al-Sham opposition local council, which piped water from wells located in eastern Daraa to the centre of the city. Second, under the watchful eyes of its security apparatuses, the state allowed support provided by several local NGOs, Syrian Arab Red Crescent as well as United Nations agencies to distribute aid and food baskets, enhance service delivery and ease the living conditions of the local population.

That being said, the state's limited authority granted locals an important autonomous sphere to launch collective initiatives to institute short-term alternatives to complete service-related responsibilities in parallel to those required from and by the state institutions. Often under the direct supervision of clan sheikhs, kinship ties, *faz'a* (rapid response for material and non-material support by relatives), collective responsibility and shared norms and customs shaped the locals' preference for collective organization, raising money and the mobilization of cross-border networks and diasporic communities to fulfil their essential needs. For example, against the backdrop of the debilitated healthcare provisions in Daraa governorate, the arrival of coronavirus to Syria in March 2020 pushed locals to launch Covid-19 response initiatives. Under the supervision of clan sheikhs, locals dipped into their savings or appealed expatriates in the Gulf states to sanitize streets, distribute ration baskets and deliver water tanks to localities like al-Jizeh, Ma'raba and Busra al-Sham.[26]

The presence of a dominant and endogenous armed actor has permitted some clan sheikhs to continue to exercise para-judicial functions. During wartime, the erosion of state judicial institutions during wartime granted clan sheikhs a degree of agency enabling them to exercise functions of conflict management, be it between ordinary civilians, between insurgents or between civilians and insurgents (Al-Jabassini 2020). The return of state judicial institutions in the post-war eopch did not deprive them of continuing to play such a revived traditional role. Due largely to the robust ties they enjoyed with a dominant and endogenous armed actor, clan sheikhs broadly intervened in the judicial realm and continued to resolve disputes through the practice of *sulh*, a traditional conflict-resolution mechanism. On numerous occasions, clan sheikhs intervened – individually or collectively through the formation of a *sulh* delegation – and succeeded in resolving disputes over agricultural land borders, robberies, debts and intentional and unintentional homicide. Due to their 'wisdom' and 'honesty', as many locals from Daraa described their qualities, *sulh* delegations succeeded in persuading parties in conflict to forego vengeance, accept fair compensation and reach reconciliation in numerous reported disputes in various localities such as Kahil, Gahsm, al-Jizeh and Busra al-Sham.[27]

In their turn, the commanders of the Eighth Brigade have been aware of the strategic importance of the role played by clan sheikhs and family elders in maintaining a degree of local order, not only in local disputes but also in the ones that rose with neighbours in the Sweida Province (Al-Jabassini and Ezzi 2021). Therefore, they have been facilitating the endeavours of mediators to launch *sulh* processes by providing transport and protection against potential kidnapping or assassination, and they operated as an executive body to enforce the outcome of the *sulh* process in cases where the offender's clan refused to submit to the final decision taken. 'Under conditions of chaos, we need a military body to help us to enforce our decisions. Without a military role, we can't preserve our social role,' explained a prominent al-Hamad clan sheikh in eastern Daraa.[28]

The Eighth Brigade has emerged as a military intermediary actor with bargaining power enabling it to voice civilian demands to local state institutions with regard to improving service provision. While civilians in eastern Daraa strongly believe that there are no alternatives to state institutions, they benefit from the presence of the Eighth Brigade and capitalize on pre-existing clan and family social networks to influence decision-making in state local institutions. On many occasions, civilians –individually or collectively, overtly or covertly – approached al-Oda and his comrades, reporting municipality staff for ignoring their complaints about, for instance, electrical faults and interruptions of water supplies, requesting their intervention. In response, al-Oda opened direct channels to local state officials and conveyed civilian demands, following up on implementation. 'The water pipes in my street were broken and the municipality ignored my request to fix it for months. I approached the Eighth Brigade and explained the situation and they promised to resolve the matter. The pipes were fixed in one week,' as stated by a local from eastern Daraa.[29] Moreover, civilians have also appealed to the command of the Eighth Brigade to investigate cases of corruption in local state institutions and to take deterrent actions. 'Al-Oda was able to transfer an officer at the recruitment center of Busra al-Sham after complaints about him demanding bribes from civilians in return for issuing official documents,' reported a local from Busra al-Sham.[30]

Conclusion

Ceasefire and local reconciliation agreements have greatly aided the Syrian state to push rebels to capitulate or recompose, and to regain control over large swathes of territory. While the ensuing general situation was often labelled as 'post conflict', the indiscriminate use of this term suggests an over-simplification of the complex and disparate realities in areas where the state has claimed victory and consequently taken back control. In the case of southern Syria, the proclaimed military victory and the physical return of state institutions did not lead to the restoration of security and stability. Unlike elsewhere in Syria, the impact of regional politics and the engagement of a third party have led to 'patchwork' strategy of state return. While the state's use of armed force coerced rebels to surrender and was able to reassert its authoritarian power, Russian-led negotiations demarcated areas of limited statehood and granted former rebels a margin of manoeuvre enabling them to continue to inflict measures of violence to maintain a status quo in the southern border region. In doing so, Russia transformed the conflict from an open insurgency to a low-intensity conflict confined to Daraa's administrative borders. The result was areas of limited statehood and devolution of functions to an array of local and diasporic actors.

The empirical case of eastern Daraa demonstrates how Russia's alteration to the agenda and the role played by former rebels have transformed the nature of the conflict, which served to limit the state authority and to thwart the expansionist aspirations of its Iranian ally. Until October 2021, Russia has remained committed to the core of the 2018 agreement, namely, to intervening and limiting the state's presence in parts of the south. The establishment of the Eighth Brigade whose backbone is made up of local former rebels at odds with the state not only helped Russia to maintain the status quo but also resulted in devolution of security affairs and a creation of an autonomous sphere for locals to contribute to managing their local affairs.

Notes

1. In this study, I use the terms 'rebels', 'rebel organization', 'rebel group', 'Insurgents', 'insurgent organization' and 'insurgent group' interchangeably. 'These are armed factions that use violence to challenge the state'. Zachariah Cherian Mampilly, *Rebel Rulers: Insurgent Governance and Civilian Life During War* (New York: Cornell University Press, 2011), 3.
2. Developed in the 1970s, the concept of 'low intensity conflict' was an attempt to define a wide range of political and military activities which were less intense than modern, conventional limited war. See Alan Stephens, 'The Transformation of "Low Intensity" Conflict', *Small Wars & Insurgencies* 5, no. 2 (1 September 1994): 143–61. However, to date, the concept lacks a universally accepted definition. For a thorough discussion on the different conceptualizations and categories, see Tin Guštin, 'Some Aspects of the Low-Intensity Conflict', *Scientific Journal of the Croatian Defence Academy* 5, no. 1 (30 June 2021): 219–41.
3. Author interview with a genealogist from Daraa residing in the United Arab Emirates, Shaykh Mohammed Fathi Rashid Al-Hariri (2017).
4. Author interviews with numerous clan sheikhs in Daraa (2015–18).
5. In May 2017, representatives from Russia, Iran and Turkey met in Astana, Kazakhstan, and agreed to set up four so-called 'de-escalation zones' within which there would be a halt of hostilities between rebel groups and the Syrian military forces. See Manhal Baresh, 'The Sochi Agreement and the Interests of Guarantor States: Examining the Aims and Challenges of Sustaining the Deal' (European University Institute, January 2019), https://bit.ly/36FEkmR.
6. Author interviews with former rebel leaders in Busra al-Sham and Tafas (September 2018).
7. The Fifth Assault Corps was established by Russia in November 2016 and fell under a joint Syrian-Russian command. See Abdullah Al-Jabassini, 'From Insurgents to Soldiers: The Fifth Assault Corps in Daraa, Southern Syria' (European University Institute, 2019), http://bit.ly/2oTzoXG.
8. Author interviews with former rebel leaders and civilian opposition figures (July–October 2018).
9. Author interviews with figures who attended the negotiations in the cities of Busra al-Sham and Tafas (October 2018). See also Abdullah Al-Jabassini, 'From Rebel Rule to a Post-Capitulation Era in Daraa Southern Syria: The Impacts and Outcomes of Rebel Behaviour During Negotiations', Working Paper (European University Institute, January 2019), https://bit.ly/2CDpflK.
10. Out of more than 30,000 rebels who operated in Daraa, only about 5,000 rebel rejectionists to the negotiations were evacuated to Syria's north-west rebel stronghold, Idlib governorate. Source: Author interview with former rebel leader in the Southern Front (June 2018). Author interviews local activists (November 2018).
11. The term 'state penetration' was originally coined and used by Zachariah Mampilly in the context of rebel governance. According to him, the history of state penetration in society affects the development of rebel governance. See Zachariah Cherian Mampilly, *Rebel Rulers: Insurgent Governance and Civilian Life During War*, 68.
12. The Fifth Assault Corps was established by Russia in November 2016 and fell under a joint Syrian-Russian command. See Al-Jabassini, 'From Insurgents to Soldiers: The Fifth Assault Corps in Daraa, Southern Syria'.

13 For a behavioural assessment of rebel leaders who took part in the 2018 negotiations, and for the assessment of the gains and/or losses of each type of behaviour, see Al-Jabassini, 'From Rebel Rule to a Post-Capitulation Era in Daraa Southern Syria'.
14 The Southern Front is a disbanded Syrian rebel alliance established in southern Syria in February 2014, which consisted of forty-nine rebel groups. See Aron Lund, 'Does the "Southern Front" Exist?"', *Carnegie Middle East Center*, 21 March 2014, http://carnegie-mec.org/diwan/55054.
15 Author interview with a senior commander in the Eighth Brigade (October 2021).
16 The author obtained an archive of documents collected by local activists in the period 2011–13 on alleged violent incidents conducted by Shi'a militant and local collaborators with Hezbollah against the Sunni population in Busra al-Sham. This includes sniping, immolation and destroying properties. The archive is supported by exclusive digital evidence and medical reports, where applicable.
17 Until the time of writing, the Shi'a families, which were displaced in March 2015 when rebel groups ousted the state and its auxiliary forces, have not been allowed to return to Busra al-Sham. Author interviews with senior commanders in the Eighth Brigade (January 2019–May 2020).
18 Author interview with a senior commander in the Eighth Brigade (March 2019).
19 Author interview with a commander in the Eighth Brigade (March 2019).
20 Author interview with a field commander in the Eighth Brigade who was deployed to Lattakia (September 2019).
21 Author interview with a senior commander in the Eighth Brigade (February 2019).
22 Author interview with a senior commander in the Eighth Brigade (February 2019).
23 For example, the Eighth Brigade deployed its forces in in June 2020 to release the former head of the disbanded opposition local council in Mahja town from detention by the State Security Apparatus. During the confrontation, armed attacks broke out and led to deaths on both sides. This was immediately followed by a series of skirmishes initiated by the Eighth Brigade against state security branch members near Kahil and Sayda towns, which forced them to evacuate their checkpoints.
24 Author interview with a senior commander in the Eighth Brigade (September 2019).
25 Author interview with a former rebel who joined the Eighth Brigade (February 2019).
26 Author interviews with twelve locals in eastern Daraa and five expatriate members of local communities in Gulf States (March–May 2020).
27 Author interviews with six locals in eastern Daraa (December 2019–March 2020).
28 Author interview with al-Hamad clan sheikh (January 2020).
29 Author interview with civilian in eastern Daraa (October 2019). Exact location withheld upon the interviewee's request.
30 Author interview with civilian in Busra al-Sham (August 2019).

Bibliography

Abu Fakher, Fandi(2005). *Khalel Rifaat Al-Hawrani, Tarekh Hawran Wa Da'wataho Al-Nahdhawya Fe Aryaf Belad Al- Sham* (Khaleel Rifaat Al-Hawrani, History of Hawran, and His Renaissance Call in Belad Al-Sham Rural Areas). Damascus: Arab Writers Union.

Adleh, Fadi, and Favier, Agnès (2017). *Local Reconciliation Agreements in Syria: A Non-Starter for Peacebuilding*. Florence: European University Institute, Middle East Directions, Wartime and Post-Conflict in Syria, January. https://bit.ly/2Um2SeL.

Al-Jabassini, Abdullah (2017). 'Dismantling Networks of Resistance and the Reconfiguration of Order in Southern Syria'. Florence: European University Institute, Middle East Directions, Wartime and Post-Conflict in Syria, October. https://bit.ly/3BX1SzH.

Al-Jabassini, Abdullah (2019). *From Insurgents to Soldiers: The Fifth Assault Corps in Daraa, Southern Syria*. Florence: European University Institute, Middle East Directions, Wartime and Post-Conflict in Syria, May. http://bit.ly/2oTzoXG.

Al-Jabassini, Abdullah (2019). 'From Rebel Rule to a Post-Capitulation Era in Daraa Southern Syria: The Impacts and Outcomes of Rebel Behaviour During Negotiations'. Florence: European University Institute, Middle East Directions, Wartime and Post-Conflict in Syria, January. https://bit.ly/2CDpflK.

Al-Jabassini, Abdullah (2020). '*Festering Grievances and the Return to Arms in Southern Syria*'. Florence: European University Institute, Middle East Directions, Wartime and Post-Conflict in Syria, April. https://bit.ly/34nt2jL.

Al-Jabassini, Abdullah (2020). 'Tribalocracy: Wartime Social Order and Its Transformation in Tribal Regions – Evidence from Daraa Governorate in Southern Syria'. PhD Dissertation, University of Kent.

Al-Jabassini, Abdullah (2021). 'Russia Rethinks the Status Quo in Southern Syria'. *Middle East Institute*. 13 August. https://bit.ly/3AAx6MZ.

Al-Jabassini, Abdullah (2021). 'The Weaponization of Service Delivery in Wartime and Post-War Daraa al-Balad'. *Journal of Genocide Research* 25(1): 122–31..

Al-Jabassini, Abdullah, and Ezzi Mazen (2021). '*Tribal "Sulh" and the Politics of Persuasion in Volatile Southern Syria*'. Florence: European University Institute, Middle East Directions, Wartime and Post-Conflict in Syria, March), https://bit.ly/3u2ZjID

Al-Rai, Ninar (2019). 'Facets of Syrian Regime Authority in Eastern Ghouta'. Florence: European University Institute, Middle East Directions, Wartime and Post-Conflict in Syria, August. https://bit.ly/3k890QM.

Baresh, Manhal (2019). *The Sochi Agreement and the Interests of Guarantor States: Examining the Aims and Challenges of Sustaining the Deal*. Florence: European University Institute, Middle East Directions, Wartime and Post-Conflict in Syria, January. https://bit.ly/36FEkmR.

Batatu, Hanna (1999). *Syria's Peasantry, the Descendants of Its Lesser Rural Notables, and Their Politics*. Princeton, NJ: Princeton University Press.

Bloomfield, David, and Reilly, Ben (1998). 'The Changing Nature of Conflict and Conflict Management'. In Peter Harris and Ben Reilly (eds), *Democracy and Deep-Rooted Conflict: Options for Negotiators* (7–25). Stockholm: International IDEA.

Börzel, Tanja A., Risse, Thomas, and Draude, Anke (2018). 'Governance in Areas of Limited Statehood: Conceptual Clarifications and Major Contributions of the Handbook'. In Anke Draude, Thomas Risse, and Tanja A. Börzel (eds), *The Oxford Handbook of Governance and Limited Statehood* (1–27). Oxford: Oxford University Press.

Ezzi, Mazen (2020). *Post-Reconciliation Rural Damascus: Are Local Communities Still Represented?*. Research Project Report. Florence: European University Institute, Middle East Directions, Wartime and Post-Conflict in Syria, November. https://bit.ly/3pJKRnS.

Galtung, Johan (1995). 'Conflict Resolution as Conflict Transformation: The First Law of Thermodynamics Revisited'. In Kumar Rupesinghe (eds), *Conflict Transformation* (51–64). New York: St. Martin's Press.

Guštin, Tin (2021). 'Some Aspects of the Low-Intensity Conflict'. *Scientific Journal of the Croatian Defence Academy* 5(1): 219–41.

Kalyvas, Stathis N. *The Logic of Violence in Civil War*. New York: Cambridge University Press, 2006.

Kalyvas, Stathis N., and Balcells, Laia (2010). 'International System and Technologies of Rebellion: How the End of the Cold War Shaped Internal Conflict'. *American Political Science Review* 104(3): 415–29.

Kriesberg, Louis (1997). 'The Development of the Conflict Resolution Field'. In I. William Zartman and J. Lewis Rasmussen (eds), *Peacemaking in International Conflict: Methods & Techniques* (51–77). Washington, DC: United States Institute of Peace Press.

Leenders, Reinoud, and Heydemann, Steven (2012). 'Popular Mobilization in Syria: Opportunity and Threat, and the Social Networks of the Early Risers', *Mediterranean Politics* 17(2): 139–59. https://doi.org/10.1080/13629395.2012.694041.

Lund, Aron (2014). 'Does the "Southern Front" Exist?"' *Carnegie Middle East Center*, 21 March. http://carnegie-mec.org/diwan/55054.

Lund, Aron (2021). 'Assad Shores Up Control in Syria's Symbolically Important South', *World Politics Review*. 16 September. https://bit.ly/2XY1ra8.

Mampilly, Zachariah Cherian (2011). *Rebel Rulers: Insurgent Governance and Civilian Life During War*. New York: Cornell University Press.

Miall, Hugh (2004). 'Conflict Transformation: A Multi-Dimensional Task'. In Alex Austin, Martina Fischer, and Norbert Ropers (eds), *Transforming Ethnopolitical Conflict* (67–89). Wiesbaden: VS Verlag für Sozialwissenschaften.

Reuters (2018). 'Rebels Agree Withdrawal Deal for Enclave Near Syria's Homs'. 2 May. https://reut.rs/32qYC0l.

Stephens, Alan (1994). 'The Transformation of "Low Intensity" Conflict'. *Small Wars & Insurgencies* 5(2): 143–61.

Syrian Arab News Agency (2018). 'Army Liberates Village of Al-Qusayr, Last Daesh Terrorist Stronghold in Daraa and Finds Israeli and American Weapons in their Dens in al-Yarmouk Basin', 1 August. https://bit.ly/2TXDgGo.

Syrian Ministry of Foreign Affairs and Expatriates (2018). 'President Al-Assad in an Interview with Al-Alam TV: The Syrian-Iranian Relationship is Strategic. The Strongest Response against Israel is to Strike its Terrorists in Syria', 13 June. https://bit.ly/30s0Pux.

Thomas Risse (2015). 'Limited Statehood: A Critical Perspective'. In Stephan Leibfried et al. (eds), *The Oxford Handbook of Transformations of the State* (152–68). Oxford: Oxford University Press.

Times of Israel (2017). 'South Syria Truce Seeks to Allay Israel, Jordan Fears about Iran', 8 July. https://bit.ly/3BIjhMX.

Tokmajyan, Armenak (2020). 'How Southern Syria Has Been Transformed into a Regional Powder Keg'. *Carnegie Middle East Center*. 14 July. https://bit.ly/2SbfyCK.

Chapter 6

DEVOLUTION OF STATE POWER IN SYRIA AND IRAQ: TRIBAL AUXILIARIES FROM THE MARGINS TO THE CENTRES

Haian Dukhan

Introduction

As a result of state atrophy in Syria and Iraq, governments in both countries have been transferring the task of preserving security in certain marginal areas to tribal militias. This chapter aims to investigate the relationship between the state and tribal militias from 2014 – the height of Daesh power Iraq and the opposition insurgent forces in Syria – to the present day. It aims to answer the following questions: How and why do the Syrian and Iraqi states rely on tribes to confront challenges? What is the impact of this on internal tribal dynamics? What are some of the consequences of solidifying tribal ties for the future of Syria and Iraq? Existing studies give the impression that the formation of all paramilitary groups in Syria and Iraq was largely a top-down process. Focusing on the rise of al-Baqer Brigade in Syria and Salaheddin Brigade in Iraq and relying on a series of detailed and probing interviews with members of the al-Baggara tribe in Syria, and al-Jabour tribe in Iraq, this chapter challenges this assumption. The chapter shows that the emergence of these tribal militias was principally a grassroots phenomenon stemming from competition over local resources. It argues that both states have seized this opportunity and outsourced some of their security and counterinsurgency tasks to these groups. Ahram suggests that often the aim is to recruit the services of tribes, to serve as what Olson calls 'stationary bandits' (Ahram 2011: 138; Olson 1993: 567–76). Relying on tribes allows the state to quickly and effectively react to local challenges, especially when fighting well-organized insurgencies that invest in building their own local institutions (Clayton and Thomson 2016; Bolte 2016). As a result, tribal militias now thrive, with support from the government. Kinship ties played an important role in recruiting tribesmen into these militias, and leaders of these military formations solicited tribal concepts and affiliations such as internal solidarity and revenge to achieve their purposes. Despite this, internal differences, social and geographic fragmentation and contested leadership, depicted through interviews, run counter to the image of the tribes as cohesive groups. Both case studies show that the tribes are internally divided, and factional rivalries and conflicts among their lineages run deep. In the case of Iraq, the chapter will show how the al-Houri lineage in al-Shirqat district secured support from the Iraqi state as part of a competition with other lineages inside the al-Jabour tribe itself to restore its position of dominance, which had been lost within al-Shirqat following the rise of Daesh. Traditional leaders were sidelined, and new leadership, organized around militiamen such as Khaled al-Hussein, the leader of al-Baqer Brigade, has emerged. One may only wonder what the consequences of this are for Syria and Iraq. Instrumentalizing tribes and tribalism for military and security gains contributes to their transformation from 'the position of neglect or disadvantage, into structural margins that manage to acquire forms of internal consistency and a political dynamic' (Al-Azmeh and Al-Bagdadi 2021: 1–24). In the process, traditional tribal values such as communal solidarity (*asabiyya*), territoriality and tribal practices such as revenge (*Tha'r*) and the eviction and expropriation of certain members of the tribal community (*Jalwa*) have been reconfigured and transferred to the context of modern military combat.[1] Often, these behaviours encourage what Jabar calls 'tribal gangsterism' which is detrimental to national unity and state integrity (Jabar 2000: 28–31).

Methodology

Research in general involved conducting a broad literature review on tribes and tribalism in the Middle East and North Africa, including debates on the structure and function of tribes. This was supplemented by further review of the available literature on the purpose of 'paramilitary groups' during conflict and their impact on state society relationships in the 'post-conflict' setting. After the broad setting was established, I started conducting precise research on the two case studies chosen for this chapter: al-Baqer Brigade and Salaheddin Brigade. Both groups are embedded in tribal communities which are built on pre-existing social networks, namely, the al-Baggara tribe and the al-Jabour tribe, respectively. Therefore, researching these two empirical examples required examination of the structure of each tribe, their geographical distribution, their leadership and the history of their interaction with the central states in Damascus and Baghdad. This required analysis at both a national and a local level.

In terms of obtaining data about the establishment of both military formations, I conducted research into reports from governments, donors and international organizations about the conflict in Syria and Iraq, and created a database derived from the information gathered about both groups. Following this, I conducted thorough searches on social media platforms such as Facebook, Twitter and YouTube and compiled another dataset on these groups. I then started comparing and contrasting these two datasets. Research was conducted using English and Arabic sources. As for obtaining data on the structure, history and distribution of the two tribes in Syria and Iraq, I surveyed a wide array of literature. This included genealogical encyclopaedias written by members of these tribes, historical narratives produced by Syrian and Iraqi historians and government reports conducted for different US institutions as part of their military presence in Iraq since 2003 and in Syria since 2014. After completing this literature review, I summarized my verified findings in a document and started drafting my interview questions.

Questions were intended to achieve multiple purposes:

1. Close any gaps in the research produced by the literature review.
2. Cross-check with my interviewees the truthfulness of the empirical narratives that I found in the literature.
3. Gain new insights from the people on the ground who have first-hand knowledge of the changes and developments that took place in their region.

Fieldwork to interview members of each tribe who had been displaced as a result of the conflict from both countries was supposed to take place in southern Turkey and northern Iraq. Due to travel restrictions following the Covid-19 pandemic, this had to be cancelled and replaced with online interviews. A research fixer from al-Hassakeh who is based in Urfa and has connections with members of different tribes in Syria and Iraq arranged fifty interviews, to be conducted via WhatsApp. Twenty-five of the interviews were to be with members of the al-Baggara tribe and twenty-five were to be with members of the al-Jabour tribe. The majority of these interviewees live in their country of origin, but some now live in Iraqi Kurdistan and Turkey. I prepared a list of questions in Arabic and the same questions were asked to all interviewees. All interviews were recorded on a mobile phone and were later transcribed into written text. The method of asking the same questions of different interviewees enabled me to verify the information through multiple sources. Of course, one could speak at length of the challenges that emerged in conducting these interviews, such as internet connection problems, issues of the building of trust and time zone differences. All this required patience and persistence, particularly in terms of establishing a rapport with the interviewees, which sometimes required me to break the ice by sharing personal information, such as tribal connections or the story of my own family's experience of Daesh and their displacement during the war in Syria. This exchange of personal stories between the interviewees and myself proved fruitful in the end and helped them open up and provide new insights unavailable from the literature.

Preliminary notes on tribes and tribalism

This chapter deals with two military formations in Syria and Iraq that are built upon existing networks of kinship ties, called tribes in this context, namely the al-Baggara tribe in the case of Syria and the al-Jabour tribe in the case of Iraq. In order to be able to understand the complexity of this phenomenon, the chapter utilizes literature on tribes and tribalism in the Middle East and the processes of establishing paramilitary groups during civil wars. Below are a few points that should be taken into consideration while reading this chapter: First, while the chapter recognizes that tribes still perceive themselves according to a standard image, realities on the ground are constantly evolving, which is illustrated in many ways in this chapter, such as by the rise of militiamen who have been competing with traditional leaders for the leadership of tribes. Second, the lineages within al-Baggara tribe and al-Jabour tribe, such as al-Bu Rhama and al-Houri, show that they have a higher degree of tribal solidarity than the larger tribal units. Tibi argues that what are perceived as 'actual' kinship relations are empirically evident within the smaller units of the tribe only: these are referred to as local lineages (Tibi,1991: 127–52). Third, tribes and lineages go through processes of cohesion and fragmentation during their military ventures as a result of many factors, such as facing external threats, building clientelist networks with external forces, geopolitical boundaries and competition for state resources and spoils of war. Last, the chapter identifies a clear disparity between tribalism with its perceived ancient customs and rules and the current resurgent form of tribalism. Therefore, we are talking about what I describe in this chapter as 'the reconfiguration of tribalism' which was triggered by many factors such as the advent of the new political system and the social change it furthered.

History of devolution of violence to tribes in Iraq and Syria

Throughout history, tribes have organized themselves militarily to protect their sources of livelihood, such as grazing lands, wells and herds, from the threats posed by other tribes that could potentially commandeer their resources to expand their power and influence in the absence of effective state control in the peripheral areas (al-Abbadi 1984: 89). This ongoing competition for resources created a system of 'political accumulation', as Brenner describes the tribal raids that were intended to increase or protect the raiding tribe's assets (Brenner 1990: 26–33). Increased Ottoman activity in Arab frontier zones, beginning in the 1830s, signalled the decline of tribal autonomy that would gradually continue with the rise of the modern state, on the edge of the periphery, which prevailed, in what Toth calls the 'last battles of the Bedouin' (Toth 2006: 49–76). The case of Sheikh Ibn Mheid, chief of the al-Fad'an in Raqqa is particularly illustrative of the increasing power of the state and the declining power of the tribes. Suleiman Khalaf tells us how Ibn Mheid publicly gathered all the criminals in his region and said to them, 'Now I cannot protect anyone' (Khalaf 1981: 93). The government police forces then entered his house in search of people who had committed public offences. In these battles, the state power had not only grown on the edges of the margins but eventually spread to the core of settlements in the margins. Despite this, central authorities in Syria, Iraq and other parts of the Middle East continued to rely on tribal leaders to recruit tribal mercenaries to quell internal disturbances, and to fight external threats as well.

In an effort to counter Mustafa Barzani and the nationalist Kurdish Democratic Party (KDP), in 1960 Abd al-Karim Qasim and his followers recruited Barzani's tribal rivals to fight in conjunction with the state (Van Bruinesses 2003: 165–83).

From 1961 to 1970, northern Iraq was going through a cycle of state-insurgent confrontation. The Iraqi government succeeded in recruiting more than 10,000 auxiliaries who could be relied upon in rural and mountainous operations (ibid). Chieftains and village heads from the Barzani's traditional tribal rivals, the Herki and Surchi, were granted the title of the state *mustashar* (consultant) (MacDowall 1996: 312). Often, this process reinforced the hierarchies of clan social structure and fed competition leading to rising tribal feuds, with government tribal auxiliaries looting the villages of rival tribes.

Apart from exploiting military tribalism against the Kurds, Saddam Hussein used Arab tribes in his long-term war with Iran. In the midst of Iran's attempt to reach Basra in 1987, Arab tribes spontaneously mobilized to protect the city, declaring their hostility to Persian invaders and loyalty to Iraq (Ahram 2011: 138). This nationalist resistance provided an opportunity for the Iraqi state to find local allies against Iranian forces. Rawqan Ghafur al-Majid, the president's nephew and aide de camp, was put in charge of efforts to approach, mobilize and arm the Arab Shi'ite tribes as a national defence force on the battlegrounds of Basra, Amara, al-Kut and the marshes (Jabar, 2000: 28-31). State media and party circulars pragmatically praised the tribes for their manhood, courage and military prowess hailing their pure Arabism in order to prevent any possible communal Shi'ite association with Iranians.

The failure of the invasion of Kuwait, and Saddam's terrible loss in the 1991 war with the United S tatesand its allies, weakened the Iraqi state's military capacity, pushing Saddam to reinforce tribal networks to bolster his grip. A newly established militia force of 15,000 to 20,000 die-hard loyalists recruited from tribes and regions considered loyal to Saddam Hussein, called Fedayee Saddam (Militants of Saddam, FS), was set up and placed under the command of Saddam's son, Qusay (Cordesman 2005: 47). This militia received rifles, grenade launchers, mortars and even howitzers from the state and was tasked with patrolling key installations in the capital and other cities in Iraq (Jabar 2003: 115-30). During the Sha'ban Intifada among Shia Arabs in southern Iraq against Saddam Hussein in 1991, Saddam needed grassroots support against Iranian infiltration and guerrilla activities. Saddam identified the potential to cultivate support from the tribes that had remained on the sidelines and abstained from the revolt. The Iraqi government organized 'popular committees', which included the members of the tribes of Khafaja in Nasiriyya, the Bani Hasan around Kufa and the Rumaytha tribe near Samawa, to maintain local security (Baram 1997: 1-31). They guarded roads and installations and 'refuted rumours'. The fact that many Shi'ite tribes did not join the revolt and some even assisted the regime made it much easier for the army and the Republican Guard to put down the uprising (ibid). After the failed revolt in the south, delegations of tribal sheikhs were honoured at the presidential palace for fighting what the Iraqi media described as 'the bands of traitors' (Jabar 2003: 115-30).

The Syrian state devolved the exercise of state violence to tribes on many occasions to face internal and external challenges. From 1979 onwards, the Syrian government faced demonstrations, strikes and escalating violence orchestrated by the Muslim Brotherhood in a way that paralyzed the country (Drysdale 1982: 3–11). Jonathan Rae describes how Jamil Al-Assad, Hafez's brother, visited Boueidar (بويدر) in the governorate of Aleppo, the stronghold of the al-Hadidyyin (الحديديين) tribe, in 1981 (Rae 1999: 173). Jamil asked the al-Hadidyyin to be the government's eyes and ears in the countryside of Aleppo and Hama and to monitor movements between the two governorates (Chatty 2010: 29–49). The al-Hadidiyin built military checkpoints around Hama, kept watch on the desert and captured some members of the Muslim Brotherhood who wanted to escape to Iraq after the bombing of Hama and handed them to the Syrian regime (Dukhan 2019: 82). In March 2004, the governorate of al-Hassakeh witnessed Kurdish riots encouraged by the American presence in Iraq. The Syrian army did not have a strong presence in the eastern part of the country, and it therefore sought assistance from the Arab tribes in the governorate (Savelsberg 2014: 58–107). The al-Jabour tribe has a strong presence in al-Hassakeh and was entrusted to protect the government buildings there. They were allowed to take up arms, surround the government buildings and protect them (Dukhan 2019: 82). The Tayy tribe, headed by Sheikh Mohammed al-Fares was entrusted with defending the other major city in the governorate, Qamishli (ibid). This revolt by Kurdish groups was suppressed, with estimates suggesting that around forty people were killed, with over a hundred injured and more than two thousand Kurds detained (Lowe 2006).

This study contends that the devolution of state control over violence to tribes is hardly new, as the aforementioned examples show. This chapter presents a more nuanced picture, with the hypothesis that the reliance on tribes for military and security purposes had previously occurred under a highly centralized conventional military structure where the state recruited the tribes as non-state actors to serve as their proxies. Often, when a particular crisis was over, a prompt return to the path of monopolizing violence by the state took place. After the American invasion of Iraq and the Syrian civil war, governing structures in both countries have become extremely fragmented, not at all resembling the highly centralized state of the very recent past. This led to a multiplicity of local actors and intermediaries being empowered during the war who will not easily relinquish their newfound autonomy (Malmvig 2018). This is not to say that the state had crumbled, but its central power appears to have been very significantly devolved and dispersed, representing a fundamental abandonment of the state's monopoly over violence and a turn towards what Robert Holden calls a reliance on 'parainstitutional violence wielders' (Holden 2004: 14).

Rising from the ashes: Al-Baqer Brigade and Salaheddin Brigade

Studies of state devolution highlight the incentives for the state in setting up militias during armed conflict as part of the state's delegation of violence to non-state actors, while often claiming that militias were mere 'puppets'. The incentives for the state to form and support militias differ, however, from the dynamics that drive community-based militia formation and mobilization (Jentzsch 2014: 8). The two case studies presented here show that al-Baqer Brigade and Salaheddin Brigade were formed by tribal communities and later received assistance from state agents to mobilize recruits. During civil wars, local communities may choose to protect themselves against wartime violence by forming militias under the umbrella of the state, which is the case for al-Baqer brigade (Blocq 2014: 710–24). The act of forming militias, as occurs in many tribal societies, can also be understood as an attempt to influence the state and compete with the government for resources, as will be shown in the case of Salaheddin Brigade.

The al-Baggara tribe in the governorate of Aleppo is a branch of the main tribe that inhabits Deir Ezzor. This segment of the tribe left Deir Ezzor in the nineteenth century as a result of a rift among its members and since then has inhabited villages in the east and the south of the city of Aleppo such as Turkan (تركان), Tell Alam (تل علم), Blat (بلاط) and Khalas (Zakariya 1945: 544). There were sporadic exchanges between the two segments in Aleppo and Deir Ezzor, and visits continued, especially on important occasions such as weddings and funerals, but each segment had developed as a separate social entity.[2] The Syrian historian Jamal Barout maintained that the relationship between the two segments became merely symbolic, where the al-Bashir sheikhly lineage, prominent in Deir Ezzor, had no power or influence in Aleppo (Barout 2013: 357). From the 1960s onwards, Aleppo, like other Syrian cities, experienced a massive demographic change with a large influx of rural incomers drawn by growing employment opportunities generated by a thriving industrial sector (Pagani 2016). Many members of the al-Baggara tribe, alongside other tribes such as al-Assaseneh, al Berri and al-Hadidiyin, moved to the eastern part of the city and inhabited the Bab al-Nayrab and al-Marjeh neighbourhoods.

Although market reforms in the 1970s, 1990s and 2000s had benefited Syria's commercial bourgeoisie in Aleppo, the regime had also cultivated and often given

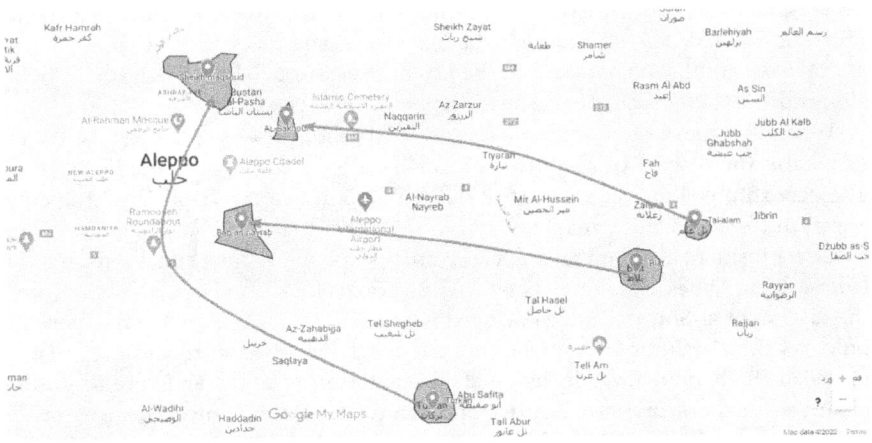

Figure 6.1 Migration of al-Baggara tribes from the rural areas of Aleppo to the city

priority to rival elites of rural and tribal origin by incorporating them into its own monopolistic economic networks and, importantly, its coercive structures and security organs (Haddad 2004: 37–76). This process was both part of the broader strategy to empower tribes in exchange for political compliance, as argued by Dukhan, and a way to buy their support for counterbalancing the traditional Sunni bourgeoisie, from which, in 1982, the Muslim Brotherhood-led revolt drew support (Dukhan 2014: 1–28). Prior to the uprising, people such as Akl al-Hamadeen of al-Baggara and Zeino Berri of al Berri became members of the Syrian Parliament (Al-Mustafa 2015). Fierce competition existed between the al-Baggara, al Berri and al-Assaseneh around smuggling routes from Syria to Jordan and Saudi Arabia for livestock, tobacco, drugs and obtaining economic concessions from the state such as the right to cultivate agricultural tracts of land (Hussein 2020).

As soon as the Syrian uprising erupted and violence intensified, al-Baggara and al Berri saw this as an opportunity to prove their loyalty and rejuvenate Assad's need for their support, and to reinforce their position locally. In Aleppo, criminal gangs called tribal ShaBbiha, from al-Baggara, al Berri and al-Assaseneh, helped quash demonstrations in the early phase of the uprising (Lund 2013: 6). By the same token, some members of the same tribes joined the Free Syrian Army to confront the state. These divisions show how the Syrian uprising and the violence that happened as a result of it created divisions in the social structure causing fragmentation among tribal networks that rely on solidarity to defend themselves (Lacher 2020). Eastern Aleppo became an area of major confrontation between loyalist and opposition forces, many of which were organized along tribal lines. Eventually, when the opposition managed to conquer eastern Aleppo, where many tribal Shabbiha originated, the conflict's brutality reached its peak (Pagani 2016). Some members of the al-Assaseneh tribe attacked the house of Hussein Al-Meri and executed him, alongside his eldest son Ali (Hussein 2020).[3] This assassination has its roots in the fact that Hussein Al-Meri was competing with other members of the al-Assaseneh to control the livestock market in Jibrin and had previously been involved in many quarrels with other members of the Assaseneh before the uprising. Khaled, one of his sons, managed to escape to western Aleppo where, after a few months, he announced the establishment of al-Baqer Brigade to fight alongside the Syrian army in eastern Aleppo (Our-Syria, 2020).

When it comes to our second case study, Al-Jabour is one of the largest tribes to inhabit the district of al-Shirqat in northern Salaheddin governorate in Iraq. They constitute about 85 per cent of the population and the remaining residents are from the Jumayli, Lughaybi, Qaysi and Luhayb tribes (Saleh 2017). Since he became president, Saddam Hussein recruited people for security positions mainly from certain tribes, notably his own (Al Bu Nasser), al-Jabour, particularly from the district of al-Shirqat, and the Ubayd (Baram 1997: 1–31). During this period, officers from al-Jabour tribe, including Asham Sabhan al-Jabouri who would later establish Salaheddin Brigade, as we shall see, were promoted and rose to senior positions in the army and security apparatus. There was, however, resentment among these officers that the levers of power and influence were dominated by Al Bu Nasser, Saddam's tribe, which they considered smaller and of lower status than the al-Jabour.⁴ In January 1990, disaffected army officers from the al-Jabour tribe planned to assassinate the president at the Army Day military parade. The instigator of this plot was Major Sattam al-Jabouri from al-Shirqat (Al-Majedi 2013). The plot was uncovered and as a result Saddam Hussein had many of the army officers from the al-Jabour tribe executed and as a precaution dismissed hundreds more, including Asham who left Iraq and stayed in Syria until Saddam was toppled in 2003. From the time of the attempted coup until 2003, al-Shirqat was forgotten by the central government in Baghdad. Local tensions and competition among the lineages of al-Jabour to exact concessions and benefits from the central government continued. To understand the significance of the inter-Jabour struggle, it is necessary to briefly introduce the major lineages of this tribe.

***The al-Jabour tribe in al-Shirqat is composed of the lineages of al-Houri (الحوري), al-Uqli (العقلي), al-Ramli (الرملي) and al-Bougzat (البوغزات).⁵ Al-Houri is considered the largest lineage and inhabits much of the al-Shirqat district west of the Tigris River. The other lineages inhabit the eastern part of the district on the other side of the Tigris River. Although all of these branches of al-Jabour affirm that they are related through common ancestors, they act as independent tribes and are not under the control of one paramount sheikh. This river acted as a geographical boundary that created a sense of division between the al-Houri and the rest of the al-Jabour lineages. The majority of the state institutions were based to the west of the Tigris River, which enabled members of the al-Houri lineage to hold influential positions in three institutions in the district: the local council, the police and the office of *qa'im maqam* (governor of al-Shirqat).⁶ Consequently, the influential people from al-Houri who held these positions secured jobs for their relatives from the al-Houri lineage.

They also used state resources to provide infrastructure and services, such as schools and health facilities, to the west of the Tigris River in al-Shirqat. This

Figure 6.2 Locations of al-Jabour lineages in al-Shirqat

situation bred resentment among other local clans and other lineages of al-Jabour, against al-Houri. On 10 June 2014, Daesh took control of al-Shirqat and caused the immediate displacement of roughly 90,000 of the estimated 210,000 residents (Saleh 2017). A popular belief among interviewees from the al-Houri lineage was that a significant segment of al-Shirqat's population, particularly other lineages of al-Jabour to the east of the Tigris River in al-Shirqat, supported and collaborated with Daesh. Martin argues that conflicts on the ground are more related to local issues than grand ideological divides, even though local rifts and issues are presented within the framework of ideological cleavage (Martin 2017: 33–57).

In 2015, displaced members of the al-Houri lineage in Erbil were discussing methods to fight back and regain the positions they had lost in al-Shirqat. They collectively agreed to ask Asham Sabhan al-Jabouri, son of the late Sheikh Khalaf al-Jabouri, Sheikh of al-Houri to travel to Baghdad and negotiate with the central government, establishing the Salaheddin Brigade to fight under the banner of Iraq Popular Mobilization forces (PMF) to liberate al-Shirqat from Daesh (Dury-Agri et al. 2017). His efforts met with success and in June 2015, he announced the establishment of Salaheddin Brigade in Samarra and started recruiting from displaced members of the al-Houri lineage who flocked to Samarra to join the brigade (Salahedin TV 2019). In May 2016, the Iraqi government issued a formal list of the tribal mobilization units that were recognized by the state. Among them was Salaheddin Brigade, which was given the official designation Brigade 51. This gave it legal status.

Studies of civil wars often depict the state as the main force behind the creation of paramilitary groups, yet closer examination of these two case studies belies such simplification. In a detailed study of the Greek civil war, Stathis Kalyvas argues that micro-level conflicts of personal and family ambitions motivate belligerent actions more than abstract political ideology (Kalyvas 2003: 475–94). From a purely political perspective, the purpose behind these community-driven militias was an attempt by the al-Baggara and al-Houri to re-establish their ousted superordinate position in a volatile region. Both the Syrian and the Iraqi states seized this opportunity to enhance their counterinsurgency against rebels.

Logic for relying on tribal militias

The Syrian and Iraqi states found a rough and ready contingent for use in their wars against their opponents in the divergent tribal interests. This also allowed them to increase their numbers and enhance their firepower during the military operations in Aleppo and Salaheddin governorates. In the context of the conflict with Daesh, Salaheddin Brigade performed many tasks. Firstly, many active Daesh militants seem to be Iraqis and natives of their respective areas of operation (International Crisis Group 2019). Members of Salaheddin Brigade were intimately familiar with the physical terrain of al-Shirqat district and the social composition of the communities residing there – crucial knowledge of who is who and where to run.[7] Akins argues that states incorporate local tribes into their counterinsurgency strategy because they possess greater knowledge of the conflict environment, enabling them to be more effective at counterinsurgency (Akins 2020: 304–22). Many of my interviewees repeated an old Arabic proverb (*Ahl Makka adra bi-shi'abiha*) 'Mecca people know the trails', asserting that local tribes know their own area best and were consequently able to identify who was a Daesh fighter and who was a fugitive from Daesh for Iraqi security forces. Secondly, the al-Houri lineage presented a 'readily available and organic social structure ideal for mobilization', to use the words of the Iraqi sociologist Dr Alwan (2020: 1–16). The role of Salaheddin Brigade was consequently that of an important resource for mobilization, used by the Iraqi state to carry forward local efforts against Daesh in al-Shirqat. Thirdly, the present research shows that the Iraqi state relies on tribes, not only out of practical necessity due to limited state capacity, but also strategically, in order to build state legitimacy among a target population where the state is perceived as being ruled by a sectarian group that wants to oppress local communities. Alongside the Iraqi army, the state also relied on PMF, an umbrella term for a group of pro-Iran Shi'ite militias, in its war against Daesh. By supporting Sunni tribal militias in its war against Daesh, including the Salaheddin Brigade, the Iraqi government might dilute sectarian tension and help legitimize the PMF in its military efforts in a Sunni-dominated region. The Iraqi government refused to arm many Sunni tribes and was selective in accepting requests to form tribal militias (El-Hamed 2015). Many of my interviewees suggested that the main reasons for the Iraqi government's reliance on tribal militias composed of members of al-Jabour tribe is due to it being a 'trans-sectarian tribe', with members who are Sunnis and others who are Shi'ites. Even at the height of sectarian tension in 2006, when Sunnis feared going to Shi'ite-dominated districts of Baghdad, members of al-Jabour tribe would travel all the way from Mosul to visit their Shi'ite relatives in Al-A'dhamiya district in Baghdad. 'As soon as they knew that I was Jabouri, they would protect me because I am their cousin,'[8] said one.

The main justification for the Syrian state's reliance on the al-Baqer Brigade expressed by members of al-Baggara tribe is that, because of war and economic crisis, the state has been debilitated and unable to preserve peace and security in the marginal areas. Defections, desertions, battle losses, the challenges of urban warfare and the war of attrition waged by the opposition in eastern Aleppo significantly depleted the number of men available to fight (The Carter Center 2013). Raised on an ad hoc basis, the al-Baqer Brigade and other tribal militias proved to be cheaper to deploy than a standing army in low-intensity warfare. Quickly becoming a template for pro-regime mobilization, the al-Baqer Brigade, like other popular committees that supported the Syrian regime across the country, spread throughout the country, manned checkpoints, searched houses for activists and opposition figures and provided local information to the security apparatus in the initial stages of the Brigade's activity (Leenders and Giustozzi 2017: 157–80).

As the conflict in Aleppo intensified and government forces came within firing range of most of the opposition in March 2014, al-Baqer Brigade, in full battle gear, was organized into an ostensibly unified entity under the command of the Syrian military, to fight against the opposition in eastern Aleppo (The Carter

Center 2013). Governments rely on pro-government militias when the local balance of power between the government and rebel groups is in the rebels' favour, or roughly equal, and the non-state groups' interests are served by an alliance with the government (Biberman 2019: 16). Between March 2014 and March 2016, the al-Baqer Brigade claimed 246 'martyrs' (Al-Tamimi 2018). This claim to many 'martyrs', which was announced by the display of posters of these 'martyrs' on Facebook pages, is significantly larger than those announced by other pro-regime militias which indicates the large size of its military participation in the battles to drive the rebels out of eastern Aleppo.

It is important to note that the purpose of cultivating support from the tribes for the Syrian state extends beyond the objective of securing local support. Since the beginning of the Syrian uprising, the Syrian opposition have used tribal ties to mobilize and direct the peaceful and armed activities of tribesmen to further their interests in their battle with the regime. Thomson argues that insurgents often use identity-based cleavages or politicize ethnicity for recruitment and tactical and political purposes (Thomson 2013: 560–73). Therefore, tribes are also instrumentalized as a means of undermining political foes and countering similar initiatives from other actors (Center for Operational Analysis and Research 2019). For example, al-Baqer Brigade called upon fellow tribesmen who joined the armed opposition to lay down their arms, surrender and join the regime's side. Thus, state outreach to tribes should not necessarily be viewed only in military terms; it should also be viewed as a form of community outreach, used to weaken the opposition, morally speaking. In a sense, this contributed to the state's policies of eliminating local support for the rebels through a combination of coercion and co-optation. Asking loyal tribal militias to penetrate the opposition host communities offered a way for the state to recruit defected local fighters from the opposition side.

Reconfiguration of tribalism

The formation of tribal militias led to the reconfigured rise of tribal sentiments, practises and values through which one can clearly see the emergence of new groupings that retain certain tribal characteristics but that are also heavily conditioned and shaped by other factors such as economy, geography and alliances with internal and external forces. Tribalism has been reconfigured along new political and military lines rather than resurfacing in its ancient traditional form.

Both al-Baqer Brigade and Salaheddin Brigade have found tribal values and practises to be a possible mode for recruitment, morale raising and method of achieving their military and security purposes. During the liberation of Tikrit, members of Salaheddin Brigade were accused of extensive looting, destruction and violence against members of Al Bu Nasir's tribe (Gaston and Derzsi-Horvath 2018). These acts were publicly blamed on southern Shi'a PMF; however, locals said Salaheddin Brigade, which originates from al-Shirqat district, was primarily responsible for these acts, using the cover of their Shi'a PMF allies to settle their own scores (ibid.). These acts were actually motivated by the desire to take revenge against members of Al Bu Nasir's tribe, not only because they contributed to the empowerment of Daesh, but because they are the tribe of Saddam Hussein, who persecuted the members of al-Jabour tribe for a long time and executed many of their relatives in the 1990s.[9]

In the same vein, one might address the issue of how the formation of tribal militias brought forward explicit claims for tribal territorial rights. Traditionally, tribes had acquired and held their territories by physical force (Al-Faour 1968: 42). Their territories had been inhabited by the same tribe for generations and had been used for animal grazing and then turned into agricultural territories at the beginning of the twentieth century. The communal land of the tribes was appropriated either by the state (in terms of farmland and waterpower resources) or by individuals (Dawood 2015). Many leaders of the al-Baqer Brigade speak of a territory marked by the seal of al-Baggara tribe called Khatt al-Baggara (The al-Baggara's domain) as expressed in the following words of Fadi al-Afees (فادي العفيس), one of the leaders of al-Baqer in Deir Ezzor: 'We will not let the Kurds occupy Khatt al-Baggara and we will fight them and take it back from the Kurds who are killing our men and raping our women' (*Euphrates Post*, 2019). Fadi Al-Afees said these words while he was addressing people from al-Baqer Brigade to mobilize them against Syrian Democratic Forces (SDF) that were occupying al-Baggara tribe territory.

Another reconfigured tribal custom associated with the rise of tribal militias is the practise of *Jalwa*. After capturing al-Shirqat from Daesh, leaders of the Salaheddin Brigade decided to deport families of Daesh fighters from the al-Shirqat district, and to approach authorities in place urging them to establish a camp for these families under the supervision of the security and intelligence services (Kittleson 2018). One of the residents of al-Shirqat told me, 'Daesh families are considered a source of threat to the security of al-Shirqat. Daesh could exploit the families to conduct future attacks against security forces which could destabilize the region again. Moreover, the families of those who lost their children at the hands of ISIS will attempt to conduct revenge against the families of ISIS fighters.' Leaders of Salaheddin Brigade told Human Rights Watch that deporting the families of Daesh fighters is in accordance with the tribal custom of *jalwa* which means banishment of a killer from the area in which the homicide took place, usually for a period of seven years following the event (HRW 2017).

Cohesion and fragmentation among tribal militias

In the formation of these militias, one observes the rise of sub-tribal solidarities where one lineage, in the case of al-Jabour, or two lineages, in the case of al-Baggara, forms the core of these military militias. Broader tribal affiliations were used only in transactional, often ephemeral, ways to appeal to other lineages in the same tribe (Mazur 2020: 151–95). In the case of al-Baqer Brigade, Khaled al-Hussein, who is the leader of this militia, recruited members heavily from his lineage al-Bu Rhama (البورحمة), which came to be known as the military wing of al-Baggara tribe.¹⁰ Prior to the civil war in Syria, the most influential lineage of al-Baggara tribe in Aleppo was Al Bu Fadel (البو فاضل), based in the village of Turkan.¹¹ The rise of the al-Bu Rhama via al-Baqer Brigade jeopardized their position close to the Syrian state. In order to hold that position, they used their maternal connections with Khaled al-Hussein to become active members of al-Baqer Brigade, making this militia highly reliant on members of al-Bu Rhama and al Bu Fadel (Mazur 2020: 151–95). For the al-Baqer Brigade, al-Baggara tribe is a source of identity and emotional attachment that is symbolically important. In many of the videos produced by the media section of al-Baqer Brigade, called Sheila (tribal songs), the performers chant a verse which glorifies the military abilities of the al-Baggara tribe and calls upon their members to defend the tribe's territory from what they describe as the 'aggressors'. The tribe here is a collective that could be activated for a specific task (Khoury and Kostiner 1991: 1–23). In the past, this was initiated by the paramount sheikh of the tribe; however, the 'traditional' system of tribal leadership broke down, giving prominence to the role of militiamen within the system during the war. The extent to which these militiamen can activate this collective depends on how much cash they can distribute to tribesmen outside their lineage as a reward for their loyalty and military support. It also depends on the personal characteristics of these men such as bravery, generosity and charisma, which can enable these men to appeal to the traditional values which bind them with the tribe in relation to external groups.

However, there is a great deal of evidence to suggest that fragmentation cuts across lineages too. Lacher argues that in civil wars, strategic conditions change constantly forcing actors to reposition themselves and enter into new alliances and enmities leaving lasting traces in the form of rifts within the social fabric (Lacher 2020). Following the victory over Daesh in al-Shirqat and the opposition in Aleppo, both solidary groups started to fragment. The most pronounced case of such fragmentation was in 2019 when Sheikh Qaddour al-Hussein of al-Bu Rhama lineage and Khaled al-Hussein, the leader of Liwa al-Baqer, clashed with each other, during which they aligned themselves with members of al-Bu Rhama lineage. According to my informants, during this period, Sheikh Qaddour al-Hussein restored the security intelligence apparatus and obtained their sponsorship to establish 'the Shield of Tribes Brigade' (لواء درع العشائر).¹² Mechanisms that promote differentiation within groups include competition among leaders to represent that group externally, and their competition in building up clienteles within the group (Lacher 2020). In 2020, a disagreement arose between Asham Sabhan al-Jabouri and one of his assistants, Sabar al-Houri (صبار الحوري), which ended with Sabar defecting and establishing his own small militia. On the surface, this was a disagreement between two individuals, but beneath the surface lie social grudges and competition for power between the families of Sabhan and al-Qarni to whom Asham and Sabar belong, respectively.¹³ Antoun argues that economic interests and social grudges lead men to line up against the majority of their patrilineal kinsmen on specific issues (1979: 162).

Despite these defections, both Khaled and Asham remain powerful within their lineages in terms of total numbers of fighters, wealth enhanced by controlling economic concessions from the state and the regular salaries their fighters receive from the state, and external actors such as Iran. Given these resources, the dominance of these leaders would be safeguarded, allowing them to practise clan paternalism by distributing resources and extending their generosity in their surroundings. The patrimonial values of tribalism play an important role in distributing the salaries among the tribesmen and in harnessing support behind the leaders. Further internal dissent is, however, inevitable as a result of continuous interlineage disputes and events.

The impact of military tribalism on intra-tribal politics

Alliances with al-Houri in Iraq and al-Baggara in Syria may have brought advantages to the state, but the relationship between tribes in both regions became fraught with tensions. The establishment of tribal militias led to sharp increases in social distance, cleavage, competition and conflict between the tribes and the clans of the region. Leaders of both the al-Baqer Brigade and Salaheddin Brigade used their militias as instruments of control and as a way to assert their authority over other tribes in their locality and even further afield. The al-Baqer Brigade attempted to hold sway over the tribes of Aleppo and other segments of society that do not belong to tribes, even in the city and its countryside (Hassan 2020). In 2018, al-Baqer Brigade organized a conference in the eastern part of Aleppo to which it invited representatives of other tribes such as al Berri, al-Hadidiyn (الحديديين) and al-Assaseneh(العساسنة) (Al-Khatib 2019). The conference represented a recognition of the hegemony of the al-Baggara tribe over other tribes in the region. This hegemony did not last long because other tribes such al Berri sought support from external patrons, in this case the Russians, to compete with the al-Baggara tribe (Ayyam Syria 2020). Therefore, the desire of tribal groups to seek out privileges for their militias to settle private scores leads to a situation in which rival clans jostle to establish their own militias and legalize them through the state in order to level the playing field (Peic 2019: 1022–49). Not only did al-Baqer Brigade try to impose its hegemony over the tribes in Aleppo, but it also attempted to rekindle kinship ties with members of al-Baggara tribe to establish itself a base there too. Dawood argues that the viability of tribes involved in the political game grows tangibly with the enlargement of their activity outside the initial sphere of their principal living (2003: 110–35). One of the leaders of al-Baqer Brigade told me, 'Upon our victory in Aleppo and the return of Sheikh Nawwaf al-Basheer to Syria in 2017, we went to visit our cousins there and we agreed to set up a branch for al-Baqer Brigade in Deir Ezzor. Things went well to start with but at a later stage, tension started to escalate as Sheikh Nawwaf al-Basheer did not want to receive orders from Hajj Khaled.[14] Sheikh Nawwaf and his followers said they are the stem of the tree, and we are just the branch and that we should follow his orders.'[15] As a result, there was political polarization involving the whole of al-Baggara tribe, which was then mirrored in the spatial location of the two main blocks in Syria. The term 'al-Sharqiyyin', or 'Easterners', came to refer to Nawwaf al-Basheer and the segment of the al-Baggara tribe located in Deir Ezzor. They arose as an opposing faction against the Gharbiyyin, or the Westerners of al-Baggara tribe, headed by Khaled al-Hussein, residing in the western part of Syria, specifically Aleppo. There are clearly two factions of al-Baqer Brigade, each resting on a different power base, each having its own separate agenda and supporting symbols. The group in Deir Ezzor was strongly associated with Nawwaf al-Basheer, and its main focus was on counterbalancing SDF supported by the United States on the eastern side while the group in Aleppo was mainly tasked with confronting the opposition forces in Aleppo.

As soon as the Iraqi army, supported by the Salaheddin Brigade, managed to drive Daesh out of al-Shirqat, tribal gatherings were organized regularly to encourage harmony, rapport and trust among the social components of the district. They often had mottos such as 'al-Jabour is one hand against terrorism' or 'al-Jabour, gathering to achieve social cohesion(التوافق) in the governorate', yet beneath the facade of intertribal co-existence and cooperation, tension and incipient conflict existed between the lineages of al-Jabour in al-Shirqat. The relationship between al-Houri and other lineages on the eastern side of the Tigris River was that of the victorious and the defeated, where al-Houri used the power of the military to impose its will on the subjugated and exact more economic concessions from the state such as a greater share of electricity, water and other services.[16] By sponsoring Salaheddin Brigade, the Iraqi state generated intra-Jabour tribal tension (Dury-Agri et al. 2017). This tension reached its peak when the al-Uqli lineage, headed by Sheikh Mohammad al-Saleh, gained approval from the Iraqi government to set up the Suqur Dijla (Falcons of Tigris) militia in their locality on the eastern side of the Tigris River.[17] The excuse was that Salaheddin Brigade did not have enough manpower to help the Iraqi government preserve peace and security across the al-Shirqat district, yet the real reason behind setting up Suqur Dijla seems to have been to break up al-Houri's monopolization of the legal, militarized tribal structure in al-Shirqat.

The banishment of the families of Daesh fighters from al-Shirqat was led by Salaheddin Brigade as previously mentioned. Locals say that the way the evacuation was conducted included significant misconduct by Salaheddin Brigade, including looting, robbery, torture and revenge killings. These acts played into existing tensions and upset local political and tribal balances, exacerbating political instability in the governorate (Gaston and Derzsi-Horvath 2018). Salaheddin Brigade has been able to operate with some degree of autonomy, both in terms of conducting evacuation operations and having little accountability. One member of al-Bougzat (البوغزات) lineage expressed his concern that Salaheddin Brigade would always use the accusation of belonging to Daesh or sympathizing with Daesh to assert its dominance over al-Shirqat residents and to silence any voices of opposition from other lineages of al-Jabour tribe.[18] As well as creating tribal tension, Salaheddin's *Jalwa* raised sectarian tension as locals accused Salaheddin Brigade of acting as a proxy for the Shiite Popular Mobilization units, who were using them to undertake the distasteful tasks that the units did not want to do themselves.

In general, creating tribal militias not only reshuffled local dynamics but also created a new state of affairs whereby these militias would attempt to impose a new order with rules intended to subjugate other social groups and enable one group to control the emerging order. Other actors would respond in different ways, resulting in successive waves of tension and instability in their local setting.

Retribalization and the curtailment of state institutions

The policies of the Syrian and Iraqi governments show that they are not only dependent on tribalism for their support but that they have actually strengthened tribal power. Mazrui defines retribalization as a process arising from the decline of nationalism which, he argues, produces a revival of tribal bonds and sentiments (Mazuri 1969: 89–105). In the face of a weak state clinging to survival rather than being concerned with development, the members of tribes begin to isolate themselves from national politics and to look to local events (Salih 1989: 168–74). The result is the absence of concepts such as nation and state at the local level.

After defeating the opposition in eastern Aleppo, al-Baqer Brigade treated the houses of the opposition fighters as war booty by occupying many of them and using them either as residences for their fighters or by stealing their furniture and selling it on the black market (Al-Nahar Al-Arabi 2021). Extortions and robbery became income-generating activities for the al-Baqer Brigade, particularly in western Aleppo. There have also been many reports of the children of wealthy merchants in Aleppo being kidnapped at military checkpoints for ransom. Many merchants were forced to pay monthly protection money to al-Baqer Brigade to continue their mercantile activities in Aleppo. One resident of al-Akramiah district in Aleppo said, 'Security forces must stop these thugs who belong to different tribes who came from the villages to the city. Their breaches of law are continuous. The state must be more serious in dealing with them and should force them to leave the city as soon as possible.'[19]

Military mobilization of the tribes became so entrenched that some government institutions began to legitimize these formations and introduce patterns of power-sharing into their workings, thus reverting to a legacy that had almost disappeared due to the transformations achieved by the modern state (Boutaleb 2012). Just as the Syrian Social Nationalist Party used its militia in Syria to push for political influence in the form of candidates for the recent Syrian parliamentary elections, so too did al-Baqer Brigade throw its weight behind an ostensibly independent candidate called Omar Hussein al-Hassan, Khaled al-Hussein's brother (Al-Tamimi 2016). Moreover, al-Baqer Brigade took control of the transportation sector in Aleppo city, where most of minibus drivers are descended from al-Bu Rhama (البورحمة) and AL Bu Fadel (البوفاضل)lineages who fought in the brigade (Ezzi 2017). The revenue from transportation services is shared between the al-Baqer militia in cooperation with the state Military Security Department (ibid.). Despite the Syrian government's knowledge of al-Baqer Brigade's leaders' criminal records, it decided to cooperate with them for the sake of short-term success in the fight against the opposition, disregarding the long-term destabilizing potential that such a strategy promised. It is obvious that Syrian state motivations were simply directed at defeating the opposition by any means necessary.

The state's attitude sent a clear message to the tribal militias implying that the government was weak and that there was no authority to check their plundering or criminal activity. Tribal gangsterism in al-Shirqat started to provoke concerns that it had become a source of embarrassment to law enforcement agencies. In 2017, members of Salaheddin Brigade assaulted an Iraqi journalist from the Iraqia TV station during his coverage of the military operations there (AlwatanVoice 2016). Apparently, the incident happened because, during his visit to al-Shirqat, the Iraqia TV journalist refused to interview Mashan al-Jabouri (مشعان الجبوري) who is of al-Houri lineage and is a friend of Asham Sabhan al-Jabouri (عشم سبهان الجبوري). The incident developed into a significant confrontation between members of Salaheddin Brigade and security forces which required the intervention of the ministry of defence.

Unclear boundaries between state institutions and tribal militias have led to direct clashes between the state agencies and tribal militias on many occasions. More than five years after the end of military operations by government forces in eastern Aleppo, supported by its loyal militias, the region is a hotbed of armed enclaves and seemingly intractable small conflicts between local tribes. The government's writ runs mainly in western Aleppo, and even there its control has been challenged by the militias recruited mostly from tribes who were armed as counterinsurgency proxies after 2013 (Orient TV 2019). The question remains whether the state can rein in the tribes, or whether they will continue to operate after combat has ceased. What must be stressed is that, in the short term at least, tribes will challenge the state's claim to central control and sovereignty, including decision-making and implementation.

Conclusion

State atrophy in Syria and Iraq has brought about the weakening of government institutions, including its security and military capabilities, which lack the efficiency to deal with opponents during civil wars. Both conflicts have witnessed a dramatic rise of non-state actors that attempted to challenge the state and overrun it, as exemplified by a wide array of armed groups such as Daesh and others. To support their counterinsurgency measures, the states in both countries have established and trained pro-government militias, such as the National Defence Forces in Syria and the PMF in Iraq. Tribal auxiliaries became a widespread phenomenon and were often treated by academics and analysts as groups formed using a calculated, top-down approach. This study contended that tribal militias represent an attempt by certain tribal groups to benefit from the weakness of the state to strengthen their position vis-à-vis other tribal groups in their surroundings. Akdedian and Hasan argue that in Syria and Iraq, newly emerged formal and informal networks have become integral to the structures enabling the state's exercise of power and control (2021: 323–31). Both al-Baqer Brigade and Salaheddin Brigade, presented in this research, helped the state regain its power in the marginal areas but in turn, both groups instrumentalized the state apparatus for their kin's interests, agenda and power.

This study challenges the organic model of tribes that defines them as coherent internally closed systems. The fluid realities of tribal belonging can hardly be represented in a fixed model. The tribes, as we have seen in this chapter, do not position themselves as a unified body, particularly in the military sphere (Digard 1991: 119). This does not mean that tribes have ceased to exist or that tribalism does not have the ability to mobilize fighters in the face of threats. Instead, it reasserts the tribe, as defined by Madawi Al-Rasheed, in that it does not denote a static socio-economic grouping, but one that changes over time (ibid.). Tribes can form and dissolve; they can grow, shrink in size or change in composition, and they can merge with other units of kin and lineage and lose their distinctive name with time (ibid.). As clearly illustrated in this study, small, localized, often primary, tribal segments were decisive units in the establishment of both military formations to an extent that they competed with other lineages as independent tribes.

Faleh Abdul Jabar warned that reliance on tribes for military purposes could become a 'Frankenstein-like' evolution in the future (Jabar 2003: 69–109). This is exactly what is happening in Syria and Iraq where discipline and order are replaced by fierce competition among tribes to gain more concessions from the state or capture state resources themselves. The shrinking of the national arena and the transfer of politics to tribal groups is a matter of major concern, not only to Syria and Iraq but to the entire region.

Notes

1. Tribal values and practices have been reconfigured along new political and military lines rather than resurfacing in their ancient traditional form.
2. Interview via WhatsApp with Abdol Mohsen Ali: one of the members of the al-Baggara tribe in Aleppo on 22 May 2020.
3. This story was narrated by many members of the al-Baggara tribe whom I interviewed for this research. Also mentioned in many Arabic news sources on the conflict in Aleppo. They are cited in this chapter.
4. Interview conducted via WhatsApp on 22 May 2021 with Abdulkarim Ali, a member of the al-Jabour tribe who lives in al-Shirqat.
5. This mapping was produced after conducting multiple interviews with members of the al-Jabour tribe in al-Shirqat.
6. An interview conducted via WhatsApp on 29 May 2021 with Ali al-Houri, a member of the al-Jabour tribe who lives in al-Shirqat.
7. An interview conducted via WhatsApp on 17 May 2021 with Abdallah Omairi, a member of the al-Jabour tribe who lives in al-Shirqat.
8. An interview conducted via WhatsApp on 14 May 2021 with Zayd Abd Rabah, a member of the al-Jabour tribe who lives in al-Shirqat.

9   An interview conducted via WhatsApp on 29 May 2021 with Ali al-Houri, a member of the al-Jabour tribe who lives in al-Shirqat.
10 Interview via WhatsApp with Sheikh Zakkour Salman, one of the members of the al-Baggara tribe who resides in Turkey on 13 May 2020.
11 Interview via WhatsApp with Ramadan Habbash, one of the members of the al-Baggara tribe who resides in the countryside of Aleppo on 2 May 2020.
12 Shield of Tribes (dir'a alqabayil). Page representing the Militia of Shield of Tribes set up by Sheikh Qaddour, *Facebook*, 2015. https://www.facebook.com/%D8%AF%D8%B1%D8%B9-%D8%A7%D9%84%D8%B9%D8%B4%D8%A7%7%D8%A6%D8%B1-530934240387528/.
13 An interview conducted via WhatsApp on 29 May 2021 with Ali al-Houri, a member of the al-Jabour tribe who lives in al-Shirqat.
14 Hajj Khaled is the name used to refer to Khaled al-Hussein, the leader of al-Baqer Brigade.
15 An interview via WhatsApp with Ali Hamadeen, one of the leaders of al-Bqer Brigade in May 2021.
16 An interview conducted via WhatsApp on 29 May 2021 with Ali al-Houri, a member of the al-Jabour tribe who lives in al-Shirqat.
17 An interview conducted via WhatsApp on 12 May 2021 with Hamid al-Jabouri, a member of the al-Jabour tribe who lives in al-Shirqat.
18 An interview conducted via WhatsApp on 8 May 2021 with Abdulrahman Tamer, a member of the al-Jabour tribe who lives in al-Shirqat.
19 An interview via WhatsApp with Mohammad Sha'ar, a resident of western Aleppo.

Bibliography

al-Abbadi, A. A. (1984). *Introduction to Study of Jordanian Tribes: Class and Analytical Studies 1921-1984. (Muqadimat li Dirasat Al-Ashair al'urduniyati: Dirasa ltahlilia wa tabaqia 1921-1984)*. Amman: Ministry of Culture and Antiquities in Jordan.

Ahram, Ariel (2011). *Proxy Warriors: The Rise and Fall of State-Sponsored Militias*. Stanford, CA: Stanford University Press.

Akdedian, Harout, and Hasan, Harith (2021). 'Conclusion'. In Aziz Al-Azmeh, Nadia Al-Bagdadi, Harith Hasan, and Harout Akdedian (eds), *Striking from the Margins: State, Religion and Devolution of Authority in the Middle East* (323–31). London: Saqi Books.

Akins, Harrison(2020). 'Tribal Militias and Political Legitimacy in British India and Pakistan'. *Asian Security* 16(3): 304–22.

Ali, Abdol Mohsen (2020). One of the members of the al-Baggara tribe in Aleppo. Interview conducted via WhatsApp, 22 May.

Ali, Abdulkarim (2021). A member of the al-Jabour tribe who lives in al-Shirqat. Interview conducted via WhatsApp, 22 May.

Allinson, Jamie (2015). *The Struggle for the State in Jordan: The Social Origins of Alliances in the Middle East*. London: I.B. Tauris.

Alwan, Fajir J. (2020). 'The Tribal Power in Contemporary Iraq: A Sociological Analysis'. *Journal of College of Education for Women* 31(2): 1–16.

AlwatanVoice (2016). 'Shocking video shows member of the Parliament Mashan al-Jabouri assault the correspondent of Iraqia TV station in al-Shirqat' (*fidyu sadim yuzhir alnaayib albarlamaniu mashan aljaburi wahu yaetadi ealaa murasil qanaat aleiraqiat fi alsharqati*). 25 September. https://www.alwatanvoice.com/arabic/news/2016/09/25/972653.html (accessed 11 October 2021).

Antoun, Richard T. (1979). *Low-Key Politics: Local-Level Leadership and Change in the Middle East*. New York: State University of New York Press.

Al-Arabi, Al-Nahar (2021). 'Disagreements Hit al-Baqer Brigade: Would It Collapse?' (*alkhilafat tudrib liwa' albaqir: hal yanhar?*). *An Naharar*. 5 January. https://www.annaharar.com/arabic/news/arab-world/syria/27042021071254445 (accessed 15 September 2021).

Al-Azmeh, Aziz, and Al-Bagdadi, Nadia (2021). 'Introduction'. In Aziz Al-Azmeh and Nadia Al-Bagdadi (eds), *Striking from the Margins: State, Religion and Devolution of Authority in the Middle East*. (1–24). London: Saqi Books.

Baram, Amatzia (1997). 'Neo-Tribalism in Iraq: Saddam Hussein's Tribal Policies 1991-96'. *International Journal of Middle East Studies* 29(1): 1–31.

Barout, Mohammed J. (2013). The Last Decade in the History of Syria: The Theory of Deadlock and Reform. (*Aleaqd al'akhir fi tarikh Suriatin: Jadaliat Aljumud wal'iislah*). *Arab Centre for Research and Policy Studies*, 357.

Biberman, Yelena (2019). *Gambling with Violence: State Outsourcing of War in Pakistan and India*. Oxford: Oxford University Press.

Blocq, Daniel S. (2014). 'The Grassroots Nature of Counterinsurgent Tribal Militia Formation: The Case of the Fertit in Southern Sudan, 1985–1989'. *Journal of Eastern African Studies* 8(4): 710–24.

Bolte, Brandon (2016). 'Pro-Government Militias and the Institutionalized Enemy'. Paper presented at the 25th annual Midwest Political Science Undergraduate Research Conference at Wartburg College in Waverly, Iowa, 11–12 March. http://public.wartburg.edu/mpsurc/images/bolte.pdf (accessed 22 August 2021).

Boutaleb, Mohammad N. (2012). 'The Political Aspects of the Tribal Phenomenon in Arab Societies: A Sociological Approach to the Tunisian and Libyan Revolutions'. *Arab Centre for Research and Policy Studies*, 8 February. http://english.dohainstitute.org/release/51b540e1-6563-46ec-9602-6aa9bd9597b8 (accessed 15 May 2021).

Brenner, Robert (1990). 'Agrarian Class Structure and Economic Development in Pre-Industrial Europe'. In Trevor Ashton and Charles Philpin (eds), *The Brenner Debate: Agrarian Class Structure and Economic Development in Pre-Industrial Europe*. (26–33). Cambridge: Cambridge University Press.

Van Bruinesses, Martin (2003). 'Kurds, States, and Tribes'. In Faleh A. Jabar and Hosham Dawood (eds), *Tribes and Power: Nationalism and Ethnicity in the Middle East*. (165–83). London: Saqi Books.

The Carter Center (2013). 'Syria Pro-Government Paramilitary Forces'. 5 November. https://www.cartercenter.org/resources/pdfs/peace/conflict_resolution/syria-conflict/pro-governmentparamilitaryforces.pdf (accessed on 23 July 2021).

Center for Operational Analysis and Research (2019). 'Tribal Tribulations Tribal Mapping and State Actor Influence in Northeastern Syria'. *COAR Global*. 6 May. https://coar-global.org/2019/05/06/tribal-tribulations-tribal-mapping-and-state-actor-influence-in-northeastern-syria/ (accessed 23 May 2021).

Chatty, Dawn (2010). 'The Bedouin in Contemporary Syria: The Persistence of Tribal Authority and Control'. *Middle East Journal* 1(64): 29–49.

Clayton, Govinda, and Thomson, Andrew (2016). 'Civilianizing Civil Conflict: Civilian Defense Militias and the Logic of Violence in Intra-State Conflict'. *International Studies*

Quarterly 3(60). https://pureadmin.qub.ac.uk/ws/portalfiles/portal/17738212/Civilianizing_Civil_Conflict.pdf (accessed 17 May 2021).

Cordesman, Anthony (2005). *Iran's Developing Military Capabilities*. Washington, DC: CSIS Press.

Dawood, Hosham (2003). 'The "State-ization" of the Tribe and the Tribalization of the State: the Case of Iraq'. In Faleh A. Jabar and Hosham Dawood (eds), *Tribes and Power: Nationalism and Ethnicity in the Middle East* (110–35). London: Saqi Books.

Dawood, Hosham (2015). 'The Sunni Tribes in Iraq: Between Local Power, the International Coalition and the Islamic State'. *Norwegian Peacebuilding Resource Centre*, September. https://reliefweb.int/sites/reliefweb.int/files/resources/Sunni%20tribes%20in%20Iraq.pdf (accessed 14 May 2021).

Digard, Jean-Pierre (2003). 'Tribus, maisons, Etats: modernité de la parenté arabe'. L'HommeNo. 166 (avril/juin): 185–92.

Drysdale, Alasdair (1982). 'The Asad Regime and Its Troubles'. *MERIP Reports* 110 (November and December): 3–11.

Dukhan, Haian (2019). *The State and the Tribes in Syria: Informal Alliances and Conflict Patterns*.London: Routledge.

Dukhan, Haian (2014). 'Tribes and Tribalism in the Syrian Uprising'. *Syria Studies Journal* 6(2): 1–28.

Dury-Agri, Jessa R., Kassim, Omer, and Martin, Patrick (2017). 'Iraqi Security Forces and Popular Mobilization Forces: Orders of Battle'. *Institute for the Study of War*. December. http://www.understandingwar.org/sites/default/files/Iraq%20-%20ISF%20PMF%20Orders%20of%20Battle_0_0.pdf (accessed 18 June 2021).

Euphrates Post (2019). 'One of the Leaders of al-Baqqer Brigade, Fadi al-Afees, Threatens to Take Over SDF Controlled Areas in Deir Ezzor' (*ahad qadat liwa' albaqir fadi Al-Afees yuhadid bialsaytarat ealaa manatiq saytarat qasad fi Deir Ezzor*). *YouTube*. 12 September. https://www.youtube.com/watch?v=kjHAh75TZ3U (accessed 18 September 2021).

Ezzi, Mazen (2017). 'The Regime and Its Militias Will Face Difficulty Disentangling from Each Other'. *Chatham House*. July. https://syria.chathamhouse.org/ar/research/2017/the-regime-and-loyal-militias-will-struggle-to-disentangle-their-relationship (accessed 23 June 2021).

Al-Faour, Fadl (1968). 'Social Structure of a Bedouin Tribe in the Syria-Lebanon Region'. PhD diss., University of London, London.

Gaston, Erica, and Derzsi-Horvath, Andras (2018). 'Iraq after ISIL: Sub-State Actors, Local Forces, and the Micro-Politics of Control'. *GPPi*. March. https://reliefweb.int/sites/reliefweb.int/files/resources/Gaston_Derzsi-Horvath_2018_Iraq_After_ISIL.pdf (accessed 14 July 2021).

Habbash, Ramadan (2020). One of the members of the al-Baggara tribe who resides in the countryside of Aleppo. Interview conducted via WhatsApp, 2 May.

Haddad, Bassam (2004). 'The Formation and Development of Economic Networks in Syria: Implications for Economic and Fiscal Reforms, 1986–2000'. In Steven Heydemann (ed.), *Networks of Privilege in the Middle East: The Politics of Economic Reform Revisited* (37–76). New York: Springer.

Hamadeen, Ali (2021). One of the leaders of al-Baqer Brigade. Interview conducted via WhatsApp, May.

El-Hamed, Raed (2015). 'Ramadi and the Debate Over Shia Militias in Anbar', *Carnegie Endowment for International Peace*. 21 May. https://carnegieendowment.org/sada/60168 (accessed 15 October 2021).

Hassan, Mohammed (2020). 'Arab Tribes in al-Hasakah and Deir ez-Zor Choose Their Allies'. *Chatham House*. January. https://syria.chathamhouse.org/research/arab-tri bes-in-al-hasakah-and-deir-ez-zor-choose-their-allies (accessed 14 August 2021).

Holden, Robert H (2004). *Armies without Nations: Public Violence and State Formation in Central America, 1821-1960*. New York: Oxford University Press.

al-Houri, Mousa (2021). A member of the al-Jabour tribe who lives in al-Shirqat. Interview conducted via WhatsApp, 29 May.

Human Rights Watch (2017). 'Iraq: Displacement, Detention of Suspected "ISIS Families"'. *HRW*. 5 March. https://www.hrw.org/news/2017/03/05/iraq-displacement-detention-suspected-isis-families (accessed 10 October 2021).

Hussein, Mansour (2020). 'Tribes in Aleppo during the Revolution' (alqabayil fi halab khilal althawra), *Jesr Press*, 16 August. https://www.jesrpress.com/2019/07/13/%D 8%A7%D9%84%D8%B9%D8%B4%D8%A7%D8%A6%D8%B1-%D9%81%D9%8A-%D8%AD%D9%84%D8%A8-%D9%88%D8%A7%D9%84%D8%AB%D9%88%D8 %B1%D8%A9-%D9%A1-%D9%A2/ (accessed 22 October 2021).

International Crisis Group (2019). 'Averting an ISIS Resurgence in Iraq and Syria'. *Middle East Report N°207*. 11 October. https://d2071andvip0wj.cloudfront.net/207-avert ing-an-isis-resurgence.pdf (accessed 10 October 2021).

Jabar, Faleh A. (2000). 'Shaykhs and Ideologues: Detribalization and Retribalization in Iraq, 1968-1998'. *Middle East Report* 215: 28–31.

Jabar, Faleh A. (2003). 'The Iraqi Army and Anti-Army: Some Reflections on the Role of the Military'. *Adelphi Paper* 43(354): 115–30.

Jabar, Faleh A. (2003). 'Sheikhs and Ideologues: Deconstruction and Reconstruction of Tribes under Patrimonial Totalitarianism in Iraq, 1968-1998'. In Faleh A. Jabar and Hosham Dawood (eds), *Tribes and Power: Nationalism and Ethnicity in the Middle East* (69–109). London: Saqi Books.

al-Jabouri, Hamid (2021). A member of the al-Jabour tribe who lives in al-Shirqat. Interview conducted via WhatsApp, 12 May.

Jentzsch, Corinna (2014). 'Militias and the Dynamics of Civil Wars'. PhD diss., Yale University, New Haven, CT.

Kalyvas, Stathis N. (2003). 'The Ontology of "Political Violence": Action and Identity in Civil Wars'. *Perspectives on Politics* 1(3): 475–94.

Khalaf, Sulayman (1981). 'Family, Village and the Political Party: Articulation of Social Change in Contemporary Rural Syria'. PhD diss., University of California, Berkeley.

Al-Khatib, Khaled (2019). 'How Did al-Baqqer Brigade Become a Stumbling Block in the Face of the Russians?' (*kayf 'asbah liwa' albaqir hajar eathrat fi wajh alruws?*). *Almodon Online*. 21 April. https://www.almodon.com/arabworld/2019/4/21/%D8%AD%D9%84%D8%A8-%D9%83%D9%8A%D9%81-%D8%A3%D8%B5%D8%A8%D8%AD-%D9%84%D9%88%D8%A7%D8%A1-%D8%A7%D9%84%D8%A8%D8%A7%D9%8 2%D8%B1-%D8%AD%D8%AC%D8%B1-%D8%B9%D8%AB%D8%B1%D8%A9-%D8%A8%D9%88%D8%AC%D9%87-%D8%A7%D9%84%D8%B1%D9%88%D8%B3 (accessed 10 October 2021).

Kittleson, Shelly (2018). 'Iraqi Police Who Fought for Tribal PMUs Won't Return to Force'. *al-Monitor*. 11 April. https://www.al-monitor.com/originals/2018/04/shirqat-pol ice-pmu-iraq.html#ixzz72T7IJKLy (accessed 15 October 2021).

Khoury, Philip, and Kostiner, Joseph (1991). 'Introduction: Tribes and the Complexities of State Formation in the Middle East'. In Philip Khoury and Joseph Kostiner (eds), *Tribes and State Formation in the Middle East* (1–23). London: Tauris.

Lacher, Wolfram (2020). *Libya's Fragmentation: Structure and Process in Violent Conflict.* London: I.B. Tauris.

Leenders, Reinoud, and Giustozzi, Antonio (2017). 'Outsourcing State Violence: The National Defence Force, "Stateness" and Regime Resilience in the Syrian War'. *Mediterranean Politics* 24(2): 157–80.

Lowe, Robert (2006). *The Syrian Kurds: A People Discovered.* London: Chatham House. https://www.chathamhouse.org/sites/default/files/public/Research/Middle%20East/bpsyriankurds.pdf (accessed 20 November 2021).

Lund, Aron (2013). 'The Non-State Militant Landscape in Syria'. *Combatting Terrorism Center*, Special issue, 6(8): 6.

MacDowall, David (1996). *A Modern History of the Kurds.* New York: I.B. Tauris.

Al-Majedi, Abdul R. (2013). 'Releasing Mashan al-Jabouri: One Day after His Arrest'. (*al'iifraj ean mashan aljaburi: baed yawm min aetiqalih*). *Elaph.* 19 December. https://elaph.com/Web/news/2013/12/859102.html (accessed 13 October 2021).

Malmvig, Helle (2018). 'Mosaics of Power: Fragmentation of the Syrian State since 2011'. *DIIS Report* 4. https://www.econstor.eu/bitstream/10419/197622/1/1030030332.pdf.

Martin, Mike (2017). 'KTO Kovo? Tribes and Jihad in Pastun Lands'. In Virginie Collombier and Olivier Roy (eds), *Tribes and Global Jihadism* (33–57). London: C. Hurst.

Mazrui, Ali A. (1969). 'Violent Contiguity and the Politics of Retribalization in Africa'. *Journal of International Affairs (New York)* 23(1): 89–105.

Mazur, Kevin (2020). 'Dayr al-Zur from Revolution to ISIS: Local Networks, Hybrid Identities, and Outside'. In Matthieu Cimino (ed.), *Syria: Borders, Boundaries, and the State* (151–95). Basingstoke: Palgrave Macmillan.

Al-Mustafa, Turki (2015). 'What Made the Majority of the Tribal Leaders Stand with Assad's Regime?' (*ma aladhi jaela ghalibiat zueama' aleashayir yaqifun 'iilaa janib nizam al'asad?*). *Zaiton.* 19 April. http://www.zaitonmag.com/%D9%85%D8%A7-%D8%A7%D9%84%D8%B0%D9%8A-%D8%AC%D8%B9%D9%84-%D8%A3%D8%BA%D9%84%D8%A8%D9%8A%D8%A9-%D8%B4%D9%8A%D9%88%D8%AE-%D8%A7%D9%84%D8%B9%D8%B4%D8%A7%D8%A6%D8%B1-%D9%8A%D9%82%D9%81%D9%88%D9%86-%D8%A5/ (accessed 24 September 2021).

Olson, Mancur (1993). 'Dictatorship, Democracy, and Development'. *American Polit. Sci. Rev.* 87(3): 567–76.

Omairi, Abdallah (2021). A member of the al-Jabour tribe who lives in al-Shirqat. Interview conducted via WhatsApp, 17 May.

Orient TV (2019). 'Al Berri Controls the Districts of Eastern Aleppo' (*Al Berri t usaytir ealaa 'ahya' sharq halab*). *YouTube.* 1 December. https://www.youtube.com/watch?v=cEPx29JxPdw&t=252s (accessed 20 May 2021).

Our-Syria (2020). 'Iranian Militias in Syria: Their Numbers and Their Distribution' (*almilishiat al'iiraniat fi suria: 'aedaduha watawzieuha*). 22 January. https://our-syria.com/8487/ (accessed 17 June 2021).

Pagani, Giovanni (2016). 'Urban Conflicts and Multiple War Narratives: The Case of Aleppo'. *Jadaliyya.* 14 September. https://www.jadaliyya.com/Details/33546 (accessed 20 October 2021).

Peic, Goran (2019). 'Divide and Co-Opt: Private Agendas, Tribal Groups, and Militia Formation in Counterinsurgency Wars'. *Studies in Conflict and Terrorism* 22(12): 1022–49.

Rabah, Zayd Abd (2021). A member of the al-Jabour tribe who lives in al-Shirqat. Interview conducted via WhatsApp, 14 May.

Rae, Jonathan (1999). 'Tribe and Rangeland Management in Syria'. PhD diss., University of Oxford, Oxford.

Al Rasheed, Madawi (1991). *Politics in an Arabian Oasis: The Rashidi Tribal Dynasty*. London: I.B. Tauris.

Salahedin TV (2019). 'Special Meeting with Ashem Sabhan al-Jabouri' (*liqa' khasun mae eishm subhan aljaburi*). *Salah El Din Satellite Channel*. 29 April. https://www.youtube.com/watch?v=uUQHa9MhQMo (accessed 17 May 2021).

Saleh, Bahra (2017). 'Iraq after ISIL: Shirqat District'. *GPPi*. 22 September. https://www.gppi.net/2017/09/22/iraq-after-isil-shirqat (accessed 19 August 2021).

Salih, Mohamed A. M. (1989). '"New Wine in Old Bottles": Tribal Militias and the Sudanese State'. *Review of African Political Economy* 45(46): 168–74.

Salman, Sheikh Zakkour (2020). One of the members of the al-Baggara tribe who resides in Turkey. Interview conducted via WhatsApp, 13 May.

Savelsberg, Eva (2014). 'The Syrian-Kurdish Movements: Obstacles Rather Than Driving Forces for Democratization'. In David Romano and Mehmet Gurses (eds), *Conflict, Democratization, and the Kurds in the Middle East Turkey, Iran, Iraq and Syria* (85–107). Basingstoke: Palgrave Macmillan.

Schubiger, Livia I. (2017). 'Repression and Mobilization in Civil War: The Consequences of State Violence for Wartime Collective Action'. PhD diss., Universität Zürich, Zurich.

Sha'ar, Mohammad (2021). A resident of western Aleppo. Interview conducted via WhatsApp, 17 May.

Shield of Tribes (2015). (*dir'a alqabayil*) Page representing the Militia of Shield of Tribes set up by Sheikh Qaddour. *Facebook*. https://www.facebook.com/%D8%AF%D8%B1%D8%B9-%D8%A7%D9%84%D8%B9%D8%B4%D8%A7%D8%A6%D8%B1-530934240387528/ (accessed 17 August 2021).

Syria, Ayyam (2020). 'How Did Russia Establish Their Own Militias in Syria?' (*kayf 'ansha'at rusia milishiatiha alkhasat fi suria?*). *Al-Ayyam Syria*. 15 February. https://ayyamsyria.net/%D9%83%D9%8A%D9%81-%D8%A3%D8%B3%D8%B3%D8%AA-%D8%B1%D9%88%D8%B3%D9%8A%D8%A7-%D9%85%D9%8A%D9%84%D9%8A%D8%B4%D9%8A%D8%A7%D8%AA-%D9%85%D8%AD%D9%84%D9%8A%D8%A9-%D9%85%D9%88%D8%A7%D9%84%D9%8A%D8%A9-%D9%84/ (accessed 15 October 2021).

Tamer, Abdulrahman (2021). A member of the al-Jabour tribe who lives in al-Shirqat. Interview conducted via WhatsApp, 8 May.

Al-Tamimi, Aymenn J. (2016) 'The Local Defence Forces: Regime Auxiliary Forces in Aleppo'. *Syria Comment*. 23 May. http://www.aymennjawad.org/18859/the-local-defence-forces-regime-auxiliary-forces (accessed 14 August 2021).

Al-Tamimi, Aymenn J. (2018). 'Who Are Liwa al-Baqir, the Pro-Regime Unit Seeking to Enter Afrin?' *Mid East Centre*. 21 May. https://www.mideastcenter.org/post/who-are-liwa-al-baqir-the-pro-regime-unit-seeking-to-enter-afrin (accessed 10 October 2021).

Thomson, Andrew (2013). 'Ethnic Conflict and Militias', In Steven Ratuva (ed.), *The Palgrave Handbook of Ethnicity* (560–73). London: Palgrave Macmillan. https://pure.qub.ac.uk/en/publications/ethnic-conflict-and-militias (accessed on 14 September 2021).

Tibi, Bassam (1991). 'The Simultaneity of the Unsimultaneous: Old Tribes and Imposed Nation-States in the Modern Middle East'. In Philip Khoury and Joseph Kostiner (eds), *Tribes and State Formation in the Middle East* (127–52). London: Tauris.

Toth, Anthony B. (2006). 'Last Battles of the Bedouin in Northern Arabia: 1850-1950'. In Dawn Chatty (ed.), *Nomads of the Middle East and North Africa: Entering the 21st Century, Handbook of Oriental Studies, Volume 81* (49–76). Leiden: Brill.

Zakariya, Ahmad W. (1945). *Tribes of the Levant (Ashair al-Sham)*. Damascus: Dar Al-Fikr.

Chapter 7

CONFLICTED COUNTERINSURGENCY: DAESH VERSUS IRAQ'S SECURITY ARENA

Jessica Watkins

Introduction

The Iraqi government's declaration of victory over Daesh in Mosul in July 2017 was a poignant moment in Iraq's post-Ba'athist history. It was the culmination of a nine-month battle for the city, during which the Iraqi army joined the federal police, counterterrorist forces, Kurdish Peshmerga, a host of Popular and Tribal mobilization forces (collectively known as the *Hashd*), and Iraq's international allies (primarily the United States and Iran) to defeat the group. By December of that year, the Iraqi government had declared victory over Daesh across the country. The group's activities were reduced to small pockets in largely rural areas. Yet, Iraqi prime minister Haidar al-Abadi's 'coalition of the willing'[1] was a motley assortment of forces with few common goals, which, in the aftermath of victory, mostly went their separate ways.

From its colonial days, Iraq has been no stranger to uprisings against the central authority, nor to sustained government-led campaigns (variously interpreted as stabilization operations, counterterrorism, counterinsurgency or outright repression) to quash them. In the years after the regime change, the US-led coalition's suppression of violence instigated by former regime loyalists, salafi-jihadist militants and overtly sectarian Shi'a militias spawned literally hundreds of English-language academic tracts, policy papers and technical manuals relating to conducting effective counterinsurgency.[2] Most were concerned with the coalition's tactical and/or cultural shortcomings, and suggested correctives along these lines, with the stated objective of asserting the coalition's authority and ultimately establishing sovereignty for the new Iraqi government. Notwithstanding the coalition's tolerance of select non-state armed groups, the ultimate goal of establishing a unitary state, in which a coherent security sector exercised a monopoly over the legitimate use of force (i.e. Max Weber's 'ideal' modern institutionalized state[3]) was frequently asserted. During those same years, however, the coalition presided over the subsidence of the Iraqi state's institutional memory and the replacement of the Ba'ath regime with a qualitatively different kind of state. Iraq today is far from the Weberian modern state. It is neither an authoritarian regime in the mould of its predecessor, nor (despite regular elections) an institutionalized competitive democracy like its former Western occupiers. Instead, the state is a network of power hubs,[4] dominated by elites defined largely along ethno-sectarian lines, whose alliances with external actors and control over armed groups are integral to their political survival.

The ease with which Daesh seized Mosul and thereafter close to 40 per cent of Iraqi territory in 2014 was particularly stunning to the outside world, given the highly publicized scale of international investment into Iraq's security sector post-2003. But Iraq's security sector only occupies part of a broader 'security arena' in which a variety of armed groups compete (Hills 2014).[5] Within this arena, the boundaries between 'state' and 'non-state' actors are amorphous, both in terms of civil law and popular legitimacy. Indeed, the popularity of certain paramilitary groups rivals that of the elected government and its coercive apparatus. The Daesh episode of Iraq's history was both a consequence of the fractured security arena, and a cause of its further entrenchment. The counter-Daesh campaign revealed the extent of the security forces' incoherence and the prevalence of ethno-sectarian and foreign agendas within them; but the roots of these trends lie in policies pursued by the US-led coalition and the al-Maliki government in the decade prior to ISIL's emergence.

This chapter offers a backstory to the conflict between Daesh and Iraq's security arena, culminating in the battle of Mosul in 2017. Iraq's chronic insecurity over the past two decades is often explained as a consequence of the consociational political settlement established by the Coalition Provisional Authority (CPA) in 2003 and 2004 and its provocation of ethno-sectarian violence, which in turn was exploited by both internal and external actors. Through an exploration of the shifting relations between the Iraqi state, society and external intervening actors post-regime change, the analysis here reinforces the impact of these factors on the evolution of the officially designated state security apparatus alongside that of other armed actors post-2003. However, it also draws attention to the way in which the coalition's pursuit of counterinsurgency (COIN) in Iraq shaped the security arena's development from the outset.

Configuring counterinsurgency

If war is a continuation of politics by other means (von Clausewitz 1997: 357) then COIN is a particular kind of political project. Khalili argues that COIN (and counterterrorism) provide technical solutions to what are ultimately political problems, making governance the work of militaries (Khalili 2015: 8). Unlike traditional warfare, COIN operations commonly entail strategies for winning over, managing and/or 'educating' civilian populations. Following the coalition's invasion of Iraq, these components of the campaign were clearly discernible, even if they were only partially successful.

As a military doctrine, COIN has an unmistakeably colonial genealogy, which permeates how it has been conducted more recently, even while the underlying political logic for waging it has shifted. In the nineteenth and twentieth centuries, Britain and France had frequent recourse to asymmetric warfare against rebels in their imperial territories, and to the current day, works by British military general Charles Callwell (1859–1928) and French army captain David Galula (1919–1967) on the subject have been incorporated into British Army and US Marine Corps manuals on COIN (Callwell 1896; Galula 1964; Galula 1963). Yet, as Alex Marshall points out, the framing rationale of classical colonial COIN was rather different. While the British in particular built the myth of imperial rule as moderate, benign and egalitarian (the classic 'liberal lie'), COIN was 'a profoundly imperial, state-centric' approach to conflict settlement which utilized population control, coercion and state-controlled economic incentives, even if it 'only rarely faced the thorny issue of sovereignty and legitimacy which bedevils and may doom these same efforts today' (Marshall 2010: 233).

In the twenty-first century, Western counterinsurgency campaigns have been premised on the Liberal Peace Theory, designed to transform fragile states into sovereign, Western-style democracies with free market economies. Within the Liberal Peace framework, since institutionalization must precede liberalization, modernization may entail coercive COIN. Yet, in practice, while contemporary liberal interventions are conducted in the name of state-building, they typically engender a largely privatized reconstruction process: deregulation and economic shock therapy which bypass the state itself. Far from fostering an institutionalized sovereign democracy with a competitive market economy, this has, in the post-Ba'athist Iraqi case at least, produced rife corruption and factionalized violence. In this context, Marshall asks:

> Are intervention forces present to actually govern the country in a neo-imperial form, to provide cover for the development of permanently dependent economic satraps, or are they there to genuinely provide support to the sovereign local government from the sidelines, while developing an effective 'exit strategy'? Who constitutes 'the enemy' in such a scenario: the terrorist with a bomb, or the corrupt government minister covertly diverting massive reconstruction funds to his own clan or ethnic community? (Marshall 2010: 247)

In Iraq, the answers have not always been obvious. The coalition's pursuit of a political settlement that has inadvertently consolidated inter-confessional tensions, its reliance on private contractors to build the new security apparatus and its rolling campaigns of COIN, in which different armed groups and parts of the population are sometimes seen as insurgents and sometimes as allies, are all components of the ill-conceived Liberal Peace. Khalili argues that in the new colonial context, the technical solutions provided by counterterrorism and COIN make governance the work of militaries. 'Conquered or subjugated populations are transformed into adversaries who are kept in good order through the application of ever-increasingly refined lethal methods of control' (Khalili 2015: 8). Yet, in Iraq's case, the assumption that the coalition might have pursued COIN with systematic precision belies the fact that its policies produced an Iraqi government comprising multiple, violently competitive factions, whose ability to conduct a coherent COIN programme in its own right is limited by the fractured nature of its coercive forces.

The Coalition and the emergence of Iraq's security arena

The alignment of coercive forces in Iraq today is intimately connected to the political settlement and the coalition's approach to COIN post-occupation. The CPA built the infrastructure for a federal governing system based on regular competitive national elections during its tenure (May 2003–April 2004). From the outset, however, the political field was dominated by a number of political entities which had existed, mostly in exile, during the Ba'athist period. Amongst the most influential were several for whom politicized sect associations (Shi'ism or Sunnism), or Kurdish ethnic nationalism, were prominent identity markers: the Islamic Da'wa Party, the Supreme Council for Islamic Revolution in Iraq (SCIRI), the Iraqi Islamic Party (IIP), the Kurdistan Democratic Party (KDP) and the Patriotic Union of Kurdistan (PUK). The CPA accorded senior members of these parties (as well as the more secular-leaning Iraqi National Accord and Iraqi National Congress), leading roles in the interim Iraqi Governing Council. The same parties continued to prevail after the election of the transitional government in January 2005, and the election of the federal government in December 2005.

The CPA initiated a consociational division of power, consolidating patronage networks along sectarian lines and establishing the Shi'a (roughly 65 per cent of the population) as politically dominant. The de-Ba'athification Programme removed much of Iraq's Sunni political class, since Sunnis had dominated the upper echelons of the party, leaving Iraqi Sunnis politically marginalized. In 2005, the leading Sunni party, the IIP, withdrew from the Governing Council in protest against the US military campaign on Fallujah, and while the IIP did contest the December 2005 national elections as part of the Iraqi Accord Front, many Sunni voters boycotted. Shi'a Islamist and Kurdish nationalist parties won most seats in the new parliament and a system of sectarian apportionment (*muhasasa ta'ifiyya*) arose, whereby ministries, state-owned enterprises, political posts and public sector jobs were divided amongst the dominant parties and their followers.[6]

As a consequence, the political spectrum was shaped by several factions defined by sect and aligned with paramilitary wings. Some were incorporated into the institutionalized political mainstream; others remained outside it (as anti-coalition insurgents), or retained one foot in the political process with the other in the insurgent camp. CPA Order No. 91, passed in June 2004, permitted armed groups that were 'identified by the Administrator … as participating in the political process leading to a peaceful, prosperous, and progressive Iraq' to continue operating. Three of the core political actors already had well-established paramilitary forces which continued to operate after the establishment of the interim government: the KDP and PUK commanded separate components of the Kurdish armed forces known as Peshmerga, in the Kurdish Region of Iraq (KRI) where the Iraqi army is prohibited from operating; whilst SCIRI's paramilitary wing, the Badr Corps, established in Iran in 1982 and trained by the Quds Force component of the Iranian Revolutionary Guard Corps, rapidly infiltrated the new Iraqi security forces (ISF). In May 2005, Bayan Jabr, a senior SCIRI member, became minister of the interior in the Governing Council and thereafter oversaw the recruitment of thousands of Badr members into the Iraq police.

On the fringes of the political process were followers of Moqtada al-Sadr, a young Iraqi nationalist cleric whose relationship with Iran has waxed and waned since 2003. The Sadrists' paramilitary wing, *Jaysh al-Mahdi* (JAM), attracted tens of thousands of young Iraqis, predominantly in Baghdad, Najaf and the southern provinces, who conducted frequent attacks on coalition forces, but pro-Sadrists also competed and won seats in the 2005 elections. JAM was integrated less thoroughly into the ISF than Badr, and the two groups frequently clashed violently, but both emerged as core protagonists in the sectarian civil war that ensued between the Sunni and Shi'a from 2005 to 2007. Badr and JAM (including members within the ISF) as well as other so-called Special Groups (hardliner anti-coalition Shi'a militant groups sponsored by Iran), were the biggest perpetrators of targeted attacks, forced disappearances and evacuations of Sunnis during that period (Cordesman 2007: 2).

Ranged against these latter groups, who identified strongly with political Shi'ism and anti-coalition sentiment, were former regime loyalists or extremists (FREs) and several Sunni Islamist groups including al-Qaeda in Iraq (AQI), founded by Jordanian Abu Musab al-Zarqawi. These groups targeted coalition forces and the newly formed ISF, but increasingly also political groups (predominantly Shi'a) participating in the political process, and the Shi'a population more broadly. In 2005–6, AQI alone staged hundreds of bombings in Shi'a districts, where unarmed civilians were the primary targets and victims. But the group also targeted Sunnis who resisted it, particularly in Anbar where AQI had its largest following.

Iraq's political field and emerging security arena, 2005–6

The coalition forces sought to configure a form of COIN that could be sustained while they hastily established the new Iraqi security sector. Following the disbandment of the Iraqi Army pursuant to CPA Order No. 2, the coalition initiated a massive train-and-equip programme for the New Iraqi Army (NIA), which was intensified when a sectarian civil war began in 2005. By 2007, 14,000 men were being recruited into the army every five weeks, and by 2009, the army had nominally reached almost 200,000 active members, even though most recruits were trained for only three to five weeks (Gaub 2016). The police, meanwhile, were not dissolved, but around half of the estimated 58,000 serving policemen deserted or were dismissed following the de-Ba'athification law. The coalition spent the

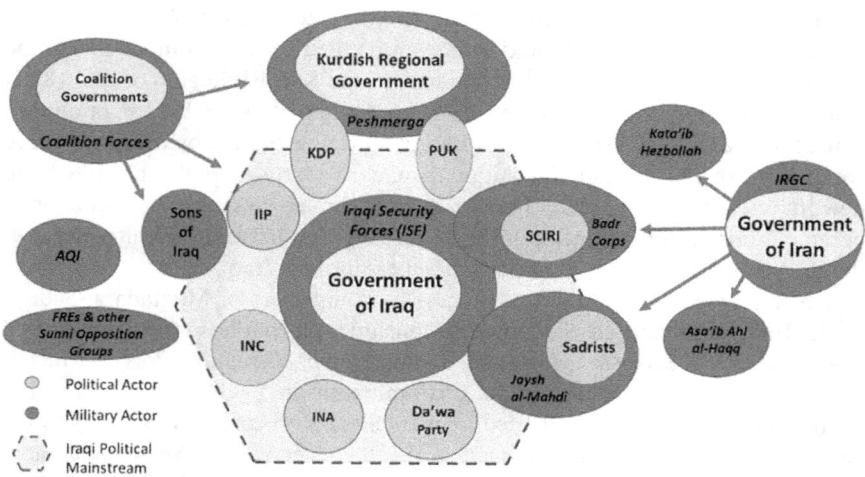

Figure 7.1 Iraq's political field and emerging security arena, 2005–6.

next eight years chasing the creation of an institutionalized, professionally trained security sector (albeit trained largely by private military companies[7]). But in the meantime, numerous former soldiers and police officers joined the growing, albeit disparate, insurgency against the coalition.

Eventually in 2007, General Petraeus implemented the US troop surge, deploying an additional 20,000 US troops to Baghdad and Anbar provinces for up to 18 months to contain insurgent activity. Petraeus's strategy was heavily influenced by his 2006 US Field Manual on Counterinsurgency, premised on protecting the population as opposed to killing insurgents. It was broadly hailed as successful in reducing the death of US troops in Iraq and improving domestic security overall; yet its success seems as much a product of the coalition's decision to work with (and renumerate) non-state armed Iraqi groups which it had previously fought against as it was to do with protecting the population. Key amongst these groups was the Anbar Awakening. From 2006, a collection of Sunni tribal chiefs across the province joined forces with the US-led coalition to combat al-Qaeda in what was known as the *Sahwat al-Anbar* (Anbar Awakening). The tribesmen recruited were known as the 'Sons of Iraq', and the initiative expanded to Diyala and Salah al-Din Provinces (McCallister 2008: 8). They are widely credited with suppressing AQI's activities in the province for several years, but to the new Iraqi government, they came to represent another problematic piece in the post-Saddam security jigsaw.

Even beyond the withdrawal of coalition combat forces in 2011, the United States promulgated COIN as a successful strategy for boosting the capacity of the Iraqi government and its security sector against Daesh. One prominent commentator on US COIN claimed, 'the anti-ISIS campaign offers a sustainable and replicative model for future US operations against terrorists and guerrillas: help allies conduct COIN with only small-scale deployments of US advisers and airpower' (Boot 2021). But while the United States commonly refers to the Iraqi government as an ally, several of its component parts are distinctly hostile towards the US agenda within Iraq and the broader region. A closer look at Nouri al-Maliki's premiership (2006–14), his inadvertent cultivation of the security arena and his approach to COIN allow us to see why.

The al-Maliki years: Suppressing the security arena

In May 2006, six months after Iraq's first post-Saddam legislative elections, Nouri al-Maliki of the Da'wa Party was appointed prime minister. Al-Maliki was a compromise candidate: acceptable precisely because he was not a big name within the predominantly Shi'a coalition (United Iraqi Alliance) that dominated the election, and because neither the United States nor Iran vetoed him. For the United States, the fact that the Da'wa Party did not have its own paramilitary force was a decisive factor. Yet al-Maliki was scarcely the malleable partner that the United States presumably hoped he would be in the institutional development of the ISF: he did all he could to foster a security apparatus that was loyal to him personally, as opposed to the Iraqi state.

Under Nouri al-Maliki's premiership, de facto, not merely de jure, control of the ISF passed from the coalition to the Iraqi government. The country also passed from what Dodge (2013: 245) referred to as 'imposed democracy to competitive authoritarianism', whereby the government sought to shape the electoral contest to its advantage and al-Maliki sought to impose himself as Iraq's new 'strongman'. The ISF was integral to this process. Al-Maliki assumed his post amidst the sectarian civil war, in which large swathes of the Ministry of Interior were implicated in targeting Sunnis. Al-Maliki took the opportunity to tighten his grip over the components of the security forces less closely associated with sectarian agendas: namely the New Iraqi Army, intelligence apparatus and counterterrorist service. He was thereby initially able to present a unitary, non-sectarian state-strengthening agenda, whilst ensuring that command positions went to individuals loyal to him (Dodge 2013: 245).

To demonstrate the efficacy of these new security services, while taking an apparent stand against militias implicated in sect-based targeting, in March to May 2008, al-Maliki authorized the 'Charge of the Knights Operation' in Basra Province to uproot JAM, which had taken control of strategic parts of the city including the port of Umm Qasr (Jabar 2012). The coalition optimistically viewed the operation as evidence of Maliki taking a stand against Iran, which had provided armaments and training to JAM.[8] The prime minister followed up the operation in Basra with similar campaigns to rout the Sadrists' paramilitary wing in other southern provinces as well as Sadr City, a slum district in Baghdad populated by an estimated two million Iraqis, many of whom are dedicated followers of Moqtada al-Sadr.

In the short term, these operations leant credibility to the narrative that al-Maliki was suppressing non-state militant activity, even if, in the long term, they earned Maliki the lasting enmity of the Sadrists and damaged his political career. Moqtada al-Sadr retreated to Iran, and in August 2008 announced that he was indefinitely suspending the activities of JAM to focus instead on developing the social and cultural aspects of the movement.

Maliki also sought to tighten the reins on the Sons of Iraq. The Iraqi government was always a sceptical partner in the US-led promotion of the Awakening, and was initially reluctant to take over responsibility (and payment) of these tribal forces from the United States. Still, Maliki backed the establishment of several parallel Tribal Support Councils in predominantly Shi'a provinces including Basra, Maysan and Najaf, which were again directly answerable to the prime minister's office, whilst making tailored agreements with armed tribal groups in Sunni provinces and suppressing others whose loyalty to him was uncertain (Parker 2009:18). In September 2008, the government did take over the administration of the Sons of Iraq Programme (which now numbered over 90,000 tribesmen) agreeing to integrate 20 per cent into the ISF, and the remainder into the staff of other government ministries. The agreement never fully materialized: by April 2010, only 9,000 had been absorbed by the ISF, and another 30,000 had been hired by non-security ministries (Wilbanks and Karsh 2010). The government reasoned that most of the tribesmen were insufficiently educated, trained or loyal to be incorporated into the security forces, particularly when the ISF was still vulnerable to insurgent attacks. After al-Maliki's State of Law Coalition prevailed in the 2010 parliamentary elections, the incentive to integrate the Sons of Iraq dwindled. According to Cordesman and Khazai (2014),

> by late 2013, many elements had aligned themselves with Al Qaeda, while others became Sunni militias with few ties or loyalty to the Shi'ite dominated central government. Iraqi Sunnis report that many have since been pushed out of their positions, marginalised or denied their wages.

Overall, the al-Maliki years were characterized by his efforts to create a security apparatus directly loyal to himself. Most outlying armed groups were suppressed, chose to lay low or made peace with the administration. This created an impression that in time, Iraq might move away from the security arena, and away from purely sectarian agendas, towards a more traditionally conceived security sector that was beholden to the state, even if it did not conform to the ideal of the liberal democratic state. In retrospect, it is apparent that this impression was largely a mirage. The prime minister's coup-proofing mechanisms produced a security apparatus which was internally at odds with itself: different units within the ISF competed for political favour rather than cooperating to achieve operational objectives, and professionalism was sacrificed in favour of cronyism and entrenched administrative corruption.

The misconduct of various components of the ISF undermined popular confidence in state institutions. Elements of the local and federal police, in particular, were found guilty of human rights abuses, torture and neglect of duty as well as corruption. This misconduct and corruption extended to the Iraqi army, which, although it retained a significant number of Sunnis at the senior level, had a predominantly Shi'a rank and file. Moreover, reflecting the *muhasasa* system, individual units within the army were affiliated with particular political parties, reducing the credibility of the army as a mechanism for national unity and integration. In April 2013, ISF raided a protest camp in Hawija, Kirkuk, staged by hundreds of residents, parallel to sit-ins in other predominantly Sunni towns, protesting what they called the policies of exclusion and marginalization pursued by al-Maliki's government. In the process, between twenty-seven and fifty people were killed, and over seventy individuals (predominantly protestors) were injured. Incidents of this kind, in addition to al-Maliki's marginalization of the Sons of Iraq, spurred the resurgence of salafi-jihadist violence across Sunni-dominant parts of the country, specifically the rise of Daesh.

Additionally, al-Maliki's efforts to monopolize the security sector did not provide the Badr Organization with any incentive to demobilize. Indeed, while Da'wa and SCIRI were political rivals, in the 2005 parliamentary elections, they stood together in the United Iraqi Alliance, and al-Maliki needed SCIRI and Badr's support to be appointed prime minister. Ceding control of the Ministry of Interior to SCIRI/Badr was a political concession that enabled Badr to monopolize part of the state security apparatus, whilst retaining its expertise in non-conventional (insurgent) warfare through ongoing links with the Iranian Quds Force. Both SCIRI and Badr evolved during al-Maliki's administration: in 2007, SCIRI's leader Abdul Aziz al-Hakim changed the party's name to the Islamic Supreme Council in Iraq (ISCI), dropping the 'Revolution' part of the name in a bid to adopt a more Iraqi nationalist image. Badr's leader, Hadi al-Ameri, changed the group's name from 'Corps' to 'Organization' to promote the impression of being integrated into the political mainstream, despite retaining its paramilitary modus operandi. Following al-Hakim's death, his son 'Ammar sought to further 'Iraqify' the party and become less heavily associated with Iran. However, al-'Ameri and the ISCI old-guard retained close links with the Quds Force, and in 2012 al-Ameri established Badr as an independent political party. In 2015, Badr emerged at the forefront of the Iranian-backed Popular Mobilization Forces (PMF), which have transformed Iraq's security arena into something way beyond the control of the Iraqi government.

The proliferation of armed coercion under Daesh

Daesh's seizure of Mosul on 10 June 2014, after a three-day fight, took the ISF by surprise. Both the 2nd Division of the Iraqi army and the 3rd Federal Police Division dissolved in Daesh's wake. Within two days, four more Iraqi army divisions had collapsed as the militants advanced to within ninety-five miles of Baghdad (Parker, Coles and Salman 2014). Following Mosul's fall, rumours abounded as to how the ISF had been defeated virtually without a fight. Iraqi government officials laid the blame for abandoning the city on General Mahdi Gharawi, the Shi'a operational commander of Ninewa Province (who had previously been widely accused of maintaining secret prisons and torturing Sunni detainees while in command of the 2nd National Police Division in Baghdad during the sectarian civil war). Gharawi, for his part, maintained that he had been scapegoated, and that the responsibility lay with the Ministry of Defence deputy chief of staff and the commander of ground forces (whose abandonment of the West Bank of Mosul on 9 June prompted mass desertions by soldiers), and with al-Maliki himself.

The failings of senior commanders during Daesh's assault may have been the proximate causes for the ISF's defeat, but several more deeply entrenched structural failings explain in a more holistic sense why the city fell. The ISF guarding Mosul were, for the most part, on unfavourable terms with the local population. Years of political cronyism and the *muhasasa* system meant that the army and police units in question were predominantly Shi'a as opposed to Sunni (or Kurdish), while the majority of Maslawis are Sunni. In the lead-up to Daesh's attack, the Ninewa Operations Command had pursued a COIN approach within the city that had further alienated the population by running oppressive checkpoints manned by poorly trained, poorly motivated and poorly disciplined soldiers (Abbas and Trombly 2014). Additionally, after years of corrupt commanders permitting the rank and file to go absent without leave whilst retaining them on the books as employees so that they could take a cut of their salaries, by the time Daesh attacked, the number of ISF actually deployed within the city was far lower than the official figure of 25,000: it was probably less than half that number (Parker, Coles and Salman 2014).

Overall, the collapse of the ISF in June 2014 resulted in the removal of nineteen Iraqi army brigades from the order of battle (five of which have since been reconstituted); six federal police brigades and six department of border enforcement brigades on the Syrian frontier also disbanded (Knights 2016: 22). Over the following few years, ISF units underwent a renewed series of training in order to lead the campaign against Daesh. The onus of responsibility fell on the Counterterrorism Service (CTS) of 'Golden Division', whose remit was extended to combat conventional warfare as well as terrorist attacks and insurgency. Despite al-Maliki's bid to assume direct control over the CTS, the service, which had been established and trained by US special forces, was widely hailed as professional and non-partisan – in Knights' words, 'The Best Thing America Built in Iraq' (Knights and Mello 2017).

Beyond the ISF, however, the defeat of Daesh was in no small part due to a collection of around fifty predominantly Shi'a armed groups known collectively as the *Hashd al-Sha'abi* (Popular Mobilization Forces or PMF). Some of these groups were established in the wake of Daesh's territory grab, following al-Maliki's call for Iraqis across the country to form armed self-defence groups to protect their neighbourhoods (De Petris 2018). Others, specifically Badr and offshoots of JAM, rebranded as the 'Peace Companies or *Sarayat al-Salam*', and former 'Iranian Special Groups', including Asa'ib Ahl al-Haqq, Kata'ib Hezbollah and the Abu Fadl al-Abbas Brigades, were already seasoned factions within Iraq's security arena, enjoying varying degrees of popularity amongst the Iraqi population. Days after Daesh's seizure of Mosul, Iraq's most senior Shi'a religious authority, Grand Ayatollah Sayyid al-Sistani, issued a fatwa (non-binding Islamic legal opinion) urging Iraqis to defend their country. The fatwa leant legitimacy to groups that might otherwise have appeared to be little more than unruly militias. Mansour, citing a senior PMF intelligence official, notes that in 2015, 75 per cent of men aged eighteen to thirty residing in the Shi'a provinces had signed up to the PMF (by early 2016 the number had stabilized at around 120,000) (Mansour 2018). While the majority of the PMF identified as Shi'a, an increasing number of Sunni tribal and ethnic minority armed groups nominally joined the overarching PMF umbrella in the fight against Daesh.

The PMF groups were instrumental in the campaign, but they also further fractured the state's coercive capabilities. Nouri al-Maliki's successor Haidar al-Abadi (September 2014–October 2018) took faltering steps to incorporate the PMF into the state's institutional framework.[9] In April 2015, he ordered the PMF be placed under the direct command of the prime minister's office. In November 2016, the Iraqi parliament passed a law legally recognizing the Commission of the PMF, whilst also recognizing that the PMF was 'an independent military formation as part of the Iraqi armed forces and linked to the Commander-in-Chief'(Law of the Popular Mobilization Authority 2016).[10] Yet, while some PMF groups limited themselves to defending their own locales, others – including those with strong Iranian affiliations – joined or even bypassed the ISF in retaking key territories. While some PMF groups worked within the ISF command structure, others acted virtually autonomously. The Iraqi government struggled to curtail the latter groups after agreeing to pay PMF members' salaries to their units rather than directly to volunteers, placing enormous budgetary control into the hands of different leaderships. Videos emerging from the battles in Tikrit and Fallujah in 2015 and 2016 showing Iran-backed PMF units committing rights abuses on Sunni residents, apparently on the basis of sect, were taken as ominous signs by the outside world (Arab Center for Research and Policy Studies 2016). However, within Iraq, the overall popularity of the PMF, who came to the country's rescue when the ISF could not, was extremely high by the time of the liberation of Mosul. In March/April 2017, national polling indicated that 74 per cent of Iraqis outside of the Kurdish region viewed the PMF favourably (Greenberg Quinler Rosner Research 2017).

The battle for Mosul and beyond

The campaign to retrieve Mosul and with it Ninewa Province ('*Qadimun Ya Ninawa!*') was a massive military offensive, undertaken by an assortment of fighting groups on multiple fronts. Leading the charge were security forces controlled directly by the Iraqi federal government (the ISF) and the Kurdistan regional government (the Peshmerga). They were supported by a US-led coalition of international forces who provided air power, logistical aid, training and intelligence. Over a dozen popular and tribal mobilization forces also participated in the offensive, in some cases supported by small numbers of Iranian military personnel (who operated with the Iraqi government's consent) and in others by Turkish troops (who operated without the Iraqi government's consent (Saada 2016)).[11] In total, an estimated 114,000 Iraqi members of this 'coalition' plus

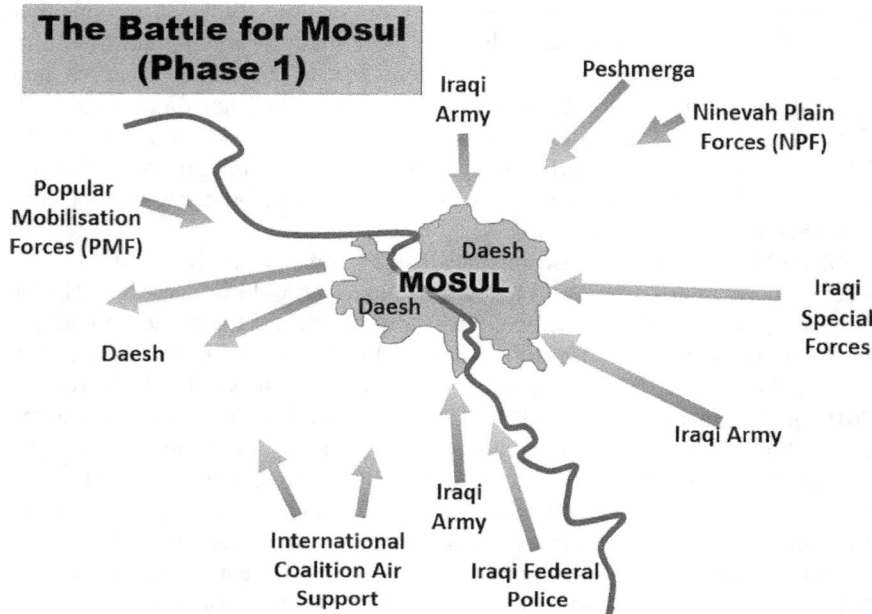

Figure 7.2 The Battle for Mosul - Phase 1: Visualising combatant forces in the Battle of Mosul, October-December 2016

their external allies faced off against an estimated 8,000–9,000 Daesh militants (Williams, Glyn and Souza 2017).[12]

The battle, which al-Abadi vowed in September 2016, would be won within three months, continued for nine (October 2016–July 2017). The ISF initially advanced on Mosul from the south and west; the Peshmerga overran Daesh-held villages to the north; the CTS captured areas north-east of Mosul and some of the PMF advanced on the western flank to block Daesh's route to Syria. On 1 November, the CTS and Iraqi Army began their assault on Eastern Mosul, and in mid-November the PMF cut off Daesh's westerly supply route to Tal Afar by seizing Tal Afar airport. Phase One ended on 15 December, with the ISF's capture of forty out of fifty-six districts in Eastern Mosul.

In Phase two (29 December–23 January), the Iraqi Army, Federal Police and CTS, accompanied by US military advisory personnel, continued to eject Daesh from Eastern Mosul. As ISF advanced on the bridges over the River Tigris from the eastern side, Daesh destroyed the connecting bridges to delay the assault on Western Mosul. The PMF continued to extend positions to the west and in the Ninewa Plains, whilst the Peshmerga concentrated on northeastern Ninewa, pushing into the Makhmur region. In the afternoon of 23 January, al-'Abadi announced the full liberation of Eastern Mosul.

Phase three (19 February–10 July) focused on Western Mosul. The ISF recaptured Mosul airport within days. By 7 March, the Rapid Response Division and Federal Police announced the capture of the governorate buildings, but throughout March, April and May, the ISF progressed slowly, fighting block by block against Daesh militants in heavily built-up areas. By June, they had reached the centre of Mosul, and finally in July, the ISF was clearing the old city. The PMF continued to focus on the outlying region, eventually cutting off Daesh's access to Tal Afar, whilst the Federal Police moved into the villages west of Mosul.

The battle was protracted by the nature of Daesh's defence of the city: their use of booby-trapped tunnels and vehicles, human shields, suicide bombers and snipers. The majority of Mosul's 2.4 million inhabitants remained in the city during the battle, and the coalition asserted that humanitarian considerations slowed their progress, although some residents cited abuses committed by their 'liberators', including sect-based targeting and indiscriminate air strikes (Hennessy-Fiske and Hennigan 2017).[13] The conflict was also prolonged by the limits of coordination between the forces involved. Each assumed areas of responsibility, which broadly aligned with their commanders' priorities.

Within Mosul city, the ground offensive was conducted by the ISF, who were also active in the outlying districts, reflecting the prime minister's objective of asserting sovereign state control over all Iraqi territory. Yet even the breakdown within the ISF was notably partisan. Iraqi ISF commanders complained about the lack of a centralized command and control system, and about the international coalition's inconsistent provision of air support: while air strikes were prolific, they were not always aligned with the ground offensive objectives. For the Kurdish Peshmerga, the priority was the territory in the north-east close to Iraqi Kurdistan, in areas where the KDP already exercised political and military influence and sought to expand it after Daesh's demise. The Kurdish regional government's commitment to a unified Iraq was clearly not a factor in its participation in the battle. A mere two months after the liberation of Mosul, the Kurdish president, Masoud Barzani, called a referendum on the independence of Iraqi Kurdistan from the rest of Iraq: 92.73 per cent voted in favour (although their aspirations were swiftly quashed by the federal government).

Meanwhile, the PMF prioritized regions in keeping with their diverse affiliations. Around half-a-dozen prominent Iranian-backed PMFs active to the west of Mosul were intent on consolidating access to aid from Iran. Amir Taheri notes that the Iran-backed components of the *Hashd* 'spent more energy on its ethnic-cleansing programme in Tal-Afar than in engaging ISIS units' (2016). Amongst the other PMFs were several Sunni tribal groups and a collection of units formed around minority ethnic identities including Yezidis, Turkmen, Assyrians and Shabak, who fought primarily for their immediate homelands and, in some cases, for autonomy from Kurdish or Iraqi federal authority. While the international coalition worked primarily alongside components of the ISF, it also supported the Peshmerga and select PMF-representing ethnic minorities, whilst Iran worked with (other) components of the ISF and PMF.

In the aftermath of victory against Daesh, many PMF members have demobilized; some have joined the Iraqi army and indeed, more recently, several units loyal to Sistani have placed themselves directly under the authority of the prime minister's office instead of the PMF Commission (Ahmed 2021). The Commission's officially-appointed chairman is Falah al-Fayadh, a former national security advisor, but until

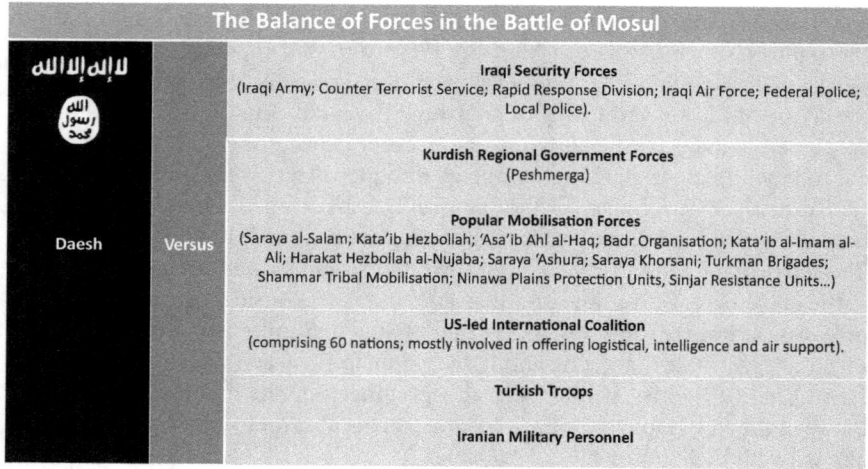

Figure 7.3 The balance of forces in the Battle of Mosul

January 2020, the deputy chairman, Abu Mahdi al-Muhandis (also leader of Kata'ib Hezbollah), was widely recognized as the de facto leader. Muhandis cooperated closely with Qassem Soleimani, the leader of Iran's Quds Force (which Muhandis had previously worked for whilst in exile in Iran), until January 2020 when both men were assassinated by a US drone attack at Baghdad airport. Hadi al-Ameri of the Badr Organization and Qais al-Khazali of *Asa'ib Ahl al-Haq*, also pro-Iran groups, were and still are highly influential within the PMF hierarchy. They are amongst the PMF members that have embedded themselves into political, economic and social structures at the provincial and sub-provincial levels, sometimes in areas other than those from which their members hail, with no intention of disbanding. Riding high on their post-Daesh popularity, a collection of seventeen factions representing the political wings of broadly pro-Iran PMFs formed a coalition (Fateh) to contest the May 2018 parliamentary elections. They won 48 out of 329 seats, making them a bloc to be reckoned with within the Iraqi government, with the political clout to insist on certain privileges for their associated armed groups, including the right to go on operating across parts of Iraq, long after the defeat of Daesh. Over time, while hostilities related to sect and ethnicity have persisted in Iraq, pragmatic deals cut between PMF leaders and local figures of influence along non-sectarian lines have contributed to the fracturing of identity-based politics, giving way to a more complex labyrinth of power structures.

The post-Weberian state of counterinsurgency in Iraq

Daesh's defeat in Mosul was a sine qua non in Haidar al-Abadi's bid to assert control over the Iraqi state, yet the disparate nature of his allies in the battle underscored the reality that Iraq is far removed from the Western and Weberian image of the sovereign institutionalized state and will likely remain so indefinitely. The status of the PMF, classified by the Iraqi parliament as part of the armed forces and yet 'independent' could be said to blur the line between what constitutes a 'state' and a 'non-state' actor: but perhaps more accurately, it calls for a reassessment of the nature of the state in contemporary Iraq. It is not, as the classic model of COIN would have it, a unified, institutionalized actor, but rather a network or arena of power nodes, each of which has recourse to coercive reinforcements.

The character and distribution of Iraq's security arena is intrinsically tied to the post-2003 political settlement, but after nearly two decades, the repercussions of that settlement have filtered down through myriad channels to virtually every level of government and governance. The removal (violent or otherwise) of particular individuals within armed groups, deemed by external actors to be exercising a particularly pernicious influence on the state, provides no solution for this root problem. Mansour, critiquing the suggestion that the PMF should simply be dissolved, provides the following argument:

> The PMF is not a symptom or even the root of the problem, but part of the array of forces that make up the incoherent Iraqi state. Its brokerage networks – those that link and negotiate between different groups – include not only fighters, but also parliamentarians, cabinet ministers, local governors, provincial council members, business figures in both public and private companies, senior civil servants, humanitarian organisations, and civilians. The diffusion of these networks means that removing one node – like Muhandis – will not change the nature of the problem. (Mansour 2021: 5)

Nonetheless, international and domestic actors continue to behave as though the state in Iraq *is* a unitary, centralized and sovereign actor, with a discrete state-sanctioned security apparatus, whilst cultivating links with particular agencies within the state that appear best placed to further their own agendas. In the post-Daesh era, the Iraqi government's focus on COIN under al-Abadi's successors (Adel Abdul Mahdi, October 2018–May 2020, and Mustafa al-Kadhimi, May 2020 to present) has diminished, but the international coalition has continued to support professionalization initiatives for the ISF premised on its ability to wage COIN (and counterterrorism). In October 2018, NATO launched a non-combat mission to Iraq 'designed to help strengthen Iraqi security institutions and forces so that they themselves can prevent the return of ISIS, fight terrorism and stabilize their country … conducted in full respect of Iraq's sovereignty and territorial integrity' (NATO 2021). In the coalition's case, this insistence on Iraq's sovereignty comprises part of the ongoing 'liberal lie' inherent in its approach to COIN in Iraq. To return to Marshall's articulation of this argument:

> While it has also begun to be acknowledged in some quarters that traditional COIN may actually run contrary to effective state-building, few have yet fully plumbed the implications of this gap, and neo-imperialist practices have in practice served to paper over the conceptual cracks. Rhetoric implies that the counterinsurgent

forces are there to support the sovereign government; actual governmental and administrative practices in fact often imply otherwise. (Marshall 2010: 247)

Outside of Iraq, in other conflict-prone states, international actors have dropped the traditional approach to COIN. In Somalia, for example, Moe describes how the state has become a renowned site of 'reworked security approaches, including counterinsurgency efforts, adapting to state fragility by moving beyond linear hierarchical state-centric forms of stabilization' (2017: 120). In this context, she claims, contemporary COIN analysts have been reinterpreting the basic conditions for political (dis)order in Somalia. Decentred forms of non-state authority, rather than being portrayed as obstacles to international intervention schemes and as a fertile breeding ground for insurgencies, can instead be seen as constituting 'key potential building blocks for effectively fighting insurgencies' (Moe 2017: 120). In this context, the very idea of state sovereignty is being reformulated, away from supposedly objective measures of legality and rationality, towards a post-Westphalian, decentralized, 'bottom-up government' entry-point for COIN (Moe 2017: 122). In Libya too, international actors appear to have given up on the idea of a unified, centralized state, although it is difficult to argue conclusively that offering support for localized factions has enhanced the security of local populations in any lasting sense.

In Iraq, however, nearly two decades after the occupation, the elusive Weberian 'ideal' state persists as a goal for the international actors, and more importantly, it appears to retain appeal for Iraqis themselves, even when they resort to particular factions under duress. For the coalition, lack of understanding of how networks of influence amongst coercive forces operate at the sub-national level remains a powerful disincentive for pursuing a less centred approach to COIN. For Iraqis, when it comes to security actors, nationwide public polling indicates that Iraqis overall want the ISF to bear primary responsibility for their security. In a 2020/2021 survey, 60 per cent indicated that amongst Iraqi security actors, the ISF had the most positive impact on their personal security. Still, the idea that the ISF might exercise the monopoly over the use of force remains doubtful. More than 31 per cent of respondents overall (and a much higher percentage of Sunnis) felt that the ISF did not protect all Iraqis equally, and less than 30 per cent of respondents felt that their own personal safety and that of their families was ensured (Clausen 2021).

The outcome of the October 2021 parliamentary elections – in which Fatah's share of seats dropped from forty-eight to seven – appeared to indicate a loss of popular support for the bloc and the Iran-backed militant groups associated with it.[14] Seizing the initiative, Moqtada al-Sadr, whose bloc outperformed all others, insisted that 'unruly' armed factions (a guarded reference to pro-Khamenei groups) hand over their weapons to the government-sanctioned PMF commission. He equally asked the PMF to purify its ranks from 'undisciplined elements' and surrender 'corrupt individuals' to the judiciary (Abdul-Zahra 2021). Sadr's demand, made from his now established position of respectability within the political mainstream, represents a volte face since his time as spiritual leader of the JAM, which was frequently called upon by the former Iraqi government to disband. Indeed, a senior representative of *Kata'ib Hezbollah* said that while, in principle, he welcomed Sadr's call to hand over weapons, it could only happen when Sadr's own armed group, *Sarayat al-Salam*, and, likewise, the Kurdish Peshmerga surrender their weapons: 'Only after these two things happen can the project of limiting arms in the hands of the state succeed'(Abdul-Zahra 2021). As long as this genre of domestic security dilemma between Iraq's main armed groups and their constituencies persists, there is little prospect of Iraqi's security arena being consolidated into a single state security sector.

Notes

1   The 'Coalition of the Willing' was how President Bush referred to the international forces that joined the United States to topple Saddam's regime in 2003.
2   Some of the more prominent amongst these include Hoffman (2004), Petraeus (2006), Berman, Shapiro and Felter (2011) and Malkasian (2008).
3   See Weber (1949: 90). Weber's 'ideal type' does not mean perfect, rather it emphasizes certain elements common to most cases of a given phenomenon, yet in liberal state-building projects, it is indeed commonly envisioned as the desired outcome.
4   For an elaboration of this characterization of the Iraqi state, see R. Mansour, 'Networks of Power: The Popular Mobilization Forces and the State in Iraq'. Research paper, Middle East and North Africa Programme (London: Chatham House, 2021).
5   The term 'security arena' was coined by Alice Hills.
6   For a detailed account of the early CPA years in Iraq, see T. Dodge, *Iraq–from War to a New Authoritarianism* (London: Routledge, 2017).
7   The NIA was initially trained by the US company Vinnell, until the United States assessed that Jordan would do a better job of the task, whilst the Iraqi police was trained by another US security firm, Dyncorps.
8   Although al-Maliki has subsequently been closely associated with Iranian agendas in Iraq.
9   In mid-August 2014, mounting domestic and international criticism forced Nouri al-Maliki to resign.
10 Law of the Popular Mobilization Authority No. (40) of 2016.
11 From early 2015, Turkey provided military training and support to Kurdish Peshmerga as well as certain Sunni tribal mobilization forces to fight Daesh. In October 2016, Turkey sent several hundred troops to Bashiqa, north-east of Mosul, in what the Iraqi government considered an illegal encroachment on its sovereignty.
12 Statistics on Daesh are taken from the Mosul Eye Website.
13 In mid-March 2017, residents of Western Mosul claimed that US-led air strikes had killed over 230 civilians.
14 Although Fatah claimed that the electoral system had been skewed against them.

Bibliography

Abbas, Yasir, and Trombly, Dan (2014). 'Inside the Collapse of the Iraqi Army's 2nd Division'. *War on the Rocks*. 1 July. https://warontherocks.com/2014/07/inside-the-collapse-of-the-iraqi-armys-2nd-division/ (accessed 19 May 2022).

Abdul-Zahra, Qassim (2021). 'Iraqi Shiite Cleric Calls on Pro-Iran Militias to Disband'. *RUDAW*. 18 November. https://www.rudaw.net/english/middleeast/iraq/18112021 (accessed 19 May 2022).

Ahmed, Omar (2021). 'Pro-Sistani Factions Leave Shia Forces, but Iraq's PM Signals They Are Here to Stay'. *Middle East Monitor*. 20 May. https://www.middleeast monitor.com/20200518-pro-sistani-factions-leave-shia-forces-but-iraqs-pm-sign als-they-are-here-to-stay/ (accessed 19 May 2022).

Arab Center for Research and Policy Studies (2016). 'The Battle for Fallujah: Winning the Battle, Losing the War'. *Assessment Report Policy Analysis Unit, Doha Institute*, June.

Berman, Eli, Shapiro, Jacob N., and Felter, Joseph H. (2011). 'Can Hearts and Minds Be Bought? The Economics of Counterinsurgency in Iraq'. *Journal of Political Economy*, 119(4): 766–819.

Boot, Max (2021). 'America Still Needs Counterinsurgency'. *Foreign Affairs*. 2 June. https://www.foreignaffairs.com/articles/afghanistan/2021-06-02/america-still-needs-counte rinsurgency (accessed 19 May 2022).

Callwell, Charles E. (1896). *Small Wars: Their Principles and Practice*. 1st edition, The Oxford Handbook of Contemporary Middle-Eastern and North African History. London: HMSO.

Clausen, Maria-Louise (2021). 'Providing Security in Iraq – What Do Iraqis Think?'. *Danish Institute for International Studies*. 27 April. https://www.diis.dk/en/research/providing-security-in-iraq-what-do-iraqis-think (accessed 19 May 2022).

von Clausewitz, Carl (1997). *On War*. Trans. J. J. Graham. Ware: Wordsworth.

Cordesman, Anthony (2007). *Iraq's Sectarian and Ethnic Violence and Its Evolving Insurgency*. Center for Strategic and International Studies. https://csis-website-prod.s3.amazonaws.com/s3fs-public/legacy_files/files/media/csis/pubs/070126_insurgency_update.pdf.

Cordesman, Anthony, and Khazai, Sam (2014). 'Shaping Iraq's Security Forces'. . *Centre for Strategic and International Studies*. June 12. https://www.csis.org/analysis/shap ing-iraq%E2%80%99s-security-forces (accessed19 May 2022).

Dodge, Toby (2013). 'State and Society in Iraq Ten Years after Regime Change: The Rise of a New Authoritarianism'. *International Affairs* 89(2): 241–57.

Dodge, Toby (2017). *Iraq–From War to a New Authoritarianism*. London: Routledge.

Galula, David (1963). *Pacification in Algeria 1956–1958, MG-478-1*. Santa Monica, CA: RAND.

Galula, David (1964). *Counterinsurgency Warfare: Theory and Practice*. New York: Praeger.

Gaub, Florence (2016). 'An Unhappy Marriage: Civil-Military Relations in Post-Saddam Iraq'. Research paper, Carnegie Middle East Center, January, 13.

Greenberg Quinler Rosner Research (2017). 'Improved Security Provides Opening for Cooperation'. *Greenberg Quinler Rosner Research*. Survey Findings, NDI. March–April. https://www.ndi.org/sites/default/files/NDI%20Poll%20-%20Mar-Apr%202017%20%28English%29.pdf (accessed 19 May 2022).

Hennessy-Fiske, Molly, and Hennigan, W. J. (2017). 'More Than 200 Civilians Killed in Suspected U.S. Airstrike in Iraq'. *LA Times*. 24 March. https://www.latimes.com/world/middleeast/la-fg-mosul-civilians-airstrike-20170324-story.html (accessed 19 May 2022).

Hills, Alice (2014). 'Security Sector or Security Arena? The Evidence from Somalia'. *International Peacekeeping* 21(2): 165–80.

Hoffman, Bruce (2004). *Insurgency and Counterinsurgency in Iraq*. Santa Monica, CA: RAND.

Jabar, Faleh A., Mansour, Renad, and Khaddaj, Abir (2012). *Maliki and the Rest: A Crisis within a Crisis*. London: Iraq Institute for Strategic Studies.

Khalili, Laleh (2015). 'Counterterrorism and Counterinsurgency in the Neoliberal Age'. In Amal Ghazal and Jens Hanssen (eds), *The Oxford Handbook of Contemporary Middle-Eastern and North African History* (365–83). Oxford: Oxford University Press.

Knights, Michael (2016). 'The Future of Iraq's Armed Forces'. *al-Bayan Centre for Planning and Studies*. March. https://www.bayancenter.org/en/wp-content/uploads/2016/03/The-future.pdf (accessed 19 May 2022).

Knights, Michael, and Mello, Alex (2017). 'The Best Thing America Built in Iraq: Iraq's Counter-Terrorism Service and the Long War Against Militancy'. . *War on the Rocks*. 19 July. https://warontherocks.com/2017/07/the-best-thing-america-built-in-iraq-iraqs-counter-terrorism-service-and-the-long-war-against-militancy/ (accessed 20 May 2022).

Law of the Popular Mobilization Authority (2016). No. (40). *LSE Middle East Blog*. 15 March 2018. https://blogs.lse.ac.uk/mec/2018/03/15/the-popular-mobilisation-forces-and-the-balancing-of-formal-and-informal-power/ (accessed 20 May 2022).

Malkasian, Carter (2008). 'Counterinsurgency in Iraq'. In Daniel Marston and Carter Malkasian (eds), *Counterinsurgency in Modern Warfare* (241–59). Oxford: Osprey Publishing.

Mansour, Renad (2018). 'The Popular Mobilisation Forces and the Balancing of Formal and Informal Power'. *LSE Middle East Centre Blog*. 15 March. https://blogs.lse.ac.uk/mec/2018/03/15/the-popular-mobilisation-forces-and-the-balancing-of-formal-and-informal-power/ (accessed 19 May 2022).

Mansour, Renad (2021). 'Networks of Power: The Popular Mobilization Forces and the State in Iraq'. Research paper, *Middle East and North Africa Programme*, London: Chatham House.

Marshall, Alex (2010). 'Imperial Nostalgia, the Liberal Lie, and the Perils of Postmodern Counterinsurgency'. *Small Wars & Insurgencies* 21(2): 233–58.

McCallister, William S. (2008). 'Sons of Iraq: A Study in Irregular Warfare'. *Small Wars Journal* 8(Sept.): 27.

Moe, Louise W. (2017). 'Counterinsurgent Warfare and the Decentering of Sovereignty in Somalia'. In Louise W. Moe and Markus-Michael Müller (eds), *Reconfiguring Intervention* (119–40). London: Palgrave Macmillan.

NATO (2021). 'Mission Iraq'. . *NATO*. 18 November. https://www.nato.int/cps/en/natohq/topics_166936.htm (accessed 19 May 2022).

Parker, Ned (2009). 'Machiavelli in Mesopotamia: Nouri al-Maliki Builds the Body Politic'. *World Policy Journal* 26(1): 17–25.

Parker, Ned, Coles, Isabel, and Salman, Raheem (2014). 'Special Report: How Mosul Fell – an Iraqi General Disputes Baghdad's Story'. . *Reuters*. 14 October. https://www.reuters.com/article/us-mideast-crisis-gharawi-special-report-idUSKCN0I30Z820141014 (accessed 19 May 2022).

Petraeus, David H. (2006). 'Learning Counterinsurgency: Observations from Soldiering in Iraq'. *Military Review* 86(3): 21.

De Petris, Daniel (2018). 'Iran's Power Play in Iraq: Will Shi'a Militias Save Maliki?'. *The National Interest*. 8 June. https://nationalinterest.org/blog/the-buzz/iran%E2%80%99s-power-play-iraq-will-shia-militias-save-maliki-10695.(accessed 29 May 2022).

Saada, Mohamed (2016). 'The Military Operation in Mosul and Its Future Repercussions'. *Middle East Observer*. 20 October. https://www.middleeastobserver.org/2016/10/20/

the-military-operation-in-mosul-and-its-future-repercussions/ (accessed 19 May 2022).

Taheri, Amir (2016). 'Liberating Mosul, the Five Weaknesses of the Battle Plan'. 2 December. https://eng-archive.aawsat.com/amir-taheri/features/liberating-mosul-5-weaknesses-battle-plan (accessed 19 May 2022).

Weber, Max (1949). *The Methodology of the Social Sciences*. Trans. and ed. Edward.A. Shils and Henry A. Finch. Glencoe,IL: Free Press.

Wilbanks, Mark, and Karsh, Efraim (2010). 'How the "Sons of Iraq" Stabilized Iraq'. *Middle East Quarterly* 17(4): 57–70.

Williams, Brian G., and Souza, Robert T. (2017). 'The Fall of a Jihadist Bastion: A History of the Battle of Mosul (October 2016 – July 2017)'. *Jamestown Foundation*, 12 October.

Part III

THE POLITICAL ECONOMY AND GEOPOLITICS OF EMERGENT ORDERS IN SYRIA AND IRAQ

Chapter 8

THE WAR ECONOMY IN SYRIA: CONSOLIDATING THE PRE-2011 DYNAMICS OF SYRIA'S POLITICAL ECONOMY

Joseph Daher

Introduction

After more than ten years of war, the Syrian state's forces control almost 70 per cent of the territory, thanks to the political, economic and military assistance provided by its allies – Russia and Iran. An estimated population of 15 million inhabitants is living in government-controlled areas, out of a total population of around 20.8 million (World Bank 2020). In addition, around six million Syrians are refugees worldwide, most of whom have been displaced to neighbouring countries with only a tiny fraction having returned to Syria. More than half of Syria's population is internally or externally displaced as a result of the war. Most Syrians – in neighbouring countries and in Syria – live with poverty, exploitation and discriminatory policies.

Despite massive support from its foreign allies and lower populations in government-held areas than in 2011 (at least according to estimates), Damascus is facing huge socio-economic and political challenges. In light of this dire socio-economic situation, the Syrian authorities have developed economic policies with the aim of consolidating their power and their various patronage networks, all while allowing new forms of capital accumulation. A central component of this strategy has been the promotion of a model of economic development that relies on Public Private Partnerships (PPPs) and the privatization of public goods as the basis for the country's reconstruction and economic regeneration.

The 'war economy' model, put forward by various analysts to portray the current state in Syria, is often presented as a new paradigm that supposedly represents a rupture with and departure from the economic dynamics that existed in Syria before 2011. Economic growth, therefore, was essentially derived from the service sector and rents, dependent on oil-export revenue and capital inflows, including remittances. However, only a very small stratum of the society benefited from this growth. In 2007, the percentage of Syrians living below the poverty line was 33 per cent, which corresponded to around 7 million individuals, while another 30 per cent were just above this level, 14 per cent of Syrians were estimated to be living under the poverty line in 2000.

In fact, the conflict has exacerbated these prior economic dynamics. It has intensified the Syrian government's pre-war neoliberal policies and orientation while reinforcing the authoritarian and patrimonial aspects of the Syrian state. The change that has occurred is in the networks of local and foreign actors that underpin and benefit from the system. Prior to the 2011 uprising, Saudi Arabia, Qatar and Turkey were among the main actors benefiting from the economic opening of Syria, whereas today it is firstly Russia and, to a lesser extent, Iran.

The present study relies extensively on multiple economic reports and data provided by international and Syrian research and economic institutions for key information and changes within the country's economy. It also makes wide use of newspaper and media articles published in Syria to examine major current economic issues and changes, as well as a significant academic literature available on the evolving structure of the Syrian economy

The Syrian economy after more than ten years of conflict

The outbreak of the war in 2011 had destructive consequences on Syria's economy. GDP declined from USD 60.2 billion in 2010 to around USD 21.6 billion in 2019,[1] while total accumulated economic losses is estimated to have reached USD 530.1 billion by the end of 2019 (The Syrian Center for Policy Research 2020). As a result of appalling war damage, the structure of the economy and of GDP changed significantly. The official numbers are not, of course, completely reliable, especially as, prior to the war, the informal economy – which accounted, according to some estimates, for about 30 per cent of employment (1.5 million individuals) and about 30–40 per cent of GDP (The International Labour Organization 2010) – has grown since 2011, notably through smuggling[2] and criminal (such as narcotrafficking) activities. These statistics nevertheless reflect the important trends and changes in the structure of Syrian economy since 2011.

Major evolutions of the Syrian GDP

The agricultural sector has become the first contributor to the Syrian GDP over the conflict years by representing for between 25 and nearly 41 per cent of GDP since 2013. The significant share of the agricultural sector in GDP is not, however, the result of its net growth, but a consequence of the large destruction that took place in other economic sectors. In 2016, the World Food Program estimated losses in Syria's agricultural sector at USD 16 billion since 2011 (e.g. almost 40 per cent in absolute term).

The manufacturing sector has been one of the sectors most seriously impacted by the conflict and is very far from the path of recovering its pre-2011 level of production. The value of damage and destruction in the public and private industrial sectors was estimated at between USD 3 and USD 4.5 billion

(Economy2Day 2019). Nationwide, in May 2021, the number of Syrian private industrial establishments had decreased to around 80,000 compared to more than 130,000 prior to 2011, while out of the 103 public manufacturing companies operating in 2011, 34 were functioning fully and 20 only partially (Hana Ghanem 2021). Similarly, to other sectors of the economy, the service sector in its diversity has been affected significantly from the destructions of the conflict, including real estate and tourism.[3]

The destructions resulting from the conflict negatively impacted infrastructures, production means and trade, while sanctions considerably curtailed trade by imposing restrictions on trade financing and accessing inputs and services from abroad.[4] The structure of imports was driven by the needs of the population for food, clothes and energy (Syrian Center for Policy Research 2020). Commodities that were produced before 2011 in amounts sufficient to meet local demand, such as oil, wheat, medicine, fertilizers and cotton have been imported to a large extent in the past few years. The balance of trade has therefore continued to be deeply negative, amounting to USD 4.5 billion in 2020. In 2020, the total value of exports was estimated at USD 900 million, while its overall value was around USD 11.2 billion in 2011.

On its side, government services' contribution to the GDP in real value decreased nearly on a constant way since 2011 as a result of the continuous and rising inflation.[5] In comparison to the 2010 GDP, the real value of government services declined in 2019 by more than 80 per cent and by half proportionally passing from 14 to 7 per cent (Syrian Center for Policy Research 2020). At the same time, after the destruction of the war, state institutions are the main providers of services and the main employer. Large sectors of the population are dependent on the state for wages or assistance, despite the state having been weakened in absolute terms compared to the period before 2011. The national average of state employment rose from 26.9 per cent in 2010 to over 55 per cent in 2015. This is explained not by a dramatic increase in state employment, but by the decrease in total employment. See the massive drop in the number of individuals registered with the Social Security Organization (SSO), which included workers from the public and private sectors and pensioners. Around 2.2 million people were registered with the SSO in 2019, while an estimated 3.7 million were registered in 2012, a decrease of 40 per cent. In 2012, there were 1.39 million state employees, 2.3 million private sector employees and 360,841 pensioners. The number of workers registered in the private sector decreased by 70 per cent, while the public sector lost 22 per cent of its workforce. The number of pensioners increased by 39 per cent (The Syria Report 2019).

International humanitarian assistance inside Syria has become increasingly crucial through the years in the last decade. In 2019, the international community's total humanitarian spending in Syria, according to the Financial Tracking service, was estimated to be USD 2.6 billion, representing 11.6 per cent of Syria's GDP (Financial Tracking Service 2021). In 2020, UN agencies allocated more than USD 200 million in contracts to Syrian companies. INGOs and UN agencies also play significant economic roles inside the country by providing jobs. Economic sectors that are not subject to sanctions – transport, agribusiness, hotels and pharmaceuticals – depend greatly on income generated by international humanitarian assistance. More generally, alongside international humanitarian assistance funds, remittances sent by Syrians outside the country,[6] and public subsidies, although massively diminishing since 2011, have been key elements of sustainability for the popular classes in Syria.

The years of war have profoundly modified the structure of the country's economy. Syria is now mostly a consumption society, with insufficient levels of production to satisfy local needs. At the same time, the size of the informal economy has expanded considerably, particularly regarding narcotrafficking. Captagon has for example most probably become Syria's most important source of foreign currency and much of its production and distribution is controlled by the Fourth Armoured Division of the Syrian army, an elite unit commanded by Maher al-Assad, Bashar's younger brother and one of Syria's most powerful men, alongside other key actors involved such as businessmen with close connections to the Damascus and Hezbollah. In the end of 2019, global captagon seizures represented a street value of about USD 2.9 billion, more than triple Syria's legal exports of USD 900 million in 2020 (Hubbard and Saad 2021). Syria's central role in the supply of this product to its neighbours and elsewhere, such as in Europe, could potentially represent an obstacle for future economic relation with these states.

Regional changes following destructions and impacts of war

The regions of Syria that were insulated from the extensive destruction and unrelenting violence occurring elsewhere in the country profited economically during the war. Syria's northwest coastal region benefited the most economically from its relative stable situation throughout the war. While large segments of the workforce in Latakia have remained dependent on state employment since 2011, diversification as a result of the large inflow of Internally Displaced People (IDPs) occurred, many of whom brought savings and continued their economic activities in the city. With the relocation of many private companies, especially small and medium enterprises (SME) from Idlib and Aleppo to Latakia city and the coastal region in general, private investments were higher than in other areas of Syria during the conflict, albeit estimated well-below their 2011 level.

Tartus observed an inflow of people fleeing other regions of the country, many of whom brought their savings with them. Investment in the province was higher than in other areas of Syria, although it was believed to be well below its levels prior to the uprising, while many private companies relocated there. However, the majority of the population of Tartus remained dependent on the state for their economic survival, whether as public servants or as employees of the army or security apparatus. Many public employees often had a second job as well. From 2012 to 2013, Tartus also witnessed the proliferation of construction sites for luxury hotels, restaurants and shopping malls.

By contrast, regions that suffered intensive destruction saw large segments of their population move to other areas outside and/or within the governorate.

Most of rural Damascus experienced internal population exchanges.[7] Cities such as Douma and Darayya experienced massive destruction and significant displacement, while Qudsaya and Muadamiyat were less affected.[8] At the same time, Jaramana remained under the domination of the government throughout the war and experienced a huge increase in its population, from 185,446 registered prior to the conflict to just under a million as of the end of 2019, half of which are IDPs, mostly from Eastern Ghouta and other areas of rural Damascus. Confronted with this overpopulation, the city suffered from a lack of public services, especially gas, electricity and water in the winter (Al-Khabr 2019).

Eastern Aleppo, and more generally Aleppo city, is facing a different situation. The city has been one of the most damaged, mainly its eastern neighbourhoods which were recaptured by the government's forces in December 2016. The city's population has remained consistent, at around 1.6 million, including 190,000 IDPs, a smaller population compared to 2.4 million inhabitants in 2011. Long-term return of civilians from eastern Aleppo has been obstructed, mostly for security reasons. In addition, the labour structure of the city changed considerably. Prior to the conflict, 76 per cent of employment was in the private sector, while in 2017, 56 per cent were employed by the public sector as the total number of working individuals decreased to 140,000 (Urban Analysis Network 2019).

The depreciation of the SYP and its impact on living conditions

The relative stability of the Syrian pound (SYP) prior to 2011 was somewhat dependent on the performance of the economy and the Central Bank of Syria (CBS). The CBS sought to use revenue from exports of oil and raw materials, tourism, private sector exports and remittances from expatriates to pay for imports – whether purchased by the public or private sector. Since March 2011, the value of the SYP has, however, fallen almost constantly, while the difference between its official rate and the black-market rate has continually increased.

The Lebanese financial crisis, which started in October 2019, has played a role in the continuous depreciation of the SYP, particularly after Lebanese banks imposed severe restrictions on obtaining and withdrawing US dollars. With Western sanctions on Syria, Syrian businessmen and traders had relied on neighbouring Lebanon and its banking system to continue their economic activities, especially trade and smuggling. Before 2019, the deposits held by Syrian individuals and companies in Lebanese banks were estimated to stand at around USD 45 billion – approximately 25.4 per cent of all Lebanese banks' assets.[9]

At the same time, the roots of this depreciation are much more structural than conjunctural and reflect the abysmal state of the economy. The economy suffered tremendously during the war in Syria, and all the factors allowing for the relative stability of the SYP were badly hit. In general, Syrian government revenue has shrunk considerably in the past decade. First, the oil industry and tourism, which were major sources of foreign currency prior to the 2011 uprising, both suffered massive destruction. In 2010, oil production contributed 9.5 per cent of Syria's

GDP according to official accounts and oil exports remained the most important source of foreign currency earnings, totalling USD 5.5 billion. Daily oil production fell from nearly 380,000 barrels before the uprising in 2011 to around 20,000 oil barrels in state-controlled areas in 2021. As for Syria's tourism industry, revenue in 2010 was estimated at USD 8.21 billion (or SYP 386 billion at the exchange rate prevailing at the time), representing around 13.7 per cent of the country's GDP. In 2017, visitors only brought SYP 7 billion, which was equivalent to a mere USD 14 million. Second, foreign direct investment (FDI), which was more than USD 8 billion between 2005 and 2011, also stopped being a source of hard currency after 2011 and its quasi absence reinforced the fall of the Syrian national currency. Finally, the massive destruction in the manufacturing and agriculture sectors as mentioned above led to a shattering of local production capacity and a decrease in the volume of exports (Daher 2019).

Between 2019 and 2021, the SYP depreciation on the black market continued, increasing the gap between the official and black-market SYP prices. The Consumer Price Index (CPI) rose from 149.02 in January 2011 to 2,700 in May 2020, demonstrating the harsh increase in prices (Mehchy 2020). In December 2020, Syria's annual inflation rate reached a record high of 163 per cent, the largest year-on-year increase in decades, according to data from the Central Bureau of Statistics. This has continued throughout the year.

In the end of 2021, cost of living continued to increase as the price of petrol, fuel oil and bread augmented following the government's reduction of subsidies on these products (Daher 2021), while long queues at petrol stations and bakeries became common in 2020 and 2021. The rise in prices of oil derivatives also negatively affects agriculture and manufacturing projects by increasing production costs, while the quantities of fuel oil and gas oil provided by the state to farmers and manufacturers at a set or subsidized price are often insufficient and/or delayed by several days.

The average costs of the basic consumption basket for a family of five in Damascus increased from 732,000 SYP in December 2020 (equivalent to USD 581 on the official rate and USD 254 on the black-market exchange rate at this period) to SYP 1,847,000 in September 2021 (equivalent to USD 735 at the official rate and USD 528 on the black-market exchange rate at this period).[10] On the other side, the monthly minimum wage was increased to only SYP 92,970 (equivalent to USD 37 at the official exchange rate) from SYP 72,000 (equivalent to USD 28.7 at the official exchange rate) in December 2021, which covers 5 per cent of costs. In comparison, prior to the outbreak of Syria's conflict, an average civil servant's wage was worth between USD 200 and USD 320, with SYP 47 trading for one US dollar.

This situation has had important consequences on the vast majority of the Syrian population. The Lebanese financial crisis since 2019 and the Covid-19 pandemic have further magnified the country's socio-economic problems, with the level of poverty estimated to have been over 85 per cent even before Covid-19 erupted in Syria in mid-March 2020. The UN World Food Program had projected that, by the end of 2021, there would be a need to support an estimated 13.4 million people in Syria.

Governmental economic policies: Change and continuity

While the conflict has fundamentally changed the structure of the economy since 2011, government policies in wartime did not break with pre-war policies. The conflict seems, if anything, to have been an opportunity to deepen them. In February 2016, the Syrian government announced a 'new economic strategy' called the National Partnership, to replace the social market economic model adopted in 2005. However, the previous model had already promoted private capital accumulation and economic liberalization, which are at the core of the 'new' strategy. The deepening of the neoliberal framework is particularly clear in the Public-Private Partnership Law of 2016 and in a series of laws about house, land and property. Governmental social policies are also a good indicator of a return to the new-old model of privatization.

Public-private partnerships to reinforce clientelist networks

The law on PPPs was enacted in January 2016, six years after its drafting. According to the economics and the foreign trade minister at this time, the law created a 'legal framework for regulating relations between the public and private sectors and meets the growing economic and social needs in Syria, particularly in the field of reconstruction', and would provide the private sector with the opportunity to 'contribute to economic development as a main and active partner' (SANA 2016). This law authorizes the private sector to manage and develop state assets in all sectors of the economy as a majority shareholder/owner, except for the oil extraction sector.

The primary objective of this law was to favour crony capitalists and to reinforce their control over the economy and over public assets at the expense of state and public interests, while also benefitting Russia and Iran. In addition to its political and economic aspects, the economic dependency of the Syrian state on Russia and Iran has considerably increased since 2011, as the two countries have supplied key commodities such as oil[11] and wheat, although their economic role and investments in Syria remain limited.

Syrian private actors close to the Assad's rule are also benefiting from these dynamics. In January 2020, Bashar al-Assad ratified laws granting three contracts to the Qaterji brothers, thus giving them a strategic role in Syria's oil distribution sector. The Qaterji Group has obtained the right to establish two oil refineries and to expand an oil terminal in the port of Tartous. Refining had remained a state monopoly until then, although before 2011 the government was seeking to attract private investment in the sector. Previously, businessman Wassim Qattan, acting most probably as a frontman for Maher al-Assad, had benefitted from multiple governmental contracts to invest in hotels and malls. More generally these types of businessmen have vested interests in maintaining the Syrian state, often the source of their wealth and/or its expansion.

The PPP law must also be seen in the context of a growing neoliberal dynamic at the regional and global level: economic sectors previously managed only by the state are now open to the possibility of capital accumulation by private actors (Hanieh 2018). Various Middle East and North Africa (MENA) countries have adopted PPP legislation to double-down on privatizations of public services and state urban infrastructure.[12] The European Bank for Reconstruction and Development (EBRD), which started its activities in the MENA region after the uprisings of 2011, has the promotion of infrastructure PPPs as one of its main objectives.

In Syria, this economic approach faces, however, many obstacles. Besides instability and destruction, projects depend largely on financing from private banks, which do not have the necessary funds. The total assets of all the commercial private-sector banks operating in the country were estimated at SYP 1.134 billion (around USD 2.6 billion at the official rate of 434 SYP/USD) in December 2019, a very low number in comparison to the costs of reconstruction. By way of comparison, in 2010, the figure had reached USD 13.8 billion. Some of the six state-owned banks, in particular the Commercial Bank of Syria, had actually larger assets than their private sector counterparts.[13] However, these banks had portfolios with much bad debt (Daher 2021).

At the same time, the decline and instability of the Syrian pound affects investment levels in the country. The inability of the Syrian government and the CBS to stabilize the SYP provokes fears among foreign investors concerning the prospect of exchange losses through currency depreciation. Moreover, the chances of rapid and medium-term returns and profits on investment in Syria are limited for political and economic reasons. There is little enthusiasm then for investment inside or outside the country.

The implementation of the PPP law in 2016 is a mean for the government to restructure and deepen economic policies from prior to 2011. It significantly increases the reach of the market in a wide range of economic sectors that had previously been dominated by the state, including energy[14] and public manufacturing[15] or state-owned food production companies. At the same time, it renewed and consolidated the authoritarianism and patrimonialism of the Assad's rule through its economic networks. However, a large number of PPP projects and the (re)construction of luxury real estate projects in Syria by private Syrian actors have not yet been implemented or have been revised down.[16] For the most part there are announcements rather than actions, demonstrating the limitations of the government's economic redevelopment plans.

Housing, land and property – deepening the Assad's control over the population

While Damascus has not disclosed any global reconstruction plan for the whole country, the government has already begun to establish and restructure the economic and regulatory environment so as to implement a partial 'reconstruction'. Government measures here respond primarily to its political, economic and security interests and those of its allies, while ignoring the needs of the populations (especially in the areas controlled formerly by the opposition).

Since 2011, the Syrian government has enacted over fifty laws 'on housing, land, and property issues'. These have given the state the right to raze areas formerly held

> **Box: Chronology of main laws pertaining to housing, land, and property (HLP)**
>
> - September 2012 – Decree No. 63 enables the government to seize the assets, including real estate property, of individuals accused of crimes against the state security, that is those who fall under the Counterterrorism Law No.19 of 2012.
> - September 2012 – Decree No. 66 allows the Damascus Governorate to expel inhabitants from two large areas in the capital, and to develop the luxury real estate project called Marota City.
> - January 2018 – Law No. 3 rules on the removal of the rubble of buildings subject to laws requiring their demolition.
> - April 2018 – Law No. 10 amends Decree No. 66 of 2012 and extends its provisions to the whole of Syria.

by the opposition. This series of laws and decrees sets the framework for property expropriation and real estate development. The first piece of this legal edifice was Decree No. 66, which was inspired by some aspects of the 2007 Damascus Master Urban Plan (whose implementation was interrupted in 2011) to raze and renovate two large areas of the capital (al-Lababidi 2019). Basateen al-Razi (Mazzeh District) and Kafr Soussa were and are still considered a lucrative real-estate opportunity. They contain undeveloped farmland and informal housing, some within walking distance from central Damascus. A key element of Decree No. 66 is the funding approach, which relies on the creation of public-private investment companies, established by local authorities. In July 2015, the government approved a law authorizing the creation of holding companies by municipal councils and other Local Administrative Units in order to manage public assets and services.[17]

In addition, Decree No. 63/2012 empowers the Finance Ministry to seize assets and property from those who fell under the 2012 counterterrorism law. In 2018, the Finance Ministry made publicly documented 30,000 property seizures in 2016 and 40,000 seizures in 2017 which, he claimed, was the result of terrorist activities. Moreover, Law No.3/2018 gives the government significant leeway to define what can be identified as damaged property. It allowed neighbourhoods to be closed off and demolished, preventing civilians from returning. This set of laws serves to consolidate the domination of Damascus on the population, as well as achieving economic gains.

However, the implementation of real estate projects is limited, though new urban master plans were adopted in Aleppo in 2017 and Homs in 2018 (Ferrier 2020).[18] So far, except for a project in the Damascus suburb of Basateen al-Razi, which remained very restricted at the end of 2021,[19] reconstruction has not focused on the rebuilding of large housing areas destroyed by the war, but on the restoration of roads and some services and infrastructure, such as electricity and water. This prioritization serves the needs of specific economic sectors – internal trade, services and industries – and allows capital accumulation within the country. The holding companies created by the governorates of Homs (2018), Aleppo (2019) and Damascus Province (2019) have, for example failed to start any reconstruction project since their establishment.

More generally, the destruction and damage to infrastructures and transport networks, together with the lack of local and international funding, are significant obstacles standing in the way of large-scale reconstruction. For example, Syria's 2,500-kilometer rail network is still severely damaged. As noted by the chairman of the Federation of Shipping Companies, if reconstruction operations started in Syria, the country would need to double the currently available transport fleet in the country, on land, sea or in terms of airports (Mahfouz 2020).

Governmental social policies

Between 2011 and 2019, the total registered employed population decreased from 5.184 million to 3.058 million, of whom just over 1 million were state employees, including in public sector manufacturing; around 760,000 qualified as private employees; and 1.2 million were classed as self-employed workers (Shirub 2020). Wages have become less and less important in the production of wealth in Syria as the war has dragged on. The share of wages as a part of national income was estimated, in July 2020, at around 20 per cent, while profits and rents represented the remaining 80 per cent (Kassioun 2020).

The government has continued to neglect, with its policies, the living conditions of the labour force. Only symbolic increases in wages have occurred in the public sector, while, in 2019, the Ministry of Social Affairs and Labor (MoSAL). amended 26 articles of the Labour Law No. 17 of 2010 with very minor effect; a small rise in wages (roughly 9 per cent) and a guarantee of entitlement to maternity leave (Tishreen 2019).

The Syrian government has also continuously reduced since 2011 subsidies on essential products, negatively affecting the living conditions of the country's poor and working class. Public subsidies decreased from 20.2 per cent in 2011 to 4.9 per cent of current GDP in 2019, according to the Syrian Center for Policy Research (Tishreen 2019). Officials have explained the diminution of subsidies, price jumps and rationing to individuals and economic sectors (both private and public) in terms of war conditions and oil shortages. However, already by the mid-2000s, Syrian officials announced, on several occasions, that most energy products, and especially oil derivatives, would be sold at market price by 2015. The uprising in 2011 only slowed this process.

In the continuation of these austerity measures, the government announced by the end of 2021 that it was seeking to exclude segments of the population, up to a total of around 500,000–600,000 individuals, from its list of beneficiaries based on income level.

To compensate for the reduction of subsidies on key products especially in oil derivatives, and subsequent rising prices, the government granted bonuses to state employees and pensioners five times between October 2020 and July 2021, increased the wages of teachers working on an hourly basis once and of all state employees and pensioners in December 2021. These bonuses came especially from the funds saved by the diminution in oil derivative subsidies. According to the Syrian minister of petroleum, between January and mid-March 2021, the government saved SYP 210 billion (USD 167 million at the January 2021 official exchange rate) through subsidy reduction, and spent SYP 120 billion (USD 95.5 million) on bonuses (The Syria Report 2021).

However, these decisions only very partially made up for the noteworthy decline in the population's purchasing power, while self-employed individuals do not benefit from any similar measures. More generally, these measures do not address the root causes of the deteriorating living conditions of workers. Workers, have been obliged, through the war years to seek out alternative sources of income to supplement monthly budgets, reverting to and reinforcing the dynamic that existed prior to 2011. Important numbers of highly skilled workers also emigrated in pursuit of better living and work conditions.

The labour force is additionally characterized by high levels of unemployment, low wages and a lack of skilled workers. High unemployment may be explained by the destruction of large segments of the economy, but it also results from threats of arrest – notably on the grounds of compulsory military conscription. This explains why many young men remain at home or seek insecure and underpaid informal daily work to avoid military service.

The continuous shortage of men in Syrian society since 2011 has created a new space for women to occupy societal niches and in a workforce that was previously male-dominated or inaccessible to women.[20] In April 2018, a MoSAL official declared that there were four times more women than men on the labour market. In the public sector, the ratio was estimated to be three to one (The Syria Report 2018). However, gender participation in the economy is far from equal, with women receiving substantially lower pay and facing significant discrimination in the workplace.

Since 2011, Syria's economic-political approach, most notably through the National Partnership strategy and the PPP law, together with the HLP framework, has been presented as a necessary and 'technocratic' measure by successive Syrian governments. These measures should, rather, be considered as a means to transform the general conditions of capital accumulation and empower economic networks linked to the Syrian state, and to achieve security objectives in the case of HLP issues. The war has been taken as an opportunity by Damascus to achieve these objectives. At the same time, governmental policies have failed to tackle the growing socio-economic problems faced by the vast majority of the population, while favouring instead a privileged and elite minority connected to the Assad's rule. Socio-economic policies are likely to exacerbate social, economic and regional inequalities throughout the country. The continuous decline in wages as a share of the national income with the concomitant rise in profits and rents illustrate this trend.

Syria's economy is therefore characterized by a series of deficiencies and limitations ranging from destructions caused by the war and their impacts on the different economic sectors to the government's policies reinforcing socio-economic inequalities in the country and the concentration of wealth and power within the presidential palace.

Conclusion

The lack of stability and the deep depreciation of the SYP reflect the more general and structural destruction of the Syrian economy. Its productive sectors have been annihilated and its main sources of revenue have been reduced significantly; see for instance the oil and tourist sectors, which brought significant amounts of foreign currency to the country before 2011. The prolonged war and sanctions also prevent any potential large-scale FDI in the country. The Lebanese financial crisis since October 2019 and the effects of the global pandemic since early 2020 have reinforced all these economic problems and shortcomings.

The economic policy of the Syrian government is tied to the patrimonial nature of the Assad's rule, something which was strengthened during the war. This will have evident consequences on the socio-economic and societal structures of the country. In recent years, this approach has fostered overdevelopment of the trade and services sector and has fuelled various forms of speculative investment, especially in real estate. This has been accompanied by a rentier-style management of resources (including non-natural resources) and corruption. The Syrian economy has been transformed into a quasi-exclusively consumption one. At the same time, smuggling and criminal activities have increased considerably in the past decade involving businessmen and personalities connected to the presidential palace. These policies reflect the significant political and economic influence of business networks close to the inner circles of the government, and are mostly active in the trade and smuggling, real estate and service sectors.

The economic and commercial interests of these new players often contrast with the possibility of revitalizing the productive sectors of the economy, particularly agriculture and manufacturing, which suffered massively from war and destruction. Trade, especially imports, have become a major source of lucrative commercial business in the country due to the very low economic output, the state's lack of investment and investment incentives in productive sectors, and the need for specific products such as food, pharmaceuticals and petroleum derivatives. Traders affiliated with the state have formed monopolies in certain products from the import trade, while they also very often developed smuggling markets. This process had already started in the early 2000s with the liberalization of the Syrian market, but traders have significantly increased their domination of the Syrian economy in these past few years, at great expense to manufacturers.

This has been accompanied by Syria's increased economic isolation as the country suffers from important sanctions, especially with the US Caesar Act, preventing or at least making significant foreign investments in the country difficult. In this context, no major policy changes are to be expected from the new US administration and therefore the pressure on Syria will most probably remain in the next years. Russia and Iran lack the financial and economic capacities for investing massively in Syria in order to boost national production and reconstruction.

An economic recovery is difficult to imagine in the near-mid-future. On the contrary, what is being witnessed is the further weakening and underdevelopment of productive sectors, the further impoverishment of large sectors of society, and massive rates of unemployment and underemployment. All this is associated with extremely high rates of migration among young graduates and a lack of work opportunities for former and/or current fighters and militiamen. This has resulted in increasing frustration among the Syrian population, which have come out in criticisms expressed on social media and small protests against the continuous deterioration of the country's economy and government policies.

However, these signs of dissent and criticisms do not automatically transform into political opportunities, especially after more than ten years of brutal conflict. They also remain highly rooted in certain regions, with few or no connections between them. The absence of a structured, independent, democratic, and inclusive Syrian political opposition which could appeal to various parts of the general population makes it difficult for the population to coalesce and challenge the state anew on a national scale.

While the Assad's rule survival has been assured, mainly as a result of the support of its foreign allies, the ability of Damascus to maintain a form of passive hegemony over large sectors of the population is far from achieved. This has meant a situation of continuous instability, which will most probably continue into the near future and possibly for a good deal longer.

Notes

1 There are still no statistics for the year 2020.
2 Smuggling activities decreased in the 2000s in some sectors following the liberalization of trade. Moreover, the 2003 US invasion of Iraq ended Syria's direct involvement in various smuggling activities, especially in oil. However, other illegal trafficking and smuggling activities emerged in this period, for example drug and weapon trafficking surged, driven by new routes. Transborder smuggling in Iraq also recovered and intensified in the years following the invasion. In most cases, the Syrian government was not able to control or curb the rise in illicit trafficking. However, unlike post-2011, this type of illegal smuggling was not a threat to national manufacturing production.
3 In contrast, the INGO and NGO services sector has expanded in the past few years in line with the rise of humanitarian needs and the insufficiency of state institutions to assist local populations and IDPs. The increase in this sector has partially played a substituting role to the state in some areas and become a meaningful employer for young individuals.
4 For more information on the effects of sanctions on the Syrian economy: Samir Aita, 'The Unintended Consequences of U.S. and European Unilateral Measures on Syria's Economy and Its Small and Medium Enterprises', *The Carter Center*, December 2020, https://bit.ly/3bSgp5R.

5 The government services include salaries to its employees which never ceased to be paid during the conflict and other expenditures in SYP, including goods and services.
6 Remittances has become without any doubt a crucial element of survival for large sectors of the population in Syria. In the beginning of 2021, a poll conducted by Al-Eqtisadi website in the cities of Damascus, Latakia, Homs and Aleppo estimated that nearly 70 per cent of Syrian families depend for their livelihoods on foreign remittances. The majority of the remittances came from Europe (45 per cent) and Arab countries (43 per cent). The sums transferred from abroad for each family ranged between 200,000 and 500,000 SYP (equivalent to between USD 159 and 398 at the official exchange rate and between USD 66 and 164.5 at the black-market rate at this period in January 2021) for 57 per cent of the respondents (Syria TV, 'Remittances Are a Source of Livelihood for 70% of Syrian Families' (in Arabic), 22 January 2021, http://bit.ly/36cQBht; Harmoon Center for Contemporary Studies, 'Foreign Remittances Are an Essential Source of Life in Syria', 5 February 2021, http://bit.ly/2Lsd1Es.).
7 The governorate is composed of nine districts but is generally divided in four geographical areas: Eastern Ghouta, South-western Ghouta, the Barada River Valley and the mountainous district.
8 The population of Darayya diminished from a population of between 80,000 and 250,000 prior 2011 to an estimated remaining of between 2,500 and 4,000 in 2016 after suffering a terrible siege. Muadamiyat was not emptied of its population and around 2,500 opposition fighters and draft evaders stayed in the city. Similarly, in Qudsaya situated roughly 10 km north-west of the Syrian capital along the Damascus-Beirut highway, more than 200,000 people remained in the city after local armed opposition forces signed an agreement with the state in October 2016. People, however, wanted for compulsory or reservist military service in the Syrian army were not allowed to leave the town.
9 Daily money transfers via Lebanon were estimated at approximately USD 4 million according to *al-Watan* newspaper in 2020. Ali Aga, 'Kinan: Syrian-Lebanese Committees to Reduce the Negative Effects of Lebanese Crisis on Syrian Economy' (in Arabic), *al-Watan*, 9 January 2020, https://bit.ly/37mL0EN.
10 The monthly minimum cost of living for a family of five in Damascus in September 2021 was about SYP 1,154,800 (equivalent to USD 460 at the official exchange rate at this period). Kassioun, 'SYP 1.8 Million Average Household Cost of Living in September 2021' (in Arabic), 19 September 2021, https://bit.ly/3lGxsvj.
11 The Iranian government has, for example, continued to supply oil to Syria at different periods since. The oil imported from Iran is not paid by the Syrian authorities and represents an important source of cash flow as it is sold on the local market.
12 In Saudi Arabia, for example, PPPs have become a fundamental element of the economic and political strategy promoted by Prince Mohammad Bin Salman in the 2020 National Transformation Program.
13 In 2020, the deposits in private banks did not exceed 35 per cent of all deposits, the majority of which remained in state-owned banks, particularly the Commercial Bank of Syria (CBS).
14 Investments in electricity infrastructure, for example, were needed to attract private investments and reduce the cost of business operations.
15 Fares Shehabi, former MP and head of the Aleppo Chamber of Industry, in a session in Parliament in October 2018, called for a deepening of the PPP process in the public industrial sector to expand investment opportunities for the private sector.

16 Only a handful of contracts on such projects have been concluded since 2016, including two with Stroytransgaz, a Russian engineering and contracting company, for the management of the Tartous Port and the General Fertilisers Company.
17 In the fall of 2016, the Damascus Cham Private Stock Company was created with a capital of SYP 60 billion, or approximately USD 120 million at the time (based on the exchange rate in 2016) and was fully owned by the governorate of Damascus. The holding is responsible for carrying out the construction of Marota City.
18 The reconstruction plan in Homs focused on three most damaged districts of the city – Baba Amr, Sultanieh and Jobar – and committed to rebuilding 465 buildings, able to house 75,000 people, at a cost of USD 4 billion. The new urbanism plan took its inspiration from the 'Homs Dream' project announced in 2007 by the former governor of Homs, Muhammad Iyad Ghazal. He planned at that time, the destruction of parts of downtown to build more modern buildings and skyscrapers.
19 The first tower in the Marota City construction project, tower 'Delta H47', has been completed in November 2021.
20 According to a study published in 2017, 82 per cent of the people who died in the Syrian war were men, the majority of whom were of working age. In addition, 1.2 million men were disabled or injured as a result of the war, making it difficult for them to return to the labour force. 'The Repercussions of the Crisis/War on the Reality of Syrian Women' (in Arabic), *Damascus Centre for Research and Studies*, May 2017, https://bit.ly/37zSkwW.

Bibliography

Aita, Samir (2020). 'The Unintended Consequences of U.S. and European Unilateral Measures on Syria's Economy and Its Small and Medium Enterprises'. *The Carter Center*. December. https://bit.ly/3bSgp5R (accessed 24 May 2022).

Aga, Ali (2020). 'Kinan: Syrian-Lebanese Committees to Reduce the Negative Effects of Lebanese Crisis on Syrian Economy'. *al-Watan*. 9 January. https://bit.ly/37mL0EN (accessed 24 May 2022).

Daher, Joseph (2019). *The Deep Roots of the Depreciation of the Syrian Pound*. Research Project Report. 16 December. Florence: European University Institute, Middle East Directions, Wartime and Post-Conflict in Syria.. https://bit.ly/35reYq5 (accessed 24 May 2022).

Daher, Joseph (2021). *The Private Banking Sector in Syria: Between Survival and Opportunity*. Research Project Report. 28 May. Florence: European University Institute, Middle East Directions, Wartime and Post-Conflict in Syria. https://bit.ly/367uU1Z (accessed 24 May 2022).

Daher, Joseph (2021). *Cuts to Oil Derivative Subsidies in Syria: Consequences for Syria*. Research Project Report. 18 October. Florence: European University Institute, Middle East Directions, Wartime and Post-Conflict in Syria. https://bit.ly/3j7YGKQ (accessed 24 May 2022).

Damascus Centre for Research and Studies (2017). 'The Repercussions of the Crisis/War on the Reality of Syrian Women' (in Arabic). Damascus Centre for Research and Studies. https://bit.ly/37zSkwW (accessed 24 May 2022).

Economy2Day (2019). 'Industrialist Wishes the Government to Support Industrialists with the Prices of Oil Derivatives' (in Arabic). *Economy2Day*. 9 February. https://bit.ly/2VX7rKl (accessed 24 May 2022).

Ferrier, Myriam (2020). 'Rebuilding the City of Aleppo: Do the Syrian Authorities Have a Plan?'. *Middle East Directions Programme* (European University Institute. Florence, Italy, European University Institute). 19 March. https://bit.ly/341VBo1 (accessed 24 May 2022).

Financial Tracking Service (2021). 'Syrian Arab Republic'. 4 June. https://bit.ly/3cjN6ZD (accessed 24 May 2022).

Ghanem, Hana (2021). 'Government Report: 34 Public Companies Are Operating Out of 103 Companies … 50 Thousand Private Companies Have Stopped Production Out of 130 Thousand Facilities' (in Arabic). *Al-Watan*. 2 June. https://bit.ly/3vMe0RC (accessed 24 May 2022).

Hanieh, Adam (2018). *Money, Markets, and Monarchies: The Gulf Cooperation Council and the Political Economy of the Contemporary Middle East*. Cambridge: Cambridge University Press.

Harmoon Center for Contemporary Studies (2021). 'Foreign Remittances Are an Essential Source of Life in Syria'. *Harmoon Center*. 5 February. http://bit.ly/2Lsd1Es (accessed 24 May 2022).

Hubbard, Ben, and Saad, Hwaida (2021). 'On Syria's Ruins, a Drug Empire Flourishes'. *New York Times*. 5 December. https://nyti.ms/3ot2WHX (accessed 28 May 2022).

The International Labour Organization (ILO) (2010). 'Gender, Employment and the Informal Economy in Syria'. *ILO*. 1 June. https://bit.ly/2Ib958X (accessed 24 May 2022).

Kassioun (2020). 'Kassioun Editorial 971: Increasing Wages is a Necessity … Humanitarian and National' (in Arabic). *Kassioun*. 21 June. https://bit.ly/2NqIjJ6 (accessed 20 May 2022).

Kassioun (2021). 'SYP 1.8 Million Average Household Cost of Living in September 2021' (in Arabic). *Kassioun*. 19 September https://bit.ly/3lGxsvj (accessed 20 May 2022).

Al-Khabar (2019). 'Jaramana Residents Complain about the Small Number of Gas Cylinders Distributed … and the Municipality: The Situation in the City is Dire' (in Arabic). *Al-Khabar*. 11 December. https://bit.ly/2Vn8vIc (accessed 20 May 2022).

al-Lababidi, Mahmoud (2019). 'Damascus Businessmen: The Phantoms of Marota City'. *Middle East Directions Programme*. (European University Institute. Florence, Italy, European University Institute). April. https://bit.ly/37mlUIi (accessed 17 May 2022).

Mahfouz, Ramez (2020). 'Kishore to Al-Watan: The Jordanian Authorities Have Not Allowed Entry of Syrian Trucks Stranded in Egypt Until Now….' (in Arabic). *al-Watan*. 25 November. http://bit.ly/3p5KbIf (accessed 20 May 2022).

Mehchy, Zaki (2020). 'On the Edge of Starvation: New Alarming Consumer Price Index Estimates for Syria'. *London School of Economy*. 26 May. https://bit.ly/2Y2rjh7 (accessed 17 May 2022).

Sabbagh, Hazem (2016). 'President al-Assad Issues Law on Public-Private Partnership'. SANA. 10 January. https://bit.ly/2TQx0gk (accessed 17 May 2022).

Shirub, Rasha (2020). 'Corona Shock … and Private Sector Workers' (in Arabic). General Federation of Trade Unions Labour Observatory for Research and Studies. 2 April. https://bit.ly/2YOUBQK>(accessed 17 May 2022).

The Syrian Center for Policy Research (SCPR) (2020). 'Justice to Transcend Conflict'. SCPR. 27 May. https://bit.ly/3dA3iEI (accessed 13 May 2022).

The Syria Report (2018). 'State-Owned Companies Report Manpower Shortages'. The Syria Report. 16 October. https://bit.ly/3fCxAHH (accessed 20 May 2022).
The Syria Report (2019). 'New Data Highlights Massive Drop in Syrian Workforce'. The Syria Report. 27 February. https://bit.ly/34SdYLt (accessed 17 May 2022).
The Syria Report (2021). 'Fuel Shortages Intensify as Iranian Oil Supply Disrupted'. The Syria Report. 7 April. https://bit.ly/3oGvDBJ (accessed 19 May 2022).
Syria TV (2021). 'Remittances Are a Source of Livelihood for 70% of Syrian Families' (in Arabic). Syria TV. 22 January. http://bit.ly/36cQBht (accessed 17 May 2022).
Tishreen (2019). 'Regime Government Amends Private Sector Labour Law'. *The Syrian Observer*. 13 March. https://bit.ly/2N326Ov (accessed 20 May 2022).
Urban Analysis Network (2019). 'Aleppo City Profile' (43–5). Urban Analysis Network. https://bit.ly/3c41S4a (accessed 20 May 2022).
World Bank (2020). 'The Mobility of Displaced Syrians: An Economic and Social Analysis'. World Bank. 6 February. https://bit.ly/2TO2BjP (accessed 20 May 2022).

Chapter 9

THE SHADOW ECONOMY OF THE SHABBIHA NETWORKS IN SYRIA

Ali Aljasem

On 3 October 2021, the Chairman of Chambers of Industry in Syria, Faris al-Shehabi, appeared on the Syrian official news channel *Alikhbaria al-Suria* to express his discontent with the unprecedented level of unlawful taxation and levies on goods (Syria Alikhbaria 2021). Al-Shehabi explained that royalties and tariffs (*atawat*) were levied from industrialists through official and unofficial checkpoints that oversaw the movement of goods and cargoes. He went on to describe how '[Checkpoints] stop people and ask for rations of goods and sums of money without providing official invoices or identifying their official affiliation to government bodies' (Syria Alikhbaria 2021). Al-Shehabi's tirade did not disclose names of suspected government branches or personnel involved in such activities even when directly inquired by the interlocutor. Such activities, often labelled as corrupt, are not new to Syria. In fact, informal and predatory economic activities are intimately connected to the Assad rule's most trusted military cronies (AlDassouky 2020). During the Syrian conflict, Elite Forces, such as the Fourth Division under the official leadership of Maher al-Assad, the youngest brother of Bashar al-Assad, accumulated an unprecedented level of capital (AlDassouky 2020).

Parallel to the increased significance of informal economic activities of the Assad rule during the Syrian conflict, there have been increased measures aiming to formalize pro-government security actors. On 5 August 2013, Law No. 55 authorized private security companies to register and operate officially in Syria. Thereafter, there was an increase in security companies operating in government-controlled areas. The Assad rule formalized its outsourcing of security functions to private companies by having them operate under the supervision of the Ministry of Interior and report to the National Security Bureau (Syrian Parliament 2013). This outsourcing of security and military operations has multiple functions. First, private security companies absorb younger Syrians avoiding mandatory military conscription thus keeping them within the government security apparatus. Second, the outsourcing of security functions introduces a greater measure of visibility and supervision of informal military formations. Lastly, by formalizing such entities, the Assad rule is better able to tap into and co-opt predatory practices of economic extraction which have been sustaining Shabbiha groups without further burdening of state capacities.

This chapter focuses on the Assad rule's efforts of creating alternative financial revenue streams to feed into its war economy through military and paramilitary formations. The main question that the chapter probes to answer is how did the emergence of Shabbiha groups and their financial activities fill an economic gap and contribute to the survival of the Assad rule in Syria? Three specific economic activities are examined: (1) the escorting of goods and people, (2) taxation of goods entering government-controlled areas from other areas of control such as opposition-controlled areas, Syrian Democratic Forces (SDF) zone, or areas under the control of Hay'at Tahrir al-Sham (HTS), and (3) The burgeoning industry of looting and scrapping (*ta'feesh*) which took place after taking control over depopulated areas or areas previously under opposition control. Findings are informed by semi-structured interviews with members of paramilitary groups, businessmen and witnesses, as well as social media posts by individuals involved in said activities. The author's field observations and relevant personal experiences are also integrated. Official documents and legislative decrees pertaining to the operation of paramilitary groups and security companies are examined where relevant and available. The chapter also relies on the available literature journalistic reports on the subject.

Al-Tarfeeq: Goods and people escorting

By the time protests spread by mid-2011, the movement of people and goods became more complicated and challenging. The armed conflict exacerbated this issue even more. With checkpoints being erected at entrances of cities and neighbourhoods, the government heavily relied on 'Popular Committees' (in Syrian colloquial *Shabbiha*) to oversee those checkpoints due to their advantage of having advanced local knowledge (Aljasem 2021b: 96–7). This created an opportunity for Shabbiha members to extract revenues through blackmail and extortion. The composition of these groups was mostly clientelist in the sense that the Shabbiha would impose order and strike in the name of security branches (Mukhabarat) while the latter would turn a blind eye to the economic and extrajudicial activities by the former. In this context, the movement of people and businesses were commodified through those checkpoints and their personnel.

During the period of peaceful anti-government mobilization throughout the years 2011 and 2012, suspicion of involvement in anti-government endeavours was enough for the Shabbiha to arrest, torture and interrogate whomever they deemed a potential threat. Hence, vigilante checkpoints created ideal circumstances for the Shabbiha to extract fortunes from the general population. Family name, place of birth, age and civil registry addresses were also used to subject specific populations to blackmail and arrest.[1] Amongst the most commonly targeted groups, for instance, were university students and young adults commuting between colleges and residential areas.

The Assad rule's priority was to nip the uprising in the bud through excessive use of violence against protestors and the identification of key mobilizers and coordinators of Local Coordination Committees on social media (admins and leaders of *tansiqiyat*). Consequently, arbitrary arrests increased rapidly in places where demonstrations were recurring. In Aleppo City, for example there were four main checkpoints at the key entrances to the city. All public and private transportation was inspected by these checkpoints searching for blacklisted and suspected individuals potentially involved in anti-government activities.[2] Those coming from farther areas like university students or people commuting for work were regularly targeted.

In 2011, the main checkpoints were mostly overseen by Mukhabarat and army conscripts. This meant that residents of a city (say Hama) would pass by a checkpoint guarded by personnel from other cities. Such encounters made the extraction of royalties more convenient as there was no intimacy between the parties of the transaction. The experience of passing through checkpoints inside the cities and from one neighbourhood to another was significantly different. Within cities, ID cards were collected by conscripts but cross-checked with local Shabbiha members who have close knowledge of localities.[3]

The situation started changing by the end of 2011 as the Assad rule started facing increased defections within the security apparatus. This was a two-edged sword. On the one hand, as pointed out by Bashar al-Assad, 'a self-cleaning and filtering process purify[ied] society to become homogeneous' (Syrian Presidency 2017). On the other hand, defections created gaps in capacities of deployments to contentious areas of the country. To fill this void, the Assad rule depended heavily on the mobilization of civilians into armed activism. Civilian recruitment was attached to Mukhabarat agencies through intermediaries (Aljasem 2021a: 4–5). This also allowed the government to deny government responsibility in acts of violence and violations committed by such groups (Alvarez 2006: 1–33). The other advantage of resorting to the Shabbiha as a primary security actor was logistical and associated with its capacities of rapid deployment.

Checkpoints 'investment deals'

Three types of Shabbiha groups appeared on the scene since the 2011 uprisings, each characterized by unique historical trajectories, hierarchical relationships of exchange and sociocultural frames. These groups did not emerge out of nothing. Their historic roots reach back to the government's fostering of 'popular organizations' and Defense Companies (*Saraya al-Difa'*) of Rifaat al-Assad of the 1980s. First, there are groups who were mobilized through tribal and clan networks (communitarianism). Second, a new group emerged that was mobilized through business and informal economic networks (cronyism). Third, the Baath Party and its auxiliary organizations such as the National Union of Syrian Students (NUSS) were mobilized as new security actors with increased capacities and prerogatives. The Assad rule enlisted citizens into these organizations, syndicates and unions like the Baath Vanguard and Youth Organizations which became key intermediaries in the mobilization process (Ismail 2018: 71). These networks were linked together in a protégé system meaning that individuals at each level would be protected by someone in a higher position through a new class of mid-level intermediaries liaising between seniors in the capital and the rank-and-file operatives in the peripheries.

Through networks of trusted acquaintances (*al-ma'aref al-mawthoqa*), Mukhabarat seniors established a system of extracting financial revenues. At the top of these bodies sits the Fourth Division's Security Bureau (*al-maktab al-amny*), established in the 1990s under the leadership of Major General Ghassan Bilal. The Bureau enjoys exceptional powers and authority over businessmen and military officers alike (AlDassouky 2020). After the Russian military intervention in September 2015 to help Assad's forces regain control and break the military deadlock at the time, the Fourth Division transitioned from predominant involvement in military operations into a growing role in economic activities. Indeed, by mid-2017 the Fourth Division has taken over all key internal and international highways by replacing previously established Mukhabarat branches like the Military and Air Force Mukhabarat. The Fourth Division allocated a percentage of checkpoint revenues to these branches as a part of the arrangement in place, thus expanding its influence on clientelist networks (Ismail 2018).

Under the Security Bureau, Ghassan Bilal created the Investment Office overseeing war-related economic activities under the banner of 'military effort support' (*da'm al-majhud al-harby*) (Ismail 2018). The investment activities include, among other things, smuggling of narcotics and people, pillaging of once-under-opposition properties, taxing and escorting of people and goods, and outsourcing of checkpoints manning. When the Fourth Division took over the responsibility of overseeing the checkpoints, the Security Bureau created clear terms of references for those collaborating with it.[4] For key checkpoints at strategic and adjacent locations, the Bureau set clear figures of how much the revenue should be at the end of each day (Alsaady 2015). There are numerous examples of what is called 'the millions checkpoints' in cities like Homs, al-Salamya and al-Zablatani.[5] Arrangements entail that Shabbiha group leaders become in-charge of checkpoints on the condition that an agreed-upon sum of revenue gets paid on rolling basis. For example, the Athria checkpoint on the Hama-Homs crossroad into Aleppo became known as 'the one-million checkpoint'(Akhbar Alaan 2016).[6]

Smuggling of people

Defections and desertion were a recurrent phenomenon until September 2015, when Russia officially intervened in Syria. The Assad rule compensated for shortages in manpower through the military might of its air force and foreign militias such as the Lebanese Hezbollah and others. This military superiority created a margin for the Shabbiha to dedicate their time for extracting financial revenues through checkpoints and the smuggling and escorting of people'.[7] This move was encouraged at the highest levels of senior officials and outsourced to the Fourth Division of Maher al-Assad when shadow illegal economy got 'reregulated then deregulated' (Haddad 2012: 11). Hence, by the time the government started regaining control over territories, it had lost to the opposition; a number of processes and tools like 'reconciliation deals' (*etifakiyaat musalaha*) were introduced to allow people to return to their homes and lands. Almost all those willing to return to their cities and villages, specially those not residing in government-controlled areas, were forced to pay royalties (colloquially dubbed as *alma'lum*) to intermediaries to facilitate their return.[8]

In 2017, Russia, Iran and Turkey agreed in the Kazakh capital, Astana, to cease hostilities on all frontlines, excluding areas of Daesh (Beals 2017). The deal postulated that no actor to the conflict, under the trio guarantors, would initiate any military operations barring deterrence of violations. Moreover, the De-escalation Agreement postulated that the international roads (M4 and M5) would be opened for the movement of civilians and goods. The significant drop of hostilities gave rise to the 'checkpoint economies' which substituted the ubiquitous wartime smuggling of weapons and materials across frontlines.[9] Consequently, opposition groups gained vested interest to maintain the status quo and reinforce their positions. However, the Assad rule, with Russian and Iranian support, continued expanding in de-escalation zones, such as Saraqeb, which opened new chapters of displacement and predatory economic activities (Alsaafin 2020).

Al-Tarseem: Levy fees and royalties

When the government reconquered vast swaths of land from opposition control, it regained the burden of service provision along with territorial control.[10] In light of the scarcity of state capacity and resources, the Assad rule effectively prioritized strategic areas and populations that it deemed crucial for its survival and power consolidation. Meanwhile, official media outlets and TV channels reiterated messages about 'restoring public order and the security for the population (*'awdat al-amn wal aman*)' (Ministry of Interior 2018). Returnees were seen as commodities that could generate revenue specifically for local Shabbiha groups and brokers of reconciliation deals who occupied a leading position in extracting fortunes from people returning to their homes, the arising transportation needs and rehabilitation of economic activities. Returnees often faced accusations of being affiliated with armed groups. Moreover, those who were living in areas under the opposition control had to, and still have to, contribute to the 'war effort (*majhood harby*)'.[11] Two types of transactions flourished after the militarization of the conflict and the restoration of control of areas under the control of Daesh and the FSA. First, royalties (*atawat*) were imposed without interruption since the onset of Shabbiha mobilization. Second, levy fees (*tarseem*) were systematized when frontlines solidified and became stable.[12] It is interesting to note that even after frontlines disappeared, some of those checkpoints, specifically in entrances and exits to big cities, continued to operate.

In a leaked document (Figure 9.1) from the Khanat al-Saan Crossing, multiple stakeholders appear to operate in parallel on checkpoints. The document also

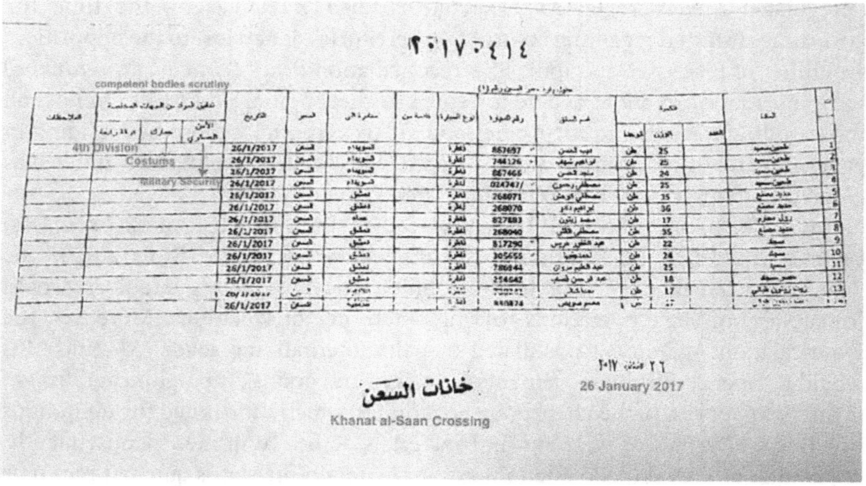

Figure 9.1 Khanat al-Saan checkpoint table showing the details of the vehicles crossing from the north and east parts of Syria into the west and south cities of the country.

shows that the movement details of vehicles, such as city of departure and destination, are also observed and documented. Another column also features the checkpoint identifying the competent bodies on the checkpoint: the Military Security, Customs and the Fourth Division.[13]

There are defined tariffs for all types of movements at checkpoints and border crossings. People's movements have different arrangements depending on destination and means of transport. If someone is travelling from Damascus to Aleppo or Latakia, passengers pay 40,000 Syrian Pounds (USD 10) which is more than half the salary of a government employee (Enab Baladi 2021). In some cases, people share a private taxi fare which is double and sometimes triple the public transport expenses and are taxed more given their perceived status.[14] The same applies for people travelling to Lebanon for work: the transportation costs are excessively high as those passengers are perceived to be enjoying a different status than 'normal people' commuting internally.[15] In an interview with a resident of Aleppo who travelled to Lebanon in August 2021, total payments made on checkpoints reached 200 thousand Syrian Pounds, three times the salary, to make it to the border and then to Lebanon.[16] Those supervising checkpoints instruct public and private transport drivers to include the checkpoint 'fees' (referred to as *alma'lum*) in the total sum of money they ask from travellers. This way, they avoid interaction with civilians and restrict their communication to defined people who become 'keys' (*mafateeh*) in future transactions.[17]

Goods and materials are subject to different processes of taxation. The Fourth Division of Maher al-Assad is the main body in charge of organizing and extracting fees and taxes on official movement of goods. First, through its Investment Office which falls under the Security Bureau, the Fourth Division issues permits for defined customs clearance companies to organize the levy fees (*al-tarseem*) processes.[18] These companies do not necessarily pledge allegiance to the Fourth Division. However, they are obliged to give away a portion of transactions taking place through the Investment Office.[19] The Castle Company for Protection and Security Services, which is owned by Maher al-Assad's associate Kheder Ali Taher (aka Abu Ali Kheder), is the main body overseeing levy fees and smuggling activities in government-controlled areas (Zaman al-Wasl 2020). At the frontline crossing of al-Tayha-al-Sukarrya, which links together the three areas of control under SDF, the Assad government and the FSA, between Menbij and Aleppo, for example, there are defined tariffs on goods. The Customs clearance for a medical truck transporting pharmaceuticals, for instance, can amount to USD 20,000 paid to the al-Areen checkpoint and broker.[20] Although the invoice does not have any reference to the official Customs Directorate in Damascus or Aleppo, the issued document, which acts as a mission order, guarantees that the objects and goods do not get confiscated by the official authorities.[21]

By resorting to such tactics, the Assad rule created a competitive environment for nurturing new warlords. Hence, the Fourth Division and the Mukhabarat branches have turned into 'rentier entities' imposing commissions on all activities. This rent extraction mechanism circulates capital in ways that render the state alienated from economic processes.

Al-Ta'feesh: Looting and plunder of properties

Syrians, pro and against the government alike, have increasingly mocked the terminology the official media outlets use to describe the Assad rule's victory over opposition by replacing the phrase 'liberation and cleansing campaigns' with 'looting campaigns' (*Hamlaat al-Ta'feesh*). It has become a norm for pro-government forces to participate in military operations to plunder houses, belongings and lands of residents previously under the control of the opposition.[22] This process takes two forms. First, houses get ransacked by military formations, mostly Shabbiha, at the end of military operations. Houses get thoroughly scraped off (*Ta'feesh*) of what can be collected and taken, including embedded electricity cables and tiles.[23] The robbed items, thereafter, get transferred to one of the safe neighbourhoods or cities which are close to the frontlines to be resold, sometimes to their original owners, in what has become known as 'al-Sunna Souq' (Orient News 2014). In other circumstances, real estate, farms and agricultural lands of people who were forced to leave their towns to other areas of control or outside the country get confiscated and later on offered for investment to the relatives of the *Shabbiha* groups or collaborators with Mukhabarat officers and members in public auctions (Syrians for Truth and Justice 2021).

When pro-government forces take control of new areas, civilians are not allowed to return to their homes immediately as those areas are zoned off as military zones with the claim that they should be de-mined and are unsafe. Meanwhile, *Shabbiha* groups get houses '[sifted] so they only leave standing walls and a roof behind them'.[24] In most cases in the neighbourhoods surrounding Damascus, the government designated vast areas as uninhabitable and subjected to reconstruction planning where civilians are not allowed to go back. Moreover, policies of appropriating properties are legalized through presidential decrees and laws such as Law No. 10 of 2018, which allows the government to appropriate private properties (Human Rights Watch 2019). The law joined an arsenal of other instruments, including Law No. 3 of 2018, which gives a government committee the power to assess and appoint buildings for rubble removal and demolitions; Decree 63 of the Counterterrorism Law of 2012, which allowed the government to freeze the assets and property of perceived opposition members under counterterrorism Laws; and the predecessor to Law 10, Decree 66 (Human Rights Watch 2019).

Mukhabarat officers together with local militias emerged as brokers and intermediaries playing a significant role in 'reconciliation deals' and the return of civilians in some areas (Araabi and Hilal 2016). This process filters out designated properties of activists or those suspected of collaborating with opposition armed groups.[25] Property marked as belonging to a suspected or designated collaborator is often offered back to the original owner or family members through a broker (Syrian Observatory for Human Rights 2019). In addition to having a financial agreement in place, the person who plans to go back to reclaim their property must secure a criminal record clearance, which would also require the payment of exorbitant sums of money.[26] This applies even to family members of militants or activists who were not necessarily involved in anti-government activism.[27]

In fertile agricultural and farming areas, the government introduced new regulations to appropriate the lands and properties of those displaced. One of these regulations is related to public auctions for investment. After the government regained control over big swaths of northern Hama and southern Idlib countryside, the majority of the population left their homes and fertile agricultural lands to escape potential hostilities and reprisals. After a while, the Security and Military Committee in Hama, reporting to the National Security Bureau, offered the seized lands for rent or investment by the means of public auctions.[28] New committees were set up, comprising local Baath Branch members, the Mukhtar and representatives from the Agriculture Directorate, to count and register lands of perceived opposition affiliates or those displaced or living abroad (Step News Agency 2020).

In line with the same rationale, the General Secretariat of Hama announced through an administrative order that it would hold a public auction for leasing pistachio farms in fourteen recently liberated towns and villages (Syrians for Truth and Justice 2021). The order outlined the terms and conditions for participating in the auction. Every applicant must deposit 70,000 Syrian pounds for every one thousand square meters for a period of one year, renewable for another year with the mutual agreement of both parties to the contract. However, the provincial council is the leasing party not the original owner of the land. After the final bid by the investor, 10 percent must be paid to the provincial council. Moreover, applicants must submit their completed applications including a non-convicted record, a residency registry, a disclaimer, a commitment document and a preliminary deposit (Syria Today 2021). This process has occurred in many newly restored areas where the Mukhabarat officers and the Shabbiha leaders accumulated fortunes through participation in the bidding themselves and later by renting these lands and properties to their original owners.[29] The revenues, as claimed by Baathist officials, will support the 'families of martyrs'.[30]

Concluding remarks

Upon his appointment as deputy prime minister for economic affairs in 2005, the Syrian economist Abdallah al-Dardari made an observation when introducing the 'Social Market Economy' by stating that '[T]oday technocrats are technocrats. Before, technocrats were politicians' (Haddad 2012: 169). After almost fifteen years, emergent business elites seem to be neither technocrats nor politicians; they are warlords.

The American Civil War novelist Margaret Mitchell noted that there are 'two times for making big money, one in the up-building of a country and the other in its destruction. Slow money on the up-building, fast money in the crack-up' (Mitchell 2021: 229). This observation applies to the Syrian case where war profiteers proliferated since 2011. The warlords have militarily contributed to the survival of the Assad rule with the latter implicitly and sometimes explicitly allowing the former to operate and flourish on condition that spoils would be shared amongst power brokers at multiple levels. Military personnel and commanders operated with an informal agreement where commanders instructed conscripts that the 'land is ours, and everything above it is yours for the taking' (Salamah 2018).

In light of the economic sanctions by the United States and the EU, the most recent of which is the Caesar Act, Syrian security figures, businessmen and state institutions bankrolling the Assad rule are under pressure (Stroul 2021). To evade sanctions and facilitate import-export activities, the Assad rule is empowering new faces. In most cases, however, these figures are only means for the circulation and accumulation of wealth for the Assad rule (*The Daily Beast* 2018).

The arrangements and transaction deals between senior leadership in the centre and local actors created a multi-layered heterarchical patronage structures. The involved entities get assimilated through brokers and intermediaries who facilitate transactions between state institutions, the Assad rule and its networks. Therefore, the Assad rule can consolidate its rule through the informal networks with the emergent class of warlords who have significant local might, militarily and economically.

As a final remark, it is worth mentioning that in 2011, the Assad rule did not grant Shabbiha groups the predatory freedoms it has now acquired. Ultimately, military formations operating as para-state entities gained and nurtured their capacities of taxation, their coercive capacity within areas where they proudly boosted to have become the state (*nehne el-dawle, wlak!*) The outsourcing of security functions directly contributed to *substituting* state authority to security actors sometimes acting on behalf of the state, but mostly acting instead of the state. The economic functions of Shabbiha networks and local warlords resuscitate the Assad rule and its capture of the state at the cost of the state as a public institution that continues to serve narrow private interests.

Notes

1. The Syrian Identification Card has extensive details about its holder like, among others, the mother's full name, date and place of birth, civil registry number and place, the full address and the landline telephone number.
2. The government was promoting the idea that there were no anti-government protests in Aleppo. If there were any, they would be incited and organized by people and students from other cities who were paid to protest. Online interview with Khalid Awad (pseudonym), a resident of Aleppo, 25 September 2021.
3. Online interview with Hassan Hassan (pseudonym), a former university student from Aleppo, 20 September 2021.
4. Online interview with Hamid Ali (pseudonym), militia member, 2 October 2021.
5. Ibid.
6. Online interview with Hamid Ali (pseudonym), militia member, 2 October 2021.
7. Online interview with Hamid Ali (pseudonym), militia member, 2 October 2021.
8. Online interview with Ziad Wasel (pseudonym), a returnee who went through a musalaha deal, 25 September 2021.
9. Online interview with Hamid Ali (pseudonym), militia member, 2 October 2021.
10. When the Assad government felt challenged on multiple frontlines, the government fortified its positions in the capital and other key cities in what was dubbed 'useful Syria'. The government purposefully aimed to challenge the opposition, local populations and the international community with the chaos associated with the new actors in providing security and governance as alternative to its rule. Moreover, it was selectively targeting FSA groups while not confronting radical groups like Jabhat al-Nusra and Daesh in the east.
11. Online interview with Abu Imad (pseudonym), head of Air Force Mukhabarat detachment, Aleppo, 28 October 2021.
12. Interview with A Kadi (pseudonym), an expert from Aleppo, Berlin, Germany, 21 October 2021.
13. The checkpoint is known as Khanat al-Saan. Al-Saan is a Syrian town located in the al-Saan sub-district in Salamiyah District, located in the Syrian Desert, fifty kilometres northeast of Salamiyah and northeast of Hama.
14. Online interview with Hamid Ali (pseudonym), militia member, 2 October 2021.
15. Interview with A Kadi (pseudonym]) an expert from Aleppo, Berlin, Germany, 21 October 2021.
16. Interview with A Kadi (pseudonym), an expert from Aleppo, Berlin, Germany, 21 October 2021.
17. Online interview with Hasan Hasan (pseudonym), a resident of a town at a frontline crossing, 23 September 2021.
18. Online interview with Hamid Ali (pseudonym), militia member, 2 October 2021.
19. Online interview with Hamid Ali (pseudonym), militia member, 2 October 2021.
20. Online interview with Shabaan Mohammad (pseudonym), businessman from Menbij, 27 September 2021. Al-Areen is a euphemistic way to avoid the colloquial term

usurpation (*tashleeh*). It has become known that the Fourth Division checkpoints at the entrances of cities are mainly snatching people and extracting levies on materials.
21 Online interview with Hamid Ali (pseudonym), militia member, 2 October 2021. Online interview with Shabaan Mohammad (pseudonym), businessman from Menbij, 27 September 2021.
22 See twitter post with first-hand photos by Asaad Hanna, 'The Process of Assad Army Is: They Attack Area, Escalate as Much as They Can to Push Civilians to Leave Their Houses, They Go inside Looting, They Sell It in Another Areas. Photos for the Market Being Opened after Stealing the Houses in Aleppo Countryside by #SAA Https://T.Co/6Cn9wYNHYR', Tweet, *@AsaadHannaa* (blog), 19 February 2020, https://twitter.com/AsaadHannaa/status/1230115860402053121.
23 Online interview with Abbas Abbas (pseudonym), militia member, 24 August 2021.
24 Online interview with Abbas Abbas (pseudonym), militia member, 24 August 2021.
25 Online interview with Abbas Abbas (pseudonym), militia member, 24 August 2021.
26 Online interview with Ziad Wasel (pseudonym), a returnee who went through a *musalaha* deal, 25 September 2021.
27 Online interview with Hamid Ali (pseudonym), militia member, 2 October 2021. It can happen that people return without any prior arrangements with a guarantee by one of the social figures that they will not be arrested at the checkpoint when they cross into government areas of control. However, in most cases, they get called later to one of the Mukhabarat branches after someone reports them. The negotiations over release start at this point.
28 The Security and Military Committee (*al-Lijna al-Amnia*) is a relatively new security formation introduced as the supreme security reference at the province level. The Committee reports directly to the National Security Bureau (NSB) in Damascus. At the beginning of the uprising, committees met daily to report update to the capital and received orders on how to react to protests and security incidents. Growingly, they gained more influence. Author's personal observations.
29 Online interview with Ziad Wasel (pseudonym), a returnee who went through a muslaha deal, 25 September 2021. Ziad had to re-rent his family's farm through entering a public auction by paying to one of the Mukhabarat officers to get his name on the bidding list.
30 ' شعبة محردة – فرع حماة – Posts | Facebook | Hama Branch – Mherda', accessed 3 November 2021, https://www.facebook.com/baath.maherda/posts/901211393690345.

Bibliography

Akhbar Alaan (2016). "الملیون" المنتشرة في سوریا | حاجز أثري.. أحد حواجز Hajiz Athria. Ahad Hawajiz "Almilyun" Almuntashirat fi Suria'. 22 February. https://www.akhbaralaan.net/news/arab-world/2016/02/22/barrier-archaeological-barrier-million-deployed-syria (accessed 13 October 2021).

AlDassouky, Ayman (2020). 'The Economic Networks of the Fourth Division during the Syrian Conflict'.. *Middle East Directions (MED), Wartime and Post-Conflict in Syria.* 24 January. http://hdl.handle.net/1814/65844 (accessed January 2022).

Aljasem, Ali (2021a). 'Queiq: The River That Streamed Bodies in Aleppo'. *Journal of Genocide Research* 25(1): 1–9.

Aljasem, Ali (2021b). 'In the Shadow of the State: The Rise of Kata'ib al-Baath at Aleppo University after 2011'. *Journal for Perpetrator Research* 3(2): 87–113.

Alsaady, Salam (2015). 'حواجز المليون في سورية | Hawajiz Almilyun fi Suria.' . *The New Arab*. 13 April. https://www.alaraby.co.uk/%D8%AD%D9%88%D8%A7%D8%AC%D8%B2-%D8%A7%D9%84%D9%85%D9%84%D9%8A%D9%88%D9%86-%D9%81%D9%8A-%D8%B3%D9%88%D8%B1%D9%8A%D8%A9 (accessed 13 May 2022).

Alsaafin, Linah (2020). 'Saraqeb Situation Fluid as Syrian Gov't, Rebel Groups Fight On'. . *AlJazeera*. 2 March. https://www.aljazeera.com/news/2020/3/2/saraqeb-situation-fluid-as-syrian-govt-rebel-groups-fight-on (accessed 8 May 2022.).

Alvarez, Alex (2006). 'Militias and Genocide'. *War Crimes, Genocide, and Crimes against Humanity* 2: 1–33.

Araabi, Samer, and Hilal, Leila (2016). 'Berghof Foundation'. https://berghof-foundation.org/library/reconciliation-reward-and-revenge-analyzing-syrian-de-escalation-dynamics-through-local-ceasefire-negotiations (accessed 16 January 2022).

Beals, Emma (2017). 'De-Escalation and Astana'. *Atlantic Council*. 15 September. https://www.atlanticcouncil.org/blogs/syriasource/de-escalation-and-astana/ (accessed 16 February 2022).

Enab Baladi (2021). 'تعرفة ركوب المواصلات في حمص تخرج من يد الحكومة | Taerifat Rukub al-Muasalat fi Hims Takhruj min Yad al-Hukuma.' 25 April. https://www.enabbaladi.net/archives/476294 (accessed 15 Febuary 2022).

Haddad, Bassam (2012). *Business Networks in Syria: The Political Economy of Authoritarian Resilience*. Stanford, CA: Stanford University Press.

Human Rights Watch (2018). 'Q&A: Syria's New Property Law'. 29 May. https://www.hrw.org/news/2018/05/29/qa-syrias-new-property-law (accessed 10 May 2022).

Human Rights Watch (2019). 'Rigging the System: Government Policies Co-Opt Aid and Reconstruction Funding in Syria'. 28 June. https://www.hrw.org/report/2019/06/28/rigging-system/government-policies-co-opt-aid-and-reconstruction-funding-syria (accessed 6 May 2022).

Ismail, Salwa (2018). *The Rule of Violence: Subjectivity, Memory and Government in Syria*. Cambridge: Cambridge University Press.

Mediany, Ahmed (2015). '[Hawajiz Almilyun fi Suria] حواجز المليون في سورية'. *The New Arab*. 13 April. https://www.alaraby.co.uk/%D8%AD%D9%88%D8%A7%D8%AC%D8%B2-%D8%A7%D9%84%D9%85%D9%84%D9%8A%D9%88%D9%86-%D9%81%D9%8A-%D8%B3%D9%88%D8%B1%D9%8A%D8%A9 (accessed October 2021).

Ministry of Interior (2018). 'قوى الأمن الداخلي تدخل جيرود وسط فرحة الأهالي بعودة الأمان بعد إخراج الإرهابيين وعائلاتهم منها | Qiwa Al-'Amn al-Daakhili Tadakhul Jirud Wast Farhat al-Ahali Bi Awdat al-Aman Ba'd Ikhraj al-Irhabiiyn Wa' Ayilatihim M.' 24 April. http://www.syriamoi.gov.sy/portal/site/arabic/index.php?node=551&nid=2022&First=172&Last=1770&CurrentPage=174&mid=&refBack= (accessed 26 October 2021).

Mitchell, Margaret (2021). *Gone with the Wind*. London: Alma Classics.

Orient News (2014). 'جمهورية "سوق السنّة" الديمقراطية | Jumhuriat "Souq Alsunna" Aldemuqratia'. 14 March. https://orient-news.net/ar/news_show/8188 (accessed 1 November 2021).

Orient News (2018). 'النظام يمنح الفرقة الرابعة صلاحيات جديدة في سوريا | Alnizam Yamnah Alfirqa Alrab'a Salahiat Jadida Fi Suria.' 8 January. https://orient-news.net/ar/news_show/144237/0/%D8%A7%D9%84%D9%86%D8%B8%D8%A7%D9%85-%D9%8A%D9%85%D9%86%D8%AD-%D8%A7%D9%84%D9%81%D8%B1%D9%82%D8%A9-%D8%A7%D9%84%D8%B1

%D8%A7%D8%A8%D8%B9%D8%A9-%D8%B5%D9%84%D8%A7%D8%AD%D9%8A%D8%A7%D8%AA-%D8%AC%D8%AF%D9%8A%D8%AF (accessed 13 October 2021).

Salamah, Rafya (2018). 'The Looting Years'. *AlJumhuriya*. 9 August. https://www.aljumhuriya.net/en/content/looting-years.

Step News Agency (2020). 'اص| مناقصة للاستيلاء على محاصيل الزيتون بـ ريف حماة الشمالي ومصادر. | وكالة ستيب الإخبارية | تكشف التفاصيل |khas| Munaqasa lilistila' ala Mahasil Alzaytun bi Reef Hama Alshamali'. 14 October. https://stepagency-sy.net/2020/10/14/%d9%85%d8%ad%d8%a7%d8%b5%d9%8a%d9%84-%d8%a7%d9%84%d8%b2%d9%8a%d8%aa%d9%88%d9%86-%d8%a8%d9%80-%d8%b1%d9%8a%d9%81-%d8%ad%d9%85%d8%a7%d8%a9-%d8%a7%d9%84%d8%b4%d9%85%d8%a7%d9%84%d9%8a/ (accessed 9 May 2022).

Stroul, Dana (2021). 'The Caesar Act Comes into Force (Part 1): Increasing the Assad Regime's Isolation'. *Washington Institute*. 5 November. https://www.washingtoninstitute.org/policy-analysis/caesar-act-comes-force-part-1-increasing-assad-regimes-isolation (accessed 8 May 2022).

Syria Alikhbaria (2021). 'مطالباً بإزالة الحواجز التي تضع الأتاوات على حركة المواد من دون أي ضوابط | Mutalban Bi'iizalat Alhawajiz 'Alati Tada' al'atawat Ala Harakat Almawad Min Dun Ayi Dawabit.' 3 October. https://www.youtube.com/watch?v=Gz341K-FWcE (accessed 4 May 2022).

Syria Today (2021). 'السوري اليوم – النظام يستولي على أراضي المهجرين ويعرضها للبيع في المزاد العلني | Alnizam Yastawli ala Aradi Almuhajarin wa Yariduha Lilibaye' fi Almazad Alalani.' 10 July. https://syrian-today.net/ar/article/1793/%D8%A7%D9%84%D9%86%D8%B8%D8%A7%D9%85-%D9%8A%D8%B3%D8%AA%D9%88%D9%84%D9%8A-%D8%B9%D9%84%D9%89-%D8%A3%D8%B1%D8%A7%D8%B6%D9%8A-%D8%A7%D9%84%D9%85%D9%87%D8%AC%D8%B1%D9%8A%D9%86-%D9%88%D9%8A%D8%B9%D8%B1%D8%B6%D9%87%D8%A (accessed 21 November 2021).

Syrian Observatory for Human Rights (2019). 'مخابرات النظام تبتز المواطنين وتستولي على مزيد من | الممتلكات والأموال في غوطة العاصمة دمشق وترفض مبالغ وصلت لـ 12 ألف دولار Mukhabarat Alnizam Tabtaz Almuatinin wa Tastawli ala Mazid min Aleqarat wal Amwal fi Ghutat Alasima Dimashque wa Tarfud Mabaligh W.' 4 April. https://www.syriahr.com/%D9%85%D8%AE%D8%A7%D8%A8%D8%B1%D8%A7%D8%AA-%D8%A7%D9%84%D9%86%D8%B8%D8%A7%D9%85-%D8%AA%D8%A8%D8%AA%D8%B2-%D8%A7%D9%84%D9%85%D9%88%D8%A7%D8%B7%D9%86%D9%8A%D9%86-%D9%88%D8%AA%D8%B3%D8%AA%D9%88%D9%84/317419/ (accessed 14 May 2022).

Syrian Parliament (2012). 'المرسوم التشريعي 63 لعام 2012 سلطات الضابطة العدلية | Almarsum Altashrie'y 63 Liam 2012 Sulutat Aldaabita Aladlia.' 16 September 2012. http://parliament.gov.sy/arabic/index.php?node=5576&cat=16218& (accessed 1 October 2021).

Syrian Parliament (a) (2012). 'القانون 19 لعام 2012 قانون مكافحة الإرهاب | Alqanun 19 Liam 2012 Qanun Mukafahat Alirhab'. 2 July. http://parliament.gov.sy/arabic/index.php?node=55151&cat=4306 (accessed 5 November 2021).

Syrian Parliament (2013). 'مجلس الشعب السوري. المرسوم التشريعي 55 لعام 2013 منح الترخيص | Almarsum Altashrieiu 55 Lieam 2013 Manah Altarkhis Lisharikat Khadmat Alhimayat Walhirasat Alkhasa.' 8 May. http://www.parliament.gov.sy/arabic/index.php?node=201&nid=4253&ref=tree& (accessed 1 October 2021).

Syrian Parliament (2016). 'المرسوم التشريعي 30 لعام 2013 فرض رسم طابع المجهود الحربي' | Almarsum Altashriei 30 Liam 2013 Fard Rasm Tabe' Almajhud Alharby.' 15 March. http://www.parliament.gov.sy/arabic/index.php?node=5592&nid=16052&First=0&Last=16&CurrentPage=0&mid=&refBack= (accessed 1 October 2021).

Syrian Presidency (2017). 'كلمة الرئيس السوري بشار الأسد في افتتاح مؤتمر الخارجية والمغتربين بدمشق ' | Kalimat Alrayiys Alsuwry Bashar Al-Assad Fi Iftitah Mutamar Alkharijia Wa Almughtaribin Bi Dimashq'. 20 August. https://www.youtube.com/watch?v=4b-BcIPp0eo (accessed 11 May 2022).

Syrians for Truth and Justice (2021). 'Hama: Syrian Government Auctions New Swathes of IDP's Lands'. 27 September. https://stj-sy.org/en/hama-syrian-government-auctions-new-swathes-of-idps-lands/ (accessed 10 May 2022).

The Daily Beast (2018). 'Top Trump Fundraiser Caught Working for Assad Ally'. 28 October. https://www.thedailybeast.com/top-trump-fundraiser-caught-working-for-assad-ally?ref=scroll (accessed 13 May 2022).

Zaman al-Wasl (2020). 'الغوار .. بائع الدجاج الذي حولته حرب الأسد إلى ملياردير يضاهي رامي مخلوف' | Alghuar .. Bayie Aldajaj Alathi Hawalath Harb al-Asad ila Milyardir Yudahi Rami Makhluf.' 23 June. https://www.zamanalwsl.net/news/article/124980/ (accessed 7 May 2022).

Chapter 10

THE STATE FROM TAHRIR SQUARE: UNDERSTANDING PROTESTORS' CONCEPTIONS OF THE IRAQI STATE

Irene Costantini and Yasmin Chilmeran

Introduction

Since October 2019 and until the Covid-19 pandemic imposed a premature end to it, Iraq witnessed an unprecedented wave of mass demonstration concentrated mostly in Baghdad, Nasiriyah, Karbala, Najaf and other cities in the south of the country. Building upon the developments of previous rounds of protest, a young and angry crowd challenged the premiership of Adil Abdul-Mahdi and the entire political system in Iraq with demands ranging from ending corruption, improving the access to and quality of service provision to reforming the country's political system away from the reach of *muhasasa ta'ifia* – a system allocating political and administrative positions based on identity/party loyalties. As the October (Tishreen) movement[1] threatened the tenure of the existing political leadership, the response against it became particularly harsh, resulting in hundreds of deaths and thousands of injuries. Since then, activists and journalists continue to be targeted through both violence by different security actors and laws that limit the space for free speech and free political discussion (Al Hassani 2021).

The significance of the October 2019 protest sparked a small but developing body of policy and academic literature exploring prospects and challenges of social mobilization in a country, like Iraq, marred by political violence and instability. This scholarship provides insights into the slogans and messaging of protestors (Mahmood and Rawai 2019), their organization, including the impact of a generational divide in civil society activism (Halawa 2020; Alshamary 2020) and the threat they pose to the existing political order in the country (Mansour 2020). Other works have highlighted the relationship the October 2019 protest has with previous protest episodes (Jabar 2018; Al-Marashi 2017; Costantini 2021) and have situated the 2019 protests in relation to processes of NGOization and the formation of a 'new civil society' (Ali 2021). Building upon this literature, this chapter examines the Tishreen movement as an instance of state imagination and enactment from the bottom up.

This chapter explores the Tishreen movement from the vantage point of the various articulations that the Iraqi state has taken since 2003. Thus, it intends to advance the literature on social mobilization in Iraq, which has only marginally acknowledged the state-centric trait of the protest. The chapter first outlines the theoretical underpinnings of investigating the Tishreen movement in relation to the development of the post-conflict state in Iraq. Secondly, it briefly presents the events linked to the 2019 protests, which serve as the background to the analysis. The final part explores four dimensions of the Iraqi state: the sectarian/civil state, the security state, the service state and lastly, the gendered state. In each of these sections, we explore how each theme acted as a mobilizing factor in the development of the protest movement in 2019 and how protestors performed their idealized version of the state in protest camps and squares. We draw on content analysis of the protest movement's platforms, as well as desk research and secondary literature, to understand the mobilization of protesters in relation to each of these four dimensions. We argue that the image of the state advanced by the Tishreen movement stands in contradiction to both the development that the Iraqi state took after 2003 and to the view that was enshrined in the international intervention in Iraq.

Iraq as a post-conflict state

The 2003 US-led intervention in Iraq has precipitated a condition of latent instability that has cyclically turned into open violence, notably during the civil war (2006–7) and in the events leading to and following the expansion of the Islamic State (2014–17). In between, the absence of large-scale violence has not meant the restoration of peaceful horizontal (at the societal level) and vertical relations (between society and authority), but rather the mere containment of simmering tensions. In Galtung's (1964) parlance, the absence of violent behaviours (direct violence) in Iraq coexisted with the continuation of violent attitudes (cultural violence) and existing contradictions (structural violence): tensions between and within communities fed by years of exclusionary politics; the continuous and marked inequality pushing people into or at the margin of poverty and strained state–society relations. Almost twenty years after the regime change, the prospects for peace are still meagre as the Iraqi political leadership has not undertaken any substantial steps to address the structural causes of violence in the country and has operated in a reactionary mode when dealing with open violence.

As a result of the factors cited earlier, Iraq has been typically classified as a post-conflict state, together with other cases ranging from Bosnia-Herzegovina to Lebanon and Rwanda. While grouping together different experiences, the category of the 'post-conflict' state is useful inasmuch as it positions countries that have experienced civil conflict along a continuum from war to peace, thus proposing a processual reading of conflict resolution, rather than a binary one that artificially distinguishes between the conditions of peace and war. On the one hand, the post-conflict state stems from the empirical evidence that proves that conflict-affected countries are more prone to a relapse into conflict (Collier and Sambanis 2002) and identifies specific threats associated with countries that have experienced conflict, though such threats are differently identified (Collier, Hoeffler and Söderbom 2008). Moreover, some scholars examining post-conflict contexts also show how the post-conflict state can be a site of heightened insecurity and violence for specific population groups, including women (Davies and True 2017; Meger and Sachseder 2020; Meintjes, Pillay and Turshen 2002). On the other hand, the label post-conflict 'usually describes a predicament in which violent social conflict changes its form and intensity, perhaps becoming more amenable to internationally sponsored reconstruction and reform efforts' (Cramer and Goodhand 2002: 886). The risk associated with post-conflict becoming a condition for international intervention is instead a teleological reading explaining a transition as a function of its (desired) result, usually associated with Western forms of statehood and liberal democratic political system.

Especially when applied to the state, the 'post-conflict' label often goes in parallel with the search for those marks left by international interventions. In countries that have seen various forms of international interventions for conflict management and resolution, the 'post-conflict' condition is highly influenced by international paradigms, policies and practices of intervention. The post-conflict state is therefore one that sees multiple transition processes, some of which are informed by international paradigms that have so far responded to the liberal peace paradigm. The literature analysing such phenomena has come to the widely shared conclusion that the result of such multiple transitional processes, influenced by endogenous and exogenous dynamics, is once again an ambiguous condition, resulting in an 'empty state', one that is built in forms, but not in practice, and is dependent on external support (Richmond 2014) or an internationalized state that is 'neither built nor formed' (Heathershaw 2012: 252).

A way to understand such a condition is to look at the encounter between statebuilding, as 'the instruments and underlying worldviews underpinning intervention in conflict-affected countries at the centre of which there is a formal, Weberian and neoliberal notion of the state' and state formation, 'a dynamic process involving a struggle for affirming state authority' (Costantini 2018: 13; de Guevara 2012; Richmond 2014). The result of such an encounter in the context of Iraq is a state that, while formally adhering to some of the precepts of the liberal state, continues to manifest modes of organization and operation that defy it. The contradictions that such an encounter generates result in a state that, in the eyes of its citizens, has repeatedly failed to serve them but remains the key referent for expressing their dissent both through pacific means and violent ones.

In such a fluid and ambiguous condition, the post-conflict state is subject to different views and articulations of the state, its functions and what it should look like. While the literature has largely focused on the form of the state postulated by international actors through statebuilding interventions (Paris and Sisk 2009; de Guevara 2012), this paper takes a bottom-up approach to investigate how the state is perceived by the population and how they present alternatives to it. Going beyond a formal understanding of the state that treats it as a unitary entity distinct from society (Mitchell 1991), this essay is instead interested in capturing how the Iraqi state penetrates society through practices and representations reproducing itself in the daily lives of ordinary citizens (Sharma and Gupta 2006). Taking a bottom-up approach enables us to see how people encounter and experience the state and, in reaction to such experience, deploy alternative views of it.

The 2019 Protests in Iraq and the state

Iraq is no stranger to social mobilization, and since 2003 has been the site of a variety of protest events that aimed to influence the broader statebuilding project as well as specific aspects of the post-2003 political order (Issa 2015; Ali 2021; Zangana 2013). The Tishreen movement began in October 2019 but the factors driving its mobilization had been developing in preceding years, as protests began around 2011 and became more frequent from 2015. These protests, and the 2019 protests that followed, challenged the state, its capacity to represent the people, to provide them with security and with an environment for sustainable development. It identifies the current political leadership as being responsible for 'failing to build state institutions' (Jabar 2018: 7).

The Tishreen movement began as a mobilization of young Iraqi university graduates who assembled near several ministries in Baghdad, protesting a lack of employment opportunities despite their education. As protests were broken up by security forces, this mobilization swelled and grew further in reaction to the government's decision to demote Lieutenant General Abdul Wahab al-Saedi, a respected commander of the Counter-Terrorism Service. Protest camps began to appear in public squares across a number of cities in the southern governorates of Iraq, including Basra, Nasiriyah, Najaf, Karbala and other centres. At their inception, the protests focused on issues of poor governance, lack of access to services (like water or electricity), unemployment and corruption – issues that also triggered previous rounds of protests. As demands and platforms developed, the protest camps became centres of organization, debate and re-envisioning what the Iraqi state could look like, its obligations to its citizens, a critique of the ruling elite and their corruption and a call for a more unified Iraqi identity, rather than one based on sectarian divisions.

The Tishreen movement marks a specific development in social mobilization in Iraq. Compared to previous rounds of protests, the majority of protestors in the Tishreen movement were younger, often unemployed and not politically affiliated (Mansour 2020), though they were largely young Shia Iraqis. They constitute a generation who has no experience of the previous regime and who grew up witnessing the gap between the expectations raised by the post-2003 transition and its (meagre) accomplishment. The overwhelming push of this younger group is what surprised not only politicians but also activists with longer experience in protests. Among them, young women joined the protests as citizens and made broad claims to their rights as Iraqis, rather than joining based on feminist grounds or a specific women's platform.

The protest camps in some ways set up territories, and this was especially visible in Baghdad's Tahrir Square, which was turned into a makeshift city with tents where protesters camped out for months, as well as tents devoted to specific activities or organizations, where workshops, meetings and other gatherings were being held. Within this camp, protesters developed both services like food distribution, cleaning, city beautification projects and healthcare units as well as spaces of education and communication, including the founding of a newspaper called Tuk-Tuk,[2] makeshift libraries or book stands and a radio channel. As one report described it, the atmosphere in Baghdad's Tahrir Square was 'festive' (International Crisis Group 2021), particularly in the early months, when the square was 'transformed into inclusive spaces ruled and managed by the population' (Ali 2019).

The following sections thus explore specific articulation of protest demands and platforms, and interpret them as articulations of an imagined state, or demands made of the state, by protesters. The reason we discuss statebuilding in such a central way in relation to the protest movements is twofold. First, accounts of the 2019 protest movement have consistently noted the state-like character and function of the protest, calling it, among other things, a 'proto-state' (Barbarani 2019) or a 'mini-state' (Aboulenein and Jalabi 2019). In such state-like spaces, demonstrators provided security, health services, food, shelter, education and even issued fake identity cards within a specific 'territory' contained in the protest squares. While certainly not the first case of social mobilization, 'the Tishreen uprising differs from protests in previous years in that months of sit-ins and demonstrations created a specific sense of belonging among activists, as well as a broad vision of what the state and nation should be and do' (International Crisis Group 2021: 5).

Secondly, protest demands highlight a specific set of imagined ideals of what the Iraqi state should provide. In the streets and squares of Baghdad, the people invoked the state (*al-dawla*) and oriented their demands towards it, thus making it a still relevant locus of expectations and aspirations. At the same time, through daily practices and representations they expressed a view of the state that is at odds with both its development since 2003 and the model that has informed the international intervention. These aspects are explored below through each section or thematic iteration of the Iraqi state in the imaginaries of the protesters. As we argue throughout this chapter, these themes articulate a variety of failures of the post-2003 Iraqi state, and ideals about what the road forward needs to be.

The security state

The protest movement of October 2019 faced unprecedented violence. As already mentioned, the government's response to people's demands has in fact been extremely violent. The crackdown has seen security forces crashing the protest by employing water cannons, live rounds and rubber bullets, causing a high number of casualties, as a result of which UNAMI/OHCHR records the death of at least 487 protesters with 7,715 injured from 1 October 2019 to 30 April 2020 (UNAMI and OHCHR 2020: 14). In the crackdown against the protest, non-official armed personnel (militias) have been heavily involved in various forms, from direct attacks through snipers to targeted assassination of key activists in the country. However, UNAMI and OHCHR attribute 74 per cent of the casualties to official security forces (UNAMI and OHCHR 2020: 14). While not all security apparatuses had an adversary relation with the protestors, the Federal Police, the Emergency Response Division and the Facilities Protection Service, all of them responding to the Ministry of Interior have been reportedly involved, albeit this varies from site to site.

Demonstrators' experience of the security state during the 2019 protests reflects the evolution of the security apparatus of the Iraqi state since 2003: the multiplicity of security actors involved; the unpredictability of the response; the absence of accountability to the people and the difficulty of separating state from non-state actors. Faced with the instability caused first by the regime change and the occupation by international forces, and later with a morphing insurgency against the occupation forces as well as the newly created political system in Iraq, the security apparatus in Iraq has developed, through large financial and political investments from external actors, foremost the United States, in the eyes of ordinary Iraqis as a main source of simultaneous security and insecurity. Death squads using security uniforms or having infiltrated the official apparatus of the state were among those responsible for the sectarian violence that peaked in 2005–7. The *Hashd al-Shaabi*, the popular mobilization forces that were employed to face the threat of the Islamic State since 2014 have been saluted by the population as heroes for their contributions against the threat posed by the terrorist organization while later becoming a threat themselves for part of the population.

In Tahrir Square, similar patterns of security/insecurity emerged. Muqtada al-Sadr's 'Blu Hats', yet another development of the cleric's security arm, charged themselves (but were not mandated by the Tishreen movement) with policing and protecting the square. The square, thus, reproduced a familiar trait of the state's security function in society: a voluntary-based non-state sanctioned security arrangement that comfortably moves in between the state/official and the non-state/unofficial realms, lacking accountability to the people and eventually turning into a threat to the protestors. In late February, after the repositioning of Muqtada al-Sadr towards the establishment and away from the protest, the 'Blu Hats' were involved in the repression of the Tishreen movement.

Patterns of security/insecurity also determined the geography of the Tishreen movement. While Tahrir Square and its vicinity gained some security guarantees, other areas were deliberately left as spaces of violence, subject to clashes between the protestors and mostly, non-state armed groups. More generally, in such security-determined areas, the infrastructure of the checkpoints throughout the country and particularly in Baghdad mirrors the ambiguous position of the security state in people's experiences, being one manifest way through which people encounter the security state in their daily lives. As recounted in the work of Martinez and Sirri (2020: 859), checkpoints and people's experience of them defy the binary interpretation of the checkpoint as an infrastructure intended to 'tame exceptional insecurity and establish normalcy' becoming instead both 'targets and facilitators of violence'. Throughout their history, urban checkpoints not only responded to different security threats and strategies but also contributed to altering the urban space as well as people's daily lives.

The checkpoint has been reproduced also in the organization of the protest movement in Tahrir Square. As the protest movement could not rely on the protection of the security apparatus, this became another field of self-organization. The practice of *taftish* (search), a common experience in the Iraqi public, has been reproduced by the demonstrators who established checkpoints at the entrance of the square to ensure that no weapons were carried inside the space inhabited by the protestors. The practice of the checkpoints was thus not contested by the demonstrators who recognized the necessity to police the protest space but was imbued with new meanings in order to create and preserve a space of non-violence inside the city. By reappropriating this security practice, people manning checkpoints restored the importance of the widely acclaimed but virtually never achieved issue of accountability to the people.

The protest square, with its many facets, mimicked some of the security mechanisms with which Iraqis have become accustomed throughout the years, such as the voluntary-based organization of security or the practice of *taftish*. They did so while upholding an alternative view of the security state – one that through security practices grants a space of peace (Tahrir Square) and one that is accountable to the people. This stands in contrast to the limits of the security advanced by the Iraqi state: on the one hand, after the US invasion, which never managed to privilege human security over externally oriented security objectives, and on the other hand, under Iraqi political elites, who moulded the security apparatus to serve parochial interests.

Demands for protection coming from the protest movement were ultimately directed to the state, demonstrating yet again its centrality in the formulation of demands from the bottom-up. As recounted by the ICG (2021: 22–3), in coincidence with the one-year anniversary of the 2019 protest, some activists presented a paper to the government to ensure peaceful demonstrations. In it, they called for a greater involvement of the Ministry of Defence and of the Counter-Terrorism Service (responding directly to the prime minister) to limit the power of the Ministry of Interior, perceived by many as too close to non-official armed forces involved in the crackdown, the banning of all non-official forces acting as self-proclaimed protection forces and the issuing of badges to the participants. Although the proposal was rejected, it nonetheless shows the demonstrators' quest for the state's role in ensuring security to the people.

The sectarian/civil state

In continuation with the 2015–16 protest movement, the defining feature of the 2019 protest has been the rejection of the *muhasasa ta'ifia* – a system allocating political and administrative positions based on identity/party loyalties – and of the main (mostly religious) political parties upholding it (Jabar 2018; Hasan

2019; Dodge and Mansour 2020). The *muhasasa ta'ifia* has been the principle dictating the evolution of Iraq as a post-conflict state since 2003, enshrined in both international plans for transition and in the Iraqi political leadership's struggle for domination. A distortion of power-sharing arrangements as a way to frame political contestation in the country and organize its governance, *muhasasa ta'ifia* has taken hold of formal rules and institutions, from the Iraqi constitution to the electoral law to preserve power in the existing political leadership and counter any attempt at reforming it. In the everyday lives of the Iraqi people, *muhasasa ta'ifia* is primarily experienced through the pervasiveness of corruption that frames people's encounters with the state.

Demonstrators' representation of the protest movement as an alternative to *muhasasa ta'ifia* was vehiculated through two main notions: the search for a homeland (*Nreed al-Watan*) and for a civil state (*al-dawla al-maddaniya*). The Iraqi flag, the visual representation of the *al-Watan* – the geopolitical locus of national identity, prevailed over other identity signifiers in Tahrir Square, without however substituting them. Through this notion, the protest's movement expressed the search for a common belonging in the Iraqi citizenship. Calls for a civil state, instead, are not related to a sense of (national) belonging, but rather to the functioning of the state. *Al-dawla al-maddaniya* is a purposefully vague representation that can accommodate multiple views of the state: one that is neither religious/sectarian nor secular, national but not nationalist, or aligned to Western-based concepts such as the rule of law (Dawood 2016). The term has indeed been used in several of the MENA contexts that experienced the 2010–11 uprisings (Lavie 2017), yet it still escapes a clear formulation to remain open to a plurality of voices. As Ali (2021) argues, *al-dawla al-maddaniya* is not only a 'post-Islamic' call, but it also demands freedom in representation as well as equality in redistribution.

The movement's employment of inclusionary framing is not only evident in the protest's representation, but also in their practices, for instance in the way the movement organized through space. Tents belonging to and expressing different voices – with some of them linked to political parties, others to civil society organizations or religious institutions – occupied the space of Tahrir Square (International Crisis Group 2021: 5). The floors of the Turkish Restaurant – an abandoned building at the core of Tahrir Square occupied by the demonstrators – were also managed by different groups taking part in the protests (Alshamary 2020: 10). The explosive spontaneity of the 2019 protest was mitigated by the organizational capacity of the various coordination committees (*tansiqiyat*), which had also operated in previous mobilization events (Costantini 2021: 9).

Despite being arguably an obstacle to its effectiveness, the protest movement safeguarded this plurality of voices, leading to a political orientation different from the past. From the ranks of the 2015–16 protests, a coalition between the Sadr movement and the civil trend in the country, mostly represented by the Iraqi Communist Party, emerged as representing and leading the protest movement (Robin-D'Cruz 2019) and transforming it into a (successful) political actor in the Iraqi electoral contestation (Mansour 2019). The 2019 protest, instead, refused to elect its own leadership, despite being pressured to do so, fearing that such a move could antagonize some of the participants and expose the movement to co-optation attempts by the established political leadership. Activists engaged with political actors mostly through advising and consulting, avoiding existing political parties, but dealing with the Iraqi presidency and the Iraqi government. The movement, thus, favoured horizontality over verticality, which sometimes has been mistakenly taken as spontaneity.

Although some elements within the protests formed new parties or joined existing political parties or their spin-offs, the protest movement in its plurality did not result in a political actor engaging in the system. Rather, the efforts of the protest movement have been targeted at reforming those same rules of the game that have favoured, or at least not countered the development of the *muhasasa taifia*. Among the 'Road Map to Save Iraq' list of demands, published in the magazine *Tuk-Tuk*, born out of the same protest, stands the reform of the electoral law in view of anticipated elections. Once the protest was successful in obtaining the resignation of Prime Minister Adil Abdul-Mahdi, attention shifted to the electoral law. Among the requests were the abolition of the eighteen provincial electoral districts and to instead have a district for each electoral seat, adopting individual nomination procedures, the lowering of the minimum age of twenty-five for being elected and the introduction of minimum educational attainments to be elected and a reform of the Political Parties Law to reduce financial and bureaucratic barriers to form new parties (al-Jaffal 2021).

The proposed reforms, together with others targeting the constitution, the High Electoral Commission and the law on local election were meant to lower the entry barrier to the political system so that a new and younger generation of activists could be represented and puncture the self-reproducing system of the *muhasasa taifia*. Between the initial draft of the electoral law proposed by President Barham Salih and the one ratified on 5 November 2020, many of the protestors' request were watered down (Jiyad 2021). However, the protest movement's requests were coherent with its own practices of social organization in the square as well as with the representation that it advanced of an alternative model of the state, one that, while preserving a unitary sense of belonging, is nonetheless capable of accommodating a plurality of voices not necessarily expressed in an ethno-sectarian way.

The post-conflict state in Iraq has marginalized the people, ordinary ones, favouring instead views of the state originating internationally and local politicians' appropriation, resistance or adaptation to them. With its heterogeneity, which makes it difficult to frame the 2019 protests as either revolutionary or reformist, demonstrators are claiming new forms of representation through the affirmation of a new subjectivity, the protest movement. The latter stands in opposition to the existing representative structure, which the political system in Iraq has rendered distant and hierarchical. Although consisting of different groups, the 2019 protest constituted a new subject, which is perhaps the most innovative trait of the Iraqi trajectory since the regime change. Rather than assessing their effectiveness, the protest's position is to present an alternative to the prevailing views of the Iraqi state.

The service state

The Iraqi state in its post-2003 iteration was developed as a neoliberal state, at odds with the expectations of protestors, and indeed of a broader Middle East citizenry that sees the state as a provider of security, welfare, employment and services. Poor services and deteriorating hospitals, schools and job markets were key features of life for Iraqi citizens since the sanctions era of the 1990s (al-Jawaheri 2008). However, rather than inverting the trend, the post-2003 era represents the failure of governance and statebuilding systems. This was exacerbated first by an extensive neoliberal agenda in the aftermath of military invasion (Hamourtziadou and Gokay 2020), second by structural factors related to Iraq's political economy (including economic mismanagement and corruption) (Dodge and Mansour 2021) and lastly, due to multiple crises (Costantini 2017; Krishnan and Olivieri 2016). This has resulted in Iraq's poorest surviving on informal and illicit economies (Banwell 2015) as well as the entrenchment of high rates of poverty. All of this is exemplified by a state that fails to deliver services like electricity, housing and clean water for many of its citizens, despite Iraq's status as a middle-income country.

As we highlight through the chapter, the Tishreen protestors have responded to the failures of the state, and in this instance, the failure of the 'service state', in two ways: in reimagining what the state could look like or provide inside protest camps, and in targeting the state itself as the focus of mobilization and a target for their demands. Given how central class issues are for the Tishreen protests, Iraq's political-economy and service failings are a natural and important issue to analyse. It is important to remember that in the lead-up to the protests, unemployment in Iraq had risen to 13 per cent (according to official figures) and was much higher in youth populations (EPIC 2021). Life in Iraq, however, was not only mired in high unemployment rates, but also in increasing private forms of accessing basic services like clean water, electricity and education. In reaction to this, protestors highlighted both what they expect from the Iraqi state as well as how they could enact the very reforms they wanted to see.

Protest squares around Iraq, and in Baghdad's Tahrir Square in particular, saw a clear performance of the proto-service state in the physical presence of protest camps and in the activities that different protestors took on. A wide variety of actors, some formal civil society organizations, others as clusters of actors (like Tuk Tuk drivers), and at times, well-intentioned individuals, took on a variety of coordination roles to deliver services to those who were camping inside the squares. For example, various CSOs arranged workshops, lectures and other educational material to help interested protestors understand the Iraqi constitution, the legal system and other campaigning skills, simulating an education system inside the camps (Al-Shadeedi, Skelton and Ali 2020). Networks of professionals, including doctors and nurses, provided healthcare services to protestors. Others appeared with food, water, washing materials to wash the clothes of protestors who were camping full time in Tahrir Square, all as a contribution to the effort to sustain protest camps and maintain it as a functioning place where life, and political activity, could take place. Volunteers in Tahrir and elsewhere also took on cleaning and beautification projects inside camps and in neighbouring areas, painting murals, collecting rubbish and fixing various things like road markers.

There is another element to this, in which protestors also challenge the sociopolitical developments that have occurred in urban centres in Iraq since 2003: the privatization of secure public spaces in which to socialize and exist in an everyday sense. Security developments, coupled with privatized development of the city, mean that urban space in Iraq is heavily segregated based on class, gender and other issues of access (Ali 2017; Sirri 2021). Omar Sirri's (2021) study clearly illustrates the inequality between beneficiaries of Iraq's post-2003 economic landscape and ordinary Iraqis who navigate the fallout of this, and how this has implications for Baghdad as a place to live. In many ways, the performance of the service state by Tishreen protestors challenges this urban reality, as so much of the camp set-up was about cleaning and beautifying the squares they inhabited. This is perhaps best exemplified by the creation of leisure spaces by Baghdadi protestors, including their building a beach on the banks of the Tigris, directly opposite Baghdad's Green Zone (Omar 2020).

In targeting the Iraqi state itself as the recipient of protest demands and a site of much-needed reform, protestors also articulated their expectations of the service state: one that provides opportunities for employment and one that provides necessary public services to sustain its population. The Tishreen protestors' demands for employment touch on an important and difficult point in the Iraqi state: a tension between the design of the neoliberal statebuilding model and its aims at shrinking the state and expanding the private sector, and the way the Iraqi state has developed since 2003, which maintains a large bureaucracy that funnels funds to specific actors only. There is a paradox in demands made of the government to provide work, in that the state itself has engendered a process in which jobs are given in ways that favour appeasing certain political and security actors, further entrenching corruption. This is true in contexts around Iraq where the oil sector becomes a primary source of employment, like Basra (see Skelton and Saleem 2020), but also true in Baghdad, where some civil servants were both involved in funnelling large amounts of funding to political parties and had a hand in slowing service delivery projects if the projects were not in line with the interests of their party. As a result, ordinary Iraqis were caught between a state that could not provide them with jobs in theory, and a state unwilling or unable to reform itself out of an unemployment and economic crisis in reality.

The gendered state

An under-examined and yet central feature of the protest movements is the commentary these protests provide on the gendered nature of the Iraqi state and Iraqi society at large, as well as how they reveal new insights into the way Iraqi women organize and mobilize. This section therefore explores the gendered state in post-2003 Iraq, as well as what the Tishreen protests represent for women's participation in broad social and political activism in Iraq, by exploring the practical and figurative roles of women inside protest squares, gendered language in slogans and what this means for the imagined Iraqi state projected from the Tishreen camps.

A 'gendered state' refers to the way in which states created specific gender norms around citizenship, belonging and security, and how gender in turn shapes the state itself in many broad and specific ways (see volume edited by Parashar, Tickner and True 2018). In part, it also relates to women's social reproductive roles in society (Chilmeran and Pratt 2019), in which women are considered as playing an important biological and cultural role in reproducing citizens and the nation itself (Yuval-Davis 1997). Gendered forms of citizenship, labour, reproduction and participation have long played a role in the way the Iraqi state organizes itself, presents itself globally and to its own citizens, as well as in the way Iraqi citizens, including women, see themselves relative to the nation. In its post-2003 iteration, the Iraqi state is a site of opportunity for women's participation in certain parameters (with a widening civil society space, and the enshrinement of a 25 per cent parliamentary quota for women in the 2005 constitution). However, the post-2003 state is also one of entrenched insecurity, inequality and alienation for Iraqi women, as previous legal gains (including in the 1959 Personal Status Code) come under renewed threat.

The presence of women in Tishreen's camps represents not only a number of issues that affect women, but also their mobilization as Iraqis. First, young women mobilized not based on feminist/gender demands, but as young Iraqis demanding employment and support from their failing state. This type of platform marks an important shift in the way women's issues are discussed in post-2003 Iraq, and a generational shift away from women's civil society, which has largely focused its efforts on issues related to advocacy of gender-based violence, protecting the personal status codes, participation in political and policy conversations and service delivery. Younger women's mobilization in Tishreen doesn't employ a specifically women's or feminist platform, but rather places the claims of young women as part of a development of new civil society activism that is less professionalized, less linked to the international system of programming and funding and more responsive to a young and dynamic population (of which young women are a part) (Halawa 2020).

The articulation of a specific women's demand, the demand of access to the spaces in protest squares, came later on in the Tishreen movement. A key factor for this development was a statement by Muqtada al-Sadr in February 2020, in which the cleric called into question the morality of those within protest camps. Specifically, he said 'the mixing between genders inside the protests' tents is not acceptable' (Abdelhameed 2020). In response, women mobilized using specific hashtags, slogans and most visibly arranging a women's march on 13 February 2021 across a number of cities that had been the sites of protests in the preceding months. During that particular protest, women took centre stage, but were supported by male protestors too, who at times provided at least a visible security ring.

The specifically gendered hashtag and slogan *banatak ya watan* (We are daughters of the nation) see women claiming a public space in the protest movement that is not only both gendered and yet broad (to claim an active role in Iraqi citizenship and nationhood), but also responds directly to al-Sadr's statements about gender segregation. Similarly, the slogan *sawt al mar'a thawra* claims that the voice of women is a revolution, in direct response to more conservative actors making statements about the impropriety of women raising their voices in public. This poses a challenge to the gendered state that religious authorities project in Iraq and presents an alternative view of the Iraqi public and political space, in which women have a stake and a contribution to make, and feel entitled to a physical and a rhetorical presence in politics. Women's visibility as protestors, as supporters and at times as leaders in person and online represents a specific articulation of a gendered state that is visibly different from Iraq as it is: more open, more accepting of women's political voices and their political presence in public space. While the protest slogans draw on relational identities that appeal to the gender norms already present in Iraqi society (as mothers of martyrs, or as daughters of a nation), there nonetheless is a clear articulation by the young men and women leading these protests of a different gender politics, and a gendered state, that they hope to see.

The Tishreen movement also shows that the following gendered norms underpinned women's participation and link this presence to culturally and historically rooted gendered identities rather than a liberal feminist call to participation: women rhetorically appeared as mothers, as daughters of the nation and as a challenge to religious norms surrounding women's presence in public space. Motherhood as a key political identity is not new in popular mobilization (Mhajne and Whetstone 2018; Richter-Devroe 2018), and it is similarly visible in Iraq's Tishreen protests as one of many ways women were visible, physically and symbolically, in protest squares (see the chapter by Abdelhameed and Alkinani 2023). A key figure in these protests and in previous depictions of womanhood and motherhood in Iraqi culture is the grieving, sacrificing mother or elderly woman *al-hejiyya* (Ali 2018; Al-Ali 2007). In the Tishreen protests, this was embodied by the figure of 'Thanwa', the mother of Safa Al-Saray (Antoon 2019), an Iraqi activist who was killed in the first month of Tishreen protests after being struck in the head with a tear-gas canister (MacDonald 2019). Thanwa herself had died of cancer in the years preceding 2019. After Safa Al-Saray's death, he was mourned as *ibn thanwa* (son of Thanwa), highlighting the significance of the figure of the mother and of mother's sacrifices, in Iraq and in Iraqi culture. Entrenched over the many decades of conflict, sanctions and renewed insecurity after 2003, this figure has been an important one for Iraqis since the 1980s. The motif of the grieving mother remains a part of women's presence in protest movements in Iraq, most recently through the activism of the mother of Ihab al-Wazni, an activist who was assassinated in 2021 (Lkaderi 2021). In appearing in this way, women across multiple generations and roles have taken up space in the Tishreen protests, deploying both traditional identities that allow them to claim a political stake in the Iraqi state and using that identity to challenge more conservative voices, as well as the status quo.

Conclusion

This chapter has taken a bottom-up approach to examining the Tishreen movement as an instance of state imagination and enactment vis-à-vis other articulations of the state that prevailed since 2003. Through space occupation, ways of organizing, daily practices and forms of representation, the Tishreen movement has enacted a view of the state in the domain of security, the economy, political representation and gender relations. The Tishreen movement's imagination and enactment of the state reflect largely the contradictions and failures left, on the one hand, by the international intervention, and on the other hand, by the political project pursued by the existing political elites – contradictions and failures that mark the post-conflict character of the Iraqi state since 2003. However, what is important to note is that while it acts as an alternative to the post-conflict state, it continues to have the state as its main referent.

As we have shown, the imagination and enactment of the state from Tahrir Square follows two directions: first, it tends to reproduce familiar state practices – those that are experienced the most by the people. The organization of security in the square or the gender norms of the mother and the daughter of the nation reflect the ways in which the state has penetrated society, over more than just the last few years. However, while reproducing such familiar state practices, the enactment of the state takes a second direction, that is, it imbues them with novel significance. Thus, the checkpoint manned by the people becomes a tool to guarantee peaceful coexistence in the square and is no longer an instrument of oppression. The formulation of *al-dawla al-madaniyya* replaces sectarianism by proposing an inclusionary, not hierarchical, form of representation. In this simultaneous reproduction and reinterpretation of the state and its envisioned processes, we begin to see a vision for the Iraqi state beyond its post-conflict iteration: where public space is accessible regardless of class, where employment opportunities are within reach for those who want them and where the state functions, as it should, in providing for the needs of Iraqis who exist outside of the elite systems of governance that are currently in place.

Notes

1 We will refer to the protest movement as the Tishreen movement, noting however that it can be referred to by other literature as the October Movement, October Uprising and October Revolution.
2 The tuk-tuk and the tuk-tuk driver became a symbol for the Tishreen protests, which were previously a mode of transport in lower socio-economic neighbourhoods. During the protests, these vehicles were visible as a way to move around the square, between the square and the front line (where protestors would clash with security forces), and as a way to transport wounded protestors to hospitals and medical tents (see Ali 2019).

Bibliography

Abdelhameed, Hadeel (2020). 'The Pink and Purple Protest: Iraqi Women Invert the Gender Game.' 1 April. *Australian Institute of International Affairs*. https://www.internationalaffairs.org.au/australianoutlook/the-pink-and-purple-protest-iraqi-women-invert-the-gender-game/ (accessed 29 May 2022).

Abdelhameed, Hadeel, and Gaith Alkinani. (2023). 'Mothering the Protest: Gender Performativity as a Communication Mechanism in the Iraqi Protest Movement'. In Loubna Hanna and Nahed Eltantawy (eds), *Palgrave Handbook on Gender and Communication in MENA* (87–106) London: Palgrave Macmillan.

Aboulenein, Ahmed, and Jalabi, Raya (2019). 'Iraqis Pour into Streets for Biggest Protest Day since Saddam'. 1 November. *Reuters*. https://www.reuters.com/article/us-iraq-protests-idUSKBN1XB3X5 (accessed 29 May 2022).

Al-Ali, Nadje (2007). *Iraqi Women: Untold Stories from 1948 to the Present*. London: Zed Books.

Al-Hassani, Ruba Ali (2021). 'Storytelling: Restorative Approaches to Post-2003 Iraq Peacebuilding'. *Journal of Intervention and Statebuilding* 15(4) : 510–27.

Al-Jawaheri, Yasmin H (2008). *Women in Iraq: The Gender Impact of International Sanctions*. London: I.B. Taurus.

Al-Marashi, Ibrahim (2017). 'Iraq and the Arab Spring: From Protests to the Rise of ISIS'. In Mark L. Haas and David W. Lesch (eds), *The Arab Spring: Change and Resistance in the Middle East*, Second edition. Boulder, CO: Westview Press.

Ali, Zahra (2017). 'Reflecting on Multiple Fragmentation in a City of Men.'" 6 November. *Jadaliyya*. http://www.jadaliyya.com/Details/34665/Reflecting-on-Multiple-Fragmentations-in-a-City-of-Men (accessed 30 May 2020).

Ali, Zahra (2018). *Women and Gender in Iraq: Between Nation-Building and Fragmentation*. Cambridge: Cambridge University Press.

Ali, Zahra (2019). 'Iraqis Demand a Country'. *Middle East Report* 292(3) (2019) https://merip.org/2019/12/iraqis-demand-a-country/.

Ali, Zahra (2021). 'From Recognition to Redistribution? Protest Movements in Iraq in the Age of "New Civil Society"'. *Journal of Intervention and Statebuilding* 15(4): 1–15. https://doi.org/10.1080/17502977.2021.1886794.

Al-Shadeedi, Hamzeh, Skelton, Mac, and Ali, Zahra (2020). 'Why Iraq's Protesters Won't Go Home: 10 Voices from the Movement'. 3 March. LSE Blogs, IRIS Brief. https://blogs.lse.ac.uk/mec/2020/03/03/why-iraqs-protesters-wont-go-home-10-voices-from-the-movement/ (accessed 30 May 2020).

Alshamary, Marsin (2020). 'Protestors and Civil Society Actors in Iraq: Between Reform and Revolution'. December. IRIS Report. https://auis.edu.krd/iris/frontpage-slider-publications/protestors-and-civil-society-actors-iraq-between-reform-and-revolution (accessed 30 May 2020).

Antoon, Sinan (2019). 'I Will Visit Your Grave When I Go to Iraq'. 16 December. *The New York Times*. https://www.nytimes.com/2019/12/16/opinion/iraq-protests.html (accessed 30 May 2022).

Banwell, Stacy (2015). 'Globalisation Masculinities, Empire Building and Forced Prostitution: A Critical Analysis of the Gendered Impact of the Neoliberal Economic Agenda in Post-Invasion/Occupation Iraq'. *Third World Quarterly* 36(4): 705–22.

Barbarani, Sofia (2019). 'Protesters Say Tahrir Square Is Everything Iraq Is Not'. 12 November. *alJazeera*. https://www.aljazeera.com/news/2019/11/12/protesters-say-tahrir-square-is-everything-iraq-is-not (accessed 30 May 2022).

Chilmeran, Yasmine, and Pratt, Nicola (2019). 'The Geopolitics of Social Reproduction and Depletion: The Case of Iraq and Palestine'. *Social Politics* 26(4): 586–607.
Collier, Paul, Hoeffler, Anke and Söderbom, Måns (2008). 'Post-Conflict Risks'. *Journal of Peace Research* 45(4): 461–78. https://doi.org/10.1177/0022343308091356.
Collier, Paul, and Sambanis, Nicholas (2002). 'Understanding Civil War: A New Agenda'. *Journal of Conflict Resolution* 46(1): 3–12.
Costantini, Irene (2017). 'A Neoliberal Rentier System: New Challenges and Past Economic Trajectories in Iraq'. *International Spectator* 52(1): 61–75.
Costantini, Irene (2018). *Statebuilding in the Middle East and North Africa: The Aftermath of Regime Change*. New York: Routledge Taylor & Francis Group.
Costantini, Irene (2021). 'The Iraqi Protest Movement: Social Mobilization amidst Violence and Instability'. *British Journal of Middle Eastern Studies* 48(5): 832–49. https://doi.org/10.1080/13530194.2020.1715788.
Cramer, Christopher, and Goodhand, Jonathan (2002). 'Try Again, Fail Again, Fail Better? War, the State, and the "Post-Conflict" Challenge in Afghanistan'. *Development and Change* 33(5): 885–909.
Davies, Sara E., and True, Jacqui (2017). 'When There Is no Justice: Gendered Violence and Harm in Post-Conflict Sri Lanka'. *International Journal of Human Rights* 21(9): 1320–36.
Dawood, Ismaeel (2016). 'Moats, Walls, and the Future of Iraqi National Identity'. 28 October. IAI Working Papers 16. https://www.iai.it/sites/default/files/iaiwp1628.pdf (accessed 30 May 2022).
Dodge, Toby, and Mansour, Renad (2020). 'Sectarianization and De-sectarianization in the Struggle for Iraq's Political Field'. *Review of Faith & International Affairs* 18(1): 58–69.
Enabling Peace in Iraq Centre (EPIC) (2021). 'The Long Game: Iraq's "Tishreen" Movement and the Struggle for Reform'. 30 September. Relief Web. https://reliefweb.int/report/iraq/long-game-iraq-s-tishreen-movement-and-struggle-reform-october-2021 (accessed 30 May 2022).
Galtung, Johan (1964). 'An Editorial'. *Journal of Peace Research* 1(1): 1–4.
De Guevara, Berit Bliesemann (2012). *Statebuilding and State-Formation. The Political Sociology of Intervention*. London: Routledge.
Halawa, Hafsa (2020). 'Iraqi Women in Civil Society'. December. IRIS Policy Brief. https://auis.edu.krd/iris/frontpage-slider-publications/iraqi-women-civil-society (accessed 30 May 2022).
Hamourtziadou, Lily, and Gokay, Bulent (2020). 'Iraq's Security 2003–2019: Death and Neoliberal Destruction Par Excellence'. 7 January. Open Democracy. https://www.opendemocracy.net/en/north-africa-west-asia/iraqs-security-2003-2019-death-and-neoliberal-destruction-par-excellence/ (accessed 30 May 2022).
Hasan, Harith (2019). 'Iraq Protests: A New Social Movement Is Challenging Sectarian Power'. 4 November. Carnegie Middle East Center. https://carnegie-mec.org/2019/11/04/iraq-protests-new-social-movement-is-challenging-sectarian-power-pub-80256 (accessed 30 May 2022).
Heathershaw, John (2012). 'Conclusion: Neither Built nor Formed – the Transformation of States under International Intervention'. In Berit Bliesemann de Guevara (ed.), *Statebuilding and State-Formation. The Political Sociology of Intervention* (246–59). . London: Routledge.
International Crisis Group (2021). 'Iraq's Tishreen Uprising: From Barricades to Ballot Box'. 26 July. Middle East Report No. 223. https://www.crisisgroup.org/mid

dle-east-north-africa/gulf-and-arabian-peninsula/iraq/223-iraqs-tishreen-uprising-bar ricades-ballot-box (accessed 30 May 2022).
Iraqi High Commission for Human Rights (IHCHR) (2020). 'Freedom of Opinion, Expression and Peaceful Demonstration'. 4 October. Special Report V. https://www.ohchr.org/en/press-briefing-notes/2019/10/press-briefing-notes-iraq (accessed 30 May 2022).
Issa, Ali (2015). *Against All Odds: Voices of Popular Struggle in Iraq*. Stanford: Tadween Publishing.
Jabar, Faleh A. (2018). 'The Iraqi Protest Movement: From Identity Politics to Issue Politics'. June. LSE Middle East Centre Paper Series 25. http://eprints.lse.ac.uk/88294/11/Faleh_Iraqi%20Protest%20Movement_Published_Arabic.pdf (accessed 30 May 2022).
al-Jaffal, Omar (2021). 'Iraq's New Electoral Law: Old Powers Adapting to Change'. 12 January. *Arab Reform Initiative*. https://www.arab-reform.net/publication/iraq-electi ons/ (accessed 30 May 2022).
Jiyad, Sajad (2021). 'Protest Vote: Why Iraq's Next Elections Are Unlikely to Be Game-Changers'. 23 April. LSE Middle East Centre Paper Series 48. http://eprints.lse.ac.uk/110201/1/Protest_vote_iraq_elections_paper_48.pdf (accessed 30 May 2022).
Krishnan, Nandini and Olivieri, Sergio Daniel (2016). 'Losing the Gains of the Past: The Welfare and Distributional Impacts of the Twin Crises in Iraq 2014', 16 February. World Bank Policy Research Working Paper No. 7567. https://ssrn.com/abstr act=2733403.
Lavie, Limor (2017). 'The Idea of the Civil State in Egypt: Its Evolution and Political Impact Following the 2011 Revolution'. *Middle East Journal* 71(1): 23–44.
Lkaderi, Sulaiman (2021). 'Mother of Assassinated Iraqi Activist Ihab al-Wazni Demands Justice'. 23 June. *Middle East Eye*. https://www.middleeasteye.net/video/mother-assas sinated-iraqi-activist-ihab-al-wazni-demands-justice (accessed 30 May 2022).
MacDonald, Alex (2019). '"He Died for a Cause": Safaa al-Saray Has Become the Face of an Uprising'. 12 November. *Middle East Eye*. https://www.middleeasteye.net/news/prof ile-martyr-who-became-face-iraqs-uprising (accessed 30 May 2022).
Mahmoud, Mohamed, and Al Rawi, Bushra Jameel (2019). 'The Slogans of the Iraqi Demonstrators Demanding Reform: Semiotics Study'. مجلة العلوم النسانية والاجتماعية – Journal of Humanities and Social Sciences (Arabic) 46(3): 228–56.
Mansour, Renad (2019). 'Iraq's 2018 Government Formation. Unpacking the Friction between Reform and the Status Quo'. 14 Febrcury. LSE Middle East Centre Report. https://eprints.lse.ac.uk/100099/1/Mansour_Iraq_s_2018_government_formation_2 019.pdf (accessed 30 May 2022).
Mansour, Renad (2020). 'Running Out of Options: Why Iraq's Elite Fails to Address Protest Demands'. October. *IRIS Commentary*. https://auis.edu.krd/iris/sites/default/files/Running%20Out%20of%20Options%20-%20RM%20-%2022%20Oct%2020.pdf (accessed 30 May 2022).
Martínez, José Ciro, and Sirri, Omar (2020). 'Of Bakeries and Checkpoints: Stately Affects in Amman and Baghdad'. *Environment and Planning D: Society and Space* 38(5): 849–66.
Meger, Sara, and Sachseder, Julia (2020). Militarized Peace: Understanding Post-Conflict Violence in the Wake of the Peace Deal in Colombia. *Globalizations* 17(6): 1–21.
Meintjes, Shila, Pillay, Anu, and Turshen, Meredeth (2002). *The Aftermath: Women in Post-Conflict Transformation*. London: Zed Books.

Mhajne, Anwar, and Whetstone, Crystal (2018). 'The Use of Political Motherhood in Egypt's Arab Spring Uprising and Aftermath'. *International Feminist Journal of Politics* 20(1): 54–68. https://doi.org/10.1080/14616742.2017.1371624.

Mitchell, Timothy (1991). 'The Limits of the State: Beyond Statist Approaches and Their Critics'. *American Political Science Review* 85(1): 77–96.

Omar, Oumayma (2020). 'Tahrir Beach, a Safe Haven for Protesters from Baghdad's Turmoil'. 22 January. Middle East Online. https://middle-east-online.com/en/tahrir-beach-safe-haven-protesters-baghdad%E2%80%99s-turmoil (accessed 30 May 2022).

Parashar, Swati, Ann Tickner, and Jacqui True (2018). *Revisiting Gendered States: Feminist Imaginings of the State in International Relations*. Oxford: Oxford University Press.

Paris, Roland, and Sisk, Timothy D. (2009). *The Dilemmas of Statebuilding: Confronting the Contradictions of Postwar Peacebuilding Operations*. London: Routledge.

Richmond, Oliver P. (2014). *Failed Statebuilding: Intervention and the Dynamics of Peace Formation*. New Haven: Yale University Press.

Richter-Devroe, Sophie (2018). *Women's Political Activism in Palestine: Peacebuilding, Resistance, and Survival*. Urbana: University of Illinois Press.

Robin-D'Cruz, Benedict (2019). 'Social Brokers and Leftist-Sadrist Cooperation in Iraq's Reform Protest Movement: Beyond Instrumental Action'. *International Journal of Middle East Studies* 51(2): 257–80.

Robin-D'Cruz, Benedict (2021). 'The Social Logics of Protest Violence in Iraq: Explaining Divergent Dynamics in the Southeast'. 19 August. LSE Middle East Centre Paper. http://eprints.lse.ac.uk/111784/2/SocialLogicsofProtestViolence.pdf (accessed 30 May 2022).

Sharma, Aradhana, and Gupta, Akhil (2006). *The Anthropology of the State: A Reader*. Oxford: Blackwell Pub.

Sirri, Omar (2021). *Destructive Creations: Social-Spatial Transformations in Contemporary Baghdad*. LSE Middle East Centre paper series (45). London: LSE Middle East Centre.

Skelton, Mac and Ali Saleem, Zmkan (2020). 'Iraq's Political Marketplace at the Subnational Level: The Struggle for Power in Three Provinces. Conflict Research Programme', London School of Economics and Political Science, London, UK. http://eprints.lse.ac.uk/105184/.

UNAMI and OHCHR (2020). 'Human Rights Violations and Abuses in the Context of Demonstrations in Iraq October 2019 to April 2020'. 27 August. Relief Web. https://reliefweb.int/report/iraq/human-rights-violations-and-abuses-context-demonstrations-iraq-october-2019-april-2020 (accessed 30 May 2022).

Yuval-Davis, N. (1997). 'Women, Citizenship and Difference'. *Feminist Review* 57(1): 4–27. https://doi.org/10.1080/014177897339632.

Zangana, Haifa (2013). 'Iraq'. In Paul Amar and Vijay Prashad (eds), *Dispatches from the Arab Spring: Understanding the New Middle East* (308–24). Minneapolis: University of Minnesota Press.

Part IV

THE BODY POLITIC RECONFIGURED:
BETWEEN SOCIAL ENGINEERING AND COMMUNITY
RESISTANCE

Chapter 11

'AL-'ISLĀM KAMĀ 'UNZIL' – ASSAD'S ISLAM: RELIGION, THE STATE AND REFITTING SYRIAN ISLAM

Hammoud Hammoud

In mid-December 2019, a report was published in the Syrian media in which it was stated that Bashar al-Assad had met with representatives of an Islamic women's movement: al-Qubaysīyāt (the name is derived from the surname of the founder, Munīra al-Qubaysī). Emerging during the 1980s, the movement, whose membership was estimated to have reached 'roughly over one hundred thousand', is very piously rigourist in outlook and disposition. Some members of the group who attended this meeting posted photos online (Omar 2013: 347, Jaber 2019). Social media posts, accompanied photos with captions written in a somewhat sycophantic style, stated: 'From the honour of the meeting with the Lord of [our] Homeland (*sayyid al-watan*).' Bashar al-Assad effusively thanked, saying: 'You have permitted our dreams to be fulfilled ... O you who are the whole of our identity'.

This is not the first meeting between members of the group and al-Assad, since al-Qubaysiyyat had received significant support from the state. The question that could be asked is, what sort of dreams led this Qubaysīya woman to consider al-Assad as 'the whole of our identity'? This chapter will address some relevant issues related to the discourse between the two sides. It is important to note that harmony between this Islamic movement, expressed in the words of Hanan al-Shaykh, and the Assad rule is not confined to this incident, but rather this is one example of the way in which Islamic discourse has been recast and foisted upon society by means of al-Assad's autocracy.

The fact that the dreams fulfilled by al-Assad could be Islamic ones reflects the religious policies of Bashar al-Assad, as he continued not only the Islamic politics of his father, Hafez, but also prioritized the politics of Islam, subjecting them to new transformations. This chapter will attempt to analyse the Assad rule's religious politics prior to, and during, the Syrian uprising. The Syria of today is confronted and occupied by many regional and international forces, and is faced by *at least* two types of Islamic activism, each being the complement of the other: the various new fundamentalist opposition movements *and* the

Islamic politics of the Baʿth which seeks to fortify its grip by promoting a specific form of Islam, creating a fertile breeding ground for present and future Islamic fundamentalism. Both loyalist and opposition types of Islamism are supported and celebrated by the matrix of foreign forces (Saudi Arabia, Qatar, Iran, Turkey), each of which pursues its own vision of the many imagined Islams. All seek to erode what remains of the secular dimension in Syria. The insurgents attempt this by claiming that they are waging *jihad* against an imagined *secular* regime, tightly imbricated with sectarian agitation, and the loyalists by pretending that they are pursuing the resuscitation of the 'original Islam' of Muhammad, in opposition to those who (according to the Baʿthist scenario) distorted the image of the 'true religion'.

Consistent with the focus of this chapter, we will concentrate only on the second group: the loyalist and Syrian state-sponsored type of Islamic activism. The issue of how the Islamic politics of the Baʿth functions and how it contributes to the production of new forms of radical Islamic disposition in the country, in contrast to the secularization that had characterized major facets of political and cultural life, will be examined within this framework. This chapter will use three case studies for its empirical material and analytical elaboration. The first considers a short historical background of Hafez al-Assad's Islamic politics during and following the Islamic Uprising of Muslim Brothers in 1980s. The second considers the new neo-Islamizing efforts of his son, Bashar, in reorganizing, recasting and institutionalizing the Sunni establishment, reshaping the already close ties between this establishment and the state. The third deals with aspects of the Shi'itization, led by Iran, of both the Alawites and the Sunnis, a major development in the socio-religious life of Syria.

It will become clear from the evidence that one of the main goals of the Assad politics of religion has been the creation of a new Sunni establishment. Correlated with this was the creation of new mechanisms of control surrounding Islam, a process also associated with Iran's policies of Shi'itization. The Islamic movements in Syria (especially the Muslim Brothers), from the 1970s onwards, contributed to the rise of new forms of fundamentalism in Syria (alongside the neo-traditionalist Islam politics of Hafez al-Assad from the 1980s). However, it can now be seen that the enduring neo-traditionalist religious politics promoted by the state, which has become the chief supporter of religious rigourism, spilled over into radical Islamic activism.

Background: The politics of Islam under Hafez al-Assad

After the Syrian Ba'th party coup of 1963, the first indicator of the way Islamic politics would be handled was the removal of Abu al-Yusr 'Abidin (1955–63) from his position as the Grand Mufti, on 30 March 1963, to be replaced temporarily by 'Abd al-Razzaq al-Himsi (1889–1981), who held this office until 1 April 1964. The aim of this replacement was not to immobilize the religious establishment, but to impede its social and religious influence, since the Mufti 'Abidin had been perceived by the Assad rule as hostile to its politics of 'nationalizations [of businesses and industries] as well as its project of authoritarian modernisation of religious institutions' (Böttcher 1997: 54, Pierret 2013a: 177). This step was then followed by other measures, which involved the marginalization and exclusion of numerous Syrian religious figures. Among those affected was the well-known rival for this post, the ultra-conservative and generically Salafi Sheikh Hasan Habannaka al-Midani. The new Syrian regime perceived him as a thorn in the flesh, as he incited Damascene public opinion against the Ba'th and its social and economic policies. These policies pertained specifically to land reform, nationalization of private banks and industries, foreign investments, and later, the draft constitution of Hafez al-Assad in 1973. In general, the dismissal of Abu al-Yusr 'Abidin was only the first move, indicating the direction of the winds then and thereafter.

The message of the Assad rule was clear: its concerns were not only with eroding the standing and influence of Sunni religious institutions, but also with reshuffling the cards of these institutions and recasting them in accordance with the regime's purposes. Accordingly, the adaptable Sheikh Ahmad Kaftaru, who would later be especially favoured by the Ba'th, was chosen for the position after seeing off his potential rival, Habannaka. That Kaftaru traditionally had no significant support among the Syrian 'ulama, seems to have been reason enough to favour him as partner to the Assad rule. As Annabelle Böttcher puts it, the next thirty years proved what an excellent partner one could find in Kaftaru (1997: 58).

In many Islamic countries, such as Egypt and Saudi Arabia, the Sunni space has a relative history of firm institutionalization around specific religious authorities (such as the al-Azhar institution). The religious authority of the 'ulama in Syria, however, was fragmented and dispersed among marginal and more prominent voices, despite certain crucial steps being taken towards more durable institutionalization of religious authority before the period of Ba'th rule. Claiming that under the Ba'th regime there was 'no longer an official, overarching religious authority. Nor was there a professional hierarchy of 'ulama, such as Egypt's al-Azhar or Saudi Arabia's Council of Senior Scholars', is historically inaccurate. The so-called unifying institutional religious authority did not exist at all in Syria, neither before nor under the Assad rule (Rifai 2020). Although Syria has always demonstrated its ability to produce religious scholars, sometimes with a significant weight in the Islamic world, the country did not produce a charismatic institution comparable to those in some countries of the Islamic world.

In Syria's complex circumstances, it has been difficult to form stable regulatory religious frameworks, due to a number of factors, including the complexity of the denominational dimension, the intervention of regional and international forces and the lack of an inherited institution. The secular state is, first and foremost, the public space that allows such processes of institutionalization to be undertaken and rooted in social and political trajectories. There is no need to stress that such a political and institutional horizon has been, and still is, absent from the history of modern Syria, irrespective of the rather cursory arrangements put in place in the shadow of the two Assads. Added to this, the regime, as Thomas Pierret has pointed out, has pursued an indirect approach to managing religious affairs since the 1960s, by neutralizing religious institutions and by suppressing and marginalizing leading religious figures (Pierret 2013b). This is one of the reasons why the Ministry of Awqaf at that time remained small, and its administrative staff declined in number after 1980; from 296 statutory functionaries in 1978, its numbers fell to 237 in 1984, and to 103 in 2000 (Pierret 2013b: 91–2). By and large, the Assad rule depended on individual religious figures from the margins, intentionally selected from minorities,[1] and attempted to empower them in cities. The regime showed no concern about relying on a religious institutio (Böttcher 2004). In my opinion, this is the most important point that embodies the Assad rule's religious policy towards the Awqaf and other religious bodies, preceding the era of Bashar al-Assad.

With the monopoly of politics in Syria, in which the state and the political field had been transformed into 'a font of patronage', and where the 'leading party' of the Ba'th has the last word, the religion of Islam had been monopolized accordingly. Aiming to secure and consolidate his power, Hafez al-Assad strengthened his ties with this loyal Sunni establishment (and with it his relations with the leading merchants in Aleppo and Damascus) (Hinnebusch 2001: 83). One aspect of al-Assad's Islamic policy was shaped by two seemingly opposing factors: on the one hand, the oppressive policy developed over the course of the struggle against the Muslim Brotherhood, where certain Islamic practices were banned, some mosques and Islamic institutes were closed, and many leading Muslim scholars were dismissed (Atassi 2016). As an example of the restrictions imposed by Hafez al-Assad on preachers, scholars and mosques, we can mention the directive by the Ministry of Awqaf that mosques remain closed between prayer times, against local custom and practice (the aim was to forestall gatherings and religious instruction). On the other hand, the state was pursuing a policy of tolerance in creating free religious spaces, with implicitly authorized forms of Islam that lend authority and legitimation to the ruling elite (Böttcher 1997: 127). As for those preachers and mosque personnel who did not conform to the direction and supervision of secret services (*muḥabarāt*), they were imprisoned and tortured – measures that earned Syria the sobriquet *état de barbarie* (Böttcher 1997: 127).

The conflict with the Muslim Brotherhood represented a major turning point in the regime's adoption of a new religious policy with which the Muslim Brotherhood might be countered. On the one hand, the Assad rule tried to undermine the authority of the traditional Syrian religious scholars who played a significant role in the production of Brotherhood ideology and rhetoric.[2] On the other, it focused on creating a new Islamist ideology, one which could be thoroughly controlled by the Assad rule, emerging from populist Sufi voices, the aim of which was to create an alternative to and a substitute for the Brothers. Trusted sheikhs such as the popular Islamic writer Muhammad Sa'id Ramadan al-Buti, Ahmad Kaftaru and Salih al-Farfur (1901–1986), to mention only a few, led this new Sunni discourse in defending al-Assad against the Brotherhood.³ However, it is important to note that their works were not entirely independent but rather shaped and manipulated to align with the political imperatives of the regime. They stood apart from traditional Damascene ʿulama, some of whom produced a critical or antagonistic discourse, such as Hasan Habannaka al-Midani.

The Ministry of Awqaf, however, was not an entirely idle instrument of government. From the early 1980s the Ministry featured both as an institutional front and a potential propaganda tool. In October 1980, in its later form, it started issuing *Nahj al-Islam*, while Muhammad Mahmoud al-Khatib was minister. It was clearly intended to be a counter-punch to the Muslim Brotherhood's publication *al-Nadhir*; this was clearly articulated by the magazine's editor-in-chief, Haitham Jalloul, as he described the Muslim Brothers as 'criminals and traitors' for abusing Islam and wearing an Islamic cloak for political ends (Khatib 2012: 100). According to Jalloul, this is why Muslim scholars must take a clear position when it comes to the separation of Islam and those who call themselves the Muslim Brotherhood (Böttcher 1997: 39).

Two processes, occurring in parallel, were involved in the Islamic politics of Hafez al-Assad. One was the de-Islamization of the Brother's Islam by stripping it of Islamic legitimacy. Witness, for instance, Jalloul's reference to the text of "*ahdunā*', 'our pledge', which was to be repeated every morning by Syrian school students: 'We pledge to confront imperialism, Zionism and atavism الرجعيّة, and to crush their criminal tool, the treacherous gang represented by the Muslim Brotherhood.' The other was establishing and formulating the Islam of al-Assad and his subjects. The matter was not confined to the critical position taken against the Brotherhood's propaganda and to commenting on current issues (e.g. the 1981 Azbakiyah bombing massacre in Damascus and the Aleppo Artillery School massacre 1979). It drew in the very functions of Awqaf Ministry, to offer Sunni Islamic legitimization to the religious sect of Hafez al-Assad, given his desire for Sunni recognition for the Alawites as Muslims, since the Alawite sect, according to the dominant Islamic dogma, was then considered heretical or 'beyond the pale of Islam' (Ajami 1986: 174).⁴ In this context, we should take into account the controversy previously raised by Assad's draft constitution of 1973, in which the stipulation that the president of the Republic be a Muslim was lifted. Since the president, according to the Syrian constitution, needs to be a Muslim, and since Hafez al-Assad was born into the Alawi sect, which was not generally recognized as Muslim, this draft constitution was an instrument to remove the heretical label from the Alawi sect and disengage the legitimacy of the presidency from religion. It is inaccurate to consider this draft as a commitment to secularism, but rather needs to be seen as an 'attempt to legitimize his authority given that he comes from a minority sect' (Aldoughli 2020: 367).⁵ Thus, it is not surprising that headlines issued by the ʾAwqaf magazine began to demonstrate the rising profile of Alawites within the ministry apparatus. The magazine had begun to speak frankly: 'Alawi Muslims belong to the Shi'ites of the House of the Noble Prophet.' Other articles talked about the virtues of Imam Ja'far al-Sadiq (Böttcher 1997: 147). These efforts of the Awqaf reflected the tension that al-Assad was experiencing in relation to its *Islamic legitimacy*.

The strategy of the politics of Islam, an element thought to attract votes from an important segment of the population, should be understood in terms of the circumstances described. It is the lack of specifically Islamic legitimacy that precipitated the emergence of new religious discourse from the regime. This lack represented a compensatory strategy to ensure a balanced operational setting to placate Sunni Muslims for the actions of the regime against other Islamic voices. In line with this, the Awqaf Ministry accelerated the building of mosques, increasing their number exponentially. Bashar al-Assad had previously boasted about his government's strengthening of the religious structure of mosques: 'In Syria', al-Assad boasted, 'since 1970 until today, eighteen thousand mosques have been built ... If secularism is against religion or we practice it against religion, how can we allow the construction of 18,000 mosques ... 220 Sharia schools and Sharia secondary schools were built ... Dozens of institutes were built to train preachers.'[6]

Hafez al-Assad not only doubled the number of mosques in Syria in this new engagement with Islam,[7] but even started visiting mosques frequently, took part in most Islamic events (such as the birthday of Muhammad) and performed a pilgrimage to Mecca. Images were disseminated publicly, showing al-Assad practicing the rituals of the Islamic pilgrimage. The expression 'the believing President' (*ar-raʾīs al-muʾmin*) came to be used occasionally by clerics such as the Syrian Mufti Kaftaru.[8] This expression is also used to describe the former Egyptian president Anwar Sadat. To this strategy, combined with an increasing religiosity of the society (e.g. the proliferation of demand for religious education and the growing number of women wearing headscarves),[9] one can add the networks known as al-Assad Institutes for the Memorization of the Qur'an (*maʿāhid al-ʾAsad li-taḥfīẓ al-Qurʾān*) (Pierret 2013a: 71, 2013b: 93). This Islamic strategy also expressed the Assad rule's attempt to use religion as a cover for its repressive practices against other religious figures opposed to it. Böttcher explains the Assad rule's desire to provide its Islamic politics with an 'institutional, controllable framework' in which the increasing religiosity of Syrian societies could be fostered and practiced (Böttcher 1997: 85).

In this context, the more repressive the Baʿthist authority was towards suspect Sunni spaces, including the Islamist voices of various stripes, the more new religious Sunni spaces were created by the regime itself, the aim being the addition of religion to the various elements of authority wielded by the Assad rule. These spaces were considered an alternative to those hitherto adopted by radical Sunnis, an inner-Islamic substitution, which in turn contributed to the production of new forms of religious extremism: traditionalist in outlook, fundamentalist in norms of social behaviour, and attempting to legitimize regnant authority with another set of instruments. The classical Islamism of the Muslim Brotherhood represented only one type of Syrian Islamic activism, the other was that fostered by the Baʿth: a fertile breeding ground for today's Islamic fundamentalism, as will be shown later.

Institutionalization and the refitting of Islamic spaces under the politics of Bashar al-Assad

Addressing Islamic scholars in a meeting during an *ifṭār* banquet in 2009, Bashar al-Assad declared: 'The importance of adopting the institutional system as a guarantee for the success of the religious institution in achieving its goals and conveying the true message of Islam to the whole world, ... because without institutional thought, the country cannot develop' (SNS 2009). The statement came after the Assad rule's decisive turn towards the re-institutionalization and de-privatization of religious bodies spread across the country. Following the replacement of Muhammad Ziyad al-Ayyubi with Muhammad Abd al-Sattar al-Sayyid as Minister of Awqaf in December 2007, the latter had declared 'the end of the era of anarchy' when 'each institute was a state within the state' (Pierret 2013b: 85). The announcement followed the Syrian government's publishing a public confession by a member of the terrorist Fatah al-Islam Organization and a former student at al-Fath Institute – a confession which underlined the relationship between what is religiously and ideologically taught at that institute and the car bomb that had been planted, and which exploded in Damascus on 27 September 2008. The manipulation of Islamic institutions turned towards religious and social control – determined, aggressive and direct – a move which sought to place all religious institutes and charities directly under the authority of the Ministry of Awqaf, which had increased its personnel to 1,500 by 2009 (Pierret 2013b: 100).[10]

It may be emphasized that there were two complementary processes which at first glance might seem contradictory. On one side, there was institutionalization, understood here as the means of reorganizing the distribution of political and religious power, and fostering new institutionalized forms of social control in social, religious and political settings. The other was the process of generating new ways of redefining Islam, which had substantial consequences for the construction of new communal spaces for religiosity and even redefined many Islamic symbols and concepts. The degree of latitude shown by the Assad rule towards the relative autonomy of some religious organisms (specifically the private institutes of shari'a such as al-Fath Institute of Damascus, founded by sheikh Salih al-Farfur (1901–86) and Badr al-Din al-Hasani Institute) was reversed, but by sheer inertia, and in an operation of devolved authority, continued in a variety of locations. The circumstances governing this change were, on the one hand, a failure of the Awqaf to manage domestic Islam, and on the other, a consequence of the many transformations that began to afflict the Mashreq after 2000, where the rigourist transformations of Islam represented the most challenging question in the Middle East and globally. Indeed, it is autonomous development, independent from official authorities, that helped form new religious groups and intensified a historical condition conducive to widespread mobilization, which emerged in Syria as 2011 progressed, leading to the release of interned jihadists released from Syrian prisons. The previously state-led management of mosques had failed to control the social dynamics, out of which many of the next generation of fundamentalist movements were to emerge.

This failure was not only related to mosques on the margins of Damascus, but even reached parts of the capital, such as the al-Rifa'i Mosque in Kafr Suse (the area was admittedly regarded as a surrounding village only a generation prior), or the very central Zayd bin Thabit Mosque in Khalid ibn al-Walid Street, with its famous fundamentalist Zayd Group, a network that had been founded by 'Abd al-Karim al-Rifa'i. He was followed by his two sons one of whom, Usama al-Rifa'i, is the current head of the Syrian Islamic Council based in Istanbul, who reportedly, in 2015 had contact with the terrorist commander of Jaysh al-Islam Zahran Alloush,[11] and his brother, Sariya, known as 'Sheikh of the Merchants'. The relationship illustrates the nexus of money and other forms of logistical support relevant to the production of religious meaning independent of authority, and sometimes allied with it (Jazmati 2020). Legally, the Zayd bin Thabit and al-Rifa'i Mosques are owned by the Awqaf, but 'their use actually "belongs" to the al-Rifa'i family and its movement' (Pierret 2013 a: 89).

The same point can be made in the case of religious institutions that had been producing hundreds of graduates, coming from many nationalities, in shari'a disciplines. Although many of these institutes and their properties are officially owned by the Awqaf, the ministry did not have the capacity, and clearly not the will, to influence, let alone to form, the religious perceptions, attitudes and sensibilities of these students. Institutes such as Badr al-Din al-Hasani, al-Fath Institute, Majma' Abi al-Nur al-Islami in Damascus and the Kiltawiyya in Aleppo are good examples of how little the authority of the ministry worked to enforce its preferences: the sheath of the sword belongs to the Awqaf, but the blade of it belongs to other religious actors.

It is therefore not surprising that leaders of many Islamist jihadist factions in Syria were affiliated with and educated in these religious spaces. This does not imply a structural relationship between these educational spaces and jihad, or even political Islamism. These spaces do not inherently embody ideological paradigms for the action of jihad. It is not that all jihadists were primarily graduates of these institutions. Most leaders of jihadist groups are not primarily graduates of Shari'a but came from new cultures that have tended to alienate themselves from the Islamic tradition itself. Generally, the point is very complicated, specifically in the Syrian jihadist context (and more specifically when it is approached from the angle of the globalized Islamism) but some graduates who have led jihadist operations and movements may be mentioned. One example would be Abdullah Azzam, the inspirer of Al-Qaeda, who studied at the Faculty of Shari'a at Damascus University. Among Syria's jihadist groups today, one observes the emergence of a new phenomenon called the 'aš-Šar'īyūn', الشرعيّون (those who study shari'a or are graduates from it), who are charged with upholding the principles and norms of jihadism, and of control in areas under jihadist control (Jusoor 2017).

Additionally, the Syrian state took a very important measure while attempting to extend its control over educational institutions and subject them to the authority of the Ministry of Awqaf. In April 2011, after the eruption of mass demonstrations,

Bashar al-Assad issued a legislative decree establishing the al-Sham Higher Institute for Islamic Studies and the Arabic Language. This was directly linked to the Ministry of Awqaf, including three Islamic bodies: the Fath Institute, the Kuftaru Academy and the Shiʻa school Ruqqaya Hawza (later in 2017, the name of this institute was changed to achieve academic rank: Bilad Al-Sham University for Shariʼa Sciences). It might be assumed that including these institutes under the authority of the state would be a gift to institutions and personalities that had proven their loyalty to the Assad rule over the decades, since these institutes had always sought formal governmental recognition, but this does not describe adequately the dynamics and conjunctures involved. The early involvement of the state was designed to curtail any possibility of establishing alliances and links between the figures of these institutes and the Islamic opposition groups, some of which joined the uprising in 2011. Aiming to win over the Sunnis following the beginning of the uprising, Bashar al-Assad criticized allegations that the Syrian state was against religion, frequently referring to the elevated religiosity of Syria, comparing Umayyad times to the Assad family's rule from 1970. Al-Assad says:

Who sent women's call to mosques? ... Who launched the first religious channel (Noor Al-Sham TV)? Who founded the Al-Sham Institute for Sharia Sciences? What about Sharia institutes, religious institutes, middle schools ... the high religious freedom that exists in Syria? These are facts. We must defend our country with these points ... Between the Umayyad state until 1970, the number of mosques in Damascus was about 4,000, and since 1970 until today, 7,000 mosques were built.[12]

Following these developments, the famous Presidential Legislative Decree No. 31 was promulgated in October 2018 and, according to the Minster of Awqaf, came into effect after a situation of 'legislative chaos' resulting from old laws (Swiss Info 2018). This can be considered part of the turn towards firmer institutionalization. Broadening the remit of the state, the minister declared in the same vein that, 'this is the first time in legislation in which regulations and standards for religious work and conditions for appointing imams and preachers are issued, and this is a great achievement for this work to be institutionalized' (Swiss Info 2018). According to this law, the mandate of the mufti, whose position has been newly abrogated,[13] is limited to three years, which is open to extension. The most important thing is that he must be appointed by decree based on a proposal submitted by the Minister of ʼAwqaf, as stated in Article 37, unlike the prior state of affairs, where only the president of the Republic could appoint the mufti, his term being unlimited.

As for recasting Islamic social spaces, the government-controlled regions witnessed, and still witness, a variety of new Islamic projects led by the state. The Virtue Project '*mašrūʻ faḍīla*' is one example. It aims to encourage adherence to the norms described as Islamic morals and values, and to combat what it describes as moral decay. Thus, specific religious teams were created, focusing on some religious sectors, such as imams and religious teachers, and working on training courses for these sectors, whose mission was to contribute to raising the standard of preachers and imams according to the dictates of the Syrian state (Sahafat al-jadid 2020). The project indicates the efforts made by the authorities to refashion Syrian communities and to redefine and control their Islam officially, with the goal 'to spread noble national and religious moral values and to spread virtue'.[14] These authorities' operations go hand in hand with Iranian religious expansion and its sponsorship of affiliated organizations, including Iran's religious authorities and militias. Added to this, the Ministry of 'Awqāf ran another project in 2014, in order to counter what it considers the extremist Islam of the oppositions. This was a set of lectures that focused on explaining the concept of terrorism: *fiqh al-azma fī muwājaht fiqh al-fitna* (The Jurisprudence of Crisis in the Face of the Jurisprudence of Discord), a subject on which the Ministry has published four volumes so far under the same title: *Fiqh al-'azma* (Sana 2014).

Such projects are not new in Syria but are receiving increased interest as an alternative strategy to that posed by many inflections of Islam, including the various Islams of militant opposition groups who, again, challenged the social and religious control of the regime. The Assad rule ultimately created its own ultimate, pure version of Islam that it believes must prevail over the anathematizing forms of fundamentalist dissidence, *takfīrī*. This is implied by the newly made physical logo of the Ministry of 'Awqāf, *al-'Islām kamā 'unzil* (Islam as Revealed), which fully expresses *al-'Islām* that government forces are trying to push as an alternative, accompanied by new groups with traditionalist, rigourist and fundamentalist leanings to face the Islams of *takfīrī* others.

De-Islamizing the *takfīrī* 'others', with whom Islam is not to be identified, means, again, intensifying the re-Islamization of the Syrian state's 'own' subjects. Both processes are closely related. One significant development in this regard is the creation of the Youth Religious Team, *al-Farīq ad-Dīnī as-Shabābī*, which received legislative recognition in Law 31, and is headed by Abdullah al-Sayyed, the son of the minister of Awqaf. Launched from the Al-Othman Mosque in Damascus in January 2016, the team has now expanded and has branches in all the major cities in Syria. In Aleppo, for example, it is directed by Sheikh Mohammed Rami Al-Obeid, who holds the position of director of Aleppo's Awqaf Department, and Ibrahim Habbash, the imam of Al-Tawhid Mosque there. Like other political parties, the team, being linked to the Ba'thist National Union of Syrian Students, has a Central Council of ten members, including three women, and directs 244 imams registered with the Ministry of Awqaf (Al-Khatib 2019). As announced by the heads of the team, its main aim is 'confronting the terrorist *takfīrī* ideology' and producing a new generation able to confront its enemies (Syrian Arab Republic 2016). Darin Suleiman, head of the National Union of Syrian Students, insisted on developing contemporary religious discourses to immunize the young, and, in line with the motto of 'Awqaf, preserve 'true Islam as revealed by Allāh Almighty' (Syrian Arab Republic 2016).

With these developments, it becomes increasingly evident what constitutes the essence of being Muslim according to al-Assad's *al-'Islām kamā 'unzil*. That al-Assad was considered the sole authority, deciding what authentic, pure Islam was, can be confirmed by a lecture delivered by the minister of ʾAwqaf who edited a multivolume exegesis of the Qurʾan (*at-Tafsīr al-Ǧāmiʿ*, *The Comprehensive Interpretation*),[15] designed in the same vein as *fiqh al-ʾazma*. The lecture was titled, 'Standards and Rules of Interpretation of the Noble Qurʾan ... according to the Intellectual Foundations of President Bashar al-Assad for Religious Reform'.[16]

Legislative Decree No. 31, the progress of Shi'itization, and other parallel initiatives represent a re-engineering of religious organisms and a response to the new religious conditions in Syria. These processes work to create new fundamentalist lobbies, in both Shi'i and Sunni forms. Contrary to their announced purposes, these are traditionalist undertakings far removed from meaningful reforms of religious thought and practice.

The aforementioned abrogation of the Grand Mufti position occupied by Ahmad Badr ad-Din Hassun can also be examined in this light. Specifically, it can be considered a new Islamic landscape in line with the strategies of Assad's Islam, even if this leads to the destruction of one of the important Islamic symbolic trajectories, despite the importance of this position within the wings supporting the Syrian regime, both inside Syria and at an international level. The move, which was followed by a counter-statement announcing the election of Sheikh Usama al-Rifaʿi as Grand Mufti of the Syrian Arab Republic Syrian Islamic Council based in Istanbul[17] (the appointment in itself embodies one of the important dimensions in the struggle over Islam in Syria), undoubtedly goes beyond Hassoun's problematic personality. He has always been one of the most vocally supportive and fawning Sunni voices of the Syrian regime. This move is completely in line with what the Assad rule was, and is, doing in recasting the Sunni Islamic landscape and imposing its own fundamentalist vision over the new realities in Syria, the Iranian aspect being the most important, as will be discussed below.

Some aspects of Shi'itization

The phenomenon of Shi'itization in Syria is structurally related to Islamic politics and re-institutionalization, however variably it may be described. It must be noted that Shi'itization in Syria is not a new phenomenon. Rather, it recurs in Syrian history and the Middle East in general, most prominently during the era of the Fatimids, who, with their Ismaili Shi'i doctrine, dominated much of the Levant and had a strong influence on eastern Syria in the 11th century. The last important traces of this era were, however, destroyed by the Mamluks and, further north, by the sixteenth-century Ottomans (Barout 2017, 2018). In modern times, its roots can be traced back to the era of Hafez al-Assad,[18] who cooperated closely with the fundamentalist mullah's regime of Iran, through the formation of the Syrian-Iranian axis, which involved considerable Iranian investments in the rebuilding of some Shi'i shrines according to conventions of 'Persian architecture' (Pierret 2013c: 103, Maltzahn von 2013). From the 1990s onwards, Iranian Twelver Shi'a became very 'visible' in Syria (e.g. in Sayyida Zaynab[19] and Sayyida Ruqayya in Damascus and Raqqa, north of Syria) with their cultural and religious activities, such as pilgrimages and religious studies, which were systematized by the Iranian Embassy and the Iranian Cultural Center in Damascus (Böttcher 2004: 140–1). This notwithstanding, Shi'itization under Hafez should neither be exaggerated nor underestimated. Despite his close cooperation with Iran, from which the sectarian dimension cannot be excluded, he remained very cautious regarding their activities inside Syria (less so in Lebanon), and the relationship was subject to the broader parameters of political and strategic relations in the region.

Under Bashar al-Assad, from 2000 onwards, Shi'itization shifted significantly, acquiring an institutional trajectory. It was reported that the Ministry of 'Awqaf began establishing schools of shari'a officially teaching the jurisprudence of the Ja'fari school, with student numbers, both male and female, estimated to reach approximately 10,000 (Mustafa 2017). In addition to the continuing establishment of *ḥawzāt* (religious seminaries), 'dozens of *husayniyyāt*' (dedicated to the remembrance of the Passion of Husayn, also acting as community centres, proselytizing and recruitment points, and meeting halls) were established in Syrian cities and villages. Campaigns of Shi'i proselytization were and are still active, particularly among the Sunni population of the Jezira, specifically in Raqqa and Deir al-Zor (Pierret 2013c: 107). Twelve *ḥawzāt* and three Shi'i colleges were established in Sayyida Zaynab. In 2005, a special directorate was established in the Ministry of 'Awqaf to supervise these seminaries (International Institute for Syrian Studies 2008: 125–6).

This massive proliferation of Shi'i learning centres was accompanied by a relentless Iranian push to Shi'itize the Alawites, and even the Sunni populations, or at least give Alawism a Twelver drift. There are dozens of reports referring to these processes closely linked to the intentional recasting of Sunni Islam. In the Jezira (specifically al-Raqqa, Deir ez-Zor, and al-Hasakah), some 6,080 people were thought to have been converted between 1999 and 2007. The overall figures for this period are estimated to be around 22,300, of whom 70 per cent are Alawites, 21 per cent are Sunnis and 9 per cent are Ismailis (International Institute for Syrian Studies 2008: 162–3).

What is being suggested here is that the politics of Islam in Syria may be approached through a number of structurally related processes, which the Assad rule felt should be institutionalized. On the eve of the Syrian uprising, the Syrian government had institutionalized religious learning by granting official recognition to Shi'i educational institutions on an equal footing with those of Sunnis. This official position of parity must, however, be weighed against the reach of Iranian authority inside many crucial organs of the Syrian state, including the Ministry of 'Awqaf.

Over the decade since the uprising began, Iran, represented by the Revolutionary Guard's Quds Brigade, recruited Alawite and Shi'i Syrians and organized them into militias,[20] alongside militias recruited from Lebanon, Iran, Iraq, Pakistan and Afghanistan, under the guise of protecting Shi'i shrines and defending what they call Axis of Resistance (Idlbi 2021: 18). These factions became most widespread in the suburbs of Damascus, in some central parts of the city and in a few other areas of the country. Recruitment centres were opened at various points along the Syrian coast, mostly led by former officers (often Shi'itzed) who chose to work with the Shi'ite militias for religious and financial reasons (high salaries were provided) (Mustafa 2017). From the beginning, Hezbollah adopted sectarian mottos with incandescent anti-Sunni historical references, such as, *lan tuslab Zaynab marratayn* (Zainab shall not be enslaved twice), the reference being to Zainab b. Ali, when she was captured by the followers of Yazid ibn Muʿawiyah during the Passion of Husayn (Idlbi 2021: 8).

Iran's strategy used a completely different trajectory from that of Russia in Syria. Iran, in addition to its militias, considers the religious and sectarian aspects with the aim that it will have the loyalty of the new generation of young people. In contrast, Russia does not care much about these sectarian dimensions, except when and if they come to harm its interests. For Iran, the religious factor represents a major ideological framework ripe for investment in the long term. Despite the fact that the characteristics of Iranian penetration in Syria vary across the religious, political, military, security, economic and cultural arenas, the sectarian religious motive remains the most ubiquitous determinant of Iranian foreign policies. This is expressed through investment in the followers of the Shi'ite sect in the region, and escalating calls for avenging and setting right *maẓlūmīya* (historical injury) of the Shi'ite sect, claimed to have been caused by Sunnis throughout history.

'Iran is handing out cash to needy Syrians, [with] a heavy dose of indoctrination in religious seminaries, scholarships to children to study in Iranian universities, free health care, food baskets, and trips to tourist spots to encourage conversion' (Vohra 2021, Idlbi 2021: 27).[21] To this religious end, new important Iran-backed organs also emerged, such as the Supreme Ja'fari Islamic Council in Syria, in 2012, headed by the Shi'i cleric Sayyid Muhammad Ali Al-Miski and designed to be similar to the Supreme Islamic Shi'i Council in Lebanon. The council has set itself several goals, the most important of which is the representation of Shi'ism and the Shi'a in Syria, supporting the spread of the principles of the Iranian revolution, and establishing religious, educational and charitable institutions (Idlbi 2021: 10). Additionally, one of Iran's most prominent missionary centres in Syria is its Cultural Center with its three branches in Damascus, Latakia and more recently in Deir Ezzor, the last being opened in 2018 under the direct supervision of the Iranian Revolutionary Guards. The centre is active in coordinating Shi'i cultural and religious events, in addition to its activity in attracting Syrian youths for recruitment (Idlbi 2021: 10–11).

Shi'itization also operates among various social and political strata. All of the developments described form part of a broader policy drive which includes the systematic policy of demographic engineering. This involves the local equivalent of ethnic cleansing, which takes place under trucial agreements, and includes the forced displacement of the Sunni population (sometimes by buying or confiscating land and real estate) from their homes in Homs, Daraya, the eastern neighbourhoods of Aleppo and Zabadani and the Qalamoon region abutting the central parts of the border in Lebanon. These populations were transported to the regions of northwest Syria around the city of Idlib. Despite the very substantial numbers of young, educated Syrians lost to war and migration,[22] and the catastrophically damaged infrastructure, al-Assad was able to assert that Syria had now gained a 'healthier and more homogeneous society'.[23] The reference to homogeneity is deceptive, of course, but demographic engineering represents one of the important strategies in Iran's Shi'ite politics.

Iran is also devoting considerable effort to spread the Persian language in Syria, as a complement to Shi'itization and to cultural and religious expansionism. The language is now taught in several universities, schools and institutes (Idlbi 2021: 27).[24] According to the *Washington Post*, 'some schools in Raqqa and Deir Ezzor provinces have already added Farsi classes to elementary and middle school curriculums' (Dadouch 2021). Reportedly, there were more than forty Iranian private schools in Damascus alone before the Syrian uprising, including about ten secondary schools affiliated with the Ministry of 'Awqaf. In 2014, the Syrian president, Bashar al-Assad, issued a decree that Shi'i doctrine would be taught alongside the Sunni equivalent, in addition to opening the first public Shi'ite school in the country in the same year under the name 'The Great Prophet' (*ar-Rasūl al-Kabīr*) which has several branches in several Syrian cities (Al-Hurra 2020).

There are dozens of other names of military and religious formations (which cannot be mentioned here), which indicates the breadth of the Shi'i re-Islamizing processes that Syrian society is now undergoing under the auspices of Iran and al-Assad's security organs. However, the most perilous Shi'i Islamizing operations affecting Syrians, from my standpoint, are those that are directed towards children and young persons who are being recruited into the corps and militias described as armies of Allāh, Muhammad, Hussein, Fatima and so on.[25] One prominent paramilitary corps is the so-called Mahdi Scouts, affiliated with the Imam Mahdi Association in Lebanon (established in Lebanon in May 1985). This association was founded in Syria only one year after the Syrian uprising by the leader of the Iranian Revolutionary Guards Hassan Shateri who was killed by Syrian rebels in 2013. The Mahdi Scouts represent a tributary to the military body of Hezbollah, as most scouts are involved in 'jihadist activity' after the age of sixteen.[26] Like the Ashbal (Lion Cubs) corps feeds into the Sunni terrorist group Daesh, the Mahdi Scouts train children in military activities, as well as instil religious education. The minds of children are particularly susceptible to the religious lessons in *husayniyyāt* where they are introduced to Shi'i ideas, dogma and sensibilities, instilling ideas of vengeance against the Sunnis (Al-Amin 2015).

These Shi'ite activities, and others, now take place under Syrian government sponsorship, and even with the conferment of official status. Bashar al-Assad himself did not hesitate to compare his 'Islamic Syria' to Iran, with its foundational political doctrine of *Wilāyat al-Faqīh*, since both countries, he said, are based on Islamic shari'a. The comparison by al-Assad came during a meeting with religious scholars of different sects: 'What is the Syrian constitution based on?' asked al-Assad, then answering: 'On Islamic law (*aš-šarī'a al-'Islāmīya*) … completely on Islamic jurisprudence. What are all the family and civil status laws in Syria based on? On Islamic law. Of course, Christians and other faiths have their particularity in this matter … Well, we are an Islamic state in this sense too. This is self-evident.'[27] Despite the presence of cognitive dissonance, it should be acknowledged that when the president declared Syria to be an Islamic state to some extent, his words were not without basis or mere rhetorical improvisation, as some critics have suggested. There were likely underlying reasons or evidence that influenced his statement. That these words came from the head of a state whose Ba'thi leaders continue to portray themselves as the secular vanguards in the region, contrary to the reactionary Arab forces (of the Arabian Gulf), is a novel condition in Syria, given the complexity of Islamic activism and its intertwining with the Islamic policies led by Iran. Assad's words, as we have seen, are currently being conveyed on the ground through Sunni and Shi'i activities, now heavily systemized by Iran.

I would like to conclude with this quote taken from a speech by former Iranian president Mahmoud Ahmadinejad in October 2010, which may illuminate some of what has been discussed: 'There are many interpretations of Islam, but [the] basis for our practice is the Iranian interpretation. The historical experience proves that the Iranian interpretation of the truth is the closest one to the truth' (Khalaji 2010). The statement may also remind us of al-Assad's Truth of *al-'Islām kamā 'unzil*. Like al-Assad, Ahmadinejad was not fabricating this Persian or Iranian nationalism and forcibly linking it to Islam out of vacuum. Rather, there was, and still is, a discourse behind it, a fundamentalist structure, which has a long history of nationalizing the Islamic religion and 'religionizing' Persian nationalism. Like the mentality that produced the discourse of *al-'Islām kamā 'unzil*, this Shi'ite fundamentalist structure conforms with practicalities on the ground. It is transposed into bloody translation in most regions of the Levant, and in Iranian support for, and the creation of, dozens of military Islamic organizations throughout the Levant and in Syria with particular intensity. It is the same structure that strives to make Iran a source of Shi'ite political Islam in all its forms, to produce theocratic *marǧi'iya*, authoritative points of reference and the Shi'ites, to whom all the Shi'ites of the Mashreq and those Shi'i affiliated sects should yield.

Conclusion

There were, and still are, countless secular forces and social and cultural dynamics in Syria, and of course in politics also, but al-Assad and the security forces – and the civil wars as well – had eliminated many and besieged others. The picture is bleak and makes it even more difficult to conceive of the rebuilding of Syria's modern and secularist heritage. There is no doubt that endeavours have been made in institutionalizing secular spaces by processes that can be observed from the middle of the nineteenth century to the middle of the twentieth century (this stage deserves independent study). These modernization processes and the extension of state power came at the expense of the authority of the sheikh and the 'ulama. The concept of religious education and religious authority has itself been subjected to secularization and institutionalization. We should not forget that the Ministry of 'Awqaf is a product of these historical trajectories (Al-Azmeh 2020). However, following the Assad rule's military takeover of all key state institutions, these processes of modernization took completely different directions, in many respects, historically speaking, driving in reverse gear.

Questions such as how the Islamic politics of the Ba'th works and how this has contributed to producing new forms of radical religious dispositions rather than furthering the secularization of Syria were examined within the existing framework. As discussed, Hafez al-Assad's dealings with the Ministry of 'Awqaf and its human entities were not based on an institutionalizing orientation, but rather on 'individual subjected entities' in the ministry, and even the manipulation of the contradictions between them and other religious sectors outside the 'Awqaf whose main role was legitimizing an illegitimate authority. As for the Islamic politics of Bashar al-Assad, specifically in the context of the Syrian uprising, his ministry has become one of the most important religious sectors through which Islam has undergone significant transformations in producing new forms of religiosity. This has been in line with *Assad's Islam,* and the construction of other fundamentalist formations, and always within the limits required by the mechanisms of authoritarianism.

Notes

1 Apparently playing on communal differences, minorities or even the contradictions within Syrian Islamic discourses, Hafez al-Assad preferred popular figures who came from the Kurdish minority: Sheikh Muhammad al-Khaznawi, the popular Islamic writer Muhammad Sa'id Ramadan al-Buti and Ahmad Kaftaru are good examples (all of these figures also belonged to the Sufi orders). This question has been well illustrated by Böttcher (2004).
2 We should, in this context, recall the intertwined relationship between the discourse of 'ulama and that of the Syrian Brotherhood, which was originally created by the charismatic Islamic scholar Mustafa al-Siba'i and his disciples and followers. In several Islamic countries we have witnessed Islamist groups that did not emerge from the official religious scholarly base associated with the state, but rather from groups against it, and thus against the official Church of 'ulama. This situation fully applies to the Muslim Brotherhood in Egypt (the Brotherhood is against al-Azhar, despite the periods of superficial cooperation between them). In Syria, the situation was the opposite: it was the 'ulama of Damascus and Aleppo themselves who contributed to the creation of the Islamist movement with a political and social charter. This can be read, for instance, through the establishment of the Faculty of Sharia at the University of Damascus through the efforts of Mustafa al-Siba'i.
3 Regardless of the details of the conflicts between the Ba'th and the Muslim Brothers, it was clear from the beginning that the battles between them were not taking place on ideological grounds, nor were they because the Brothers were very *Islamic,* and the Ba'th very *secular.* The issue of secularism was itself not the focus of the discussion. Overall, authority and power was the compass of the struggle, not secularism, as the Brotherhood's literature at that period would like to convince us.
4 Unsurprisingly, this aspiration for Islamic confirmation that Alawites represent a branch of Islam has been followed by a fatwa provided by the Iranian Shi'ite leader active in Lebanon, and founder of the Amal movement: Musa as-Sadr (Ajami 1986), in which the Alawite's religion was recognized as Islam (Szanto 2013: 4.). The Alawites were henceforth referred to as Muslims of Twelver Shi'ite confession (Kramer

2017: 199–200). There were also previous efforts towards Alawi-Shi'ite rapprochement and the possibility of recognizing Alawites as Muslims (Pierret 2013c).

5 The draft constitution was not sustained, but nevertheless it triggered a wave of protests in Syria. The 'ulama and the Muslim Brotherhood coordinated their rejection and organized large demonstrations across the country. For details, see esp. Pierret (2013a: 184).

6 Bashar al-Assad's interview with the *Syrian News* channel, broadcast on 17 April 2013. http://www.presidentassad.net/index.php?option=com_content&view=article&id=1112:17-2013&catid=305&Itemid=469.

7 Hence the criticism that the Mamluks, who ruled (Syria) in the thirteenth and fourteenth centuries, and the Alawites under Assad, had more mosques built than any other rulers in Syrian history. See Shora (2009: 235).

8 For example, he spoke on the occasion of the condolences for the death of al-Assad in 2000: 'The Arab and Islamic nations have lost, with the passing away of the faithful president, Hafez al-Assad, a prominent historical leader' (Al-Yahya 2011).

9 This Syrian tendency towards religiosity needs to be understood in its broader international context, which, in the 1980s, witnessed the rise of Iranian fundamentalist Khomeini. Distinct new religious identities arose, including the resultant Saudi turn to rigourism after 1979, and of course the awakening of fundamentalism globally, from the local and international spread of American Evangelism on to Hindu fundamentalism and Hindu nationalism. There are many important studies on this point, see, for example, Al-Azmeh (2021, 2015.

10 According to *al-Thawra* newspaper, 6 February and *Nahj al-Islam*, August 2009, 82.

11 Reportedly, Sheikh Usama had been visited secretly by Alloush. Some photos were published of the meeting. See, for example, Orient News (2015).

12 From a speech delivered by Bashar Al-Assad in front of a group of Islamic scholars 25 August 2011. https://www.youtube.com/watch?v=RcJEf2N3BoM.

13 According to the Presidential Decree No. 28 issued on 19 November 2021, where the task of issuing fatwas was entrusted to the Jurisprudence Council of the Ministry of 'Awqaf.

14 From one of the 'Sessions of the Syrian People's Assembly' http://www.pministry.gov.sy/contents/12017/categories/40/الجلسات20%جميع.

15 *At-Tafsīr al-Ǧāmi, (The Comprehensive Interpretation)*. https://mow.gov.sy/ar/tafseer/pdf.

16 On the Syrian Ministry of 'Awqaf's Facebook page: https://www.facebook.com/awkafsyrian/posts/2238815322812487.

17 https://youtu.be/9hIgR0N5Evg.

18 The most relevant example of Shi'i activities is the foundation of the Ali Murtada Association by Hafez's brother, Jamil al-Assad, in 1981 during the war with the Muslim Brothers. Although the association had built branches in many Syrian cities and villages and many Syrians joined it, it was soon closed by a presidential decree in 1983 in retaliation against Jamil, who had supported Rifaat al-Assad in his struggle for power with his brother Hafez. See International Institute for Syrian Studies (2008: 42). https://almoslim.net/documents/IISS-7.pdf.

19 Just as Najaf had in Iraq and Qom had in Iran, Sayyida Zaynab attracted students from the Middle East, Africa, South Asia, Southeast Asia as well as North America (Szanto 2018: 96). Reportedly, from 1995 onwards, this suburb witnessed the construction of several *ḥawzāt* (religious seminaries), and it appeared that the area was going to become the 'Qom of Syria', since in the period between 1995 and 2000,

more than five *ḥawzāt* were constructed (International Institute for Syrian Studies 2008: 77). Szanto, however, argued that the seminaries held there 'concurrently aided the questioning of authoritative religious edicts and opinions emanating from Iranian and Iraqi centres of learning' (Szanto 2018: 96).
20 The number of Iranian-backed Shi'i militias in Syria has reached around 50, amounting to nearly 100,000 fighters, according to Iranian statements. They often bear provocative sectarian names, on this see Idlbi (2021: 18).
21 The number of scholarships for postgraduate studies in Iranian universities reached about 100 in 2017, and the number of scholarships offered by Iran to Syrian students increased to 200 in 2018, see Idlbi (2021: 27).
22 See the shocking figures up to 2015 (Balanche 2015).
23 Bashar al-Assad's speech at the opening of the conference of the Ministry of Foreign Affairs and Expatriates, 19 August 2017. https://www.youtube.com/watch?v=4b-BcIPp0eo.
24 See also the report: https://www.youtube.com/watch?v=C2YR4iTRinE. In 2005, Tehran succeeded in establishing the first Persian language department at Damascus University. It was followed by the universities of Homs and Aleppo and a large number of Syrian universities in other cities (Al-Hurra 2020).
25 An example can be seen from this small clip regarding the 'Scouts' march on the forty days of Imam Hussein': https://www.youtube.com/watch?v=ai1p__S5eUc.
26 On 10 November 2019, the opening of a branch of the Imam Al-Mahdi Scout in Deir ez-Zor was officially announced, see Ruqaiya and Othman (2021).
27 Al-Assad, Bashar, an excerpt from Al-Assad's meeting with religious sects, 2014. https://www.youtube.com/watch?v=ZczHkDXKrHg&t=11s.

Bibliography

Ajami, Fouad (1986). *The Vanished Imam: Musa al-Sadr and the Shia of Lebanon*. New York: Cornell University Press.
Al-Amin, Wissam (2015). 'Malaf hizbullāh (2): Kaššāfat al-Mahdī … [Hezbollah file (2): The Mahdi Scouts …]'. *Janoubiyya*. 26 April. https://janoubia.com/2015/04/26/-ملف (2)-حزب-الله-٢-كشافة-المهدي-خزان-المقا/ (accessed 10 June 2022).
Al-Azmeh, Aziz (2015). *Sūriya waṣ-ṣ'ūd al-'uṣlī: 'an al-'uṣūlīya waṭ-tā'fiya waṯ-ṯaqāfa* [Syria and the Fundementalist Surge: On Fundamentalism, Sectarianism and Culture]. Beirut: Riyāḍ Al-Rayyis.
Al-Azmeh, Aziz (2020). *Secularism in the Arab World: Contexts, Ideas and Consequences*. Edinburgh: Edinburgh University Press.
Al-Azmeh, Aziz (2021). 'Introduction'. In Nadia Al-Bagdadi, Harout Akdedian and Harith Hasan Aziz al-Azmeh (eds), *Striking from the Margins: State, Religion and Devolution of Authority in the Middle East* (1–31). London: Saqi Books.
Aldoughli, Rahaf (2020). 'Departing "Secularism": Boundary Appropriation and Extension of the Syrian State in the Religious Domain since 2011'. *British Journal of Middle Eastern Studies* 49(2): 360–85.
Al-Hurra (2020). 'Madaris wa-luġa fārisīya wa-ḥusayniyyāt … '. *al-Hurra News*. 18 February. https://www.alhurra.com/iran/2020/02/18/-مدارس-ولغة-فارسية-وحسينيات-حرب ناعمة-تشنها-إيران-في-سوريا/ (accessed 10 June 2022).

Al-Khatib, Majd (2019). 'Al-qānūn 31.: Al-ʾIslām kamā yarāh al-ʾAsad [Law 31: Islam as Seen by al-Assad]'. *Syria Untold*. 3 July. https://syriauntold.com/2019/07/03/-31-القانون- الإسلام-كما-يراه-الأسد/ (accessed 10 June 2022).

Al-Yahya, Mohammed Abdul Rahman (2011). 'Ṣafaḥāt min tārīḫ sūrīya al-muʿāṣir [Pages from Syrian Contemporary History]'. *Syria Noor*. 16 October. https://syrianoor.net/article/71 (accessed 10 June 2022).

Atassi, Ahmad Nazir (2016). 'Al-Baʿth wa al-ʾIslām fī Surīya: sultat al-Asad fī muwājahat al-ʿulamāʾ [The Bʿth and Islam in Syria: The Assad Lineage against the ulema]'. The World Institute. 1 July. http://alaalam.org/ar/religion-ar/item/321---البعث-والإس لام-في-سوريا-سلالة-الأسد-مواجهة-العلماء20%في (accessed 10 June 2022).

Böttcher, Annabelle (1997). *Syrische Religionspolitik unter Asad*. Freiburg: Arnold-Bergstraesser-Institut.

Böttcher, Annabelle (2004). 'Official Islam, Transnational Islamic Networks, and Regional Politics: The Case of Syria'. In Dietrich Jung (ed.), *The Middle East and Palestine: Global Politics and Regional Conflict* (125–50). New York: Palgrave Macmillan.

Balanche, Fabrice (2015). 'Ethnic Cleansing Threatens Syria's Unity'. Washington Institute. 3 December. https://www.washingtoninstitute.org/policy-analysis/ethnic-cleansing-threatens-syrias-unity (accessed 5 June 2022).

Barout, Mohammed Jamal (2017). *ḥamalāt Kisrwān fī at-tārīḫ as-syāsī li-fatāwa ʾIbn Taimīya*. Doha: Arab Center for Research and Policy Studies.

Barout, Muhammad Jamal (2018). *aṣ-ṣirāʿ al-ʿutmānī aṣ-ṣafawī wa-ʾataruh fī aš-šīʿīya fī Šamāl Bilād aš-Šām*. Doha: Arab Center for Research and Policy Studies.

Dadouch, Sarah (2021). 'After Backing Assad, Iran and Russia Compete for Influence and Spoils of War'. *Washington Post*. 20 May. https://www.washingtonpost.com/world/middle_east/syria-war-russia-iran-influence/2021/05/19/7d26851e-a9d1-11eb-bca5-048b2759a489_story.html. (accessed 5 June 2022).

Hinnebusch, Raymond (2001). *Syria: Revolution from Above*. London: Routledge.

Idlbi, Omar (2021. 'Ad-dawr al-ʾIrānī fī ʾiʿādat handast al-muǧtamʿ as-Sūrī [The Iranian Role in Re-engineering Syrian Society]'. *Haramoon for Contemporary Studies*. 8 September. https://www.harmoon.org/en/researches/irans-role-in-re-structuring-the-syrian-societ/ (accessed 10 June 2022).

International Institute for Syrian Studies (2008). *Al-baʿth al-shīʿī fī Suriyya: 1919–2007* [The Shiʿi Revival in Syria: 1919–2007]. s.l., 2008, p. 17. http://www.mediafire.com/?nmkdjmm3mzm (accessed 13 April 2010).

Jaber, Hanin (2019). 'al-Qubaysiyyāt fī ḍiyāfat al-ʾAsad mujddadan [Al-Qubaysīyāt are again hosted by al-Assad]'. *al-Ittihad Media*. Accessed Dead Link: https://aletihadpress.com/?p=158214.

Jazmati, Hussam (2020). 'Thawrat mashāyiḫ Dimashq [The Revolution of Sheikhs of Damascus]'. *Syria TV*. 26 October. https://www.syria.tv/ثورة-مشايخ-دمشق (accessed 10 June 2022).

Jusoor (2017). 'Sharia Leaders in Syria: Mentality and Role'. *Jusoor for Studies*. 28 November. https://jusoor.co/details/Sharia-Leaders-in-Syria-Mentality-and-Role/338%20/en (accessed 6 June 2022).

Khalaji, Mehdi (2010). 'A Marriage of Convenience'. Washington Institute. 18 November. http://www.washingtoninstitute.org/policy-analysis/view/a-marriage-of-convenience (accessed 5 June 2022).

Khatib, Line (2012). *Islamic Revivalism in Syria: The Rise and Fall of Secularism in Ba'thist Syria*. New York: Routledge.

Kramer, Martin (2017). *Arab Awakening and Islamic Revival: The Politics of Ideas in the Middle East*. New York: Routledge.

Maltzahn von, Nadia (2013). *The Syria–Iran Axis: Cultural Diplomacy and International Relations in the Middle East*. London: I.B. Tauris.

Mustafa, Hazem (2017). 'As-Sāḥil as-Sūrī: hal waqaʿa fī faḫ at-tašīīʿ as-syāsī [The Syrian Coast: Has It Fallen into the Trap of Political Shiitization?]'. *Syria Untold*. 11 April. https://syriauntold.com/2017/04/11/الساحل-السوري-هل-وقع-في-فخ-التشييع-السي/ (accessed 10 June 2022).

Omar, Sara (2013). 'Al-Qubaysiyyāt Negotiating Female Religious Authority in Damascus'. *Muslim World* 103(3): 347–62.

Orient News (2015). 'Ẓuhūr mufājiʾ li-Zahrān ʾAllūš fī Turkīya yuthīr at-tasāʾulāt! [Sudden Appearance of Zahran Alloush in Turkey Raises Questions]'. *Orient News*. Accessed Deadlink: https://www.orient-news.net/ar/news_show/86784.

Pierret, Thomas (2013a). 'Karbala in the Umayyad Mosque: Sunni Panic at the "Shiitization" of Syria in the 2000s'. In B. Maréchal and S. Zemni (eds), *The Dynamics of Sunni-Shia Relationships: Doctrine, Transnationalism, Intellectuals and the Media* (99–116). London: Hurst.

Pierret, Thomas (2013b). *Religion and State in Syria: The Sunni Ulama from Coup to Revolution*. Cambridge: Cambridge University Press.

Pierret, Thomas (2013c). 'The State Management of Religion in Syria: The End of 'Indirect Rule'. In Steven Heydemann and Reinoud Leenders (eds), *Middle East Authoritarianisms: Governance, Contestation, and Regime Resilience in Syria and Iran* (83–106). Stanford: Stanford University Press.

Rifai, Laila (2020). 'The Sunni Religious Establishment of Damascus: When Unification Creates Division.' Carnegie Middle East Center. 19 June. https://carnegie-mec.org/2020/06/19/sunni-religious-establishment-of-damascus-when-unification-creates-division-pub-82107 (accessed 6 June 2022).

Ruqaiya, al-Abadi, and Othman, Fatima (2021). 'Kaššāfat al-Mahdī: waqāʿ taǧnīd mīlīšiāt ʾIrānīya al-ʾṭfāl fī Sūrīya wa-Lubnān [Mahdi Scouts: The facts of Iranian militias' recruitment of children in Syria and Lebanon]'. Daraj Media. 6 May. https://daraj.com/71559/ (accessed 10 June 2022).

Sahafat al-jadid (2020). 'مدير أوقاف حلب لـ الثورة: التحصين الذاتي هو السلاح الأمضى في الدفاع عن الوطن [Director of Awqaf in Aleppo to the Revolution: Self-Preservation Is the Strongest Weapon to Defend the Nation]'. *Sahafat al-jadid*. 17 December. https://oman.sahafahn.net/news/10047566. (accessed 10 June 2022).

Sana (2014). 'fiqh al-ʾazma fī muāǧaht fiqh al-fitna'. *Syrian Arab News Agency*. 21 December. http://sana.sy/?p=117722 (accessed 10 June 2022).

Shora, Nawar (2009). *The Arab-American Handbook: A Guide to the Arab, Arab-American and Muslim Worlds*. Seattle: Cune Press.

SNS (2009). 'Al-ʾAsad yuqīm maʿdubat ifṭār li-rijāl ad-dīn' [Al-Assad Hosts Fast-Breaking Banquet for the Men of Religion]'. *Syrian News Station*. 17 September. http://www.sns.sy/ar/node/18187 (accessed 10 June 2022).

Swiss Info (2018). 'Ar-Raʾīs as-Sūrī yuṣdir qānūnan li-tanẓīm al-ʾAwqāf… [The Syrian President Issues a Law Regulating Endowments]'. *Swiss Info*. 13 October. https://www.swissinfo.ch/ara/44471/الرئيس-السوري-يصدر-قانونا-لتنظيم-الأوقاف-يحدد-ولاية-مفتي-الجمهورية 414 (accessed 10 June 2022).

Syrian Arab Republic (2016). 'Al-ʾAwqāf tuṭliq al-muntadā al-ḥiwārī li-Farīq ad-Dīnī as-Shabābī [Awqaf Launches a Dialogue Forum for the Youth Religious Team]'.

Ministry of Information. 26 April. http://www.moi.gov.sy/index.php?content=2&article=NjQzMg== (accessed 10 June 2022).

Szanto, Edith (2013). 'Beyond the Karbala Paradigm: Rethinking Revolution and Redemption in Twelver Shi'a Mourning Rituals'. *Journal of Shi'a Islamic Studies* 6 (1): 75–91.

Szanto, Edith (2018). 'Challenging Transnational Shi'i Authority in Ba'th Syria'. *British Journal of Middle East Studies* 45(1): 95–110.

Vohra, Anchal (2021). 'Iran Is Trying to Convert Syria to Shiism'. *Foreign Policy*. 15 March. https://foreignpolicy.com/2021/03/15/iran-syria-convert-shiism-war-assad/ (accessed 6 June 2022).

Chapter 12

DILEMMAS OF INTERVENTIONS IN NORTHERN SYRIA: REFUGEE RETURN, RECONSTRUCTION AND DISPLACEMENTS

Zeynep Sahin-Mencütek and Osman Bahadir Dinçer

Introduction

The repercussions of the uprising in Syria quickly transformed into a humanitarian crisis due to the harsh crackdown by the Assad rule. Along with mass violence and destruction, waves of migration and displacement in and out of the country swept across Syria and the region (Shaery-Yazdi and Üngör 2021; Kingsley 2015). More than half of Syria's population[1] has been displaced since 2011 (Ferris 2015; Ferris et al. 2013). Besides internally displaced persons (IDPs), around 6.5 million Syrians living in neighbouring countries, mainly in Turkey, Lebanon, and Jordan have faced dire living conditions and precarious legal status.[2] Traditionally, three main solutions have been proposed to address the circumstances of refugees – integration, resettlement and voluntary repatriation. The latter has often been deemed the most desirable by host countries, while they have approached formal integration impossible due to domestic concerns (Sahin-Mencütek 2018). Many externally displaced Syrians, however, do not consider returning to Syria a safe option.[3]

The return of the displaced is a crucial component of post-conflict agendas. The narrative of the safe return of refugees and displaced persons often suggests that circumstances in the countries of origin have returned to normal. Furthermore, such narratives also signal preparedness for post-war reconstruction, rehabilitation and progress towards developmental goals, which reinforce the post-war legitimacy of those who emerged victorious (Petrin 2002; Black and Koser 1999). The return of displaced persons is considered an indicator of the wellbeing and maturity of a post-war state, signalling the success of a political settlement (McDowell and Eastmond 2002: 2–3). From this point of view, whether or not refugees will return to Syria could provide clues about the future of Syria and its politics.

Though the Assad rule has maintained control over much of the Syrian territories, many parts of Syria remain beyond its grasp. Northern Syria, for instance, remains under the control of non-state actors (HRW 2021), primarily supported by Turkey. In some parts of the northeast, pro-Kurdish forces have maintained a presence. Power holders, including the Assad government, Turkish-backed Interim Government, Idlib-based Salvation Government or Democratic Federation of Northern Syria in Rojava and their partners (e.g. the local councils) ultimately lack substantial legitimacy and capacity to carry out full-scale governing functions (al-Meehy 2021; Hoffman and Makovsky 2021; Kamel 2017). Economic deterioration and the collapse of central service infrastructure have had ruinous consequences across the country (Azmeh 2021; Asseburg 2020; Daher 2018). In addition, there is significant concern about demographic engineering parallel to the ethnic, religious, and sectarian changes of the Syrian population in general and within local communities in northern Syria in particular, alongside the confiscation of properties (Ghosh-Siminoff 2020; Osmandzikovic 2020; Gardner 2019). Within this political and security context, urging the immature return of Syrian refugees exposes potential returnees to fragile and harmful circumstances, including security concerns, social and political challenges, lack of livelihood opportunities, and the destruction of properties. Even if a political solution is achieved with the Assad rule, this will not guarantee the safety and security of returnees. Nevertheless, despite the challenges on the ground, neighbouring countries continue to advocate for the repatriation of Syrian refugees back to Syria. Turkey's position is critical in this context as it hosts 3.7 million displaced Syrians.[4]

This chapter aims to scrutinize Turkey's changing policies regarding the return and reintegration of displaced Syrians to northern Syria: the regions under the control of Turkey or Turkish-backed groups. The focus is on the practices of the Turkish state regarding displacement, repatriation, and formal and informal initiatives in negotiating the future of Syrian refugees. These themes are addressed within a broader context, including the transformations in Turkey's approach to the Syrian crisis and its military interventions.[5] Empirically, the chapter is informed by desk research and the authors' fieldwork in cities along both sides of the Turkish-Syrian border over the past decade. Interviews were conducted with Syrian returnees and key community members (e.g. local council representatives, officers and bureaucrats) to get a sense of the realities on the ground. We also contacted the diaspora organizations and networks of Syrian groups taking a leading role during different phases of the displacement. This research is also based on secondary sources, particularly the reports of international organizations[6] and the analyses of public statements by the ruling Justice and Development Party (AKP) and Turkish authorities representing the Turkish state. Notably, the speeches and statements of Turkish President R. Erdogan and former Interior Minister S. Soylu (2016–23) – the two leading names that shaped the refugee policy framework – and the declarations of the National Security Council (NSC) are studied as the primary sources to analyse Ankara's approach in the period between 2015 and 2021. These multiple data sources complement each other to provide a comprehensive analysis of Turkey's refugee policy and its correlations with military interventions in northern Syria since 2016.

The chapter argues that Turkey's return policies regarding Syrians are fluctuating and paradoxical, and reflect its domestic and foreign policy imperatives. Refugee management (specifically repatriation to country of origin), geopolitics (particularly border control and local electoral politics) and domestic politics (rising anti-immigrant and anti-Syrian dispositions) are inseparable in the case of Turkey (Tziarras and Harchaoui 2021; Siccardi 2021). Turkey's politics and policies aim to encourage the return of refugees while also taking active steps towards laying the groundwork for the unilateral repatriation of refugees through military, administrative and economic interventions inside Syria. More specifically, the Turkish government seeks to control demilitarized zones, close to what is labelled as the 'safer' border regime on its southern front, by sponsoring opposition groups on the ground that also counter Kurdish forces. Since concluding its operations, namely the Euphrates Shield in March 2017 and Peace Spring in 2019, Turkey has provided control along the length of the border to prevent the formation of a geographically contiguous Kurdish autonomous zone. It has taken advantage of the vacuum in the northeast by imposing itself in Syrian territories through 'Operation Peace Spring', which established a 'safe zone' of 460 km on the Syrian-Turkish border, while promising to repatriate Syrian refugees in these designated areas. Turkey's reconstruction and development projects introduced cross-border administrative measures and included involvement in local initiatives in areas ranging from aid delivery, security, and the provision of education, health and municipal services (Adar 2020; Sahin-Mencütek 2021). 'An alternative local elite [in northern Syria] loyal to Ankara', hampers any Kurdish self-administration agendas close to Turkey's border and consolidates its power and bargaining power in the Syrian conflict (Asseburg 2020: 13; Adar 2020).

Regarding domestic politics, the growing public predispositions against Syrian refugees, with anti-immigrant narratives becoming more politicized, propelled the return of Syrian refugees as an urgent policy matter, especially during elections (Icduygu and Nimer 2020). Both public and political elites are no longer incentivized to carry the humanitarian 'burden' of the Syrian conflict. Public surveys show that most Turks are unsympathetic to the idea of coexistence with Syrians and support solutions such as 'putting them in safe zones inside Syria', 'deporting them' and 'establishing a Syrian-only city' (Erdogan 2020). Turkey's operational use of refugee policies raise fair concerns about the instrumentalization of refugees for purposes of demographic engineering and long-term cross-border interventions.

Turkey and the Syrian displacement crisis

In the early 2000s, the southern border of Turkey was of pronounced geostrategic importance and was once seen as a site of opportunity for economic and cultural integration with the rest of the region. However, following the Arab uprisings, it has slowly become an ongoing source of challenges that are characterized by unprecedented instability and turmoil (Dinçer and Hecan 2016; Ferris 2015). Turkey has gradually assumed the position of an isolated actor facing allegations of fuelling the civil conflicts, primarily in Syria and Libya, instrumentalizing and politicizing refugees in both domestic and foreign policies (Jennequin 2020; Badi 2021; Gottlieb and Kedar 2020; Speckhard 2019).

Turkish authorities followed an open-door policy at the very beginning of the events and, therefore, unconditionally accepted all forcibly displaced people from Syria (Ferris and Kirisci 2015). The people who took refuge in Turkey not only came from the regions close to the border but from all over the country, including from frontline areas near Damascus in Southern Syria (Güçer, Karaca and Dinçer 2013: 36). In October 2011, the Turkish government introduced de facto 'temporary protection' for Syrians, which reflected Ankara's open-door policy and commitment to ensuring basic humanitarian services for refugees.[7] However, as refugee numbers continued to grow, the Turkish government started taking measures to limit entry, leading to the emergence of more than twenty makeshift camps along the Syrian side of the border for those waiting to gain admission to Turkey (Dinçer et al. 2013: 12). For example, some of these makeshift camps, Atmeh, Bab al-Hawa and Bab al-Salame, eventually became semi-permanent fixtures along the border and were provided with aid from the UN and other humanitarian organizations based in provinces of Turkey (e.g. Gaziantep, Kilis).[8] In the meantime, a growing number of Syrians fleeing the violence began to enter Turkey through so-called unofficial border-crossings and joined fellow Syrians inside Turkey.[9] Interview data reveals that some of these IDPs indeed preferred to remain in Syria to enjoy easier access to their property and family back home, yet, the growth in the number of refugees in Turkey suggested that many Syrians continued to enter Turkey unofficially. While some of them legalized temporary protection status by registering in the provincial Directorate of Migration Management branches, many others did not and attempted onward migration to Europe, which reached its peak in the summer of 2015.

Meanwhile, Turkish authorities have largely turned a blind eye to the very real possibility that the ever-growing presence of refugees could have incited societal and political tension. In other words, the authorities underestimated the size of the problem for an extended period, believing that the presence of Syrians would be temporary, and cultural/religious affinity would lead to seamless socio-economic integration.[10] The AKP initially adopted an *Ensar-Muhacir* discourse because of its Islamic approach to the refugees (Kaya et al. 2021).[11] As the conflict intensified and the resources of the Turkish government became stretched, questions started to arise about the limits of Turkey's capacity to host refugees and the costs of its self-assigned leadership role in shaping the Syrian war (Dinçer et al. 2013). Turkey's approach began to gradually change thereafter (Kiniklioglu 2020). Over time, the Turkish government sought ways to use the refugee issue as a blackmailing tool against European countries. It also started to adopt coercive measures against Syrians (e.g. impeding access to services, limiting travel mobility, deportation) after ignoring their presence in urban areas across a country devoid of a well-planned monitoring mechanism for several years (Sahin-Mencütek 2021, 2021a). Sending Syrians back to Syria might be illegal and impractical, but the government voiced such plans, reflecting growing discontent among Turkey's citizens.[12] Although refugee matters should ideally be assessed through the humanitarian prism, the security perspectives of refugee-hosting countries often prevailed.[13]

Turkey's changing approach towards the Syrian crisis: Policies and consequences

Ankara's strategic priorities about Syria fluctuated according to developments on the ground and the parallel patterns of simultaneous coordination and contestation with the United States, Russia and Iran, and anti-Assad armed groups. Accordingly, the adverse spill-over effects of Turkish foreign policy jeopardized Turkey's relations with major regional powers, such as Russia and Iran, prior to reaching precarious settlements of de facto cooperation (Köstem 2020; Özertem 2017). Likewise, Turkey's relations with the United States plunged into a cold stalemate due to the two countries' diverging political priorities in Syria (Gülmez 2020; Barkey 2016).

Ankara initially adopted a cautious and constructive approach to ensure a soft transition in Damascus, mainly convincing the Assad rule to make the demanded reforms.[14] After the Assad rule's failure to reform and the militarization of the Syrian uprising, Ankara began providing logistical support to Syrian opposition armed groups, which ultimately made Turkey a de facto part of the Syrian civil war. As a highly influential regional player, it was not an option for Turkey to stay neutral in Syria. Various factors accounted for Turkey's early and daring decision to support the opposition against the Assad rule, including Turkey's overconfidence in its foreign policy initiatives in the Middle East at that time (Demir 2017; Davutoglu 2013; Kuru 2015; Bank and Karadag 2013). However, despite supporting armed groups, Turkey did not plan any military cross-border operations in Syria until August 2016. In pre-2016 period AKP deliberately prioritized soft power instruments over coercive hard power capabilities (Yesiltaş and Balci 2013: 10).

Unlike its Western allies, Turkey maintained that the removal of Assad was central to its Syria policy for a longer time. Nevertheless, increasingly negative repercussions such as the refugee crisis, the spread of the Democratic Union Party (PYD) forces and a growing number of irregular armed groups ultimately changed Turkey's priorities in its Syria policy. Subsequently, Turkey started to have a more ambiguous hierarchy of priorities as the management of new challenges became more pressing, from a security perspective, than the removal of Assad (Dinçer and Hecan 2016). After September 2015, Russia's high-pitched military intervention generated new waves of displacement while shifting the course of the war in favour of the Assad rule (Fahim and Samaan 2015). Tens of thousands of Syrians mobilized towards the border with Turkey as the Syrian government launched operations to retake Aleppo city and its surroundings from opposition forces in collaboration with Russia, Iran and Hezbollah. In this context, Turkey was forced to shoulder most of the humanitarian burden. Turkey has started to seek pragmatic solutions through increased engagement with Russia, Iran and even the Syrian government.

Significant shifts in the country's established Western-oriented alliances also influenced patterns of cooperation in Turkey's Syria policies. Turkey found itself having a rapprochement with Russia and Iran. Despite internal opposition to Russia and Iran within the Turkish state, in January 2017 Ankara officially became a part of the Astana process. This constituted a major shift in Turkish foreign policy by effectively abandoning the Geneva process. Ankara gained a military presence in northern Syria, including in Idlib, and it has been trusted to restrain anti-Assad groups 'even though supporting the anti-Assad opposition has been the primary source of leverage in Syria thus far' (Dinçer and Hecan 2021: 272). The humanitarian crisis effectively helped Russia and the Assad rule by placing new pressures on Turkey and Europe with regards to their anti-Assad commitments and the extent of military involvement.

Cross-border military operations: Euphrates Shield, Olive Branch and Peace Spring

Given the high level of commitment to regime change in Syria from the AKP elite, some may question why Turkey did not decide to use military force until the summer of 2016. Retrospectively, some may argue that the interventions of Russia and Iran in Syria, the two actors supporting the Assad rule, prove that Turkey did not have sufficient power to deter this involvement, and that its ability/experience to lead a proxy war was not on par with Iran or Russia. Regardless of military capacity, Turkey did not use force due to a number of other reasons. These include domestic political preferences, the resistance of key factions within the army as well as geopolitical power dynamics in the Middle East. No matter the specific reasons behind the absence of force prior to 2016, the nature of the conflict as an all-out civil war played further into the hands of regional and international actors who were committed to using overt military force to support the Assad rule. Ankara's foreign policy tools were limited by the military engagement of other regional and international powers. Ankara's recent efforts to salvage its already tarnished image as an integral part of the relevant geopolitical network, namely the unilateral military operations, have not only widened the existing gap between Ankara's desires and abilities but also created many questions about its power and military status in the region and beyond (Altunisik 2020).

Apart from the joint operation with other coalition members against *Daesh*, Turkey has carried out three major unilateral military operations into the northern Syria so far: Euphrates Shield (2016–17), Olive Branch (2018) and Operation Peace Spring (2019). These operations were intended to eliminate the permanent presence of any type of Kurdish force on its southern border, expand its sphere of power/influence inside Syria and open space for refugee relocation (Siccardi 2021; Yüksel and van Veen 2019). It is worth noting that Turkey has been allowed to take these operations into the north of Syria with the approval of Russia and in line with the interests of the Syrian government. Changes in Turkey's military leadership and power structures also paved the way for military operations inside Syria.

Following the 'failed coup attempt' on 15 July 2016, the purge in the Turkish army removed officers who aligned with NATO and who opposed military intervention in Syria (Ataman 2019; ODATV 2017).

Spheres of influence and displacement

The unprecedented escalation by Turkish forces in the northeast reshuffled strategic partnerships in the region. For instance, even in August 2016 when the stated objective was to capture *Daesh* strongholds, Turkey's military involvement in northern Syria was to push the Democratic Union Party (PYD) to withdraw to the eastern side of the Euphrates River (Arango et al. 2016). Ankara views the main Kurdish component of the Syrian Democratic Forces (SDF) as a security threat because the gains of People's Protection Units (YPG) and its political counterpart, the PYD, could benefit the Kurdistan Workers' Party (PKK). PKK is a terrorist organization recognized by NATO as such, and has had long-lasting armed conflict with Turkey. Turkey consistently claims that the YPG-PYD is tied to the PKK through its party cadres, PKK-trained Kurdish fighters and volunteers who entered Syria to join the battle against *Daesh* (ICG 2020). Western countries consider the PYD and PKK legally distinct entities that are linked historically and operationally (Stanicek 2019). Due to its security perceptions, Turkey's main military aim in Syria has been to prevent the YPG-PYD from establishing an autonomous area (Yüksel 2019). Since 2018, some YPG controlled areas have fallen to a combination of Turkish and Turkish-affiliated Syrian forces after the operations mentioned above that the United States and Russia tolerated due to strategic calculations (ICG 2020).

Turkey's National Security Council (NSC), the central state body shaping the foreign and security policies of Turkey, underscores the role of Turkey's operations in 'cleansing' and 'emancipating' Turkey's southern borders from 'the terror threat' and 'preparing the region for returns of displaced Syrians' (NSC 2019b, 2020). Despite efforts to legitimize operations with humanitarian and security narratives, the Turkish government could not garner the expected international support. The EU criticized the last incursion into northeast Syria because it led to new waves of displacement, and security threats linked to *Daesh* foreign fighters present in Syria (Heinemann-Grüder 2019). The EU repeatedly called for the Syrian state's unity, sovereignty and territorial integrity while threatening Turkey with the cessation of arms sales by the EU and suspension of accession talks (Gurnini 2020; Stanicek 2019).

While reacting to the emergence of a Kurdish fait accompli, Ankara has been in the process of creating its own protectorate (de facto administration and statelet) along the immediate border, inside Syria. As of mid-2021, Turkish-backed armed rebel groups (a coalition of armed groups) have been operating in the areas identified with the operation names: the region of Operation Euphrates Shield (area between Azaz, al-Bab, and Jarabulus) and Operation Olive Branch (Afrin district) areas in northern Aleppo governorate, and of Operation Peace Spring area between Tall Abyad (ar-Raqqa governorate) and Ra's al-'Ain (al-Hasakah governorate) (EASO 2020: 37; also see Hoffman and Makovsky 2021).

As Yetim and Kaşıkçı (2021: 194) note, 'Turkey's support ... started with just sheltering the organization's [FSA] leaders in Turkey and increased gradually to financial and military aid, training, guiding, and lastly, combating together within the Syrian borders.' In 2017 the FSA was rebranded as the Syrian National Army (SNA). The alliance between Turkey and the FSA-SNA rests upon mutual gains. From the point of the FSA-SNA, the alliance with Turkey has been crucial for overcoming the groupings' organizational weaknesses and logistics (Yetim and Kaşıkçı 2021; Yüksel 2019). From Ankara's point of view, the FSA-SNA addresses Turkey's security concerns, expands its sphere of influence and contributes to the creation of a 'safe zone' inside Syria (Reuters 2016). Besides extending its control over Kurdish forces close to its borders, Ankara plans to manage the situation of Syrian refugees inside Turkey by creating a so-called safe zone where Syrians may repatriate (Sahin-Mencütek 2021). The National Security Council also announced its commitment to take 'further steps' to 'realize' this project in 2019 (NSC 2019a). The NSC also called on 'the international community' to 'support Turkey's attempts' to achieve 'safe and voluntary returns' and a 'dignified return of Syrian sisters and brothers' (NSC 2020). In line with this, in September 2019, Turkish President Erdoğan officially stated during the 74th UN General Assembly that the Turkish government

> intend[s] initially to establish a peace corridor with a depth of 30 kilometres and a length of 480 kilometres and enable the settlement of two million Syrians there with the support of the international community ... With this safe zone we have the chance to resettle 1–2 million immigrants and refugees easily. If the US, coalition forces and Iran cooperate on this issue, we can move the refugees from tent- and container-towns to this safe zone (AA 2019).

Although the plan lacks international legitimacy and support, international actors have not yet strongly rejected it.[15] In his visit to Turkey in November 2019, UN Secretary-General António Guterres stated that the UNHCR would 'immediately form a team to study the proposal and engage in discussions with Turkish authorities, in line with its mandate' (UN News 2021). Nevertheless, there is no bilateral or multilateral readmission or tripartite agreement to facilitate the return of Syrians, which would require the involvement of the UNHCR and Syria's current government. Policymakers from the Turkish ruling party tend to frame the return issue gradually and selectively to lay the conceptual groundwork for the future course of action that aims to appease domestic constituencies and the international community (Sahin-Mencütek 2021a). To do this, *reconstruction* and *local embeddedness* are prerequisites.

Returns practices and experiences of returnees

Turkey's national migration agency, the Directorate General of Migration Management (DGMM), is primarily responsible for repatriation, according to the 2013 Law on Foreigners and International Protection, and the Temporary

Protection Directive of 2014, which lays out the rules and procedures about the return of foreigners, irregular migrants and those under temporary protection (mainly Syrians). The DGMM commits to ensuring the 'voluntariness' of return, collaborating with multiple actors, including UNHCR, and completing paperwork to this end and providing in-kind and monetary support to those who apply for voluntary returns (LFIP 2013).

For Syrians, Turkey encourages repatriation by using ad-hoc practices as Syria is not a safe country for returnees (Sahin-Mencütek 2019). One practice is Turkey's use of short-term visit permits to Syria, particularly for visits during religious holidays (up to three months). By doing so, Syrians leave Turkey, assess conditions in their home areas and check on their vacated properties. If they wish, they could choose to remain in Syria. This arrangement is not based on the legal framework that came about after 2011 but is rather a government decision implemented by the DGMM and border authorities issuing temporary travel permits (Sahin-Mencütek 2019). The DGMM revokes temporary protection status if Syrians fail to return within the permitted period. In 2017, 40,000 Syrians (15 per cent of those who departed) remained in Syria, while it increased to 252,000 Syrians (57 per cent) in 2018 (Daily Sabah 2018).

Another method is the provision of logistical and information assistance to facilitate returns. Assistance is delivered at the local level with coordination between municipalities and provincial DGMM offices. The targets are the most densely Syrian-populated municipalities. After arrival at the border, returnees are assisted by two Turkish agencies (Kızılay and AFAD) working inside Syria, who escort returnees to cities under Turkey's control (Sahin-Mencütek 2019). Turkish authorities occasionally force repatriation and deportation, under the mask of voluntary returns (Sahin-Mencütek 2021b). These are justified by claiming that the returnee has been accused of being a 'terror/security' threat or a 'threat to public order' (HRW 2019) or lacking proper documentation (Sahin-Mencütek 2023). Reports of human rights organizations and watchdog journalism attested that some Syrians were forced to sign voluntary return forms under duress from state officers (HRW 2019; Sahin-Mencütek 2021b). UNHCR are not involved in return procedures. Turkish Kızılay representatives sign off on voluntary return paperwork (Sahin-Mencütek 2019).

Syrians in Turkey choosing to return without assistance or coercion mention multiple facets of their decision. The main pull-factor is an improvement in safety conditions. Returnees also reported other factors such as care responsibilities towards parents or the protection of land and property from squatters. 'Patriotic' considerations are also amongst the factors voiced by returnees. However, push-factors in the host country were voiced more frequently by returnees. The push-factors are (1) economic and livelihood challenges, particularly losing jobs in the informal sector with the pandemic, increase in food prices, rents, bills and debts, (2) the growing widespread hostility of local Turkish communities, rising anti-refugee political discourse towards Syrians, (3) losing prospects for onward migration to Europe, (4) language barriers and lacking a sense of belonging. Returnees have lost their hope for a better future in Syria due to such factors.

Turkey's Interior Minister noted 414,061 'voluntary' returns to Syria prior to 2020 (TRT-Haber 2020). Turkish authorities do not specify the source of these return figures, but they note that these returns occurred in the so-called safe zone controlled by Turkey and its Syrian allies.

Reconstruction attempts in Northern Syria

The plans proposed by the Turkish presidency in 2019 regarding the so-called safe zone return and reconstruction have been gradually put into practice (see Yüksel and van Veen 2019). Ankara now controls a long stretch of Syrian territory along its southern border. In addition to the Jarabulus-Afrin line, some north-east areas, Tall Abyad and Ra's al-'Ain towns, which were Kurdish-populated before the intervention, have also been controlled by Turkey's allies since the military operations. The plan sought to relocate over a million Syrians between Tall Abyad and Ra's al-'Ain, and build housing units, universities, schools and hospitals (Reuters 2019; Sahin-Mencütek 2021a). After significant investments, along with the political and military risks Ankara took, the activities of Turkey and Turkish-backed groups along the immediate border create many questions for the original residents of those areas and its political status (Yüksel and van Veen 2021: 5–6). There are significant questions as to whether Turkey's presence is temporary or if the current status implies a permanent stay. It seems that there is no well-planned military and political long-term plan or strategy but at the same time Turkey does not seem to have an exit plan either. In other words, it is not clear what Turkey will do with its Syrian allies in northern Syria. Northern Syria's political and military landscape manifests a de facto protectorate, and Turkey acts as its patron state. Unlike Idlib, Turkish-controlled areas in northern Syria are primarily administered by Turkish civil servants and indeed are being integrated into the Turkish economic government (Hoffman and Makovsky 2021: 10). It would not be an exaggeration to claim that northern Syria has been in the process of turning into a political entity like northern Cyprus, a Turkish protectorate through military and economic domination (Yüksel and van Veen 2019; Yanarocak 2018).

Besides military control, finding local embeddedness is critical for Turkey's presence and control in northern Syria. Turkish-backed actors have co-opted or supported local institutions. Turkish authorities have replicated their administrative divisions and implanted many state agencies to operate in the service sectors (e.g. religious, postal, safety, water, shelter, communication, health and education). In the words of Yüksel and van Veen, 'Turkey has been setting up institutions that mirror Turkish structures and practices' (2021: 5).

One particular type of key actor that Turkish authorities work with is the 'local councils'. Local councils are governing bodies that have emerged throughout Syria to fill a need for social and governmental organizations in areas where the Assad rule has relinquished control (al-Meehy 2021). Turkey created or supported existing local councils in large cities with smaller subordinate councils in surrounding towns and villages. Ankara imposed its influence on Syrian local councils[16] by tying each region to an adjacent Turkish province (Kilis, Antakya, Gaziantep, Hatay) (al-Hilu 2021). Deputy governors of the adjoining Turkish provinces intervene in the administration in Syria (Gall 2021). For governing the local services, Ankara supports Syrian local councils to manage the affairs of towns and villages in its zones of influence. At least nineteen were established, such as in Afrin (2018), al-Bab, Azaz, Jarabulus, Ra's al-'Ain (2019), Tall Abyad (2019).[17] For example,

> There are ten local councils in Syria's 'Euphrates Shield' region, overseen by the Turkish provinces of Gaziantep and Kilis. These are the councils of *al-Bab, Jarabulus, Azaz, al-Ra'i, Marea, Akhtarin, Suran, Qabasin, Bazaa* and *al-Ghandoura*, and smaller secondary councils subordinate to them. In each of these councils, the Turkish authorities have appointed a person to serve as their deputy who mediates between the council and the relevant Turkish province. (al-Hilu 2021: 11)

Local councils also attracted foreign funds and subcontracted private agencies referred to as 'implementers'. The funds are for institution-building projects or humanitarian aid delivery; many of these agencies operate from Gaziantep in Turkey (Khalaf 2021: 53). The council members (around twenty to twenty-five) are elected from powerful local families, tribes and ethnic groups, seen as 'prominent people in the city'. These councils and associated security forces provide public services with the help of Turkish officials' funding, oversight and training (Blanchard 2022: 4). Notably, in Afrin, Tall Abyad and Ras al-Ayn, Ankara seeks to ensure the formation of loyal local councils and to exclude all opponents or even neutral parties. Local projects (including those in IDP camps) are asked to run with either the supervision of 'Turkish advisors' or with permission from Turkish institutions present there, such as ministry representatives (e.g. AFAD, Ministry of Education and Turkish Intelligence Agency). Turkish Kızılay and AFAD provide humanitarian aid to the people living in the IDP camps.

Turkish institutions (deputy governors and mayors of bordering cities, relevant ministries, directorates, companies, NGOs, etc.) build or repair infrastructure, health and education facilities. Hence, 'the basic services provided to civilians in northern Syria include the maintenance of water networks, the operation of bakeries, the installation of telecommunication and internet infrastructure and the restoration of hospitals in major cities and provision of them with necessary equipment and appliances. Moreover, the Turkish government has restored schools and returned them to operation' (al-Hilu 2021: 13). Businesses become involved through Turkish border cities (backing the electrical grid, cell phone lines and currency). The Turkish government has also run projects to build temporary housing in areas like Idlib for newly displaced Syrians (Aydıntaşbaş 2020).

There are numerous concerns about the local councils. Each armed group has its own 'local council', declared one interviewee. Local observers also emphasized during interviews that even though the local councils have the authority to run the cities in theory, the armed groups controlling the area have the ultimate practical authority due to their armed power. Besides, as acknowledged by many, 'people are not happy with the local councils and are demanding they be changed because the councils are considered corrupt' (al-Khateb 2020).

Although the overall security is under Turkish-backed armed groups, there are micro patronages, as interview data reveals that returnees have to pay bribes on checkpoints while they are returning to their hometowns, meaning that responsibility-sharing became fluid in practice after returnees crossed the Turkish border. The role of local councils is not fully clear; instead, it seems to carry out some subsidiary functions in the post-return stages by filling the gaps in service provisions. They depend on vice governors of bordering Turkish cities for permission for reconstruction projects, to address council-related problems or meet basic demands (al-Khateb 2020). In the Turkish-controlled areas, interviewees noted that an eclectic governance architecture is present, as the municipal services, for instance, are provided by local councils affiliated with armed groups, and local NGOs, with funds coming from international projects.[18] In the words of one returnee, 'While local councils deliver the services, the internal security is provided by *Shurta al-madaniyye*, a police department affiliated with the local council in Tall Abyad.'[19]

Challenges encountered by returnees in northern Syria

The eclectic governance structure in northern Syria makes safety and survival difficult for returnees, requiring them to navigate the complex system and power dynamics to access basic services in challenging security, humanitarian and economic situations. The threat to security and safety is the primary concern for people living there, IDPs, and returnees in northern Syria. Insurgent attacks under Turkish-backed armed groups continue, including assassinations and car bombs against Turkish and SNA forces. The targets of most of these attacks may have been the military, but the victims also include Syrian civilians (ICG 2020). In October 2019, a resolution of the European Parliament reported that 'there are specific reports of killings, intimidation, ill-treatment, kidnapping, looting and seizure of civilians' houses' by Turkish-backed armed groups, with civilians accused of affiliation with specific Kurdish groups reportedly being forcibly removed from their homes or seized at checkpoints by members of these groups (European Parliament 2019). The OHCHR notes grave violations and a rise in criminality in the areas under the control of Turkish forces and Turkish-affiliated armed groups, including Afrin, Ra's al-'Ain, and Tall Abyad. These regions observe 'increased killings, kidnappings, unlawful transfers of people, seizures of land and properties and forcible evictions. The victims are people perceived to be allied with opposing parties or as being critical of the actions of the Turkish-affiliated armed groups or those wealthy people that may pay a ransom' (OHCHR 2020: 1). There is a lower reporting rate of arrests, detention, torture and rapes than in government-controlled areas. Moreover, an estimated 151,000 people were uprooted from their homes by fighting in the Afrin region, due to the Turkish Olive Branch military operation in January 2018 (UNHCR 2018). According to our interviews, Kurdish families had to flee to other areas inside Syria or northern Iraq. These areas continue to be the primary source of instability and escalatory cycle of violence (ICG 2020).

The changing dynamics around power-holders also impede the return of refugees and IDPs to their 'homes'. Even in places where there is a ceasefire, like Idlib, internal displacements of people occur during the clashes between armed groups and during the escalation of tensions. There are incidents in which civilians, including children, are killed and injured due to the ongoing hostilities. These circumstances also challenge the safety of returnees on the way home and upon arrival. That is to say, interview data confirms that the return journey is also a risky endeavour. The risks range from 'checkpoints' and 'investigation' by armed groups on the ground to the power struggles that easily turn into clashes and which 'happen between them, which leads to unstable feelings', and the imposition of 'forced conscription by fighting parties'.

Turkey identifies the regions under its control as 'safe', and encourages the return of Syrian refugees in Turkey, denying accusations about the demographic change in the areas under control. The European Parliament, however, 'raises serious concerns about the safety of people displaced by the conflict and those that could be relocated from Turkey' as well as noting signs of 'demographic and ethnic changes' (European Parliament 2019). Arab interviewees limitedly focused on claims about demographic changes during our conversations. One returnee who works as a police officer in Tall Abyad said, 'My relatives live in Raqqa/Maden, controlled by government forces and Iranian militants; thus, the social fabric was changed.'[20] Another said, 'Ayn Issa is under PKK control; thus, I returned to another place in Syria; first I returned to Jarabulus, then Tall Abyad.'[21]

Turkey's control in previously Kurdish-dominated areas and the ongoing fighting seem to be the main impediments for Kurds returning to Syria, particularly those fleeing to Northern Iraq (Hoffman and Makovsky 2021: 23). At the same time, the ongoing militarization (and recruitment) of PYD also worsens the conditions of returnees. Kurdish interviewees have been more outspoken about demographic change and their multiple displacements. One told us:

> We lost our areas and cities. [The] Turkish army destroyed all our historical places and changed them demographically. We are displaced in our country. We are only just 45 km far away from our origin place and cannot even visit it. We cannot return to our city because of the Turkish occupation. We are waiting for the withdrawal of the Turkish forces and the Syrian Arab militias that occupied our city so that the indigenous people can return to their areas in addition to providing basic services, returning property, providing safety and job opportunities. We can return to our original areas.[22]

Besides the security and safety challenges, the lack of access to livelihoods, high food prices and the low purchasing power of locals create additional problems. One returnee summarized the situation by stating that 'the average income for the employee in Syria nowadays is around 50$, but you need at least 200$ to manage your life'.[23] According to interviewees, some start-up businesses seem to survive but are very fragile due to the harsh economic conditions (mainly inflation) and the problems in the supply of goods. Remittances from family members in Turkey, Europe (mainly Germany) and Gulf countries seem to have been the primary sources of capital for restarting lives in Syria. The remittances are used for repairing houses, 'starting up new business, like opening shops', and meeting basic needs, as mentioned by interviewees. Accordingly, many observers acknowledge a need for humanitarian aid across the country. The problems in the distribution of humanitarian assistance by the World Food Program and international NGOs are severe, and are worsened by local authorities' blockages and cuts in the supply lines of trade goods. Two local council representatives from Tall Abyad and Ra's al-'Ain that we interviewed complained about the lack of international or EU humanitarian aid in their regions, particularly noting the non-recognition of the areas in north-eastern Syria. They believe that EU funds would alleviate the service provision problems.[24]

Service infrastructure is also a problem. Impeding access to water, sanitation and electricity has also been used by Turkish affiliated forces and SDF forces as a weapon, endangering the lives of a large numbers of people (OHCHR 2020: 1). Even for the regions less impacted by fighting, education infrastructure is the most severe problem affecting children. 'There are villages with schools but without teachers', according to an interviewee from Tall Abyad.

The literature widely acknowledges that House-Land-Property (HLP) rights are critical for returnees. The Syrian government and many non-state armed actors have been accused of HLP violations based on ethnic and sectarian discrimination. In northern Syria, the *Daesh* had an open policy of confiscating the property of those who opposed it, to house its fighters and administrators. Kurdish forces in the north have also been accused of displacing local non-Kurdish populations. Turkey-backed local militias have also been criticized for confiscating the properties of Kurds (ILAC 2020). For example, after Turkey's Operation Olive Branch, individual fighters from Syrian armed factions started to bring their relatives from opposition-controlled Idlib and northern Aleppo. They settled them in the empty houses in Afrin. Since Afrin had been effectively carved up between different Olive Branch (National Army) factions, looting and confiscation in a particular location generally depends on the group, or set of individuals, in control (Bauman 2019: 128). Nevertheless, Turkey seems to have been responsible for the HLP violations in Afrin 'as the state actor that launched, coordinated and led the operation' (Hoffman and Makovsky 2021: 23; Bauman 2019: 15; HRW 2019). The original ownership of the areas planned for housing by Turkish authorities is not clear. It is also known that some villages were entirely inaccessible to civilians because the Turkish military had appropriated them to use as bases, while other sites were off-limits on the grounds of unexploded ordnance contamination (Bauman 2019: 129; also see al-Ghazi and Hamadeh 2021).

Returnee interviewees from Turkey did not explicitly note HLP violations in their cases. Still, it was implied. Avoidance in addressing HLP violations can be attributed to the characteristics of the interviewee sample, as they are mainly people relocating to the north through Turkish assistance. When asked about HLP issues upon return, interviewees noted that their family and tribe protected their lands and homes when they were abroad. Few said that 'their property was untouched as they did not involve any fighting'.[25] Some noted that previous land certificates are still valid. Others said they regained their houses and lands upon arrival because their families stayed in Syria and kept their territories.[26] Few returnees from Turkey reported that their lands had been captured by the fighting groups such as YPG.[27]

It is worth noting that some Syrians re-migrate to Turkey after their return. They mentioned concerns about their family's future, the lack of adequate safety or lack of proper functioning state institutions. Some were very regretful in returning to Syria in the first place; as one interviewee said, 'It is better to die at the sea while crossing Europe than return to Syria.'[28] Thus, the interviewees experience multiple displacements (internal, regional and international). Many returnees consider themselves IDPs since they no longer stay in their original residence. At the same time, they can be regarded as returnees as they have returned from a country they emigrated to, to the country where they previously lived.[29] Interview data reveals that the statistics and official framing of returns as voluntary must be treated with caution. The word 'return' suggests that individuals and families typically return to their previous place of origin/residence, which is often not the case.

Conclusion

The return of refugees and internally displaced persons to their homes and communities is deemed one of the desired, durable solutions for the problem of conflict-induced displacement, as in the case of Syria. International humanitarian organizations and peacebuilding/development actors consider the return of the displaced as a fundamental requisite for the rehabilitation of war-impacted countries. It is considered an essential prerequisite for fostering peace, justice and reconciliation in post-conflict societies undergoing a political and socio-economic transition. As discussed in the literature, the return-peace nexus is a complicated political process (Bradley 2013; Shutzer 2012; Long 2010). The critical dilemma is which comes first: return, peace or reconstruction (Stein and Cuny 1994: 180). Repatriation is framed as the prerequisite for national elections or referendums for new regimes in some peace settlements. Governments face international pressure to accept and endorse returns to claim peace and stability. Politico-military factions may be interested in refugee returns for electoral outcomes, power-sharing or building strong relations with the hosting country (Fakhoury 2020). In line with this, returns signal the end of a conflict. Katy Long presents a counterargument to the return-reconstruction nexus by underlining the possible unprecedented impact of premature returns: 'Especially in fragile post-conflict states with inadequate capacity to meet their citizens' basic social and economic needs, and the return may harm reconstruction efforts by exacerbating state fragility' (2010: 1). There is also the risk that returnees will encounter persecution upon returning because refugees are often regarded as politically hostile to the home country's government or local powers in place (Rogge and Akol 1989: 196).

Reintegration is also emphasized as a critical component of repatriation policies in contexts mainly shaped by inter-group violence, leading to population strategies of demographic engineering. Post-war Bosnia stands out as an example of a facilitated return, although various deterring factors considerably impeded the reintegration of returnees. Similar efforts are currently underway in Iraq to establish sustainable conditions addressing reconstruction and peacebuilding challenges in communities of return. Syria also experiences massive displacement and destruction followed by confiscation of properties and demographic engineering. There is an alarming concern that the existing ethnic and religious/sectarian change in the Syrian population might become permanent, cemented by targeted policies disrupting the return of displaced.

Turkish government aims to send the refugees it has hosted for years back to Syria due to the increasing costs and political tensions within the country. To that end, Ankara has been conducting cross-border military operations and creating space for returns. However, despite all this, it is evident that the vast majority of Syrians living in Turkey will not return to their previous places of residence due to the aforementioned reasons. It has to be realized that the great majority of Syrians will not return to their country even if the civil war ends and a political solution is reached. The presence of refugees in Turkey will continue to present political risks no matter how they are integrated. Under the current conditions, a safe return is not an option. It remains unclear how stability and functional state institutions can come about when financial economic commitments are lacking.

Notes

1 About 6.8 million Syrians are refugees and asylum-seekers, and another 6.7 million people are displaced within Syria. This means 13.5 million Syrians in total have been forcibly displaced. https://www.worldvision.org/refugees-news-stories/syrian-refugee-crisis-facts.
2 The presence of refugees in Turkey is symptomatic of a much broader displacement crisis. Much less is known about IDPs than refugees; even estimates of their number are uncertain. International reports and the interview data reveal, however, that displacement is widespread and dynamic, with people moving multiple times in search of safety and assistance. For details about IDPs see EASO (2020).
3 See UNHCR's Survey series (six surveys) on Syrian Refugees' Perceptions & Intentions on Return to Syria. Surveys cover Lebanon, Jordan, Iraq and Egypt. https://reliefweb.int/sites/reliefweb.int/files/resources/68443.pdf. For Syrians' intentions in Turkey, see Syrians Barometer, Murat Erdogan. https://www.unhcr.org/tr/wp-content/uploads/sites/14/2020/09/SB2019-SUMMARY-04092020.pdf.
4 Turkish official migration agency statistics, last updated 25 October 2021. https://www.goc.gov.tr/gecici-koruma5638.

5 This study is not intended to provide a detailed account of Turkey's changing Syria policy or the main drivers behind its approach to the Syrian crisis. Instead, this chapter aims to examine the implications of these policies on the ground, principally within the scope of refugee returns and regional geopolitics. Existing literature already offers compelling explanations for Turkey's changing foreign policy and its limits (Kutlay and Önis 2021, Dinçer and Hecan 2021, Tetik 2019). Nevertheless, the issue of return and reintegration has been understudied.
6 A range of different published documentary sources include: Syrian and regionally based media and social media reports; international and NGO human rights reports; academic publications and think tank reports; and reports produced by various bodies of the United Nations and European Union (EU).
7 Turkey avoided granting them the proper refugee status envisioned in the 1951 Refugee Convention, considering them temporary, and the national asylum regime does not recognize asylum seekers from non-European countries as refugees (Sahin-Mencütek 2018).
8 One of the authors' fieldwork observations in these makeshift camps across the border.
9 It is important to note that the border between Syria and Turkey has always been a very porous one. While during the Cold War era of the 1950s landmines were laid along parts of the border, they did not seem to act as a deterrent to cross-border movements of people and goods. Cross-border smuggling was commonplace long before the Syrian displacement crisis began, although it has increased as the number of Syrians seeking to cross has escalated.
10 This is one of the findings of the authors' fieldwork on refugees in southeast Turkey in 2013.
11 *Ensar*, a word connected to the local people of Medina who welcomed the Prophet Mohammed and his followers and helped them. *Muhacir*, a term used originally to refer to the first Muslims who had to migrate from Mecca to Medina in order to escape religious persecution.
12 See Stephensen (2019).
13 Here, the term 'security' needs to be understood in the broadest sense of the word, including traditional understandings of national security, and also societal security as well as the security of refugees.
14 One of the authors' personal communication with the former Turkish president Abdullah Gül, 2012, Ankara.
15 The European Parliament rejected Turkey's plans to establish a so-called safe zone along the border in northeast Syria, and stresses that any forcible transfer of Syrian refugees or internally displaced persons (IDPs) to this area would constitute a grave violation of conventional international refugee law, international humanitarian law and the principle of non-refoulement. The EU also recalls that any return of refugees must be safe, voluntary and dignified and that the current circumstances are such as to categorically prevent such movements, and insists that no EU stabilization or development assistance be delivered to such areas. Additionally the EU stresses that ethnic and religious groups in Syria have the right to continue to live in or return to their historical and traditional homelands in dignity and safety. https://www.europarl.europa.eu/doceo/document/TA-9-2019-0049_EN.html.
16 For local councils' background, see https://www.mei.edu/publications/between-ankara-and-damascus-role-turkish-state-north-aleppo#pt1;https://omranstudies.org/publications/papers/the-political-role-of-local-councils-in-syria-survey-results.html; https://www.refworld.org/pdfid/5416e7d14.pdf.

17 For local councils located in Turkey-controlled areas, see https://www.suriyegundemi.com/fkh-zdh-ve-bph-bolgelerindeki-yerel-meclisler-1; https://www.suriyegundemi.com/afrin-gecici-yerel-meclisi; https://www.al-monitor.com/originals/2021/08/protests-against-turkish-backed-local-councils-northern-syria-expand-over-bad; https://www.aa.com.tr/tr/baris-pinari-harekati/rasulaynda-yerel-meclis-kuruldu/1638496; https://www.aa.com.tr/tr/baris-pinari-harekati/tel-abyadda-yerel-meclis-kuruldu/1627893.

18 Interview with Syrian Arab man who had been displaced to Turkey, then returned to Tall Abyad, 11 July 2021.

19 Interview with Syrian Arab man who had been displaced to Turkey, then returned to Tall Abyad, 13 July 2021.

20 Interview with Syrian Arab man who had been displaced to Turkey, then returned to Tall Abyad, 16 July 2021.

21 Interview with Syrian Arab man who had been displaced to Turkey, then returned to Tall Abyad, 16 July 2021.

22 Interview with Syrian Kurdish man who had been displaced to Northern Iraq and interviewed in al-Hasakah, Syria, 19 July 2021.

23 Interview with Syrian Arab man who had been displaced to Jordan, then returned to Damascus and interviewed in Jordan, 22 February 2020.

24 Interview with Syrian Arab man who had been displaced to Turkey, then returned to Tall Abyad, Syria, 10 July 2019.

25 Interview with Syrian Arab who had been displaced to Turkey, then had returned to Syria, then remigrated to Turkey, 10 June 2019.

26 Interview with A Syrian Arab who had been displaced to Turkey, then had returned to Syria, then remigrated to Turkey, 15 June 2019.

27 Interview with Syrian Arab who had been displaced to Turkey, then had returned to Syria, then remigrated to Turkey, 11.06.2019.

28 Interview with Syrian Arab who had been displaced to Turkey, then had returned to Syria, then remigrated to Turkey, 11 June 2019.

29 Interview with Syrian Kurdish man who had been displaced to Northern Iraq and then returned to al-Hasakah, Syria, 28 July 2021.

Bibliography

AA (2019). 'Erdogan Speaks at 74th UNGA on Safe Zone in Syria'. 24 September. https://www.youtube.com/watch?v=Dc8at5RnRdU (accessed 4 June 2022).

Adar, S. (2020). 'Introduction Repatriation to Turkey's "Safe Zone" in Northeast Syria', *SWP Comment*, January. https://www.swp-berlin.org/fileadmin/contents/products/comments/2020C01_ada.pdf (accessed 4 May 2022).

Akdedian, H., and Hasan, H. (2020). 'State Atrophy and the Reconfiguration of Borderlands in Syria and Iraq: Post-2011 Dynamics'. *Political Geography* 80: 1–10.

al-Azmeh, N., al-Bagdadi, N., Hasan, H., and Akdedian, H. (eds) (2021). *Striking from the Margins: State, Religion and Devolution of Authority in the Middle East*, London: Saqi Books.

al-Ghazi, S., and Hamadeh, N. (2021). 'Part 2: Violations by Nongovernment Actors', *Tahrir Institute for Middle East Policy*, 4 February. https://timep.org/explainers/part-2-violations-by-no (accessed 8 June 2022).

al-Hilu, K. (2021). *The Turkish Intervention in Northern Syria: One strategy, Discrepant Policies*. Middle East Directions (MED), 2021/01, Wartime and Post-Conflict in Syria. https://cadmus.eui.eu//handle/1814/69657 (accessed 7 June 2022).

al-Khateb, K. (2020). 'What Stops Return of Syrians in Turkey to Area Held by Turkish forces?'. *Al-Monitor*. 17 January. https://wwwal-monitor.com/pulse/originals/2020/01/peace-spring-syrian-refugeeshumanitarian-relief.html (accessed 10 November 2021).

al-Meehy, A. (2021). *Mapping Local Governance in Syria: a Baseline Study*, United Nations Economic Social Commission for Western Africa. E/ESCWA/CL3.SEP/2020/TP.4. https://www.researchgate.net/publication/348279474_Mapping_Local_Governance_in_Syria_A_Baseline_Study (accessed 4 June 2022).

Ataman, M. (2019). 'The Impact of July 15 on Turkish Foreign Policy'. *Daily Sabah*, 17 July. https://www.dailysabah.com/columns/ataman-muhittin/2019/07/17/the-impact-of-july-15-on-turkish-foreign-policy (accessed 8 June 2022).

Altunisik, M. (2020). 'The New Turn in Turkey's Foreign Policy in the Middle East: Regional and Domestic Insecurities'. IAI Papers, 17 July. https://www.iai.it/en/pubblicazioni/new-turn-turkeys-foreign-policy-middle-east-regional-and-domestic-insecurities (accessed 14 November 2021).

Arango, T., Barnard, A., and Yeginsu, C. (2016). 'Turkey's Military Plunges into Syria, Enabling rebels to Capture ISIS Stronghold'. *New York Times*, 24 August. https://www.nytimes.com/2016/08/25/world/middleeast/turkey-syria-isis.html (accessed 11 December 2021).

Asseburg, M. (2020). 'Reconstruction in Syria Challenges and Policy Options for the EU and Its Member States'. SWP Research Paper, 11 July. https://ec.europa.eu/commission/presscorner/detail/en/qanda_20_1707 (accessed 30 May 2022).

Aydıntaşbaş, A. (2020). 'A New Gaza. Turkey's Border Policy in Northern Syria'. European Council on Foreign Relations, 28 May. https://ecfr.eu/publication/a_new_gaza_turkeys_border_policy_in_northern_syria/ (accessed 4 June 2022).

Badi, E. (2021). 'To Advance Its Own Interests, Turkey Should Now Help Stabilize Libya'. *War on the Rocks*, 24 May. https://warontherocks.com/2021/05/to-advance-its-own-interests-turkey-should-now-help-stabilize-libya/ (accessed 5 June 2022).

Bank, A., and Karadag, R. (2013). 'The "Ankara Moment": The Politics of Turkey's Regional Power in the Middle East, 2007–11'. *Third World Quarterly* 34(2): 287–304.

Barkey, H. (2016). 'Syria's Dar Shadow over US-Turkey Relations'. *Turkish Policy Quarterly* 14(4): 25–36.

Bauman, H. (2019). 'Reclaiming Home: The Struggle for Socially Just Housing, Land and Property Rights in Syria, Iraq and Libya', *Friedrich Ebert Stiftung*. http://library.fes.de/pdf-files/bueros/tunesien/15664.pdf (accessed 4 November 2021).

Black, R., and Koser, K. (eds) (1999). *The End of the Refugee Cycle?: Refugee Repatriation and Reconstruction* (Fourth edn). New York: Berghahn Books.

Blanchard, C. (2022). *Armed Conflict in Syria: Overview and the U.S. Response*, CRS Report, November. https://crsreports.congress.gov/product/pdf/RL/RL33487(accessed 20 December 2022).

Bradley, M. (2013). *Refugee Repatriation: Justice, Responsibility and Redress*. Cambridge: Cambridge University Press.

Daher, J. (2018). 'The Political Economic Context of Syria's Reconstruction: A Prospective in Light of a Legacy of Unequal Development'. *Middle East Directions (MED), Wartime and Post-Conflict in Syria*, December http://hdl.handle.net/1814/60112 (accessed 2 November 2021).

Daily Sabah. (2018). '50,000 Syrians Remain in their Homeland after Leaving Turkey for Eid', 5 September. https://www.dailysabah.com/turkey/2018/09/05/50000-syrians-remain-in-their-homeland-after-leaving-turkey-for-eid(accessed 4 June 2022).

Dal, E. P. (2019). 'Status-Seeking Policies of Middle Powers in Status Clubs: The Case of Turkey in the G20'. *Contemporary Politics* 25(5): 586–602.

Davutoğlu, A. (2013). 'The Three Major Earthquakes in the International System and Turkey'. *International Spectator* 48(2): 1–11.

Demir, I. (2017). *Overconfidence and Risk Taking in Foreign Policy Decision Making: The Case of Turkey's Syria Policy*. London: Palgrave.

Dinçer, O. B., and Hecan, M. (2015). 'The Changing Geo-Strategy of Turkey's Foreign Policy along Its Southern Border'. *Institute of Strategic Dialogue*, June. https://www.isdglobal.org/wp-content/uploads/2016/07/ISDJ4677_Turkey_R2_WEB.pdf (accessed 28 June 2015).

Dinçer, O. B., and Hecan, M. (2016). 'Turkey's Changing Syria Policy: From Desired Proactivism to Reactivism'. In A. Kudors and A. Pabriks (eds), *The War in Syria: Lessons for the West* (147–68). Riga: Latvia University Press.

Dinçer, O. B., and Hecan, M. (2021). 'Turkey's Syria Policy: The Political Opportunities and Pitfalls of the Syrian Conflict'. In A. al-Azmeh, N. al-Bagdadi, H. Hasan and H. Akdedian (eds), *Striking from the Margins: State, Religion and Devolution of Authority in the Middle East* (255–81). London: Saqi Books.

Dinçer, O. B., Federici, V., Ferris, E., Karaca, S., Kirişci, K., and Çarmıklı, E. (2013). *Turkey and the Syrian Refugees: The Limits of Hospitality*. Washington, DC: Brookings Institution. https://www.brookings.edu/wp-content/uploads/2016/06/turkey-and-syrian-refugees_the-limits-of-hospitality-2014.pdf (accessed September 2013).

Dukhan, H. (2019). *State and Tribes in Syria: Informal Alliances and Conflict Patterns*. New York: Routledge.

Erdogan, M. (2020). *Turkey: Syrian Barometer 2019: A Framework for Achieving Social Cohesion with Syrians in Turkey*. UNHCR. https://data2.unhcr.org/en/documents/details/78901 (accessed 5 June 2022).

European Asylum Support Office (EASO) (2020). *Syria Internally Displaced Persons, Returnees, and Internal Mobility: Country of Origin Information Report*. April. https://euaa.europa.eu/sites/default/files/publications/easo-coi-report-syria-idps-returnees-internal-mobility.pdf (accessed 4 November 2021).

European Parliament (2019). *European Parliament Resolution of 24 October 2019 on the Turkish Military Operation in Northeast Syria and Its Consequences*. (2019/2886(RSP). 24 October. https://www.europarl.europa.eu/doceo/document/TA-9-2019-0049_EN.html (accessed 4 November 2021).

Fahim, K., and Samaan, M. (2015). 'Violence in Syria Spurs a Huge Surge in Civilian Flight'. *New York Times*. 26 October. https://www.nytimes.com/2015/10/27/world/middleeast/syria-russian-air-strike-refugees.html (accessed 4 June 2022).

Fakhoury, T. (2020). 'Refugee Return and Fragmented Governance in the Host State'. *Third World Quarterly* 42(1):162–80.

Ferris, E., Kirisci, K. (2015). 'What Turkey's Open-Door Policy Means for Syrian Refugees'. *Brookings Institution*. 8 July. https://wwwbrookings.edu/blog/order-from-chaos/2015/07/08/what-turkeys-open-door-policy-means-for-syrian-refugees/ (accessed August 2015).

Ferris, E., Kirisci, K., Shaikh, S. (2013). 'Syrian Crisis: Massive Displacement, Dire Needs and a Shortage of Solutions'. *Brookings Institute*. 18 September. https://www.brookings.

edu/research/syrian-crisis-massive-displacement-dire-needs-and-a-shortage-of-soluti
ons/ (accessed October 2013).
Gall, C. (2021). 'In Turkey's Safe Zone in Syria, Security and Misery Go Hand in Hand'.
New York Times. 27 August. https://www.nytimes.com/2021/02/16/world/middleeast/
syria-turkey-erdogan-afrin.html (accessed 3 November 2021).
Gardner, D. (2019). 'Syria Is Witnessing a Violent Demographic Re-Engineering'.
Financial Times. 2 October. https://www.ft.com/content/e40cb754-e456-11e9-b112-
9624ec9edc59 (accessed 2 June 2022).
Ghosh-Siminoff, S. (2020). 'Demographic Engineering in Syria Sets the Stage for Future
Conflicts'. *Newlines Institute*. 13 March. https://newlinesinstitute.org/governance/
demographic-engineering-in-syria-sets-the-stage-for-future-conflicts/ (accessed 4
November 2021).
Gottlieb, D., and Kedar, M. (2020). *Turkey and the Libyan and Syrian Civil Wars*.
BESA Center Perspectives Paper No. 1, 548. 4 May. https://besacenter.org/tur
key-libya-syria-civil-wars/ (accessed 20 November 2021).
Gücer, M., Karaca, S., and Dinçer, B. (2013). *The Struggle for Life between Borders: Syrian
Refugees*. Ankara: USAK.
Gulmez, D. B. (2020). 'The Resilience of the US-Turkey Alliance: Divergent Threat
Perceptions and Worldviews'. *Contemporary Politics* 26(4): 475–92.
Gurnini, F. (2020). 'Turkey's Unpromising Defense Industry'. *Sada*. 9 October. https://
carnegieendowment.org/sada/82936 (accessed 6 June 2022).
Heinemann-Grüder, A. (2019). 'Die Deutsche Angststarre: Syrien und das Scheitern der
EU-Menschenrechtspolitik'. *Blätter für deutsche und internationale Politik* 12: 59–66.
Hoffman, M., and Makovsky, A. (2021). 'Northern Syria Security Dynamics and the
Refugee Crisis.' *Center for American Progress*. 26 May. https://www.americanprogress.
org/article/northern-syria-security-dynamics-refugee-crisis/ (accessed 28 June 2021).
HRW (2021). 'Syria: Returning Refugees Face Grave Abuse'. 20 October. https://www.
hrw.org/news/2021/10/20/syria-returning-refugees-face-grave-abuse(accessed 3
June 2022).
HRW (2019). 'Turkey: Syrians Being Deported to Danger'. 24 October. https://www.
hrw.org/news/2019/10/24/turkey-syrians-being-deported-danger (accessed 4
November 2021).
Içduygu, A., and Nimer, M. (2020). 'The Politics of Return: Exploring the Future of Syrian
Refugees in Jordan, Lebanon and Turkey'. *Third World Quarterly* 41(3): 415–33.
ICG (2020). 'The SDF Seeks a Path toward Durable Stability in North East Syria'.
International Crisis Group, 25 November. https://www.ecoi.net/de/dokument/2041
372.html (accessed 4 November 2021).
ILAC (2020). 'Resolving the Property Issue in Syria Technically Possible, Politically
Challenging and Central to Accountability'. December. https://ilacnet.org/wp-cont
ent/uploads/2021/01/ILAC_Syria_2020_DiscussionPaper_webb-1.pdf (accessed 2
November 2021).
Jennequin, A. (2020). 'Turkey and the Weaponization of Syrian Refugees'. Policy Brief,
Brussels International Center. January. https://www.bic-rhr.com/research/turkey-and-
weaponization-syrian-refugees (accessed 30 May 2022).
Kamel, L. (ed.) (2017). *The Frailty of Authority Borders, Non-State Actors and Power
Vacuums in a Changing Middle East*. Rome: Istituto Affari Internazionali (IAI). https://
www.iai.it/sites/default/files/newmed_authority.pdf (accessed 4 November 2021).

Kaya, A., Rottmann, S. B., Aras Gokalp, N. E., and Şahin Sahin-Mencütek, Z. (2021). *Koruma, Kabul ve Entegrasyon: Türkiye'de Entegrasyon* [Protection, Reception and Integration: Refugeehood in Turkey]. Istanbul: Bilgi Yayınevi.

Khalaf, R. (2021). 'Governance without Government in Syria: Civil Society and State Building during Conflict'. *Syria Studies* 13(1): 33–82. https://ojs.st-andrews.ac.uk/index.php/syria/article/view/2293 (accessed September 13 2023).

Kingsley, P. (2015). 'The Journey'. *The Guardian*. 9 June. https://www.theguardian.com/world/ng-interactive/2015/jun/09/a-migrants-journey-from-syria-to-sweden-interactive (accessed 4 June 2022).

Kiniklioglu, S. (2020). 'Syrian Refugees in Turkey: Changing Attitudes and Fortunes'. *SWP*. 5 February. https://www.swp-berlin.org/publications/products/comments/2020 C05_Kiniklioglu.pdf (accessed 5 June 2022).

Köstem, S. (2020). 'Russian-Turkish Cooperation in Syria: Geopolitical Alignment with Limits'. *Cambridge Review of International Affairs* 34(6): 795–817.

Kuru, A. (2015). 'Turkey's Failed Policy toward the Arab Spring: Three Levels of Analysis'. *Mediterranean Quarterly* 26(3): 94–116.

Kutlay, M., and Önis, Z. (2021). 'Understanding Oscillations in Turkish Foreign Policy: Pathways to Unusual Middle Power Activism'. *Third World Quarterly* 42(12): 3051–69.

LFIP (2013). *Law on Foreigners and International Protection Law No: 6458*. The amended version. https://www.mevzuat.gov.tr/MevzuatMetin/1.5.6458.pdf (accessed 4 November 2021).

Long, K. (2010). *Home Alone? A Review of the Relationship between Repatriation, Mobility and Durable Solutions for Refugees*. UNCHR/PDES Evaluation Report, PDES/2010/02. https://reliefweb.int/report/world/home-alone-review-relationship-between-repatriation-mobility-and-durable-solutions (accessed 1 November 2021).

McDowell, C., and Eastmond, M. (2002). 'Transitions, State Building and the "Residual" Refugee Problem: East Timor and Cambodian Repatriation Experience'. *Australian Journal of Human Rights* 8(1): 7–29.

NSC (2019a). 'Press Release'. Milli Güvenlik Kurulu Genel Sekreterliği, 30 September. https://www.mgk.gov.tr/index.php/30-eylul-2019-tarihli-toplanti (accessed 1 November 2021).

NSC (2019b). 'Press Release'. Milli Güvenlik Kurulu Genel Sekreterliği, 26 November. https://www.mgk.gov.tr/index.php/26-kasim-2019-tarihli-toplanti (accessed 1 November 2021).

NSC (2020). 'Press Release'. Milli Güvenlik Kurulu Genel Sekreterliği, 2 June. https://www.mgk.gov.tr/index.php/02-haziran-2020-tarihli-toplanti (accessed 1 November 2021).

ODATV (2017). 'TSK'da Avrasyacı subaylar belirleyici çoğunlukta' [Eurasian officers in the Turkish army have a decisive majority]. 14 September. https://odatv.com/tskda-avrasyaci-subaylar-belirleyici-cogunlukta-1409171200.html (accessed 8 June 2022).

OHCHR (2020). 'Syria: Violations and Abuses Rife in Areas Under Turkish-Affiliated Armed Groups – Bachelet'. 18 September. https://www.ecoi.net/en/document/2037973.html (accessed 1 November 2021).

Osmandzikovic, E. (2020). 'Forced Demographic Change as a Geopolitical Tool in the Post- War Syria'. *Trends Research*. 20 January. https://trendsresearch.org/insight/forced-demographic-change-as-a-geopolitical-tool-in-post-war-syria/ (accessed 12 November 2021).

Özertem, H. (2017). 'Turkey and Russia: A Fragile Friendship'. *Turkish Policy Quarterly* 15(4): 121–34.

Özpek, B. (2021). 'How Russia Exploited Nationalism in Turkey to Expand Its Influence in Syria'. *Middle East Policy* 28(2): 109–18.
Petrin, S. (2002). 'Refugee Return and State Reconstruction: A Comparative Analysis'. UNHCR Working paper No 66, August. https://www.unhcr.org/research/working/3d5d0ec94/refugee-return-state-reconstruction-comparative-analysis-sarah-petrin.html (accessed 4 May 2021).
Reuters (2016). 'Turkey-Backed Rebels Could Push Further South in Syria, Erdogan Says'. 19 September. https://www.reuters.com/article/us-mideast-crisis-syria-turkey-erdogan-idUSKCN11P0HL (accessed 2 June 2022).
Reuters (2019). 'Erdogan Says Turkey Aims to Settle 1 Million Refugees in Syria Offensive Area'. 9 December. https://www.reuters.com/article/us-syria-security-turkey-idUSKBN1YD27R (accessed 2 June 2022).
Rogge, J. R., and Akol, J. O. (1989). 'Repatriation: Its Role in Resolving Africa's Refugee Dilemma'. *International Migration Review* 23(2): 184–200.
Sahin-Mencütek, Z. (2018). *Refugee Governance, State and Politics in the Middle East*. London: Routledge.
Sahin-Mencütek, Z. (2019). 'Turkey's Approach to Encourage Returns of Syrians'. *Forced Migration Review* 62: 28–31.
Sahin-Mencütek, Z. (2021a). 'Governing Practices and Strategic Narratives for the Syrian Refugee Returns'. *Journal of Refugee Studies* 34(3): 2804–23.
Sahin-Mencütek, Z. (2021b). *Turkey's Return Policies to Syria and Their Impacts on Migrants and Refugees' Human Rights*. Brussels: EuroMed Rights. https://euromedrights.org/wp-content/uploads/2021/03/EN_Chapter-7-Turkey_Report_Migration.pdf (accessed 4 December 2021).
Sahin Mencutek, Z. (2023). The Geopolitics of Returns: Geopolitical Reasoning and Space-Making in Turkey's Repatriation Regime. *Geopolitics*, 28(3): 1079–105.
Shaery-Yazdi, R., and Üngör, U. Ü. (2021). 'Mass Violence in Syria: Continuity and Change'. *British Journal of Middle Eastern Studies* 49(3): 397–402.
Shutzer, M. A. (2012). 'The Politics of Home: Displacement and Resettlement in Postcolonial Kenya'. *African Studies* 71(3): 346–60.
Siccardi, F. (2021). 'How Syria Changed Turkey's Foreign Policy'. *Carnegie Europa*. 14 September. https://carnegieeurope.eu/2021/09/14/how-syria-changed-turkey-s-foreign-policy-pub-85301 (accessed 4 June 2022).
Speckhard, A. (2019). 'Is Turkey Fueling a New Jihad in Northeast Syria?'. International Center for the Study of Violent Extremism. https://www.researchgate.net/publication/337196647_Is_Turkey_Fueling_a_New_Jihad_in_Northeast_Syria (accessed 4 November 2021).
Stanicek, B. (2019). 'European Parliament Briefing: Turkey's Military Operation in Syria and Its Impact on Relations with the EU'. *EPRS*. November. https://www.europarl.europa.eu/EPRS/EPRS-Briefing-642284-Turkeys-military-operation-Syria-FINAL.pdf (accessed 6 November 2021).
Stein, B. N., and Cuny, F. C. (1994). 'Refugee Repatriation during Conflict: Protection and Post-Return Assistance'. *Development in Practice* 4(3): 173–87.
Stephenson, H. (2019). 'Why Is Turkey Pushing Refugees to Return to Syria'. *Tufts Now*. 9 October. https://now.tufts.edu/2019/10/09/why-turkey-pushing-refugees-return-syria (accessed 4 June 2022).
Tetik, M. O. (2019). 'The Construction of Containment Anxiety: A Critical Geopolitical Analysis of Turkey's Military Intervention into Syria'. *New Middle Eastern Studies* 9(1): 69–95.

TRT Haber (2020). 'Bakan Soylu: 414 bin 61 Suriyeli gönüllü olarak ülkesine döndü'. 15 October. https://www.trthaber.com/haber/gundem/bakan-soylu-414-bin-61-suriyeli-gonullu-olarak-ulkesine-dondu-523516.html (accessed 4 June 2022).

Tziarras, Z., and J. Harchaoui (2021). 'What Erdogan Really Wants in the Eastern Mediterranean'. *Foreign Policy*. 19 January. https://foreignpolicy.com/2021/01/19/turkey-greece-what-erdogan-wants-eastern-mediterranean-sovereignty-natural-gas/ (accessed 4 November 2021).

UN News (2021). 'Guterres in Turkey'. 1 November. https://news.un.org/en/story/2019/11/1050451 (accessed 4 June 2022).

UNHCR (2018). The Comprehensive Protection and Solutions Strategy: Protection Thresholds and Parameters for Refugee Return to Syria, UNHCR, February. https://data2.unhcr.org/en/documents/download/63223 (accessed 12 November 2021).

Yanarocak, H. (2018). 'The Cypriotization of Northern Syria'. Jerusalem Institute for Strategy and Security. 20 August. https://jiss.org.il/en/yanarocak-the-cypriotization-of-northern-syria/ (accessed 3 June 2022).

Yesiltas, M., and Balci, A. (2013). 'A Dictionary of Turkish Foreign Policy in the AK Party Era. A Conceptual Map'. SAM Papers 7, 1 May. http://sam.gov.tr/sam-papers-07-en.en.mfa (accessed June 2018).

Yetim, M., and Kaşıkcı, T. (2021). 'Re-adapting to Changing Middle Eastern Politics: The Modification in Turkey's Actor Perception and Turkey-Free Syrian Army (FSA) Relations'. *Contemporary Review of the Middle East* 8(2): 193–209.

Yüksel, E., and Van Veen, E. (2019). 'Turkey in Northwestern Syria Rebuilding Empire at the Margins'. *Clingeldael Institute*. 4 June. https://www.clingendael.org/publication/turkey-northwestern-syria (accessed September 2020).

Yüksel, E. (2019). 'Strategies of Turkish Proxy Warfare in Northern Syria'. *Clingeldael Institute*. November. https://www.clingendael.org/pub/2019/strategies-of-turkish-proxy-warfare-in-northern-syria/ (accessed September 2020).

Chapter 13

CIVILIAN RESISTANCE AND ITS LIMITS: THE CASE OF DEIR HAFER

Harout Akdedian and Ali Aljasem

Armed groups need the support and cooperation of local communities to survive war (Kalyvas 2006). Rebel formations and government forces alike lack sufficient resources, comprehensive knowledge and understanding of areas under their control. Consequently, they often need local knowledge and involvement to maintain human resources, administrative capacity and order. In other words, effective control during armed conflict is not contingent upon coercive capacity (technologies of violence) alone (Arjona 2016). Effective control is also contingent upon broader ability to draw civilian cooperation, eliciting material resources, recruits and information by maintaining order and livable conditions for the local population through the provision of protection and services – medical, fuel, food and other basic supplies (Kalyvas 2006: 147; Gutierrez-Sanin 2017; Arjona 2016: 11).

With the ability to coerce and deploy violence, armed groups have greater capacity to influence and impose themselves than civilian entities or community organizers. Weinstein argues that 'rebel groups that emerge in environments rich in natural resources or with the external support of an outside patron tend to commit high levels of indiscriminate violence; movements that arise in resource-poor contexts perpetrate far fewer abuses and employ violence selectively and strategically' (Weinstein 2007: 7). This pattern is decisively influenced by the armed groups' level of need for local cooperation and resources (Weinstein 2007: 7). In circumstances of protracted conflict, similar to that of Syria, where resources are scarce, foreign support is conditional and limited and armed groups need local cooperation, there are possibilities for local communities to take independent measures of community protection, depending on the level of organizational capacity within respective communities and modalities of violence at play. Civilian entities, with the minimal leverage they possess, may try to expand the space for civilian autonomy, community protection and bargaining processes in various ways (Kaplan 2017). The case of Deir Hafer in Aleppo province helps us understand these processes and discern opportunities and challenges for civilian resistance against dynamics of war and conflict.

Community protection efforts take a variety of forms and can be clustered under three categories: (1) Survival and coping strategies, (2) Adaptive and mitigating strategies and (3) transformative strategies (Menkhaus 2013: 2; UNDRR 2015; Kaplan 2017; Cadier, Capasso and Eickhopp 2020). Survival and coping strategies are aimed at self-preservation in the face of violence and fragility. They stand for efforts of escaping from violence (Kaplan 2017).[1] Adaptive and mitigating strategies are aimed at taming and reducing the impact or scale of violence. Unlike coping strategies, which seek to avoid violence, adaptive strategies require *engaging* with sources or manifest forms of violence in an effort to reduce the level of harm.[2] Transformative strategies aim at addressing sources of conflict fragility. Transformative strategies can, in turn, take on different forms, such as: (1) addressing structural sources of conflict and violence towards preventing conflict and achieving justice; (2) recovery steps such as reconstruction and trauma-informed psycho-social support to address experiences of harm or (3) strengthening resiliency by learning from past experiences and addressing existing vulnerabilities in strategies, capacities and structural conditions (Cadier, Capasso and Eickhopp 2020; Kaplan 2017; Menkhaus 2013).[3]

Specific measures and strategies of community protection vary based on prevailing conflict dynamics and circumstances such as geostrategic location, local socio-economic conditions, presence of armed forces (including number of armed groups and balance of power), local resources and patterns of militarization and recruitment (Kalyvas 2006; Arjona 2016). Civilian efforts of community protection in Deir Hafer primarily stemmed in response to local conditions of state atrophy and local security threats. This chapter provides a documentation of such examples in Dar Hafer, and focuses on four main variables that shaped the nature and outcome of civilian community protection efforts: (1) the nature and scale of violence against civilians, (2) organizational capacity of civilian community organizers, (3) their local autonomy and (4) social trust within the areas examined. The chapter answers the following key questions: (1) What is the range of threats and shocks that civilians confront under conditions of state atrophy as witnessed in Deir Hafer? (2) What strategies for community protection were employed by civilians in an attempt to protect themselves and their communities from dynamics of state atrophy (militarization, sectarianization, the expansion of the religious domain and decline in state capacity to perform public functions such as service provision)? (3) What conditions limited civilian efforts of community protection? The chapter depicts local circumstances, patterns of community mobilization throughout the conflict and variables that eventually undermined efforts to resist, cope and adapt to rapidly escalating circumstances of armed conflict.

Strategies of civilian community protection in Deir Hafer include negotiating for safe spaces, bargaining with armed groups (state and non-state actors), developing norms of civilian non-collaboration to resist militarization against other communities, assisting in procurement and distribution of relief and creating civilian-led bodies to adjudicate disputes among civilians and between civilians and armed actors. The experiences of the communities in the area reflect a broader range of threats experienced by communities across the country since the onset of violence. Specific examples of threats range from economic insecurity and diminished livelihoods to direct communal attacks and indiscriminate violence. While civilian community organizers initiated and led community-protection efforts, their success and level of endurance depended upon local and trans-local multilateral arrangements involving armed groups, state or state-like institutions and stakeholders within the international aid industry.

The majority of community protection efforts surveyed in this study fall under the categories of survival and coping strategies of self-preservation in the face of violence, where communities tried to evade violence and conflict-fragility. There are fewer instances of adaptive and mitigating strategies aimed at taming or reducing the scale of violence. It is noticeable here that civilian arrangements and negotiated agreements to protect civilian infrastructure were not the outcome of organized negotiations by civilian organizers but rather the outcome of personal initiatives by intermediaries in positions of power. Transformative strategies, on the other hand, which aim to address structural conditions to provide more options for civilian organizers or expand the boundaries of possible social and political actions (such as community protection) hardly featured at all. This predominance of reactive approaches in efforts of community protection reveals the overwhelming structural conditions that undermined and restrained expressions of civilian agency. Overall, most civilian actions and efforts were reactive in the sense that they did not have a transformative outlook to change the circumstances they operated within. Rather they worked within the conditions available to them. This is the manifest limits to collective civilian agency under conditions of state atrophy – civilians under conditions of state atrophy in Deir Hafer operated within the options available to them but were unable to bring about structural changes that can introduce new pathways or options for civilian mobilization.

Community protection in Deir Hafer: An overview

Deir Hafer represents an 'influential case' as it provides examples of community resistance at the local level against specific threats and instances of violence manifesting within and around the area (Gerring 2010: 567). The area gained geostrategic significance throughout the conflict and was directly targeted by violence. Civilians experienced mass displacement from peripheral areas with regional administrative dependencies on centres of power beyond the locale (George and Bennett 2005: 67).

Various groups controlled Deir Hafer for extended periods since the onset of the uprising in 2011. This had significant implications for patterns of continuity and change in local civilian actors, civilian autonomy as well as levels of harm and patterns of violence within the area. The violence and destruction that Deir Hafer experienced was relentless and persistent. Deir Hafer sustained civilian casualties, scattered trajectories of evacuation, dispersed displacement and continues to pose existential threats to potential returnees. Civilian initiatives in Deir Hafer offer examples of local efforts to maintain autonomy, develop non-violent conflict-resolution mechanisms and procure the necessities for preserving living conditions.

Threats to civilians have been shaped by a combination of local circumstances and vulnerabilities as well as broader conflict patterns and dynamics in Syria more broadly. The year 2014 witnessed significant shifts in the balance of powers and patterns of violence in the Syrian conflict, which negatively impacted civilian community organizers. Preceding this period – between 2012 and 2013 – Deir Hafer exhibited many examples of community protection. There was no major factional infighting, civilian initiatives flourished (albeit in a limited capacity, such as local newspapers, conflict resolution committees and peaceful protests) and vital infrastructures were protected from destruction through informal agreements and arrangements with government forces.

By late 2013, however, it is evident that civilian initiatives gradually diminished and armed groups have increasingly emerged as the sole security and safety providers. As discussed in the next section, a sense of fatigue increased, manifesting in different forms, including the normalization of threats and vulnerabilities by civilian community organizers and increased sense of detachment from risks and responsibilities (Sonnentag 2011; Ackerman 2011). Furthermore, in the first half of 2014, the area witnessed unprecedented levels of active contests over territorial control, which introduced new shocks, increased the level of violence against civilians, exposed pre-existing vulnerabilities and created additional vulnerabilities that diminished civilian capacities to resist conditions of war. As an interviewee from Deir Hafer summarized:

> As soon as [Daesh] took over, the campaign against us [activists] escalated to an unprecedented level – the majority of us were either coerced out of activism, were intimidated and fled or ended up being coopted. We had no means to resist or organize ourselves ... They [Daesh] took away internet routers and monitored social media channels closely. On top of that, public executions spread fear amongst everyone; even their [Daesh] followers. From then on, every one of us was just trying to survive. There was no room for activism or to organize ourselves.[4]

It is a challenge to retrospectively examine, quantify and provide scientific measurement of social trust, fatigue and trauma levels, specifically while conflict fragility and vulnerability remain uninterrupted and baseline studies are unavailable (Klarić et al. 2007). However, findings from interviews and focus group discussions suggest that Deir Hafer's armed factions and civilian structures welcomed Daesh's charitable activities and much-needed assistance in local administrative matters before its military takeover. As detailed in the next section, this was due to local fatigue from constant bombardment, lack of resources and limited administrative capacity. Although it was impossible for anyone to predict the forthcoming brutality of Daesh, it is clear, in retrospect, that the growing reliance on its cadres diminished the role and centrality of local civilian structures.

Throughout the period between 2011 and 2017, Deir Hafer witnessed kidnappings, aerial attacks by artillery and warplanes and violence by armed factions against the population. Deir Hafer witnessed the loss of more than a third of its population, increased social mistrust, a diminished sense of safety and the exacerbation of pre-2011 elements, such as limited civilian autonomy which continues to diminish civilian capacities to mobilize.

Evacuation patterns for Deir Hafer were uncoordinated and depended upon military developments in the area during moments of forced displacement. For instance, when the local armed group, *katibat abou dujana*, took over in 2012, many of those who left headed westward towards Aleppo city.[5] Those displaced later, when the situation in Aleppo city had also deteriorated, headed north (within the Syrian Arab Republic and beyond).[6] After government takeover, many residents left to the north-east towards SDF controlled areas.[7] The obstacles to the voluntary return of the displaced are many. In addition to economic challenges and mandatory military service and conscription, serious security concerns and fear of vengeance or punitive actions by state security apparatus persist.

By 2014, heightened episodes of violence effectively overpowered and overwhelmed civilian capacity for community protection. Experiences in Deir Hafer suggest that regardless of how 'native' or 'local' the armed forces and security apparatus are, such features do not always translate into effective protective measures for the civilian population. Further, despite emerging sociopolitical divides within the areas studied, social trust and cooperative dispositions for purposes of community protection persist at the neighbourhood level but are inconsequential without organizational structure and autonomy to mobilize. That said, the case study also suggests that resilience has its thresholds – determined by the scale of violence faced, and the limitations posed to civilian capacity (which easily becomes overburdened and overwhelmed during protracted armed conflicts). In fact, the lack of transformative strategies or capacities is a direct indication that civilians under conditions of state atrophy operate within the options available to them but are unable to bring about structural changes that can introduce new pathways or options. The scale of violence prevented vital opportunities for transformative strategies to address local sources of conflict and fragility, and to recover from shocks. This was primarily due to the relentless pressures of the broader conflict, which local actors had little influence over. Civilian protection gradually and increasingly depended upon conditions that were beyond the influence of civilians.

Conflict dynamics

Deir Hafer, situated in Aleppo province approximately 50 kilometres east of Aleppo City, is among the major cities of Aleppo's countryside, along with Manbij and al-Bab. Deir Hafer emerged as a fiercely contested area with significant geostrategic position due to its proximity to the military airport of Kweiris, the air force academy within its premises and the thermal power plant, located halfway between Aleppo and Deir Hafer, which provides electricity province-wide (Enab Baladi 2019). The city is at the entrance of a primary corridor connecting the coast, Aleppo City and the major highway M5 (Damascus–Aleppo) – to Raqqa, practically granting access to both Syria's north-east and the vast *badiya* extending across the Syrian-Iraqi borders. As a result of these geopolitical qualities, the city witnessed multiple episodes of violence and was contested by multiple military actors until the government takeover in 2017 (Hasan 2018). Different armed opposition groups controlled the town and its vicinities for various intervals and each order brought in new patterns of violence and vulnerabilities.

By the second half of 2012, a local armed faction was formed in Deir Hafer under the name 'Katibat Abu Dujana'. According to residents, no significant clashes were recorded. Government forces vacated the city by mid-2012 to concentrate their presence in the city of Aleppo (Hasan 2018).[8] In the period prior to that, however, the city witnessed multiple clashes between protestors and the local security apparatus, specifically by the personnel of the Political Security Directorate in the city, in addition to local intelligence offices and other branches from nearby towns such as Maskana's Military Security that were mobilized to suppress demonstrations.[9] In terms of violence and threats, by the end of 2012, kidnappings and extortion had become widespread.

Prior to the withdrawal of government forces in 2012, kidnappings and detentions by the local security apparatus aimed to suppress activists and protestors. Other acts of kidnapping targeted those with known wealth, in order to collect ransom. Such incidents continued to take place after the local faction took over.[10] 'Kidnappings had become more rampant unfortunately', declared a previous resident who supported the local faction.[11] Participants also revealed how ransom was a factor in both government detentions and kidnappings by militiamen alike, as multiple respondents described how friends or family members detained by militants or the security apparatus were released in return for large sums of money.[12] There were also mentions of additional kidnapping incidents motivated by vengeance for previous acts of injustice or against potential government collaborators.[13]

When the Syrian government's security forces vacated the city of Deir Hafer, they left behind a sizeable governance and security vacuum for the approximately forty thousand residents in the city proper and its surrounding villages in the *nahiya*.[14] As armed opposition groups in the area ramped up operations against the military airport of Kweiris between 2012 and 2013, the city of Deir Hafer came under heavy fire (Hasan 2018).[15] Violence towards civilians shifted considerably. According to residents in the area, along with every attack on the Kweiris airport, air raids targeting the civilian population of Deir Hafer intensified significantly.[16] 'The bombing was aimed at punishing civilians, to push them against the local faction [participating in besieging and attacking the Kweiris airport]', declared a local activist.[17] He continued, stating,

> 'air raids against the city not only did not discriminate between combatants and non-combatants, but intentionally targeted residential areas and city centres'.[18]

The range of missiles that were used varied and included artillery attacks as well as barrel bombs. For local activists in support of the local armed group, however, 'without besieging Kweiris, the city would have been more easily and more repeatedly targeted'.[19] Attacks on Kweiris rendered the airport un-operational and air raids came from military airports further away, such as the T-4 airbase in Homs.[20]

This lack of security drove many civilians to seek protection by joining existing military factions. By late 2012 and early 2013, the broader area of Deir Hafer, Maskaneh and al-Bab had multiple military groups that were organized and active on significant fronts, such as the Kweiris airport. Among the most noteworthy were Liwa' al-Tawhid's eleventh division in Masakaneh and Deir Hafer, the Islamic State of Iraq and the Levant (Daesh) predominantly in al-Bab and Harakat Ahrar al-Sham (AlJazeera 2017; Lund 2013).[21] By the first half of 2013, despite the expansion of Daesh in nearby areas such as al-Bab, the area of Deir Hafer and its local factions remained largely under the banner of the Free Syrian Army and maintained amicable relations with all factions.[22] As explicitly declared by one of the most high-ranking representatives of Katibat Abu Dujana at the time, Atallah al-Wasmi, to prevent infighting the faction repeatedly refused to commit to fighting against other armed opposition groups, including Daesh.[23] According to interviewees, 'Daesh, at the time, was similar to any other armed group in the region', and did not show signs of brutality towards the populace.[24] Moreover, the organization prided itself on its commitment to providing social services and ending corruption in areas held by armed opposition groups.

Economic vulnerability in the area was one of the main reasons Daesh was eventually capable of taking over Deir Hafer with great ease. Even local agricultural production became expensive as irrigation and transportation required fuel and diesel, which became more expensive with the fluctuation of the Syrian pound, decline in local oil extraction and refinement and extortionist trade practices driving prices up. Food produced in the area witnessed an exponential spike in price as efforts to impose a ceiling on essentials proved futile (Shabakat Halab News 2013). Farmers and traders were also genuinely unable to fix their prices due to the Syrian pound's fluctuations, and many trade centres such as that in al-Bab or in Turkey started trading in United States Dollars (USD).[25] These factors, combined with the decline of local employment opportunities, created ideal circumstances for Daesh's takeover, specifically after its expansion in Iraq and the resources commanded as a result.

After Daesh clashed with Ahrar al-Sham in Maskana in early 2014, taking over Deir Hafer, the local faction of Abu Dujana split with many of its members joining Daesh while others remained with Ahrar al-Sham but withdrew from the area.[26] Throughout such retransitions and shifts in local military powers in the area, social mistrust and tribal divisions became more prominent. Sudden transitions in local military hierarchies and sudden shifts in exclusionary leadership structures continuously fuelled competing tribal networks and kinship ties.[27]

With the takeover of Deir Hafer by Daesh, the town was renamed Dar al-Fath as a symbolic expression of the organization's ambitions to radically reconfigure the city. Deir Hafer's circumstances under Daesh were not different from those of Raqqa. Daesh transformed its approach from cooperative and submissive to locals, to coercive and brutal.[28] Aside from brutal punishments and exclusionary practices, Daesh also transformed the local infrastructure through the introduction of field hospitals, improvised military factories and a public platform in the centre of the city to stage punishments. The scale of violence upon community escalated with the annulment of previous arrangements (which were made through intermediaries to save local infrastructure from aerial bombardment). As a result, the local surgical hospital, for instance, was bombed in April 2015 (Mu'asasat Taht el-Mjhar 2015).

Furthermore, Daesh used both coercive and enticing methods to create its new local cadres.[29] 'Their salaries were significantly high compared to salaries at the time and they could provide privileges and clout to those they wanted to coopt.'[30] The organization also tried to make an example of those who were difficult to co-opt, and abused them with either coercion or punishment for their stance.[31] Local actors with previous administrative capacity, experience or expertise faced such alternatives (alDeri 2014). All civilian structures were abolished and new ones were created (*dawawīn*) under Daesh's direct command. Extortion by Daesh recruits was rampant. Media activists feared for their lives and all satellite routers and internet equipment were confiscated. The need for protection as well as financial incentives motivated some locals to join. Ultimately, the organization successfully stifled all avenues for potential dissent or organized opposition against its rule.[32]

In this context, it is important to highlight the events of Tal Ayoub in 2014 because they represent a negative turning point for civilian autonomy and those who opposed the organization. In May 2014, a series of clashes, detentions and killings by Daesh forces in and around the town of Tal Ayoub began after Daesh's futile attempts at co-opting a local military commander with the *nom de guerre* of Aba a'isha – a farmer who had mobilized and commanded less than thirty friends and family members, such as his sons, to fight against government forces in the region (alDeri 2014). After refusing to join Daesh, surrender weapons or vacate the area, a large number of Daesh troops with approximately forty military vehicles, equipped with medium-to-light weaponry, surrounded the village from all directions and conducted a terror campaign against residents.[33] Aba a'isha's house was attacked and clashes ensued, ending with the capture of his son, who was later executed and displayed in the centre of Deir Hafer.[34] Concurrently, Daesh troops proceeded with a campaign of detentions in the wider area including the town of Rasm al-Abed where the renowned medical doctor Khamis al-Yousef was detained, tortured and interrogated.[35] Dr al-Yousef himself reveals that 'during the time, Daesh had brought a detainee from Tal Ayoub and decapitated him in Rasm al-Abed'.[36] The terror campaign was similar to other extreme measures and spectacles of violence adopted by the organization to establish control and domination (Akdedian 2019).

Government forces replaced the reign of Daesh in February 2017 after a week-long siege and intense aerial bombardment by the Russian forces. Daesh fighters abandoned their positions. Since then, the government issued multiple statements calling for the return of local residents to Deir Hafer (SANA 2017). The city has also regularly featured on state TV channels to portray local development and investment in rehabilitating its infrastructure and promoting agricultural activities (SANA 2017). The government also continued efforts to reorganize tribal groups and create new networks of patronage. Such efforts are widely condemned by the Majlis al-Qaba'il wal-Wujaha' Fi al-Dakhel al-Souri through statements signed by more than fifteen local tribes and clans (Syria Call 2018). Tribal leadership continues to be contested: 'Many who were previously connected to the Government and did not take part in any civilian or military activism [between 2012 and 2017] are returning to local leadership positions.'[37]

Those who had any role in local organizational and administrative efforts during armed opposition groups' control face uncertainties and existential threats.

Community protection

There were only few skirmishes between Katibat Abu Dujana and government forces during the withdrawal. The artillery and air force of Kweiris airport started targeting the city, specifically in late 2012 and early 2013, when opposition groups ramped up operations against the military airport of Kweiris (Hasan 2018).[38] Air raids against the city did not discriminate between combatants and non-combatants. As a result of the violence, many residents vacated their homes and moved to safer areas. The countryside was targeted less than the city.[39] Given the limited means of self-protection against such scales of violence, most efforts consisted of personal measures such as people abandoning the central areas of the Deir Hafer township and moving towards the countryside, to relatives or family farm lands.[40]

When violence struck, those unable to leave would either run to the basement of their house or towards a centrally located room away from balconies, windows or the outermost façades of buildings.[41] As bombardments reoccurred, most locals became familiar with the sounds and patterns of bombings. As helicopters or fighter jets were heard approaching, residents would identify their trajectory and head towards areas away from their path.[42] Residents and first responders also learned the bombing patterns, in which the same target was often attacked twice at a brief interval.[43] In the face of indiscriminate mass violence, these basic and personal initiatives were all that locals could do for self-protection.[44] Interviewees expressed that civilian councils and military factions either did not pay attention to them or simply could not do anything in the face of such violence. 'No one asked about us, there were no shelters, there was nothing', echoed multiple participants.[45]

As a result of the shelling in Deir Hafer, many residents vacated their homes and moved to safer areas. The most targeted areas were those closest to the Kweiris military airport on the western side of the Nahiya.[46] Some residents, who had no safe place to go to, remained in their houses,[47] but towns, such as Rasm Abboud, were usually vacated during attacks on the Kweiris airport by armed opposition groups. These evacuations were temporary and uncoordinated; families simply learned the pattern of violence and noticed military preparations ahead of time and vacated beforehand, temporarily leaving their towns.[48]

Permanent mass displacements took place in Deir Hafer during transitions of power and shifts in territorial control between armed opposition groups. Displacement patterns for Deir Hafer were uncoordinated and depended upon military developments in the area. For instance, when the local armed group took over in 2012, many of those who vacated headed westward towards Aleppo City.[49] Those displaced later, when the situation in Aleppo City had also deteriorated, headed north (within the Syrian Arab Republic and beyond).[50] During the rule of Daesh, the organization did not allow people to leave for extended periods of time and planted mines along the road to the north-east towards areas controlled by the SDF to prevent people from leaving.[51] Upon government return, those who vacated headed towards the SDF controlled north-east.

Among the most noteworthy community-protection efforts throughout the violent episodes of the conflict were focused on the city's most vital infrastructures. For instance, the only surgical hospital in Deir Hafer was privately owned by Syrian Parliament member, Fahmi al-Hasan, at the time.[52] Reportedly, the owner received a part of the hospital's income, which incentivized him to protect the building from bombardment utilizing his bargaining capacity within the government.[53] This implicit, de-facto agreement remained in place even after Katibat abu-Dujana pledged allegiance to Ahrar al-Sham. Furthermore, some residents living close to the hospital would go there for protection from shelling.[54] What is noteworthy here is that the protection of the hospital was not only incentivized for purposes of community protection but also through the positionality and personal financial gains of those who had authority and power to ensure the safety of the facility. In other words, given that Fahmi al-Hasan had a level of influence within state structures and in opposition-held areas, he was in a position to broker such arrangements. At the same time, he had personal gains from protecting such facilities. This highlights the need to identify individuals who can fulfil such functions and the importance of incentivizing civilian community protection and the protection of civilian infrastructures.

The situation of the local industrial bakery (*al-furn al-ali*) was similar as it was not bombed, and its diesel and flour were provided by the government in return for local wheat and a portion of the bakery's revenues.[55] The employees (those employed before the withdrawal of government forces in 2012) continued to receive their salaries provided that they travelled to areas held by the government to receive their pay cheques from the respective government centres.[56] Interviewees also shared how those who did travel to collect their pay cheques were interrogated by government forces.[57] When they returned to their areas, 'they also received harassment from local factions because their loyalty was questionable. It was suspected that they were working as informants but the truth is they were working at the bakery and had nothing to do with the armed factions'.[58]

This example illustrates how bargaining and negotiating with opposing factions can create spaces that are comparably safe (thus preserving vital community functions such as food, shelter, etc.).

Civilian structures

To address issues of widespread kidnappings at the time, local notables, such as elderly tribesmen, were reportedly asked to intervene and mediate in efforts of releasing the kidnapped. These mediations however neither provided protection nor addressed the drivers behind the kidnappings. The efforts of tribal notables remained limited to mitigating harm and attempting to mediate with kidnappers who were willing to negotiate or engage.

Civilian-led initiatives enjoyed more freedoms after 2012, and took on leading roles in organizing the locality and address arising vulnerabilities. The most notable initiatives came about through the structures of the post-2012 local civilian council, which included multiple offices and branches directly aimed at addressing local needs and safety concerns. The most notable branch for the purpose of this study is the 'reconciliation committee' (*Lijnat al-Musalaha*), which worked on diffusing tensions and addressing local disagreements to prevent conflict escalation. The committee was active between 2012 and 2014 as a civilian conflict-resolution and de-escalation body.

Between 2012 and 2014, a number of unprecedented media initiatives were employed by local youths within the armed opposition groups. They formed local newspapers (*al-bayan*) and relied on social media, specifically, Facebook pages such as *Tansiqiyet Deir Hafer*, to raise awareness and provide safety guidelines in the area.[59] For instance, according to one of the administrators, the Facebook page would post information about recent attacks and advise residents to avoid areas under attack or in danger of potential air raids.[60] In addition, new local civilian structures were formed under the umbrella of the civil councils.

Deir Hafer's council, similar to other local councils in areas beyond the control of the government, comprised multiple specialized offices, such as the relief office and the judiciary office. The judiciary included both a religious council and a legal office composed of religious judges, as a well as lawyers and judges from public law. The Lijnat al-Musalaha (the 'reconciliation committee' mentioned earlier) was also within the legal office, with its main office in the centre of the town.[61] The committee's mode of operation was such that when disagreements arose among local citizens, the committee would mediate and try and help find adequate solutions.[62] Often, when the religious court received a case, it immediately forwarded it to the committee.[63] As an informal arbitration court of first instance, 'we always preserved the right to forward the case to [the formal court] al-mahkama al-Shar'iyya that had the backing and enforcement provided by armed forces in the area'.[64]

According to members of the committee, 85 per cent of the cases brought before the committee were solved without the need to forward the file to the court.[65] Cases brought before the committee included issues and disagreements of inheritance, divorce and marriage, payment of debt, property rights, agricultural matters of land and labour management and rentals.[66] Many interviewees expressed how the committee prevented conflict escalation and avoided potential violence in the city: 'they [the committee] did a great job and they were much needed. They did the best they could'.⁶⁷

The committee was headed by local notables from a variety of tribes in the area – namely, representatives from the al-Hadidiyin, al-Kharraj and Bani Jamil. Professionally, the individuals who formed the groups were renowned teachers and esteemed tribal and religious figures.⁶⁸ The committee members, comprising a lawyer, a judge, a religious judge and two other reputable members from the community, were among those often viewed as neutral and fair regardless of their tribal affiliation.⁶⁹ As an informal arbitration court of first instance, it always preserved the right to forward the case to the formal court (al-mahkama al-Shar'iyya) operating with the backing and enforcement provided by the armed forces in the area.

Among the many challenges that the committee faced was that its office was no longer operational due to air raids but the personnel remained active and visited people in different places.⁷⁰ According to a high-ranking member of the committee, one of the glaring challenges the committee faced was that armed factions intervened in its operations and competed for influence within.⁷¹ This took place despite the committee's structure, which was designed to protect it from interventions. Ultimately, the religious court was the primary authority in judicial matters and it was directly appointed and enforced by the armed factions in place. Given its relative distance from armed factions, compared to the religious court for instance, the committee enjoyed relatively more leeway and autonomy. However, individuals accepting the mechanism and outcome of the process of the committee might have done so to avoid standing before the religious court and not due to a satisfactory performance by the committee. For the people in Deir Hafer's silent majority, for instance, who had frictions with the armed groups in place, the reconciliation committee was the best option around, and many avoided such processes altogether assuming they would not find justice. This also influenced local perceptions of the committee that, despite the reputable standing of its personnel, was perceived by many as lacking autonomy.⁷² Many of those who welcomed the idea behind the reconciliation committee also hypothetically projected its restricted autonomy due to the influence of local armed forces even when they had not accessed or worked with the committee.⁷³ Only two interviewees out of twenty-one explicitly stated they did not know about the committee at all.⁷⁴

As mentioned, the local military faction later integrated with Ahrar al-Sham in 2013, before effectively dissolving in the aftermath of the takeover by Daesh in 2014. Daesh had been in charge of al-Bab since late 2013 and had a broad presence in Deir Hafer as well (AlJazeera 2017). It did not, however, attempt to exclude other factions and establish hegemonic rule, and its military presence was limited. With its complete takeover of Deir Hafer and beyond in 2014, the situation of the city and local power relations changed dramatically. Until then, civilian-led institutions enjoyed more freedoms than before and took on leading roles in organizing the locality and address arising vulnerabilities. The most notable initiatives came about through the structures of the local civilian council, which included multiple offices and branches directly aimed at addressing local needs and safety concerns. The most notable branch for the purpose of this study is the 'reconciliation committee' (Lijnat al-Musalaha), which worked on diffusing tensions and addressing local disagreements to prevent conflict escalation. The committee was active between 2012 and 2014 as a civilian conflict-resolution and de-escalation body.

Economic vulnerability

The dire economic circumstances in the area are one of the city's most notable local vulnerabilities. Even local agricultural production became expensive as irrigation and transportation required fuel and diesel, which became more expensive with the fluctuation of the Syrian pound, a decline in local oil extraction and refinement and the extortionist trade practices, which drove prices up. Food produce in the area witnessed an exponential spike in prices and efforts to impose a ceiling on essentials proved futile (Shabakat Halab News 2013). Beyond greed, farmers and traders were also genuinely unable to fix their prices due to the Syrian pound's fluctuations, and many trade centres such as those in al-Bab or in Turkey started trading in United States dollars (USD) (Shabakat Halab News 2013).[75] These factors, combined with the decline in local employment opportunities, created ideal circumstances for a takeover of the area by a potent armed group with resources.

Despite these challenges, there was sufficient autonomy for locals to organize peaceful protests against the inflated rates imposed by traders within Deir Hafer.[76] The relief office and other charity organizations in the city were barely capable of providing food supplies (oil, rice, sugar, etc.) and basic necessities (such as milk for infants) to maintain the most elementary conditions of liveability for families in need (Shabakat Halab News 2013). These efforts, however, were no match to the needs and socio-economic vulnerabilities in place.

In light of this situation, Deir Hafer grew more dependent on neighbouring city, al-Bab, as the gateway towards the relief and humanitarian organizations in Turkey. This reinforced pre-existing dependencies between the two cities, which intensified regional tensions. According to interviewees who had a role in the local council's relief office, most humanitarian aid came through al-Bab.[77] It had become common practice for al-Bab officials to withhold part of Deir Hafer's aid.[78] Furthermore, many kidnappings according to interviewees were traced to individuals and factions from al-Bab.[79] As local agricultural produce declined in winter in Deir Hafer, al-Bab became the centre for merchandise and goods coming through Turkey (Shabakat Halab News 2013). Prices soon increased along with Deir Hafer's dependency on al-Bab's markets, and Deir Hafer residents bore the brunt, while those in al-Bab with access to trade routes in Turkey benefited. It was in the given economic circumstances and after expanding into Iraq and securing capital and military equipment that Daesh was able to not only impose itself militarily on other factions, but also recruit more people with enticing salaries and create more capable administrative structures.

Stifling civilian-led community protection efforts

Before taking over Deir Hafer in 2014, Daesh had already established itself in the city in all ways except militarily. Its strategy in Deir Hafer was similar to its strategies elsewhere east of Syria: wherever it lacked military capacity and found itself in areas contested by multiple factions, Daesh adopted a cooperative stance to help alleviate local conditions, fight corruption and establish order through services and administrative structures. It made itself useful to civilians and military factions alike. The local Da'wa office was explicitly aimed at improving the organization's image. Given the massive lack of capacity and personnel in civilian structures, Katibat Abu Dujana welcomed the organization provided that it limits its operations to administrative matters and respects its local authority. By late 2013, Daesh recruits ran the local 'Islamic police', Da'wa office, local clinics and other services in the city, and explicitly stated their membership to Daesh in a civilian capacity (Shabakat Halab News 2013). After Daesh clashed with Ahrar al-Sham in early 2014 in Maskana, it turned towards Deir Hafer and took over the area without any notable clashes. The local faction of Abu Dujana split with many of its members joining Daesh while others remained with Ahrar al-Sham but withdrew from the area.[80]

Throughout transitions and shifts in local military powers in the area, tribal leadership changed significantly. Sudden transitions and exclusionary leadership structures continuously created tensions within kinship and tribal ties in the area. Such tensions, similar to the post-2011 dynamics, could play an important role in future conflict recurrence and remain one of the most important features of persisting vulnerabilities.

The biggest tribal group in the area has been and remains the Hadidiyin. Before 2012, the Assad government provided privileges and access to power to the tribe's senior figures due to their wide networks and expansive social ties (Dukhan 2019).[81] This harked back to Assad Senior's policies of creating a broad coalition of farmers, peasants and tribesmen in rural areas to extend his reach and power (Dukhan 2019). Among the most famous and iconic of such figures nationwide is Diab al-Mashi, who served in the Syrian Parliament from 1954 until his death in 2009 (Amiralay 2011; Dukhan 2019).

The Hadidiyin in Deir Hafer remained in power with Daesh as the organization capitalized on a sense of relative marginalization, which had been festering since 2012. With the broad coalition of cross-tribal representation within Katibat Abu Dujana, the Hadidiyins' previous clout diminished between 2012 and 2014. Daesh successfully appealed to members of the tribe by providing the opportunity for a return to its previous status.[82] Before 2012, many members of the Hadidiyin and al-Kharraj had joined the Baa'th party and filled security branches locally as well as in other parts of the Aleppo province, such as Aleppo City.[83] Locals from Deir Hafer were often recruited and filled the state apparatus elsewhere. For instance, Abd al-Hanan Hajjo – from Deir Hafer and the tribe of Bani Sa'id – was appointed chief of police in Idlib city and later in Aleppo City.[84] Member of Parliament, deputy vice president and owner of Deir Hafer's only surgical hospital, Fahmi

Hasan was also from the region of Deir Hafer (born in Rasm Abboud) and from the Hadidiyin tribe.[85]

From the standpoint of Deir Hafer's political economy, the state and the Baa'th were the biggest employers, either through direct government positions or through subsidiary entities such as the farmers' union and other centralized agricultural planning initiatives. Through clientelistic allocations of wealth, services, privileges and positions, the Assad government captured the state and established patrimonial relations even beyond its immediate reach. Locally privileged tribal figures nurtured their own clientelist networks by employing and appointing their kin and tribal affiliates within state departments and institutions under their influence (Dukhan 2019).[86] This created a level of hierarchy within the tribal systems where tribal affiliation became a factor in the residents' opportunities and privileges.

This has not rendered each tribe a monolith, of course. Within each, varied groups and topographies of power existed depending on nature of kinship and proximity to those recruited in significant positions within the state apparatus. In 2012, when Deir Hafer effectively joined the opposition, it was rebelling against an older generation of local tribal leaders as much as it was against the government. These two classes of authority were intimately linked. Katibat Abu Dujana was composed of various tribes, but the majority were a younger generation that by default, and through the takeover of Abu Dujana, created new local leadership that put aside the old guard. The conflict from a local standpoint was a revolt against these classes and could only succeed by depriving them of influence.

After Daesh took over, the majority of the Hadidiyin who were members of Katibat Abu Dujana joined Daesh, whereas the majority of Bani Jamil tribesmen remained with Ahrar al-Sham.[87] In fact, according to those who closely witnessed the transition of power from Abu Dujana to Daesh, the local Da'wa office and Daesh personnel grew more acquainted to local tensions through their presence in the city prior to the organization's military takeover.[88]

With the takeover of Deir Hafer by Daesh, the town was renamed Dar al-Fath. Deir Hafer changed not only in name but also in nature. Beyond local tribal dynamics, developments in Deir Hafer were similar to that of Raqqa. Daesh transformed its approach and stance from being cooperative and submissive towards locals to becoming coercive and brutal.[89] Aside from brutal punishments and exclusionary practices, Daesh also transformed the local infrastructure by introducing field hospitals, improvised military factories and a public platform in the centre of the city to stage punishments. The primary difference in patterns of violence impacting the community was that all previous arrangements through intermediaries to save local infrastructure from aerial bombardment were annulled; as a result, the local surgical hospital was bombed in April 2015 (Taht elMjhar 2015).

Among the casualties was the city's famous doctor, Dr Radwan al-Umar, who died in the raid. Before his death, Daesh held the doctor in detention for denouncing its methods. In fact, Daesh used both coercive and enticing methods to create its new local cadres.[90] Their salaries were significantly high compared to salaries at the time and they could provide privileges and power to those they wanted to co-opt. The organization tried to make an example of those who were difficult to co-opt and abused them with either coercion or punishment for their stance.[91] Local actors with previous administrative capacity, experience or expertise received such treatment.[92] All civilian structures were suspended and new ones were created under its direct command. Extortion by Daesh recruits was rampant.

Every interviewee had personal stories about their suffering under Daesh. Media activists were under pressure and all satellite routers and internet equipment were confiscated. The need for protection as well as financial incentives motivated some locals to join. However, the events of Tal Ayoub in 2014 represented the point of no return for civilian autonomy and those who opposed the organization.

The incidents of Tal Ayoub began with Daesh attempting to co-opt a local military commander with the nom de guerre of Aba 'a'isha – a farmer who had mobilized and commanded less than thirty friends and family members, such as his sons, to fight against government forces in the region (alDeri 2014)[93] After refusing to join Daesh, surrender weapons or vacate the area, a large number of Daesh troops with approximately forty military vehicles, equipped with medium-to-light weaponry, surrounded the village from all directions and conducted a terror campaign against residents.[94] Aba 'a'isha's house was attacked and clashes ensued, ending with the capture of his son, who was later executed in the centre of Deir Hafer where his body was displayed.[95] At the same time, Daesh troops proceeded with a campaign of detentions in the wider area including the town of Rasm al-Abed where the renowned medical doctor Khamis al-Yousef was detained, tortured and interrogated.[96] Dr al-Yousef himself reveals how Daesh during the time had brought a detainee from Tal Ayoub and decapitated him in Rasm al-Abed.[97] The terror campaign was similar to other extreme measures and spectacles of violence adopted by the organization to establish control and domination (Akdedian 2019).

In February 2017, government forces took over the area after a week-long siege and intense aerial bombardment by Russian forces. Daesh fighters abandoned their positions. Since then, the government issued multiple statements calling for the return of local residents to Deir Hafer (SANA 2017). The city has been featured regularly on state TV channels, showing local development and investment in rehabilitating the infrastructure of the city and promoting agricultural activities (SANA 2017). The government also continued its efforts to reorganize tribal groups and create new networks of patronage. Such efforts are widely condemned by the Majlis al-Qaba'il wal-Wujaha' Fi al-Dakhel al-Souri through statements signed by more than fifteen local tribes and clans (Syria Call 2018). Tribal leadership continues to be contested and organizational capacity continuously shifts based on the patronage in place. Many who were previously connected to the government and did not take part in any civilian or military activism between 2012 and 2017 are reportedly returning to local leadership positions.[98] Those who had any role in local organizational and administrative efforts during opposition control face uncertainties and existential threats.

Limits to civilian autonomy: Identifying structural conditions

Community Protection Measures	Deir Hafer	Description
Shelters	Limited presence	Limited presence, not on par with the scale of nature of threats and scale of violence
Evacuation (organized)	Limited presence	Lack of organized displacement jeopardized vulnerable members of the community such as the elderly and those without property or kin nearby
Cohesion in exile (organized)	Limited presence	The displaced from Deir Hafer face numerous obstacles to voluntary return
Early warning systems (organized)	Absent	There were no organized early warning systems; limited information sharing technologies among the civilian population
Warning signals of imminent threats (unorganized)	Present	Deir Hafer predominantly relied on personal observations of military movements
Mobilization of international networks	Limited presence	Deir Hafer enjoyed limited connections and the aid received was inconsistent and insufficient
Bargaining and negotiating with armed groups (state and non-state) for safe spaces	Present	Deir Hafer managed to protect vital infrastructure from conflict, despite the fact that underlying agreements were precarious
Non-violent conflict resolution mechanisms	Present	Deir Hafer's civilian council had an office dedicated to arbitration and mediation
Civilian autonomy (vis-à-vis armed groups)	Limited presence	Greater space for civilian administrative and operational autonomy in Deir Hafer post-2011 – prone to the interference of armed factions
Armed protection (self-defence)	Limited presence	Limited militarization with insufficient capacity to resist violence against civilians

Based on the threats and efforts of community protection in Deir Hafer, a number of strengths and weaknesses can be pointed out with regard to civilian efforts of community protection. Interviewees who had an active role in local efforts of community protection expressed a need to maintain and expand the civilian space for disaster preparedness and community protection. Despite admitting the lack of transformative outlooks and relying predominantly on reactive responses to evolving threats and vulnerabilities, civilians lacked coordinated early warning and evacuation systems aimed at community protection and preservation. Deir Hafer had active community organizers with significant local knowledge, but those civilian community organizers exhibited greater need for organizational experience and preparedness for purposes of community protection during conflict.

Overall, there was a gradual decline in civilian roles and responsibilities for community protection since the second half of 2013. In addition, centre–periphery dependencies provided shifting opportunities and restraints based on conflict dynamics, but ultimately restrained the autonomy of civilian actors. Especially during moments of geographic isolation, centre–periphery dependencies proved decisively consequential. As explained later in this section, repercussions of centre–periphery dependencies during conflict were compounded by pre-existing economic vulnerabilities and lack of disaster-informed and sustainable models of economic development in the area. This significantly harmed and exacerbated the fragility of local communities and their capacity to withstand threats. By 2014, increasingly overwhelming levels of violence decisively undermined civilian capacities. Such vulnerabilities persist. This section examines some of the structural conditions that shaped the community protection efforts listed in the previous section and their influence on community protection outcomes.

Local autonomy

Local autonomy for civilian community actors in Deir Hafer is directly linked to prevailing institutional structures and power relations in context. Institutional structures and power relations between key societal, military and political actors and community-based organizations delimited the level of autonomy and decision-making capacity for local civilian actors. Power dynamics between civilian community organizers and non-civilian power groups in place (military groups within localities and centre–periphery dependencies between neighbouring areas) have delimited the space for civilians to plan, mobilize and implement community protection measures. In Deir Hafer, civilian autonomy was shaped by the level of intervention of military groups in the work of civilian community organizers. This gradually and effectively diverted decision-making responsibilities to military authorities.

In the period between 2012 and 2014, civilian entities in Deir Hafer had unprecedented operational space to organize and take initiatives such as publishing new local magazines and engaging in social media activism. The local Shoura Council emerged as a contested space among local notables to express different ideas and compete for influence in local matters.[99] Undoubtedly, such civilian spaces were not entirely accessible to everyone, as activists who mobilized and filled such ranks were concerned about infiltration. Given the dangers in place and the possible eventuality of government return, many also decided not to join these ranks out of fear of guilt by association, or of any sign that might incriminate them in the eyes of the Syrian government. After the marginalization of the old tribal leadership, relations of kinship were used as trust networks to fill local administrative structures. These two combined factors determined the cross-tribal but narrow cadre of emergent civilian structures. Given the codependencies between local factions and civilian structures in matters of administration, enforcement and protection, the two bodies were closely linked, not only operationally but also through kinship ties between the two organisms.[100] This further increased the influence of armed groups over civilian structures.

In addition, Katibat Abu Dujana often intervened in civilian matters – as in the case of Lijnat al-Musalaha. Nevertheless, given that the local faction did not have the capacity to run administrative or civil institutions, a level of de facto autonomy and operational space existed despite interventions and pressures from armed opposition groups. When Daesh took over, the landscape changed drastically, as all civil institutions were replaced by Daesh offices and recruits.

Organizational capacity

Organizational capacity and local autonomy are interdependent, specifically with regard to decision-making capacities. Regardless of resources at hand, without the autonomy to carry out decisions and strategies, resources have little consequence. Similarly, without organizational resources, decisions and strategies are impossible to carry out and implement regardless of the nature and limits of local autonomy. Organizational capacity refers to the conditions that enable or constrain protective strategies and shape their outcomes. These include organizational reach within localities and beyond, resource availability and procurement ability, organizational size (number of employees or members), institutional knowledge and memory in relation to areas of operation and information processing mechanisms to inform strategies and methods. According to the UNDP's Capacity Assessment Methodology, leadership structures, knowledge accountability and institutional arrangements, such as budget management, 'define the scope of [organizational capacity] assessment' (UNDP 2008: 6). Despite the flexibility and variations in assessment models, organizational capacity ultimately depends upon the objectives and deliverables of specific initiatives and efforts (UNDP 2008: 6). In other words, organizational capacity is measurable only in relation to the efforts and objectives of each specific organizer and each initiative (Abrutyn and Turner 2011).

Civilian entities in Deir Hafer after 2012 emerged in response to local needs. This has influenced the resources and abilities of civilian organizers, as the new leadership did not have pre-existing networks, partnerships and experiences that translate into resources during conditions of heightened vulnerability. Most civilian structures emerged throughout the conflict and public services, such as the industrial bakery, garbage collection and the thermal power plant, continued operating with reduced personnel and capacity. Some of those who had worked in the respective institutions took on bigger responsibilities with limited experience and training. The civilian council emerged in 2012 but did not enjoy established trans-local partnerships and connections. Efforts of outreach and building connections had to be improvised and nurtured during rapidly changing circumstances and volatile conditions.

Centre–periphery dependencies strongly existed in Deir Hafer. Economic activities were based on agriculture and trade. Despite the area providing wheat and electricity nationwide, it only received a marginal share of the revenues. Deir Hafer, similar to the other towns of Aleppo's countryside, experienced relative deprivation of benefits or resources while urban centres such as Aleppo City and Damascus were further reinforced as sites of concentrated capital and investment (Azmeh 2014; al-Khafaji 2016). Nearby cities such as al-Bab and Manbij fared better than Deir Hafer economically during the conflict as they emerged as economic centres due to access to the Syrian-Turkish border (Khadour 2017).

In 2008, Decree 445 administratively separated Deir Hafer from the region of al-Bab to form the new administrative region of Deir Hafer composed of Nahiyat Deir Hafer, Nahiyat Rasm alHirmil alimam and Nahiyat Kuweiris Sharqi. As a distinct administrative area, Deir Hafer received its own security branch, whereas previously it was unified with al-Bab and effectively governed from there. A number of new government jobs and administrative ranks were available for distribution within Deir Hafer. This measure diminished Deir Hafer's historic reliance and administrative subordination to the city of al-Bab, while creating new positions of power locally. These arrangements created new dependencies between smaller towns in Deir Hafer, such as Hmeyme, on the city of Deir Hafer. During the conflict, Deir Hafer became a centre for other regional townships the same way that al-Bab once again became a centre for Deir Hafer. According to interviewees from Deir Hafer's civilian council and a member of Mercy Corps' local office supporting the local bakery in Hmeyme, the local bakery in Hmeyme came under significant pressure from Deir Hafer's civilian council to relocate its operations to Deir Hafer if it was to continue to operate.[101]

Although Deir Hafer was dependent on other centres, they were also centres in and of themselves to other peripheries, such as Hmeyme. This strongly points out the need for regional policy approaches that connect multiple localities to address equitable labour relations and sustainable economic planning and management. This would minimize economic deprivation during conflict and reduce relative deprivation, which could become a source of social strife and compromise cooperative dispositions. Despite the area being now reconnected to its previous economic and administrative centre in Aleppo City, Aleppo City no longer functions as it did prior to the conflict, given the socio-economic reconfiguration and physical harm it sustained throughout the conflict (Khadour 2017).

Social trust

Social trust is a binding relational force defined by cooperative predispositions and favourable views towards other individuals, groups and institutions (Cadier, Capasso and Eickhoff 2020: 11). During armed conflict, social trust is consequential for collaborative action which may include sharing sensitive information, coordinating safety plans, mobilizing other members of the community in high-risk contexts and maintaining organizational unity (Wilson 2014: 8). In the context of armed conflict, with ruptures and transformations to the existing social fabric, networks of social trust often serve as pathways of cooperation and mobilization – —creating what Wilson describes as 'lock-in' effects that shape pathways and strategies of community protection (Wilson 2014: 10). Wilson's point is not to condemn collaborative endeavours of community protection to predetermination. Rather, his point is that in a context of conflict fragility and radical socio-economic transformations, patterns of continuity and change in social trust and collaborative networks inform trajectories of community mobilization at the local level. Findings from surveys conducted in Deir Hafer tell a similar story. Rapid shifts in perceptions of trust or mistrust often rendered collective action more restrained without rendering them impossible.

Throughout the conflict, social trust, in terms of perceptions of in-group relations, relations between groups as well as trust relations with institutions and organizations in place reveal significant changes and transformations in outlook and predispositions (Borzel and Risse 2016). The survey results show that 77.3 per cent of respondents from Deir Hafer do not consider most residents of their respective communities trustworthy. The fact that more than three-quarters of survey participants expressed blanket mistrust towards their own community is a strong indication that local trust is compromised. When asked whether trust among residents had changed throughout the conflict, 63.9 per cent of respondents from Deir Hafer answered that 'the level of trust amongst residents has gotten worse'.

The surveys indicate that the presence of communal threats and insecurity do not automatically lead community members to fuse together, trust one another and self-organize. When asked whether the level of violence or danger has changed since the major episodes of violence up until 2014, 69 per cent of respondents from Deir Hafer answered that risks increased (47.4 per cent said 'increased a lot'; 21.6 per cent said 'slightly increased'). Among the threats that communities face, for instance, 81.4 per cent of respondents from Deir Hafer answered that they are concerned about theft in their areas. Furthermore, 88.7 per cent of respondents from Deir Hafer declared that they keep the doors and windows of their houses locked at night.

In the daytime, however, 53.6 per cent of respondents from Deir Hafer declared that they keep their doors and windows unlocked. The respondents' positions reflect a level of awareness that the dangers and threats faced are contextual and contingent upon circumstantial factors and not inherent regional or social features. For example, in relation to specific areas of danger, 54.6 per cent of respondents from Deir Hafer declared that there are specific neighbourhoods within the area that they deem unsafe and avoid. In line with this, among the most noticeable areas of strengths that exhibited through the surveys was the scale of trust and cooperation at the neighbourhood level. In other words, when asked if respondents would leave their kids with neighbours to attend urgent matters, 73.2 per cent of respondents from Deir Hafer answered 'yes'. In line with findings from interviews and discussion groups, the surveys show that neighbourhood level communities comprise extended family members and intimately connected acquaintances. This trust, however, did not translate into an organizational shape and was neither consequential nor integral to efforts of community protection.

When responding to what social differences often cause problems, political opinion (19.4 per cent), ethno-linguistic (16.5 per cent) and residential status (displaced vs. resident – 14.1 per cent) featured the highest. In terms of wealth disparity and class divisions, 82.5 per cent of respondents either agreed or strongly agreed that people in the community mainly 'look out for their personal welfare' without much concern for 'community welfare'. Findings from focus group discussions, semi-structured interviews and surveys from Deir Hafer also voiced that although there were no significant levels of poverty in the area, wealth disparity and relative deprivation on regional level (between Deir Hafer and surrounding areas) exist.

In relation to cooperative dispositions within Deir Hafer, 72.2 per cent of respondents claimed that members of their community (56.7 per cent 'often'; 15.5 per cent 'sometime') work and interact with other communities in Deir Hafer. Whereas only 13.4 per cent claimed that members of their community do not interact with other groups. 'Trade and work relations' (22.5 per cent) and 'common interests and goals' (20.6 per cent) top the list of motivators for cooperation.

Furthermore, among all answers to the open-ended question about obstacles to the return of the displaced from Deir Hafer, the most prominent were: 'lack of security' (18.6 per cent) and 'unemployment, poverty and lack of social services' (14.4 Per cent). Respondents also mentioned 'military service' (11.3 per cent) and 'regime oppression' (8.2 per cent) as additional obstacles to the return of the displaced.

Examining patterns of inclusion in accessing resources as well as trust relations with decision-makers and local leadership, the dataset indicates that participants faced exclusion when accessing services or activities essential for community protection: 13.7 per cent of respondents from Deir Hafer answered yes to being excluded from 'financial aid', 13.2 per cent from 'equal employment opportunities', 12.8 per cent from 'food and relief' and 12.8 per cent from 'voting and participation in political activities'. When asked about the reasons behind such exclusion, the three highest-ranking factors were: 'level of income' (24.7 per cent), 'political views or affiliation' (18.5 per cent) and both 'religious belief' and 'occupation' at 12.3 per cent.

In communities where social exclusion and mistrust are on the rise, avenues of change and access to decision-makers are crucial to bringing about social change or act collectively. When asked whether participants are able to meet with community leaders and organizers within their locality, 22.7 per cent of participants from Deir Hafer answered 'yes, with most community leaders', 63.9 per cent answered 'no, with only few or none' and 13.4 per cent of participants refrained from answering. In tangent, participants were also asked if they thought their 'community should be organized differently': 46.4 per cent of participants answered 'very differently' and 39.2 per cent answered 'slightly differently'. Despite the desire for change, most participants expressed lack of access to local leaders and decision-makers.

Social trust is often compromised in the aftermath of "contentious politics and … social mobilization based on identity" (UNDP 2020: 17). The survey points out that despite ethno-religious divides, social trust was not primarily defined by sectarianization alone. Furthermore, despite the prominence of sect-based and religious actors, sociopolitical action and behaviour was neither exclusively guided by nor exclusively manifested in sectarian terms.

Conclusion

Civilian efforts during conditions of state atrophy are often guided by norms and objectives of community protection. However, the limitations in place are tied to capacity and structural conditions (Kaplan 2017: 307). For example, the majority of efforts mentioned in this study fall under the category of survival and coping strategies of self-preservation in the face of violence, where the population in the area tried to evade violence and conflict-related stressors. There are fewer instances of adaptive and mitigating strategies aimed at taming or reducing the scale of violence. Transformative strategies, on the other hand, which aim to address structural condition and local sources of conflict and provide more options for civilians hardly featured at all. This predominance of reactive approaches in efforts of community protection reveals the limited options and stifling institutional conditions of state atrophy.

Patterns of threats and violence, which undermined civilian initiatives in Deir Hafer, were shaped by a combination of local circumstances and vulnerabilities as well as broader conflict patterns and dynamics in the Syrian Arab Republic. The year 2014 witnessed significant shifts in the balance of powers in the Syrian conflict. Until late 2013, armed opposition groups were increasingly successful in mobilization nationwide. Territorial control by government forces, specifically before the military intervention of its foreign allies, consisted of a territorial patchwork of detached urban centres, increasingly under pressure from myriad armed opposition groups in urban outskirts and the hinterland. The decisive involvement of the Russian Army and Lebanese Hezbollah forces by 2014, along with the expansion of Daesh into Iraq, shifted the dynamics of the conflict considerably. Armed opposition groups shifted attention and resources towards combatting Daesh as the latter threatened and overwhelmed other factions in its areas of presence. Deir Hafer fell to Daesh in these circumstances. The primary challenge for fostering coping mechanisms lies in the unpredictability of conflict dynamics and the nature of violence and harm civilians are subjected to. Threats in Deir Hafer evolved in ways that no civilian efforts would have been able to withstand.

Appendix

Survey sample characteristics: Deir Hafer

Categories	Frequency	Percentage
Place of residence during survey		
Deir Hafer	32	33.0
Germany	10	10.3
KSA	4	4.1
Netherlands	7	7.2
Turkey	11	11.3

Categories	Frequency	Percentage
Jarablus	4	4.1
Azaz	9	9.3
Al Rai	4	4.1
Al Raqqa	2	2.1
Afrin	4	4.1
Other	7	7.2
No answer	3	3.1
Total	97	100.0
Ethno-religious belonging		
Muslim Arab Sunni	90	92.8
Muslim Kurdish Sunni	1	1.0
Other	4	4.1
No answer	2	2.1
Total	97	100.0
Gender		
Male	77	79.4
Female	17	17.5
No answer	3	3.1
Total	97	100.0
Age		
16–24	5	5.2
25–35	56	57.7
36–55	31	32.0
Above 55	1	1.0
No answer	4	4.1
Total	97	100.0
Highest level of education		
Illiterate	1	1.0
Primary	15	15.5
Secondary	29	29.9
Tertiary	33	34.0
Postgraduate	6	6.2
No answer	13	13.4
Total	97	100.0

Notes

1 These include developing early warning systems, avoiding casualties, evacuation plans and managing shelters and sanctuary spaces.
2 Such strategies include establishing dialogue channels with armed opposition groups, organizing protests against local aggression, shaming the security apparatus, coordination committees and solidarity norms, organizational structures based on local networks that resist outside policing, operating local justice systems and managing links and interactions with external non-governmental or

intergovernmental organizations (NGOs and IGOs) for various purposes such as humanitarian and relief efforts (Kaplan 2017).
3 Transformative strategies include negotiating peace zones void of weapons, restrictions on recruitment, collaborative agreements between different towns, addressing local grievances and relative deprivation, ensuring greater inclusivity and representation in local decision-making, redistribution of wealth and aid and developing equitable labour to capital relations such as between labourers and landowners in pastoral and agricultural areas.
4 Interview 21B.
5 Interviews 5B; 6B; 20B.
6 Interviews 1B; 21B.
7 Interview 21B.
8 Interviews 2B, 6B; The state security apparatus in Aleppo countryside prioritized Aleppo City and concentrated its presence there.
9 Interview 10B.
10 Interviews 16B; 21B.
11 Interview with Majlis personnel.
12 Interviews 10B; 21B.
13 Interview 14B.
14 The *nahiya* includes Hmeyme Koubra and Hmeyme Soughra, 'akoula, Mab'ouja, southern Rasm el-Hermel, Tal Ayoub, Oum al-Mura, Oum Zalila and Zoubeida (Central Bureau of Statistics 2009).
15 Interview 17B.
16 Interview 21B.
17 Ibid.
18 Ibid.
19 Interview 17B.
20 Ibid.
21 See official statement on YouTube: https://www.youtube.com/watch?v=wBMV HbqnMRI.
22 See official statement on YouTube: https://www.youtube.com/watch?v=ny6jlUOYkv4.
23 See official statement on YouTube: https://www.youtube.com/watch?v=5UK5L4p6jgk.
24 Interviews Daesh victims.
25 Ibid.; Interviews 2B, 11B.
26 Interviews 8B, 21B.
27 Indicators and processes of social trust are discussed in more depth in the next section.
28 Interviews 2B; 4B; 8B; 20B.
29 Interviews 2B; 4B; 8B; 20B.
30 Interview 21B.
31 Interviews 4B; 6B; 13B.
32 Interview 21B.
33 Interviews 5B; 6B; 21B.
34 Interview 6B.
35 Interviews 5B; 6B; 21B.
36 Interview 6B.
37 Interviews 15B; 21B.
38 Interview 17B.
39 Interviews 6B; 10B.

40 Interviews 6B; 8B; 10B.
41 Interviews 8B; 10B.
42 Interview 8B.
43 Interview 8B.
44 Interview 19B.
45 Interviews 14B; 19B.
46 Interviews 2B; 21B.
47 Interview 21B.
48 Interviews 2B; 5B; 6B; 21B.
49 Interviews 5B; 6B; 20B.
50 Interviews 1B; 21B.
51 Interview 21B.
52 Interviews 1B; 14B.
53 Interview 1B.
54 Interview 19B.
55 Interviews 1B; 8B; 11B; 21B.
56 Interviews 11B; 21B.
57 Interview 11B.
58 Interview 21B.
59 Interviews 4B; 16B; 21B.
60 Interview 21B.
61 Interviews 7B; 16B; 19B.
62 Interviews 1B; 6B; 7B.
63 Interview 7B.
64 Interview 19B.
65 Interview 19B.
66 Interviews 6B; 7B.
67 Interviews 1B; 3B; 6B; 7B.
68 Interview 6B.
69 Interview 1B; 7B; 19B.
70 Interview 21B.
71 Interviews 3B; 7B.
72 Interviews 13B; 14B; 15B; 16B.
73 Interviews 13B; 14B; 19B.
74 Interviews 4B; 12B.
75 Interviews 2B; 11B.
76 Interviews 6B; 21B.
77 Interviews 12B; 21B.
78 Interviews 12B; 21B.
79 Interview 16B; 21B.
80 Interviews 8B; 21B.
81 Interview 18B.
82 Interview 3B; 8B.
83 Interviews 3B; 10B; 15B; 18B.
84 Interviews 21B.
85 People's Council of Syria, "وضع مجلس الشعب: فهمي حسن," *Syrian Arab Republic: The People's Council*, http://www.parliament.gov.sy/arabic/index.php?node=211&nid=1162&RID=26&Last=252&First=0&CurrentP

age=0&FName=&LName=&City=&Cat=&Mem=&Com=&Aso=&or=& (accessed 20 May 2020).
86 Interviews 3B; 10B; 15B; 18B.
87 Interviews 1B; 2B; 4B; 6B; 7B; 8B; 10B; 14B; 15B.
88 Interview 21B.
89 Interviews 2B; 4B; 8B; 20B.
90 Interviews 2B; 4B; 8B; 20B.
91 Interviews 4B; 6B; 13B.
92 Interview 21B.
93 Interview 6B.
94 Interviews 5B; 6B; 21B.
95 Interview 6B.
96 Interviews 5B; 6B; 21B.
97 Interview 6B.
98 Interviews 15B; 21B.
99 Interviews 15B; 21B.
100 Interviews 15B; 21B.
101 Interviews 14B; 21B.

Bibliography

alDeri, Abbas (2014). 'ISIS Stormed the Village of 'Tal Ayoub' in the Countryside of Aleppo and Executed the Revolutionaries on Charges of Apostacy!' *Orient News*, 21 May. https://www.orient-news.net/ar/news_show/79180/0/%D8%AF%D8%A7%D8%B9%D8%B4-%D8%AA%D9%82%D8%AA%D8%AD%D9%85-%D9%82%D8%B1%D9%8A%D8%A9%D8%AA%D9%84-%D8%A3%D9%8A%D9%88%D8%A8%D8%A8%D8%B1%D9%8A%D9%81-%D8%AD%D9%84%D8%A8-%D9%88%D8%AA%D8%B9%D8%AF%D9%85-%D8%A7%D9%84%D8%AB%D9%88%D8%A7%D8%B1-%D8%A8%D8%AA%D9%87%D9%85%D8%A9-%D9%85%D8%B1%D8%AA%D8%AF%D9%8A%D9%86 (accessed 14 June 2022).
Abrutyn, Seth, and Bryan Tuner (2011). 'The Old Institutionalism Meets the New Institutionalism'. *Sociological Perspective* 54(3): 283–306.
Ackerman, Philippe (2011). *Cognitive Fatigue: Multidisciplinary Perspectives on Current Research and Future Applications*. Washington DC: American Psychological Association.
Akdedian, Harout (2019). 'On Violence and Radical Theology in the Syrian War: The Instrumentality of Spectacular Violence and Exclusionary Practices from Comparative and Local Standpoints'. *Politics, Religion & Ideology* 20(3): 361–80.
al-Khafaji, Issam (2016). 'De-Urbanising the Syrian Revolt'. *Arab Reform Initiative*. 6 March. https://www.arab-reform.net/publication/de-urbanising-the-syrian-revolt/ (accessed 15 June 2022).
Amiralay, Omar (2011). 'A Flood in Baath Country'. Available on *YouTube*. 30 July. https://www.youtube.com/watch?v=GWAu22K8uuE&t=17s; (accessed 15 June 2022).
AlJazeera (2017). 'albab Mouftah alshamal alsouri'. 13 February. https://www.aljazeera.net/encyclopedia/citiesandregions/2017/2/13/الباب-مفتاح-الشمال-السوري (accessed 15 June 2022).

Arjona, Anna (2016). *Rebelocracy: Social Order in the Colombian Civil War.* Cambridge: Cambridge University Press.

Borzel, Tanja, and Risse, Thomas (2016). 'Dysfunctional State Institutions, Trust, and Governance in Areas of Limited Statehood'. *Regulation & Governance* 10(2): 149–60.

Cadier, D., Capasso, M., and Eickhopp, K. (2020). 'Researching Resilience: Implications for Case Studies in Europe's Neighbourhoods'. *EU-LISTCO* 5: 1–40.

Central Bureau of Statistics (2009). *Census for Nahiyat Deir Hafer.* Damascus: Government of Syria.

Dukhan, Haian (2019). *State and Tribes in Syria: Informal Alliances and Conflict Patterns.* London: Routledge.

Enab Baladi (2019). 'Mahttat kahrouba' Halab fi 'ihda 'aqd Irani murtaqab lilmazid'. 11 June. https://enabbaladi.net/archives/340690#ixzz6LDaRWpNv (accessed 15 June 2022).

Gerring, John (2010). 'Case Selection for Case-Study Analysis: Qualitative and Quantitative Techniques'. In Janet Box-Steffensmeier, Henry Brady and David Collier (eds), *The Oxford Handbook of Political Methodology* (645–84). Oxford: Oxford University Press.

George, Alexander, and Bennett, Andrew (2005). *Case Studies and Theory Development in the Social Sciences.* Cambridge: MIT Press.

Gutierrez-Sanin, Francisco (2017). 'Organization and Governance'. In Anna Arjona, Nelson Kasfir and Zachariah Mampilly (eds), *Rebel Governance in Civil War* (246–63). Cambridge: Cambridge University Press.

Hasan, Abdullah (2018). 'Deir Hafer: From Daesh to the Revolutionary Guard'. *A'ayn al-Madina.* 14 September. https://ayn-almadina.com/public/details/%D8%AF%D9%8A%D8%B1%20%D8%AD%D8%A7%D9%81%D8%B1..%20%D9%85%D9%86%20%D8%AF%D8%A7%D8%B9%D8%B4%20%D8%A5%D9%84%D9%89%20%D8%A7%D9%84%D8%AD%D8%B1%D8%B3%20%D8%A7%D9%84%D8%AB%D9%88%D8%B1%D9%8A/4627/ar (accessed 15 June 2022).

Kalyvas, Stathis (2006). *The Logic of Violence in Civil War.* Cambridge: Cambridge University Press.

Kaplan, Oliver (2017). *Resisting War: How Communities Protect Themselves.* Cambridge: Cambridge University Press.

Khadour, Kheder (2017). 'Consumed by War: The End of Aleppo and Northern Syria's Political Order'. *Friedrich Ebert Stiftung.* October. https://library.fes.de/pdf-files/iez/13783.pdf (accessed 15 June 2022).

Klarić, M., Klarić, B. Stevanovic, A., Grković, J., and Jonovska, S. (2007). 'Psychological Consequences of War Trauma and Postwar Social Stressors in Women in Bosnia and Herzegovina'. *Croatian Medical Journal* 48(2): 167–76.

Lund, Aron (2013). 'Syria's Salafi Insurgents: The Rise of the Syrian Islamic Front'. Swedish institute of International Affairs. 28 February. https://www.ui.se/globalassets/ui.se-eng/publications/ui-publications/syrias-salafi-insurgents-the-rise-of-the-syrian-islamic-front-min.pdf (accessed 15 June 2022).

Mu'asasat Taht el-Mjhar (2015). 'Victims Are among the Dead and Wounded in the Bombing of Deir Hafer Hospital, and among the Victims Is a Doctor'. 23 April. http://www.almjhar.com/ar-sy/NewsView/2212/92467.aspx (accessed 15 June 2022).

Menkhaus, Ken (2013). 'Making Sense of Resilience in Peacebuilding Contexts: Approaches, Applications, Implications'. *The Geneva Peacebuilding Platform.*

https://www.gpplatform.ch/sites/default/files/PP%2006%20-%20Resilience%20to%20 Transformation%20-%20Jan.%202013_2.pdf (accessed 15 June 2022).

SANA (2017). 'Hundreds of Residents of Deir Hafer Area and Its Surroundings Return to Their Homes in the Eastern Countryside of Aleppo'. 20 July . http://www.sana.sy/?p=593189 (accessed 15 June 2022).

Syria Call (2018). 'Syrian Tribes and Clans Deny Participation in "Deir Hafer" Meeting'. *Syria Call*. 5 June. Deadlink.

Sonnentag, Sabine. (2011). 'Recovery from Fatigue: The Role of Psychological Detachment'. In Philippe Ackerman (ed.), *Cognitive Fatigue: Multidisciplinary Perspectives on Current Research and Future Applications* (253–72). Washington, DC: American Psychological Association.

Shabakat Halab News (2013). 'Jawla fi madinat Deir Hafer'. *YouTube*. 24 September. https://www.youtube.com/watch?v=Bfx9mZSV_To (accessed 15 June 2022).

UNDRR (2015). 'Resilience. United Nations Office for Disaster Risk Reduction'. https://www.undrr.org/terminology/resilience (accessed 15 June 2022).

UNDP (2008). 'Capacity Assessment Methodology'. New York: United Nations Development Programme. https://www.undp.org/content/dam/aplaws/publication/en/publications/capacity-development/undp-capacity-assessment-methodology/UNDP%20Capacity%20Assessment%20Users%20Guide.pdf (accessed 15 June 2022).

UNDP (2020). 'Strengthening Social Cohesion: Conceptual Framing and Programming Implications'. https://www.undp.org/publications/strengthening-social-cohesion-conceptual-framing-and-programming-implications (accessed 15 June 2022).

Weinstein, Jeremy (2007). *Inside Rebellion: The Politics of Insurgent Violence*. Cambridge: Cambridge University Press.

Wilson, Geoff, A. (2014). 'Community Resilience: Path Dependency, Lock-In Effects and Transitional Ruptures'. *Journal of Environmental Planning and Management* 57(1): 1–26.

INDEX

Note: Endnotes are indicated by the page number followed by "n" and the endnote number e.g., 20 n.1 refers to endnote 1 on page 20

al-Abadi, Haidar 117, 127, 130
Abdul Jabar, Faleh 109
Abdul-Mahdi, Adil 171, 179
'Abidin, Abu al-Yusr 192, 193
Abu Mahdi al-Muhandis 66, 130
al-Afees, Fadi 103
Afghanistan 202
   post-conflict register in 21
Afrin district 219, 223, 224, 226
aggressive counterinsurgency campaign in conflict-affected states 21
Ahmadinejad, Mahmoud 205
Ahram, A. 91
Akins, H. 100–1
Alawites 206 n.4
Aleppo (city) 52, 96, 98, 105, 107, 142, 147, 148, 152 n.6, 159, 162, 195, 200, 226, 241–2, 246, 250, 255
   rural areas of 97f
Aliyev, H. 61
Alwan, F.J. 101
American Evangelism 207 n.9
al-Amiri, Hadi 130
anti-immigrant narratives 215
Arab Mashriq 2, 4, 5, 45
Arjona, A. 60
Arnaut, K. 61
al-Assad, Bashar 78, 82, 145, 159, 191
   aspects of Shi'itization 201–5
   civilian recruitment 159
   government 48, 49
   Islamic spaces under politics of 197–201
   al-'Islām kamā 'unzil 205
   local agreements 51
   rule, Shabbiha in 62, 158
al-Assad, Hafez 51, 191, 206 n.1
   politics of Islam under 192–6

al-Assad, Jamil 96, 207 n.18
al-Assad, Maher 142, 145, 157, 160, 162–3
al-Assad, Rifaat 159, 207 n.18
al-Assaseneh 98, 105
asymmetric warfare 76
authoritarianism 3, 63, 146, 206
al-Ayyubi, Muhammad Ziyad 197

Ba'athist period 120
al-Baggara tribe 92, 93, 98, 103–4
   migration of 97f
Baghdad 92, 99, 101
al-Baqer Brigade 92, 96–100, 105–6
Barkawi, T. 46
Barout, M.J. 97
Barzani, M. 129
al-Basheer, Sheikh Nawwaf 105
Berghof Foundation 31
Berri clan 52, 97, 98, 105
Blue Hats{spelling needs to be changed in text}
   by Muqtada al-Sadr 176
Böttcher, A. 193, 196
al-Bougzat lineage 99, 106
Brenner, R. 94
Al Bu Fadel lineages 104, 107
Al Bu Nasir's tribe 102–3
al-Bu Rhama lineage 94, 103–4
bureaucratization 7, 34
Bush, George W. 4, 133 n.1
Busra al-Sham city 53, 78, 81, 82
al-Buti, Muhammad Sa'id Ramadan 194–5

Callwell, C. 119
Cambodia
   post-conflict register in 21
Chabkoun, M. 63
China 36

Civico, A. 68
civil society organizations 25–7, 31
civil war 1, 52, 61–3, 77, 78, 97
    American 165
    in Greece 100
    in Iraq 96, 172
    localized agreements use 50
    paramilitarism 66
    sectarian 121, 123
    Syrian 46, 54 n.3, 104, 217
    violence of 47
civilian resistance and its limits 237
clan 77, 95, 105
    leaders 68
    local tribes and 245, 252
    networks 159
    political 24
    sheikhs 76, 77, 84
Coalition Provisional Authority
    (CPA) 118
cohesion
    and fragmentation 103–5
    social 6, 7, 19, 77, 106
Cold War 1, 19, 27, 30, 31, 33, 229 n.9
Community protection 238
    adaptive and mitigating strategies 238
    coping strategies 238
    survival and coping strategies 238
    transformative strategies 238, 261 n.3
community-based organizations
    (CBOs) 31
conflict transformation 6, 8, 23, 27, 28
    in Arab Mashriq 45
    processes in Syria 11
consociationalism 6, 7
Consumer Price Index (CPI)
    of Syria 144
Cordesman, A. 124
cost of living
    in Syria 144
counter-Daesh campaign 118
counterinsurgency (COIN) 117
    configuring 118–20
    in Iraq 118
counterterrorism 117
Cousens, E.M. 33
Covid-19 pandemic
    in Syria 144
criminality 63

culturalism 9–10, 20, 32, 33, 124, 182
culture 4, 5, 28, 53, 67, 183, 198
    of peace 34, 38

Daesh (ISIS) 2, 9, 12, 65, 79, 91, 92, 93,
    100–3, 104, 106, 108, 226, 250
    armed coercion, proliferation
        under 125–7
    vs. Iraq's security arena 117, 118–20
daily oil production
    in Syria 144
Damascus 77, 92, 152 n.6, 162, 202
    political challenges of 139
    socio-economic challenges of 139
Daraa
    Central Negotiations Committee
        (CNC) 79–80
    clan sheikhs in 84
    Covid-19 response initiatives 84
    Eastern Daraa 81
    Eighth Brigade and state 82–5
    in southern Syria 77–9
    violent incidents and fatalities in 81f
Dawood, H. 105
death squads 60
de-Ba'athification Programme 120, 122
de-escalation Agreement, in Syria 161
de-escalation zone, in Syria 77, 86 n.5
Deir Ezzor 97, 103, 105, 106, 204
Deir Hafer 238
    civilian structures 247–9
    civilian-led community
        protection 250–4
    community protection in 239–241,
        245–6
    conflict dynamics 241–5
    economic vulnerability 249
    local autonomy 254–5
    organizational capacity 255–6
    social trust 256–8
democratization 7, 19
Denskus, T. 38
devolution
    of security functions 82–3
    of state authority 91
    of violence to tribes 94–6
disarmament, demobilisztion and
    reintegration (DDR) schemes, by UN
    6, 19, 22–5

in East Timor 24
in Manila 24
in the Philippines 23
in Sri Lanka 24
Dodge, T. 123
dual state 67, 69 n.6
Dudziak, M. 47

economy 102
  development of 20, 21, 24, 29
  political 49, 180, 251
  reintegration of 6, 7, 19
  Syrian 63, 149–150
  tributary 204
  war 139
Egypt 193
Eido, I. 2, 3
Enhanced Comprehensive Local
    Integration Program (E-CLIP)
    23–4
Ensar 216, 229 n.11
Erdogan, R. 214
Euphrates Shield (2016–17) 218–19

al-Farfur, Salih 194–5, 197
First World War (1914–18) 30, 46
foreign direct investment (FDI) 150
  in Syria 144
Fraenkel, Ernst 67, 69 n.6
fragmentation
  cohesion and 103–4
  and devolution 75
  of state functions in post-war southern
    Syria 75

Galtung, J. 30, 31, 46, 47, 172
Galula, D. 119
geopolitics 3, 11, 215
Germany 36
  Berghof Foundation in 31
Giustozzi, A. 63
governmental social policies
  in Syria 148–150
Grinstead, N. 63

al-Hadidyyin tribe 96, 105
al-Haj Saleh, Yassin 49
al-Hasan, Fahmi 246
Hasan, H. 108

al-Hashd al-Shaabi (popular mobilization
    force) 66, 176
Hay'at Tahrir al-Sham (HTS) 9, 158
Heathershaw, J. 35
Hills, A. 133 n.5
al-Himsi, 'Abd al-Razzaq 192
Hindu fundamentalism 207 n.9
Hindu nationalism 207 n.9
Holden, R. 96
home guards 60
Homs (city) 62, 147, 148, 152 n.6, 160, 243
al-Houri lineage 92, 99–101, 105, 108
al-Houri, Sabar 104
housing, land, and property (HLP)
  laws pertaining to 147
  in Syria 146–8
Hristov, J. 60
human development 20, 21, 32
humanitarian-development-peace nexus
    20, 32–3
al-Hussein, Khaled 103, 104
Hussein, Saddam 64, 95, 103

Idlib (city) 9, 79, 142, 203, 218, 222, 250
inflation rate
  in Syria 141
institutional
  peace-builders 20, 30, 37
  peace-building 27, 37
instrumentalism, in Shabbiha model
    appraoch 63
Intergovernmental Authority on
    Development (IGAD) 28
internally displaced persons (IDPs) 142,
    151 n.3, 213, 229 n.15
international aid industry 7
international nongovernmental
    organizations (INGOs) 21, 24, 27, 31,
    37, 151 n.3
international peace-building 20–1,
    25, 27, 32
  depoliticization of 37
  repoliticization of 37
Iran 9, 52, 53, 77, 78–9, 82, 145, 161,
    192, 202
  paramilitarism 66
Iraq 1, 171, 202, 249
  Ba'athist period 120
  battle for Mosul 127–130

civil war 96
coalition and emergence of 120–1
counterinsurgency in 130–3
de-Ba'athification Programme 120, 122
devolution of state power in 91
gendered state 181–3
Hashd 66
al-Houri in 105
al-Jabour tribe in 91, 93
military abatement in 2
al-Maliki years 123–5
motherhood in 183
paramilitaries in 64–6
political field (2005–6) 121–5, 122f
Popular Mobilization forces (PMF) 100
as post-conflict state 172–4
Salaheddin Brigade in 91
sectarian/civil state 177–9
security arena *vs.* Daesh and 118–120
security state 175–7
service state 180–1
social mobilization in 174
state institutions, retribalization and curtailment of 107–8
Sunni political class 120
and Syria 5–7, 8–10
tribal militias 91
tribes and tribalism 93–4
2019 Protests in 174–5
unemployment in 180
US invasion in 2003 64
violence to tribes in 94
womanhood in 183
Iraqi Ba'ath party 64
Iraqi Communist Party 65
Iraqi Islamic Party (IIP) 120
Ireland 32
Islam 192
Islamic Da'wa Party 120
Islamic pilgrimage 196
islamisation 191–5, 200–5
Islamism 192
Israel 78

al-Jabour tribe 92–4, 98, 99–100, 106, 109 n.5
Jalloul, Haitham 195
Jaysh al-Mahdi (JAM) 121
jihadism 3, 198

Jordan 54, 78, 213

Kaftaru, Sheikh Ahmad 194–5
Kalyvas, S. 60, 100
Kaşıkcı, T. 220
Kata'ib Hezbollah 66
Kataeb al-Baath 51–2
Kenya 28
    Uwiano Platform 29
Khalaf, Suleiman 94
Hajj, Khaled, 105
Khalili, L. 118, 119
Khanat al-Saan checkpoint 166 n.13
al-Khatib, Muhammad Mahmoud 195
Khatt al-Baggara tribe 103
al-Khazali, Qais 66
Khazai, S. 124
Klem, B. 48
Knights, M. 126
Kurdish militants 9
Kurdistan Democratic Party (KDP) 94, 120

Lacher, W. 104
Latakia 142, 152 n.6, 162
Lebanon 1, 6, 54, 202, 206 n.4, 213
    banking system 143
    financial crisis 143, 144
Lederach, J.P. 26, 27–8, 31
Leenders, R. 63
Left-wing sovereignism 36
liberal (ism) 20, 21, 30, 35, 36, 119, 124, 173, 183
liberal peace paradigm 173
Liberal Peace Theory 119
liberal peace-building paradigm 19–20, 30, 35
Libya 132
'localization' 20, 25, 37
low intensity conflict 76, 85, 86 n.2

al-Maliki, Nouri 66, 123–5, 133 n.8
    government 118, 123–5
Manila 24
Mann, M. 68
Mansour, R. 131
Marshall, A. 119
Martin, M. 100
Martinez, J.C. 176

mass violence 48
materialism 63
Mazrui, A. 107
Mecca, pilgrimage to 196
Al-Meri, Hussein 98
Mexico 67
Middle East and North Africa (MENA) countries 2, 146, 178
Migdal, J. 68
militarization 11, 161, 217, 225, 238
military tribalism 95
    on intra-tribal politics 105–7
militias 52, 60, 62, 82, 96, 97, 123, 160
    distinction between paramilitarism and 59–60
    in Iraq 9
    in Philippines 24
    paramilitaries and 61
    Shabbiha militias 64
    Shi'ite militias 69 n.4, 101, 202–3
    Shia 65, 117
    and state 59
    in Syria 62
    tribal 65, 91, 100–8
    in Turkey 226
    types of 61
    see also paramilitarism
Miller-Idris, C. 2
Mitchell, M. 165
Moe, L.W. 132
Moro Islamic Liberation Front (MILF) 23, 24
Moro National Liberation Front (MNLF) 23
Mosul, battle for 127–130
    balance of forces in 130f
Muhacir 216, 229 n.11
al-Muhandis, Abu Mahdi 130
muhasasa system 125, 126
muhasasa ta'ifia (system) 171, 177–8
    notions of 178
Mukhabarat 62
Myanmar 67

narcotrafficking
    in Syria 142, 151 n.2
National Guard (*Haras al-Qawmi*), in Iraq 65
National Partnership

    in Syria 145
National Union of Syrian Students (NUSS) 159
nationalism 5, 107
    economic 36
    ethnic 36
    Hindu 207 n.9
    Iranian 66, 205
    Persian 205
    secular 64
    Shia 66
negative peace, *see* violence
Nepal 11, 21
    national peace infrastructure 29
'new economic strategy'
    of Syria 145
Newman, E. 35
Nicaragua 27, 36
nongovernmental organizations (NGOs) 21, 26, 31, 33–4, 151 n.3
normalization 23, 24
northern Syria
    dilemmas of interventions in 213
    reconstruction and displacements 213
    reconstruction attempts in 222
    refugee return 213
    returnees, challenges encountered by 224–7
    unilateral military operations into 218–19
    see also Syria

Obama, Barack 4
Al-Obeid, Sheikh Mohammed Rami 200
October movement, *see* Tishreen movement
al-Oda, Ahmad 78, 80, 82, 85
Olive Branch (2018) 218, 224–5
Olson, M. 91
Operation Peace Spring (2019) 218

Paffenholz, T. 25
Pakistan 202
paramilitarism 11, 59
    global 67
    and the state 59–61
    'state-manipulated' 60
    'state-parallel' 60
    in Syria and Iraq 59

types of 60
  see also militias
paramilitary armies 60
patrimonial 140, 150, 251
  values of tribalism 105
patrimonialism 146
Patriotic Union of Kurdistan (PUK) 120
patronage 9, 12, 59, 62, 68, 80, 120, 139, 165, 224, 245, 252
Pavlović, D. 25
peace
  and conflict studies 20
  infrastructures for 27–9
  negative 21, 29, 46
  positive 21, 29
peace-building 6, 19, 35, 47
  agencies of United Nations system 30–1
  civil society organizations 31
  depoliticization of 36
  ecosystem 30–1
  frameworks 7
  institutionalizing 27–9
  international 20–1, 25, 27, 32
  post-conflict 23
  repoliticization of 36
  research institutions 31
  states 32
  with state-building 20
Pearce, J. 68
Philippines 11, 21, 36
  DDR programmes 23
  Office of the Presidential Adviser on the Peace Process in the Philippines (OPAPP) 29
  PAMANA programme 29
Pierret, Thomas 194
political engineering 11
politicization-depoliticization-repoliticization 21
  cycle of 34
'Popular Army' (al-*Jaysh al-Shaabi*) party militia 64–5
post-conflict reconstruction 7, 12, 19
post-conflict register 21
  Afghanistan 21
  appropriation of 34–8
  Cambodia 21
  emergence of 29–34
  past and post of, in Syria 46–9
  South Africa 21
'post-liberal peace' 6
post-war transition 48
private actors
  in Syria 145–6
private-sector banks
  in Syria 146
protests 82, 171–2, 184 n.2
  movements in Syria 12
  in Iraq 174–183
proxy(ies) 9, 51, 53, 82, 96, 108
pseudo-civil society organizations 27
Public Private Partnerships (PPPs) 139

Al-Qaeda 121, 122, 198
Qasim, Abd al-Karim 94
Qatar 140, 192
al-Qubaysīyāt 191
Quneitra governorates 77–8
Quwwat Shabab al-Sunna (QSS) 78

Rae, J. 96
al-Ramli lineage 99
rebel groups 53
reconciliation 11, 19, 52, 54, 161, 164
  agreements in Syria 45, 49, 50, 78, 85
  committee (Lijnat al-Musalaha) 247–9
reconfiguration
  of polities 8
  of tribalism 94, 102–3
reconstruction 6, 7, 12, 50, 119, 139, 145, 146, 213
  in Northern Syria 222–4
refugee management, in Turkey 215
religion 4, 192, 196, 199, 205
  of Islam 194
  reconfiguration of 102
religious field, expansion of 12
religious institutions 178, 193–4, 198
research institutions 19, 30, 31
retribalization
  and curtailment of state institutions 107–8
right-wing sovereignism 36
Russia 52, 75–9, 82, 83, 145, 161
  and Syria conflict 51

Sadat, Anwar 196
'Saddam's Men of Sacrifice' (*Fedayeen Saddam*) 65
al-Sadr, Moqtada 124, 132, 182–3
   'Blu Hats' 176
safe zone 229 n.15
Sahwat al-Anbar (Anbar Awakening) 122
Salafi-Jihadi 8
salafi-jihadist militants 117
salafism 3, 8, 125, 193
Salaheddin Brigade 92, 96–100
al-Salamya 160
Samaha, N. 53
Al-Saray, Safa 183
Saudi Arabia 140, 152 n.12, 192, 193
al-Sayyid, Abd al-Sattar Muhammad 197
Scarry, E. 45
Second World War (1939–45) 46
sect 4, 120
sectarianism 3, 4, 63, 184
sectarianization 3, 4, 7, 63, 66
security sector reform (SSR) 6, 19, 22
security services 22, 75, 80, 123, 163
sexism 63
Shabbiha networks 62, 64, 98, 165
   activity in Homs 62–3
   investment deals 159–160
   smuggling of people 160–1
   in Syria 157
shadow economy, *see* Shabbiha networks
Shami, S. 2
al-Shaykh, Hanan 191
Al-Shehabi, Faris 157
sheikh 77
Sheila (tribal songs) 104
Shi'ism 120
Shi'ite militias 9, 101, 117, 87 n.16
Shi'itization 192
   aspects of 201–5
   Iran's policies of 192
   nationalism 66
al-Shirqat district 92, 100–1, 106, 108
   al-Jabour lineages in 99f
al-Siba'i, Mustafa 206 n.2
Sirri, O. 176, 181
smuggling and criminal activities
   in Syria 140, 151 n.2
social cohesion 77
social engineering 12, 20, 32

social justice 31
Social Security Organization (SSO)
   in Syria 141
socialization 8
Somalia 27, 132
South Africa
   ACCORD 31
   post-conflict register in 21
southern Syria
   archipelago of political orders 79–81
   Daraa governorate in 77–9
   fragmentation and devolution of state functions in post-war 75
   Shi'a population hub in 82
   state return to Daraa governorate 77–9
   see also Syria
sovereignism
   left-wing 36
   right-wing 36
Soylu, S. 214
Sri Lanka 11, 21, 36, 54 n.1
   DDR and SSR processes 24–5
   Secretariat for Coordinating the Peace Process (SCOPP) 29
stalemate 3, 217
   military 11–12
   political 61
Staniland, P. 60
the state
   in Iraq 64–6
   paramilitarism and 59–61
   shadow in 67–9
   in Syria 61–4
   and tribal militias 91
state capture 25
state penetration 86 n.11
state security 21
Stojanović-Gajić, S. 25
Striking from the Margins (SFM) 4, 5
Suleimani, Qasem 66
sulh delegation 84
Sunni (ism) 101, 120
   establishment 192
   Muslims 196
   political class 120
Supreme Council for Islamic Revolution in Iraq (SCIRI) 120, 125
'sustaining peace' agenda 20, 37
Sykes-Picot agreement 77

Syria 1, 54, 192, 196
  al-Baggara tribe in 91, 93, 105
  al-Baqer Brigade 91
  Bashar al-Assad government 48
  ceasefires in 45
  civil war in 48, 96, 104
  conflict transformation processes in 11
  Consumer Price Index (CPI) 144
  cost of living 144, 152 n.10
  Covid-19 pandemic 144
  daily oil production 144
  devolution of state power in 91
  economy after more than ten years of conflict 140
  evolutions of GDP 140–2
  foreign direct investment (FDI) 144
  foreign remittances 152 n.6
  governmental economic policies 145
  governmental social policies 148–150
  housing, land and property 146–8
  inflation rate 141
  and Iraq 2, 5
  land and property in 49
  legalizing processes of displacement 49–51
  mandating decentralized security 51–3
  military abatement in 2
  Ministry of Social Affairs and Labor (MoSAL) 148
  monopoly of politics in 194
  narcotrafficking 142
  'new economic strategy' 145
  paramilitarism in 61–4
  Persian language in 204
  political economy 139
  post-conflict register in 46–9
  post-war transition 48
  private actors 145–6
  private-sector banks 146
  public-private partnerships 145–6
  refugees and asylum-seekers 228 n.1
  regional changes after war 142–3
  Shabbiha in 61–4
  Shabbiha networks in 157
  smuggling and criminal activities 140
  Social Security Organization (SSO) 141
  state institutions, retribalization and curtailment of 107–8
  Al-Ta'feesh 163–5
  tourism industry 144
  tribal militias 91
  tribes and tribalism 93–4
  unemployment 149
  violence to tribes in 94
  war economy model 139
  war *vs.* peacetime 45
  see also northern Syria; southern Syria
Syrian Ba'th party 192
Syrian crisis
  Turkey's changing approach towards 217
Syrian Democratic Forces (SDF) zone 103, 158
Syrian pound (SYP) 152 n.5
  depreciation of 143–5, 150

Al-Ta'feesh 163–5
taftish (search), practice of 177
Taher, Kheder Ali 163
Taheri, Amir 129
Tahrir Square 175
  protest movement in 177
Tall Abyad 223
Al-Tarfeeq 158–161
Al-Tarseem 161–3
Tayy tribe 96
terror, global war on 36
Thailand 36
Thomson, A. 102
Tibi, B. 94
Tilly, C. 68
Timor
  DDR programmes 24
  DDR and SSR processes 24–5
Timor-Leste 11, 21
Tishreen movement, in Iraq 171–2
Toth, A. 94
tourism industry
  in Syria 144
transitional justice and reconciliation 19
Tribal Army (*Jaish al-Asha'ir*) 65
Tribal gangsterism 92, 108
tribal militias 91
  cohesion and fragmentation among 103–5
  relying on 100–2
tribalism
  reconfiguration of 102–3

tribe 68, 91, 98, 101, 102–3, 109
   Arab 65
   al-Baggara 91, 92, 94–6
   Iraq 65, 91, 92, 94–6
   al-Jabour 91, 92, 94–6
   sect and 4
   in Syria 91, 92, 94–6
   and tribalism 93–4
Tuk-tuk (magazine) 175, 179, 184 n.2
Tunisia 62
Turkey 67, 77, 93, 140, 161, 192, 213, 215, 249
   cross-border military operations 218–19
   Directorate General of Migration Management (DGMM) 220–2
   military involvement in northern Syria 219
   National Security Council (NSC) 219
   policies and consequences 217–18
   reconstruction attempts in northern Syria 222–4
   refugee management in 215
   refugees in 228 n.2
   relations with US 217
   returnees, challenges in northern Syria 224–7
   Spheres of influence and displacement 219–20
   and Syrian displacement crisis 215–17

UN Peacebuilding Architecture (PBA) 31
United Kingdom 36
   Saferworld in 31
United nations (UN) 21
   and European Union (EU) 229 n.6
   system 30–1
United Nations Development programme (UNDP) 28
United States 6, 36, 54, 124
al-Uqli lineage 99, 106

Venezuela 36
violence 7, 8, 28, 59, 63–4, 95, 237, 242, 244
   of civil war 47
   cultural 172
   direct 172
   large-scale 46–7, 172
   mass 48–9, 213, 245
   monopoly of 22–5, 60
   oligopoly of 60
   open 172
   organized 46–7
   paramilitary 59, 67
   physical 46, 47, 53
   political 3, 171
   reciprocal 46–7
   by Shabbiha 63
   structural 172
   in Syria 46

Wajir Peace and Development Committee 28
war and peace 46
   distinction between 46–7
warlordism 63
warlords 1, 163, 165–6
weak state theory 68
Weber, M. 38
   modern state 117–18, 133 n.3
Weinstein, J. 237
Western counterinsurgency campaigns 119
Wilāyat al-Faqīh 204
World Bank 31

Yetim, M. 220

al-Zablatani 160
Zambelis, C. 63
Zionism
   and atavism 195

www.ingramcontent.com/pod-product-compliance
Lightning Source LLC
Chambersburg PA
CBHW052218300426
44115CB00011B/1733